David M. W. Powers
Macquarie University, Sydney

Christopher C. R. Turk
University of Wales, College of Cardiff

Machine Learning of Natural Language

Springer-Verlag
London Berlin Heidelberg New York
Paris Tokyo Hong Kong

David M. W. Powers, ThC(Hons), PhD, MACS, MIEEE
Senior Research Fellow, FB Informatik, University of
Kaiserslautern; Honorary Associate in Computing, MPCE,
Macquarie University, Director, IMPACT Ltd, 259A Trafalgar St.,
Petersham, New South Wales 2049, Australia

Christopher C. R. Turk, MA (Cantab), DPhil (Sussex)
'Bentwys', Llanbair Discoed, Near Chepstow, Gwent NB6 6LX,
UK

ISBN 3–540–19557–2 Springer-Verlag Berlin Heidelberg New York
ISBN 0–387–19557–2 Springer-Verlag New York Berlin Heidelberg

British Library Cataloguing in Publication Data   *QA*
Powers, David
    Machine learning of natural language.   *76.9*
    1. National language computer systems
    I. Title   II. Turk, Christopher (Christopher C. R.)   *N 38*
    006.3′5
    ISBN 3–540–19557–2   *P68*

                                                                   1989
Library of Congress Cataloging-in-Publication Data
Powers, David (David M. W.)
    Machine learning of natural language/David Powers and Christopher Turk.
        p.   cm.
    Includes bibliographical references.
    ISBN 0–387–19557–2
    1. Natural language processing (Computer science)   2. Machine learning.
I. Turk, Christopher.   II. Title.
QA76.9.N38P68   1989
006.3′4—dc20   89–38887
                                                                   CIP

Printed and bound by The Alden Press, Osney Mead, Oxford

2128/3916–543210 Printed on acid-free paper

Preface

We met because we both share the same views of language. Language is a living organism, produced by neural mechanisms relating in large numbers as a society. Language exists between minds, as a way of communicating between them, not as an autonomous process. The logical 'rules' seem to us an epiphenomena of the neural mechanism, rather than an essential component in language.

This view of language has been advocated by an increasing number of workers, as the view that language is simply a collection of logical rules has had less and less success. People like Yorick Wilks have been able to show in paper after paper that almost any rule which can be devised can be shown to have exceptions. The meaning does not lie in the rules.

David Powers is a teacher of computer science. Christopher Turk, like many workers who have come into the field of AI (Artificial Intelligence) was originally trained in literature. He moved into linguistics, and then into computational linguistics. In 1983 he took a sabbatical in Roger Shank's AI project in the Computer Science Department at Yale University. Like an earlier visitor to the project, John Searle from California, Christopher Turk was increasingly uneasy at the view of language which was used at Yale.

His attention was drawn to an article by David Powers in the SIGART Journal which seemed to reflect the same views. An extended correspondence then followed, which culminated in a Ph.D. written by David. This was marked by Christopher, and David spent his sabbatical in 1988 at the University of Wales, Cardiff, working with Christopher. The idea of the book had been discussed before, and during this visit it became reality.

The basic academic research was done by David Powers as part of his successful Ph.D. thesis. Christopher Turk added some material, and re-wrote most of the book. But it reflects a strongly held joint view of language, and a joint view of the way forward in computational 'understanding' of language. In recent years it has become obvious that a living organism such as human language can only be re-produced by a mechanism which follows the same path of learning. We are still at an interim stage in this development. But detailed understanding of the neural mechanisms, and the human learning process, are the only way we shall be able to reproduce human language on a mechanical system.

Our book sees language as complex and dynamic. There is far more subtlety in language than can be uncovered by hand crafted grammars, and programs to re-produce them. We take the path of engineering by plagiarism from nature. We try to glean as much as possible from the natural, biological and behavioural sciences. We also try to learn as much as we can about the neural mechanisms which support language from the Philosophy of Science.

Our focus is on the way a child learns language. The work is directed at an engineering solution, but we feel that the natural way natural language is acquired is what we must re-produce. We know of no effective algorithm other than the one which we observe, but cannot adequately explain, in the development of the human child. This algorithm, and its mysteries, is the source of our insight.

The research program reported in Chapter Fourteen was not aimed at building a system, so much as increasing our understanding of the processes involved in language learning. The small programs are simply experiments. Our book is in the end a collection of information and hypotheses about language and learning from many different disciplines. Our apology for such a wide range of interest is only that we do not know where the vital clue lies. Somewhere in this voyage through the archipelago of language we hope we have shown other travellers a good place to land.

Acknowledgements

David Powers wishes to acknowledge the benefit of discussion and argument, both personally and in letters, with many colleagues. Amongst these Ken Pike, and colleagues at the Department of Computer Science at the University of New South Wales, and the University of Wales Institute of Science and Technology stand out. Michael Wise was willing, and available, to discuss many obscure comments. Professor Murray Allen and Graham McMahon have given continued moral support and warm encouragement.

Christopher Turk wishes to acknowledge many colleagues, particularly at Yale and Wales. Larry Birnbaum and Roger Shank at Yale, Robin Fawcett and David Young at Wales talked and argued about the ideas. Maghi King of ISSCO at the University of Geneva also listened and argued. Jenni Lloyd and Rachael Jones were an invaluable help as secretaries during the preparation of the manuscript. Catherine Aldred gave me support in the early stages, and an increasing amount of free time to finish the book.

Contents

Chapter One

Art, Science and Engineering

Our subject is the acquisition of Natural Language (NL) by computers. NL is not, in our view, a surface expression, or epiphenomenon, of a deeper, underlying cognitive process in the human brain. It is rather fundamental to, and pervasive of, cognition itself. For this reason we think that language is not the sole preserve of linguists, but is pivotal in all our interactions with the world, in our science, and in our thought.

Language, on this principle, is at the centre of every human intellectual discipline. It is learned, and so is studied by psychologists. It is a function of our brains, and so is studied by neurologists. It is itself a powerful structure combining simplicity and complexity, and so its conundrums have challenged our mathematicians and philosophers throughout the centuries. But in this electronic age, language is increasingly the province of workers in the fields of cognitive psychology and Artificial Intelligence (AI), who record, transmit, simulate and analyze its every form and representation. There are senses in which language is both more and less than cognition: more because it is a medium for communicating between cognitive entities; less because it is only a medium, a mechanism or a tool, serving other processes.

This view of language is the starting point and the focus of the ideas we describe in this book. But our attention is mainly directed to the question of how computing machinery can acquire the cognitive structures which erupt in NL. Work in this field in the last thirty years has moved from a posture of confidence about the possibility of NL processing by machine, through clever programs which were, in the end, seen to be emulations, even pastiches, of the actual processes of understanding, to criticism of the very concept of machine understanding (best represented by John Searle's discussions of "intentionality"[1] — Christopher Turk hopes to describe this view in more detail in a future book — *Natural Language and Artificial Mechanisms*[2]).

At this time (1989), we do not, as a scientific community, know quite how this will be done. But we are sure that insight into this process will require very basic thinking about the nature of cognitive processes, and the methods of scientific thought which have tried to purify the researcher's perceptions of reality. For this reason our book begins with a fundamental summary of basic views of methodology, and only then moves on to bring together linguistic, scientific, neurological, and related cognitive approaches. We end by describing experimental learning mechanisms, some of which are simplifications of the way a general NL acquisition system might be built. We emphasize, however, that it is still early in the process of understanding NL and its acquisition by an automaton. We do not pretend to complete answers, only a prospective trawling of the problems. At this stage we claim that thinking in detail about first principles is the best way forward.

The start of this exploration is the realization that the integrity of Science demands that any research should be undertaken in the context of our entire heritage, irrespective of disciplinary divisions. The researcher in this field should consider topics lying in the intersection of Psychology, Linguistics and Computer Science, along with the underlying sphere of Neurology. The disciplines listed in this figure under Artificial Intelligence and Psycholinguistics are not new to workers in these fields, but the scope of what we include under the heading of Natural Language Processing (NLP) is wider than normal. The area known to AI as "Natural Language" is itself broad and nebulous, and it is not always clear whether NL programming is meant, or NL database queries, or NL deduction systems, or question answering, or system control, or machine translation, or what. Our argument is that computers and language go hand in hand, and it is helpful to have the widest perspective, both in terms of which language processing functions can already be performed, and those which cannot yet be achieved satisfactorily.

The direction for NL research we take here is thus a multidimensional vector of contributing interdisciplinary insights. The exploration of these insights and their background, discipline by discipline, is the subject of the first dozen chapters. The most useful of these insights are brought together and summarized in Chapter Thirteen, and are used in Chapter Fourteen to develop a research program and a collection of computational experiments.

This choice of a broad approach is not without problems. In the preface to *Modelling Language Behaviour*, Narasimhan points out the necessity and the pitfalls of this approach:

> By its very nature the study of language behaviour calls for an interdisciplinary effort. There are obvious dangers in attempting a monograph on an interdisciplinary subject. For no one individual can be a practicing specialist in all the disciplines ... judgement of what is relevant and what is not, which issues are central and which ones are not, and so forth, depends on the overall understanding one has of the field in question. I leave it to the practicing specialists to decide to what extent my judgements of ongoing-work in the various fields dealt with in this book are sound.[3]

We feel a similar doubt, and for this reason have always given precise references for material. Wherever possible we quote the authors' own summaries of methodology, suppositions, results and conclusions. The task of presenting this topic from the perspective of each of the relevant disciplines and collating all the relevant data is gargantuan, and hence we feel that this work represents only a beginning in an important field.

In this chapter we start to look at the nature, structure and purpose of both language and cognition. We do this by looking at the language we use to formalise our analysis, description and checking of the world around us. This gives clues to the breadth of our linguistic and cognitive capability. The corresponding systems of thought demonstrate mechanisms which are effected for development of an understanding of the world. These could have some relationship to the development of our ability to communicate such understanding through NL. Our interest diverts into the Arts, Sciences and Technology whose perspectives distinguish, signify and explain our thinking. We move from naïve relationship to scientific causality, from naïve guess to scientific hypothesis, from naïve failure to scientific refutation, from naïve metaphor to scientific method. We see in this chapter that language has many facets to its dynamic relationship with cognition and ontology and is anything but arbitrary in the way it expresses the structure and biases of our perception of our reality. This chapter looks at some of the principles which recur throughout human intellectual work, and so recur in different guises throughout our book. The reader will perceive that what is presented in this chapter as a trivial and universally accepted principle of Science or Art, appears in later chapters as a novel principle of behaviour, learning, or neural organization which we can then build on in designing a NL acquisition system. We discuss the principle here simply because formal methodologies are basically enhanced reflections of the natural ontological processes which are our subject.

In this chapter, we divide the discussion of these basic principles into those which concern the way we look at the world and categorize it; those which concern how we quantify or qualify what we observe; those which arise from control of our propensity to classify and measure; and finally some more pragmatic and some more esoteric examples.

Cognitive Structures: the Natural Cognitive Divisions

We divide up and classify our experiences in various ways. It is characteristic of both Art and Science that we divide them also into different "disciplines". In this section we consider the ways in which we typically divide up our world, and the basis and naturalness of these approaches to our complex environment. The basic division apparent in these criteria can be characterized as vertical versus horizontal, but there are also considerations of continuity and discreteness, contingency (or *coincidence*) and independence.

The usual criteria for separating the areas of study seem to be primarily vertical: each field has a variety of depths and levels of detail. Another dimension of classification which, by historical "accident", can seem to be the primary division is the horizontal metaphor: division on the basis of complexity or level of detail. For example, whilst once Chemistry and Physics would have been regarded as completely independent, today they are seen as differentiated only in level of detail, perspective and focus. Where the horizontal metaphor is appropriate, we find that the explanations of one science are based on phenomena which are themselves objects of the research of another science. Science is thus primarily a *top-down* process in which phenomena are explained in terms of lower level "facts", although theory and the "scientific method" are essentially *bottom-up* mechanisms.

The relevance of divisions to our discussion of cognitive, and therefore language, structures in this book is reflected in the debate over which distinctions may or may not be reflected in the way language is acquired. Not only Science, but all our behaviour and experience, is structured in terms of vertically and horizontally delimited hierarchies and levels. Nowhere is this more clearly and formally set out than in Linguistics, giving rise to a prevalent linguistic/parsing metaphor for such structures. In Chapter Eight we argue that this linguistic metaphor is not just fortuitous, since language takes on a structure by correlation with the sensory-motor environment.

Pike sees linguistics as being properly concerned with universals of human behaviour and a multiplicity of hierarchies.[4] In particular, he identifies three interlocking but partly independent hierarchies in language: a referential hierarchy; a phonological hierarchy; and a grammatical hierarchy. The referential hierarchy reflects our sensory-motor ontology and determines the concepts we talk about. The phonological hierarchy concerns spoken speech, and for written language there is a corresponding (but not isomorphic) lexical/orthographic hierarchy.

Pike sees each of these hierarchies as subject to the part-whole structuring which is characteristic of traditional linguistics. But if language is a function of a multiplicity of hierarchies, its description must be more complex than simple phrase structure, since it must admit of relationships between the hierarchies. Traditional linguistics tends to think in terms of only a single hierarchy whose levels are for convenience subdivided into various strata. Thus Lamb writes:

> For most spoken languages, there are at least four structural strata. We may call these [the] *phonemic*, the *morphophonemic*, the *morphemic* and the *sememic*. In addition, there is another stratum, the *phonetic*, which lies adjacent to the phonemic stratum but is outside the linguistic

structure. The term *tactics* is widely used for the analysis and description of arrangements, and the term *syntax* is traditionally used with reference to arrangements on the morphemic stratum.[5]

It seems to us essential to recognize the multiplicity of independent structures underlying the interplay of relationships responsible for the richness of our experience and our linguistic and non-linguistic capabilities. The emergence of Psycholinguistics has led to a "rediscovery that language is structured"[6] and a new awareness of its functional importance.[7] Furthermore, recent psycholinguistic research recognizes the structure in language processing which makes it apparent:

> that children process linguistic information at (at least) two levels: (a) the level of initial processing, which occurs in short-term memory shortly after children have been exposed to the input; and (b) the level of post-initial processing, which occurs at some later time when children are attempting to interpret, organize, and consolidate information.[8]

The structure of intelligent processes is part of all sciences, including Psychology and (especially) Psycholinguistics. Interestingly, it has probably been most thoroughly and formally studied in disciplines such as Management Science and Software Engineering, rather than in the study of language and cognition. This insight is in itself justification for our broadly based approach to our subject.

Cognitive Structures: Taxonomy and Constituency

The nesting relationships in the hierarchies we have been discussing are *part-whole* relations, and define *constituency hierarchies* which "are not to be confused with the *specific-generic* relations which may be called *taxonomic hierarchies*".[9] The taxonomic hierarchy is exemplified in Hayes' discussion of:

> finite exhaustive lists of the various type or categories of a kind of thing or of the possible states of a thing ... ways of being supported, kinds of physical states, possible states of a fluid.[10]

Pike also recognizes how important such relationships are, but sees them as part of a wider perspective, specifically as special cases of a relational or field perspective. He shows the advantages and disadvantages of the taxonomic hierarchy with a tree capturing a "20 Questions" like analysis:

> It has the advantage of leading to clear-cut logical definition, but the disadvantage of imposing (for the moment at least) one viewpoint, one set of priority criteria; and it may conceal implicitly some characteristics—important for other purposes—shared by twigs far removed from each other in the diagram.[11]

The constituent hierarchy illustrates two other perspectives, the *static* or *particle perspective* focussing on the individual parts, and the *dynamic* or *wave perspective* viewing a composite as a whole.

Any mental concept or event rarely consists of a set of contemporaneous and unsequenced components. This implies *distribution in sequence* in which Pike's particle and wave perspectives are applicable. In this way, we can refer to particular *states* as if they were static and the transitions were quantum leaps; we can similarly characterize *stages* in a process as if they were dynamic and the progression was continuous. In general, stages can be identified empirically. States, on the other hand, require knowledge of the mechanism, and sharp, often self-evident, discrimination. States exist in a system of transitions, and stages in a system of transformation. However, the existence of thresholds or other hurdles will frequently blur the distinction. Stages and states will participate as identifiable units in hierarchies and relationships, which we will discuss in Chapter Nine.

The concept of stages also plays an important part in psycholinguistic research, particularly in the work of Piaget. Language acquisition is a *process*, and a valid model must be tested to see if it conforms with the observed stages. Incidentally, the importance of states and stages has been recognized for some time in the frames and scenes of AI, although they are not nearly dynamic enough. Hayes writes:

> The now-classical approach to describing actions and change ... is to use the concept of *state* or *situation*. This is thought of as a snapshot of the world at a given moment: actions and events are then functions from states to states. ... What we need is a notion of a state of an event which has a restricted spatial extent. By a *history* I mean such an object, viz. a connected piece of space-time, typically bounded on all four dimensions, in which "something happens". ... Histories can be related to one another in various ways ... [12]

The problem of coming to grips with this aspect of intelligence is one of the most general and fundamental problems of AI.

Cognitive Structures: Models and Abstractions

The rationale for the divisions we have been considering is in a word, "simplicity": simplicity out of complexity. Humans can *perceive* patterns in complexity — in fact it is probably the most basic and consistent of all our cognitive attributes. This allows us to *recognize* constellations where we would otherwise just see a myriad stars. This recognition is a particular human propensity: the thousands of stars are separated from us and from each other by many light-years, and the constellation is purely within "the eye of the beholder". This is a very important point in Piaget's thinking: humans are "designed" to recognize patterns, but the patterns need not be "real" in the sense of causal or proximal relationship or even permanence.

Science on the other hand is interested in explanation, in other words in patterns which reflect underlying "truth". The process of mapping from a complex structure or process to a simpler more understandable one is *modelling*: a "model" may or may not reflect the underlying relationships or laws, but is intended "to make the study of a system more tractable"[13]. The attempt to produce a truth-preserving simplification, although it can never be complete, is *abstraction*. Piaget's proposed psycholinguistic processes preserve apparent rather than true relationships, and he uses a "reflection" metaphor for the human abstraction and internalising process:

> It is, in fact, possible to distinguish three different kinds of abstraction. (1) Let us call "empirical abstraction" the kind that bears on physical objects external to the subject. (2) Logico-mathematical abstraction, in contrast, will be called "reflective" because it proceeds from the subject's actions and operations ... We have two interdependent but distinct processes: that of a projection onto a higher plane of what is taken from the lower level, hence a "reflecting", and that of a "reflection" as a reorganization on the new plane—this reorganization first utilizing, only instrumentally, the operations taken from the preceding level but aiming eventually ... at coordinating them into a new totality. (3) We will speak finally of "reflected abstraction" ... as the thematisation of that which remains operational or instrumental in (2); phase (3) thus constitutes the natural outcome of (2) but presupposes in addition a set of explicit comparisons at a level above the "reflections" at work in the instrumental utilizations and the constructions in process of (2). It is essential, therefore, to distinguish the phases of reflective abstractions, which occur in any construction at the time of solution of new problems, from reflected abstraction, which adds a system of explicit correspondences among the operations thus thematised.[14]

Piaget's "reflective/reflected" distinction may be characterized in terms of novel *bottom-up* perceptive (sensory-motor) analysis of a pattern versus extant *top-down* constructive (abstracted) recognition of a concept. Obviously, this clearly needs a process leading from one to the other. Piaget describes this as follows:

> Reflective and reflected abstractions, then, are sources of structural novelties for the following reasons: In the first place, the "reflecting" on a higher plane of an element taken from a lower level ... constitutes an establishment of correspondences, which is itself already a new concept, and this then opens the way to other possible correspondences, which represents a new "opening". The element transferred onto the new level is then constituted from those that were already there or those that are going to be added, which is now the work of the "reflec-

tion" and no longer of the "reflecting" ... As a rule, all reflecting on a new plane leads to and necessitates a *reorganization*, and it is this construction, productive of new concepts, that we call "reflection".[15]

Piaget's "reflection" suggests some of the known and proposed neural mechanisms discussed in Chapter Seven.

Abstractions form the basis of models. A scientific model is usually a construction, a new instance, embodying the general principles of the abstraction. The abstraction identifies the properties to be examined (it is logically a set of assertions), and the model identifies an isomorphism between the problem and an independent system (the model itself). Science is prepared to sacrifice a measure of precision for a measure of understanding, and uses various ways to assess the worth of a theory. These include utility (especially in the sense of ability to predict), simplicity, and generality. A given abstraction will always map some details and obscure others. Thus an abstraction allows, or forces the focus to, a particular level of detail; and a model constrains to, and arises from, a particular perspective or viewpoint.

NL research in AI has always been rather ambivalent about the question of modelling. This is highlighted by the deficiencies recognized by Winograd in his work:

> [SHRDLU is] not a model ... reflecting the underlying process ... It seems likely that more advanced models will move towards overcoming these deficiencies. As we learn more about the organization of large complex systems, we may well be able to model language in ways which are more complex, clearer, and closer to psychological reality.[16]

Schank, on the other hand, has founded his research on a deliberate intent "to imitate the human understanding process".[17] And Goldschlager is aiming to produce a:

> unified, coherent theory of brain function ... to extract the main concepts ... developed and found useful in describing the human brain ... and to produce a computational model which embodies ... concepts.[18]

Psychological research employing computer modelling often has this viewpoint; indeed one of the foremost researchers in the area sounds the following warning:

> Since computer models actually mimic the behaviour they predict, they are supposed to specify all aspects of the behaviour and to leave nothing unsaid ... I know of no other science where this is seriously attempted ... Science progresses because of decisions to abstract out and focus on certain measures of the phenomena at hand. This abstraction reflects the scientist's judgement about what is important and what is tractable. Other scientists may differ with him in their judgement on this matter, but all must agree that abstraction is necessary.[19]

Cognitive Structures: Dichotomies and Spectra

Earlier in this chapter, we distinguished continuous as opposed to discrete perceptions of reality in our analysis of the world. Humans seem to find dichotomies easier to grasp than spectra, and so are inclined to impose absolute and precise criteria on the world, whereas in Science, and in "reality", alternatives are seldom so black and white. The desire for parsimony in explanations may lead us to prefer one mechanism over another, but frequently interesting phenomena are best explained by using two or more independent mechanisms. Occasionally, in fact, certain apparently independent laws *are* shown to have a common basis; to cite a language-related example, Kuczaj asks why children engage in language practice, and responds:

> One answer assumes that children do so because such behaviour helps them to learn their mother tongue ... Another answer assumes that they do so because language play is intrinsically rewarding to children ... These two answers are not mutually exclusive. Children might find language practice pleasurable and might also use it to facilitate their acquisition of their native language.[20]

Sometimes wanting to take an intermediate or compromise position is seen as weakness by other workers. Battle fever, or this human propensity for dealing in dichotomies, still tends to result in a hard core of extremists pushing their hard-line view. But we should remember when considering *ad hominem* argument, that the question of choosing between dichotomy or spectrum is not so much a methodological argument, as an epistemological and empirical one. Whilst parsimony may seem to prefer a single mechanism, this can be false economy. A better explanation for a phenomenon may include a number of simple components and a balance of interdependent mechanisms — we will see several examples in relation to neural mechanisms in later chapters. This is not an argument for compromise, but an observation that the structure of cognition necessarily involves an interaction of mechanisms to grasp, and explain, reality.

Scientific Method *vs* Naïve Intuition

In the rest of this section and its sequel we turn our attention away from the four basic types of cognitive structures, and concentrate instead on the next stage of our argument. We now move on to explore how we *describe* the world we have perceived, or grasped, by these cognitive structures.

In this section, then, we discuss aspects of how we measure, what we measure in relation to, how we determine such measures, and how fundamental such measures are. Here we emphasize metrics in their scientific guise, but their significance to the argument we are building up means we must compare scientific metrics with those of natural common sense.

In writing about the difference between intuitive and scientific approaches, or "naïve" *vs* "empirical" observation, we quote Narasimhan's characterization of the relation between these two:

> A scientific theory ... must determine at a phenomenological level what properties and relationships call for explanation in terms of an articulated theory ... Experiments enable us to delimit phenomenological relationships to account for which theories are invoked (or constructed ...). The statements or consequences derived from theory are verified by experiments ... A theory is applicable to a naïvely observed situation to the extent to which the latter approximates the relevant experimental situation. If the approximation is good, predictions based on theory are verified; otherwise, not ... It is this fact, that situations of the open-ended naïve world approximate more or less situations of an experimentally controlled world, that gives rise to naïvely observed regularities of the external world. The popular view that scientists study and attempt to explain the naïvely observed uniformities or regularities of nature is clearly somewhat simplistic ... The popular saying "every rule has an exception" literally applies to the rules inferred from the naïvely observed behaviour of the open-ended world. Part of the objective of science is precisely to account for these exceptions.[21]

The common version of the aphorism Narasimhan is discussing is: "the exception *proves* the rule". The meaning comes from a now marginal definition of proof. When gold- and silver-smiths proved their metals in the crucible, this "proof" was in one sense a purity test (any impurities would collect and oxidize at the surface when the metal melted). But the main purpose of the "proof" was to improve the purity of the metal (since the impurities were gradually oxidized out or skimmed off as dross). The result was that the metal had been *proven* pure.

So the misunderstood proverb actually concerns the testing and improving of "the rule"; this is reflected in both common sense and science, where "rules" and "hypotheses" are refined by "experience" and "counter-example". The main difference is one of methodology: science goes out looking for its difficult cases, whilst naïve common sense stumbles over them by accident. The term "naïve" is used of "observed" rules and relationships independent of the identification of an actual causal relationship. Simple naïve relationships are thus the stuff of human ontology, and hence the basis of NL.

Laws, Norms, Relationships and Universals

In an important sense, "laws" are the focus of our book: in each subsection we are discussing a set of related "laws". In this section, we emphasize the fundamental law that there are "laws" which govern our environment, and "universals" which are fundamental to human cognitive behaviour. This point is the centre and focus of Pike's linguistic theories. He writes, at length and in considerable breadth, on "Language in Relation to a Unified Theory of the Structure of Human Behaviour". The principles he establishes are the basis of his Tagmemics text,[22] and are very influential in our discussion in this chapter and in Chapter Eight. Neither language, nor the science of language (linguistics) can be divorced from the total of human behaviour. Language is not merely comparable to, but is a fundamental part of, intertwined and continuous with, nonverbal behaviour.

In this section we are offering several different ways of viewing these behavioural characteristics. At the simplest level, we have *relationships*. We can see, from what we have said about characteristic human cognitive structures earlier in this chapter, that a relationship will be perceived, and therefore exist, at two different levels: at the level of naïve perception and at the deeper level of causal relation. We distinguish naïve relations (which may not hold through to the deeper level), intuitive relations (which stand up to scientific examination), and un-intuitive relations (which when discovered or postulated by science are hard to accept or defy our powers of observation). We will use the word *law* for a relationship which holds at the deeper level.

Next, we can distinguish relationships which have been noted in a specific context, system, or individual, and those which apply in or underlie all contexts, systems, or individuals. These latter are the *universals*. Particularly when concerned with living systems, we find a class of universal which does not admit precise formulation; here we can describe the relationship as typical rather than inviolable. In this case we term the relationship a *norm*, and it frequently becomes a basis for measurement or comparison. Thus, "man has five fingers to the hand" is inviolable (other than by "accident" of genetics or environment, which gives rise to an *abnormality*), whilst "man grows to six foot tall" is *normative* (although extremes of variation will still be regarded as abnormal).

Norms are fundamental to the human conceptualization of the world. The whole basis of such words as "big" and "small", or even "black" and "white", is normative. Our understanding depends on whether the word is applied to a man, a mouse, or a motor-car. This is reinforced by the existence of qualifiers, such as "very", "rather" and "unusually". Indeed, in Pike's very persuasive view (which we share) language is entirely normative:

> Rules of grammar are cultural norms; like other norms they are descriptive of certain regularities of behaviour within a community, and they also are prescriptive in recommending this behaviour to new members of the community.[23]

The Scientific Measurement of Reality: Parsimony and Generality

The basis of the discovery of laws and principles can be described as generalization from specific cases. Science has developed a specific methodology for this purpose; and even in our naïve intuitions about relationships, there are evidently two basic principles at work: we look for the simplest, as well as the most general relationships. These are the principles of parsimony and generality. At this level *sufficiency* and *completeness* are the keys: an explanation must be just sufficient to explain the complete set of positive instances known. It does not appear that *soundness* or *necessity* are factors in the naïve generalization process; these are achieved by other mechanisms, if at all. In a sense parsimony is a weaker substitute for necessity, whilst generality can sometimes be a trade-off for soundness.

The principle of parsimony (the original "law" is usually attributed to William of Occam, hence *Occam's Razor*), is one of the cornerstones of modern science. Science is always looking for the smallest set of axioms which will explain the phenomena being considered. This is then construed as most likely to be the "correct" explanation of the phenomena, because of the law of parsimony. In practice, the principle of parsimony is used to choose between theories which are otherwise equally plausible. But as Anderson writes the application of parsimony is highly subjective:

> It would be foolish to propose a metric for measuring the simplicity of a theory or to expect that there will always be consensus about which of two theories is the simpler. However, there is considerable consensus in extreme cases. Despite its subjective nature, no one can deny the importance of parsimony to the acceptance of a theory.[24]

Parsimony is undoubtedly the single best known principle of scientific methodology, yet few people have recognized its position as a "law of nature". Parsimony is in this sense a universal applicable in many contexts. An example of one of these is genetics and "evolution", where it is not only a principle of scientific discovery, but also a principle found in the genetic mechanisms. Thus for example, Jacobson points to "more parsimonious use of genetic information"[25] and Anderson makes the same point about language acquisition, suggesting that "parsimony could probably serve to select some model", and asking "How much credibility can we give to the claim that nature picked the simplest form?"[26]

The principle is also evident in other developmental processes, including cultural development and linguistic development. This looks self-evident, but while some writers have come very close to this observation, they have often phrased it in a rather ambiguous or indefinite way. The discussion has tended to remain at a level where, whilst advocating that the grammar should be parsimonious, it does not make the clear connection to an hypothesis that the child's acquisition process is parsimonious, although this is sometimes implicit in the acquisition model proposed[27]. Kelley is the first writer to say clearly "the child will evaluate the alternatives in terms of an initial simplicity metric"[28], but it was Brown and Fraser who suggested a specific principle that looks very like parsimony:

> That grammar is preferred which predicts what does occur while predicting as little as possible what does not occur. Therefore, the less general grammar will be better than the more general one if it is equally successful in predicting what happens.[29]

This is really a somewhat different principle, which points up an important tension in the science of linguistics. Usually the principle of parsimony carries with it the idea that the most general theory is best: the one with the most universal scope, and able to predict the broadest range of phenomena, is the most useful. Brown and Fraser's principle suggests that the least general grammar is preferred, and they do not think at all about the question of the complexity of the formulation of the grammar.

This principle comes from a more general principle, that theories (or grammars) should predict only correct instances. So it is thus only an heuristic for minimizing the possibility of overgeneralization, and seems to be an instance of what in AI is called "conservative focussing". The goal of generality is thus related to the goal of parsimony, but is even more closely related to the processes of generalization and abstraction. We could also argue, in passing, that the need for generality is illustrated by common complaints about Linguistics such as:

> The box labeled "MISCELLANEOUS" contains more than all the rest.[30]

Scientific Measurement: Comparison and Precision

If we leave aside for the moment questions about causality, logical dependency, comprehension, and so on, we can consider the naïve viewpoint on sensory-motor and temporal relationships. The relationships people observe will usually be norms; the fundamental human propensity behind such "normal" observation is that of comparison—with the norm functioning as a form of average. Somehow, for each variable, every child quickly and systematically determines a context-dependent expectation of distribution. For each instance, and for any variable, he or she can thereafter state whether or not it deviates from the norm, and if so, by how much (relative to what would be a "normal" deviation). Humans also seem to have a natural asymmetrical instinct for assigning direction to our norms; we always talk of "more" and "less" deviation. In Clark's view, there is a universally agreed positive axis for each norm.[31]

The norm is often the measure of the world around us, and from this we get our ability to give quantities to the variables of the world. The most obvious use of norms is probably as measures of distance (for example the hand, the foot, the cubit, the mile, and so on). We also use norms to measure time (for example the day, the month, the season, the year, and so on). In this way, we can achieve an arbitrary precision by using multiples and sub-multiples of such standards. For many normal purposes, however, we use non-standardized norms—an example of this is the subjective discriminations of sound intensity which have little relationships to scientific units. On the other hand, in science we often use quite obscure norms—for instance the metre and the second have been defined in terms of the circumference of the earth and the frequency of a particular atomic light emission. Consideration of norms and comparison is fundamental to language, and in fact the majority of open-class words correspond to norms or grades.

Probably the most common general word we meet in discussions of concepts and their relationships is *context*. We can define the essence of context like this: in order to properly understand a concept we must either take into account the full scope of its interrelationship with the universe, or else, more commonly, delimit that scope. Put briefly, we can say that the designated scope of relationships is the context for the concept.

The ideas of *concept* and *context* are basic to all the other ideas we have discussed in this chapter. Three particularly closely related ideas are *metaphor* (which is the subject of chapter two), and *paradigm* and *perspective* (which we discuss in this section). We can say that metaphor is the substitution of one context by another whilst retaining the same concept. On the other hand we can think of paradigm as substitution of one concept by another whilst retaining the same context. In a similar way, perspective is the selection of particular, presumably significant, portions of the context.

Perspective is ubiquitous and unavoidable in the following sense. Man has five or so physical senses, science includes countless domains, and art utilizes myriads of different media. In most usage in these fields, language and cognition are used to link perspectives: all of our sensory-motor experience is accommodated in language and coordinated through cognition. Thus we find that paradigm is characteristic of the language acquisition process. Both first language learners (in language play or practice), and second language learners (in grammatical actions such as conjugation and declension and so on), make extensive use of paradigms. Indeed, traditional Phrase Structure Grammar (PSG) is built on paradigm, and in Tagmemics this is even more apparent. The point is obvious, but we think it worth repeating — it is clear from the orderliness of language that substitutionary processes are at work, and that the role of paradigm in Language and Learning is fundamental.

The Conceptual Context: Absolute and Relative

Up to this point in our discussion, we have emphasized relationships, or concept in relation to concept. This is the relative viewpoint which gives rise to norms; but we must now admit briefly that the opposite, absolute viewpoint also exists. Let us ask the rhetorical question "can science ever deal in absolutes absolutely?" As soon as we try to measure something, we must quantify relative to some unit, and as soon as we want to classify something we must qualify relative to various norms. The most absolute thing we can do is claim that there is absolutely no exception to some law, but this is precisely what science is never prepared to do (although mathematics and logic strive to). We find that even in the abstract there are limitations on our capability to answer even yes-no questions about well-defined systems.

Another source of confusion is the question of "how well" *versus* "how cheaply". More formally, these can be phrased "how *effectively*" and "how *efficiently*". Computer science often uses this distinction in AI, where many problems do not admit of a practically effective algorithm. The archetypical AI domain is search: often exhaustive search is theoretically inefficient, and heuristics can produce an algorithm which is practically effective.

In the case of cognitive modelling, we already have a practically effective system — the human brain. The researcher is searching for algorithms and heuristics, preferably related to neurological and psychological mechanisms, which effectively duplicate the various cognitive processes. To say, as some do, that various suggestions are theoretically inefficient, is to miss the point. It may be that modifications, heuristics, or mechanisms can be found, as for the case of search, which result in a practically effective, if theoretically impure, algorithm.

Another principle of science is the "novelty" or "surprise" value of information. To communicate, we also need to establish terms of reference by way of context and protocol, since information can only be relative to a shared context. Science is a quest for information — but it is only one manifestation of the human propensity for exploration. "Curiosity" may indeed have "killed the cat", but it "made the man". The young of most higher species have an inquisitiveness in their most formative periods, which is a quest for information; the baby's interest is directly related to novelty. He or she will be interested in a phenomenon while it has surprise value, but will become bored once it has become familiar. Thus "curiosity" is directly related to "fun" and is a positive motivation. Even the adult explorer, indeed every researcher, is motivated by fun and curiosity.

It is most helpful if this natural curiosity is directed to useful ends in useful ways; there are bounds on the allowable *complexity* and *distance* of a phenomenon for it to excite interest. Neither the baby nor the scientist can deal meaningfully with remote irrelevancies. Irrelevance may be equated with either absence or tenuity of connection in a hierarchy; spatial distance is subsumed as a specific instance. These considerations of information and relevance have obvious applicability to Language.

Thus, as Schank says, we must assume that every utterance is intended either "to communicate something, or to gain some desired effect".[32] The question of the conveying of information in communication is discussed by Winograd in expounding his SHRDLU model:

> It can check a possible interpretation of a question to see whether the asker could answer it himself from his previous sentences. If so, it assumes that he probably means something else ... We are always basing our understanding on the answer to questions like "Which interpretation would make sense given what I already know?" and "What is he trying to communicate?[33]

Consistency and Inconsistency: Rules and Exceptions

One way of defining the goal of linguistic grammatical research is that it wants to be able to find a set of rules which formally define the grammar of a language. Substituting "generate" for "define" and "sentences" for "grammar" gives us the familiar catch-cry of the Generative Grammarian. The aim of any empirical science is essentially the same: the target may be any form of behaviour, animate or inanimate, and in this sense "grammar" becomes "theory" and the fundamental common feature is that there must be no behaviour (or "sentence") which in fact occurs yet is not predicted by the theory, or which does not occur but is predicted by the theory.

Various methodologies have been designed to try to capture the generalities, or this consistent set of rules. The most influential tries to find the inconsistencies in our theories, discovering what disproves the rule and using this to improve the rule. Whilst there may be a degree of arbitrariness or non-determinism in the world, science does not lightly take "meaningless" for an answer! Thus the currently accepted methodology believes that exceptions to our postulated laws are useful, and lead to a more accurate understanding of the actual laws.

In the case of NL acquisition, one law of behaviour is, paradoxically, that we expect to find rules and exceptions, or at least that we hypothesise rules, expecting exceptions. This is often ignored in conservative models which discard rules as soon as exceptions are found. The human way is more often to "patch" rules to allow them to handle new problems, and subsequently to re-generalize the specific "patchwork" if possible. Negative information is useful information, and overgeneralization is far more common in child NL acquisition, and evidently far less problematic, than overpruning.

In an earlier part of this chapter we looked at the basis for measurement and classification in the scientific understanding of the world. Now we want to look at the particular mechanisms used to choose a classification, whether intuitive or scientific.

Categories and classification are extensively discussed throughout scientific, philosophical, linguistic and mathematical literature. In each subject there is a well established theoretical base, and here it is necessary only to clarify the place of *classes* in relation to context, analogy and paradigm. Pike defines class firstly in terms of distribution over substitution, and secondarily in terms of similarity of function:

> A unit is a member of a *filler* class (a set) of items which may appropriately occur (be distributed) in the same *slot* in a particular structure; each member of the class has the same *function*. Two units substituting for one another in such a slot are *analogous* in their relation to the containing structure; and the two instances of the containing structure are *in proportion*.[34]

An example of inappropriate substitution, in violation of proportion, is Chomsky's well known "John is easy to please" *vs* "John is eager to please" — consider who is pleased in each case.[35] Thus we establish a class in relation to a slot in a paradigm. By corollary, we establish a class by relating members to each other by analogy of function.

This section has propounded a linguistic, and primarily grammatical, definition of class, which is extensible (by metaphor) to any hierarchy. We can also note here that there is a deep analogy between the grammatical class and the ontological category which is the basis for much of the argument in Chapters Seven and Eight, as well as for the hypotheses and experiments of Chapters Thirteen and Fourteen.

Positive and Negative; Symmetry and Asymmetry

The basic type of classification is the simple binary one, and in particular, the positive-negative distinction. Some of the most important linguistic research in this area is due to the Clarks.[36] The Clarks' observations come from looking at the mapping between *physical* space (*P-space*) and the *linguistic* system (*L-space*), and an initial hypothesis of a Cartesian-like coordinate system. As we live on a roughly two-dimensional surface in a three-dimensional world, there is one obvious reference plane, the ground, and one obvious direction defined by gravity, the vertical. The question of which direction is positive and which negative is decided by them on the basis of the "asymmetries of perceptual space". Thus, in the case of the vertical:

> [As] everything above ground level is perceptible and nothing below it is, upward is naturally positive and downward is naturally negative.

Similarly, within the horizontal plane,

> [A] property of all [human] senses is that they are most sensitive to stimulation in front of the body, and least sensitive to stimulation in back of the body ... The perceptual apparatus therefore defines a clear plane of *asymmetry*, the vertical plane running through the body separating front from back ... The forward direction can be considered the positive perceptual direction, and backward the negative one.[37]

Note that, by contrast, left and right are symmetrical and thus give rise to no perceptual preference for one over the other. This is supported by the difficulty of some people, adults included, in distinguishing left from right—which is often solved at a motor level according to which is the writing hand, or which wrist carries the time. An ancient expression to describe illiterates is "persons who do not know their right hand from their left".

The significance to language of these assignments can be seen by a study of the mapping between P-space to L-space; also (as we said earlier) by looking at norms and "points of reference" as they occur in L-space. The way in which norms generalize from "points of reference" is illustrated by Clark:

> Consider the adjectives "high" and "low". To say "the balloon is high (or low)" is really to say "the balloon is high (or low)" off the ground. Implicit in such simple statements is a zero point, an origin, the point of reference from which all measurement is taken. *High* and *low* happen to have a particular reference plane—ground level ... This origin or

zero point is called the primary point of reference. Adjectives also have a secondary point of reference. *High* and *low* ... both refer to height off the ground, but *high* indicates a distance that surpasses some implied standard, and *low* indicates a distance that fails to meet that standard. This standard depends very strongly on what exactly is being measured ... a balloon is high in a room when ... perhaps 6 feet high, but in a large auditorium perhaps only when ... 10 to 20 feet high.[38]

In referring to a dimension such as *high-low*, one of them is linguistically "marked" and used both "as the name of the scale defining the positive direction and as the term labeling an excess in that direction". In this case *high* leads to *height*, and 'lowth' is not used. When a secondary scale name is used, such as "shortness":

> [It] is defined only with respect to the secondary point of reference ... a defective scale extending only from that secondary standard in a negative direction to the zero point [of no length], the primary point of reference.[39]

Similar conditions can be applied, by use of metaphor, to non-spatial attributes such as time. In the case of time, though, there is an obvious asymmetry, since time only moves in one dimension. However there are at least two possible metaphors, since we can either see ourselves as moving forward in time, or we can conceive of time as moving past us. But notice that virtually all the adverbs, adjectives and prepositions of time are taken from spatial terms using one metaphor or other.

Language about Quanta: Discrete *vs* Continuous

Categorization needn't always be consistent with a single metaphor. As we pointed out earlier, the viewpoint, sensory mode, or implied observer, has an important role in the interpretation of what is perceived. Heisenberg's uncertainty principle and Quantum Mechanics had their origins in this principle. The intertwined metaphors of particle, wave, and field are also central to Pike's consideration of the observer's relation to the observed:

> PERSPECTIVE: The observer becomes an element of the theory; no fact is treated without reference to him ...

> STATIC (PARTICLE) PERSPECTIVE: The observer can look at the world as made up of "things" ... In some sense this is treated as the basic or normal perspective ...

> DYNAMIC (WAVE) PERSPECTIVE: The observer can look at a series of "discrete" events and treat the whole as a single dynamic moving entity; and any single unit can be viewed dynamically, as having beginning (initial margin), middle (nucleus), and end (final margin) ...

RELATIONAL (FIELD) PERSPECTIVE: The observer can eliminate from the center of his attention the form or content or extension
of the units as such, and focus instead on the relationships between
them. The unit, in this case, contracts to a point in a network (or field)
of relationships.[40]

We want to focus again here on the importance in human cognitive
structures of the discrete *versus* the continuous, in other words the particle *versus* the wave. We continually emphasize the importance of relationships throughout this book, since they are at the root of cognitive
structures, and therefore of language and its acquisition. Pike sees the
particle perspective as the normal one, and the binary perspective of discrete quanta as somehow basic. As the Clarks' show, concepts may be
bounded by reference points in arbitrarily many dimensions, whether
spatio-temporal or otherwise. In language, events are captured in a spatio-temporal particle perspective. But in reality the borders between
events or subevents may often not be clear, and they may overlap and
merge.

Our tendency towards the particle is so strong that even if events
overlap, that still does not prevent us from perceiving them as *particular*
events. Conversation over dinner in a restaurant is quite a good
example of this: the separate events of eating and talking overlap in
space (at the one table) and time (at the one hour) as well as organs or
instruments (*e.g.* the mouth; perhaps also the hands, the eyes, the cutlery
etc.) If people are impolite and talk with a mouthful, the events may
become hard to distinguish (as well as the conversation).

The question of which cognitive perspective is adopted in such an instance depends, according to Pike, on the significance attributed to the
distinguishable potential units (the *etic* segments). From a static perspective, overlapped units may be confused, and additional insignificant
units perceived. The grammars (in language and other hierarchies) describe the composition of the larger perceived units in terms of smaller
distinguished units (*emic* segments). These are static formulations,
which are related by transformation to potentially overlapped dynamic
complexes in which the discreteness of the composing segments is not in
view. Morphophonemic modification is a prime example (*e.g.* /in/ +
/possible/ = /impossible/).

Such complexity is a necessary consequence where transformation
takes place between properly distinct hierarchies which are not mere reflections of each other. The problem of discovering the *emic* units of one
hierarchy by means of *etic* observations mediated by another hierarchy is
an essential problem for the language learner at all levels, and therefore
also for automatic language acquisition. This is the major source of the
complexity which makes our extended discussion of classification in this
chapter non-trivial.

System and Environment: the Dynamic *vs* the Static

We defined context very generally in earlier sections in terms of relating a concept to everything else. In this sense we saw a concept as statically embedded in a context which was viewed as basically independent. But taking a systems viewpoint, we can see that there must always be a relationship between an entity within a system and the rest of the system.

The relations which make up the context of a cognitive event are described as its environment. The entity/environment relationship is one of mutual influence; the entity affects the environment, and the environment affects the entity. The result is a system, which we define as a *dynamic* unit which contrasts with the more static unit implied by the concept/context relationship. The concept in the case of the dynamic system is that of an open system, affected and effected by other systems. Normally, any subsystem is an open system. The universe itself, as a final contrast, is in this sense a closed system which has no inputs or outputs. Any other system is seen by science as a subsystem within the universe.

It is obviously not practical for science to take as its universe for modelling and explanation the actual Universe itself, so in practice science usually defines a smaller universe which is a good enough approximation to the real thing for its purposes. Such a universe can be either like a separate system which is assumed to be closed, or it can be an open system, with the inputs and outputs modelled too. Recognizing this second version of the principle was the basis of the conceptual breakthrough which lay behind "Generative Grammar".

Another worker who used this concept was Pike, who elaborated his particle and wave perspectives using the alternate terminology of static and dynamic. In our earlier discussion of this, we merely noted that the static viewpoint was insufficient to resolve the emic/etic problem in relating one hierarchy to another. Now we can go further, and make the point that a static approach is insufficient to handle the mapping between different levels and hierarchies.

Consider the problem of distinguishing between phonological words and grammatical words; there is logically no way that the grammatical words can be identified from the phonetic data without the help of the grammatical rules. This implies a circular recognition process, and shows that language learning must be a dynamic, iterative process. The mechanism which is presumed here is *feedback*, which is of course also fundamental to the neurological discussions of Chapter Seven, and is at the basis of Cybernetics.

Somehow, preliminary (presumably phonologically motivated) hypotheses are tested at higher cognitive levels for their usefulness as units in the hypothesised grammatical rules. Feedback about the success or otherwise of the hypothesis is then returned to the lower level as the acquisition process proceeds. The most useful form of this feedback is generally negative feedback, and this gives rise to a *correction* paradigm, which we discuss in Chapters Three and Four. There is also a role for a positive form of feedback, not necessarily a retrospective reinforcement, but what may better be characterized as feedforward, the role being one of expectation. These points form the substance of our later chapters.

Summarising the Basic Cognitive Structures

In this chapter we have taken a preliminary look at the basic structuring devices typical of all human cognition. Some of this will have inevitably seemed obvious, just because these structures are so universal in all language and thought that they reappear at every stage. But we have thought it worth making explicit these patterns at the beginning of our book, since we recur to a discussion of these patterns at virtually every stage of our argument. The discussion in this chapter has ranged widely over a number of aspects of basic cognition. The model we have taken for much of the discussion has been scientific method, because this represents a formalization of useful perceptive processes, and is therefore the most direct access to universal cognitive patterns.

Most of these cognitive structures take the form of divisions, and similar divisions are made in both the arts and the sciences. It seems natural for the human mind to perceive the world in a particular mode — preferring dichotomies to spectra. We are familiar enough with this natural propensity in the contentious partisanship so common in linguistics. But the same native structures are used to understand the world in scientific method by a system of taxonomy based on the measurement of differences. These cognitive strategies are used in the formation of models of the world, and the abstractions on which generalised rules are built. The law of parsimony is as prevalent in human cognitive structures as the preference for dichotomy, and we were able to hint at the influence of such rules on the child's language acquisition. By the end of this chapter we had established a consistent view of human cognition sufficient to support the exposition of the work of the Clarks on the asymmetry of the world as described in the norms and deviations forming the basis of language.

We return to most of these points during the following chapters, since they underline our view that the characteristic and repeated cognitive structures native to the human mind form the basis of our language, and must be understood and reproduced in any automatic language acquisition system. This chapter forms, then, the basis of the argument about cognition and language. In the next chapter, the argument progresses through the disciplinary threads which we have already seen intertwine inextricably in our analysis of cognition and language.

Notes to Chapter One

1. John R. Searle, "Minds, Brains, and Programs", *Behavioural and Brain Sciences*, Vol.2 (1980), pp. 417-424.
2. Christopher Turk, *Natural Language and Artificial Mechanisms* (Ellis Horwood, forthcoming).
3. Narasimhan, R., *Modelling Language Behaviour* (Berlin, Springer-Verlag, 1981), p.6.
4. Pike, Kenneth L., *Language in Relation to a Unified Theory of the Structure of Human Behavior* (Mouton, The Hague, Holland, 1967); Kenneth L. Pike, *Grammatical Analysis* (Summer Institute of Linguistics and University of Texas at Arlington, Dallas, Texas, 1977); Kenneth L. Pike, "Here we stand creative observers of language", in *Approches du Langage*, eds Maurice Reuchlin et Frederic Francois (Publications de la Sorbonne, Serie "Etudes" Tome 16, Paris, 1978); Kenneth L. Pike, *Linguistic Concepts: An Introduction to Tagmemics* (University of Nebraska, Lincoln and London, 1982).
5. Lamb, Sydney M., "On the Mechanization of Syntactic Analysis", *Conference on Machine Translation and Applied Language Analysis* (Her Majesty's Stationery Office, London, 1961), p.675f.
6. Kelley, K.L., *Early Syntactic Acquisition* (Rand Corporation technical report, Santa Monica CA, November, 1967), p.1.
7. Braine, D.S., "On Two Types of Models of the Internalization of Grammars", in Dan I. Slobin (ed.), *The Ontogenesis of Language* (Academic Press, 1971), p.171; David S. Palermo, "Research on Language Acquisition: Do We Know Where We Are Going?", in L. R. Goulet and P. B. Baltes (eds) *Life-Span Developmental Psychology: Research and Theory* (1970), p.47.
8. Kuczaj, Stan A., *Crib Speech and Language Play* (Springer-Verlag, New York, NY, 1983), p.167.
9. Pike, Kenneth, and E. G. Pike, *Grammatical Analysis* (Summer Institute of Linguistics, University of Texas at Arlington, 1977), p.3.
10. Hayes, P.J., "The Naive Physics Manifesto", in D. Michie, ed. *Expert Systems in the Micro-electronics Age* (Edinburgh University Press, Edinburgh, Scotland, 1979), p.262f.
11. Pike, Kenneth L., *Linguistic Concepts: An Introduction to Tagmemics* (University of Nebraska, Lincoln and London, 1982), p.123, Fig.1.
12. Hayes, P.J., "The Naive Physics Manifesto", in D. Michie, ed. *Expert Systems in the Micro-electronics Age* (Edinburgh University Press, Edinburgh, Scotland, 1979), p.257f.
13. Kelley, K.L., *Early Syntactic Acquisition* (Rand Corporation technical report, Santa Monica, CA, November 1967), p.7.

14. Piaget, Jean, "The Psychogenesis of Knowledge and Its Epistemological Significance", in M. Piatelli-Palmarini, ed., *Language and Learning: The Debate between Jean Piaget and Noam Chomsky* (Routledge and Kegan Paul, 1979). p.27.

15. *Ibid.*

16. Winograd, Terry, "A Procedural Model of Natural Language Understanding", in Roger C. Schank and K. M. Colby, eds, *Computer Models of Thought and Language* (Freeman, 1973), p.186.

17. Schank, Roger C., "Identification of Conceptualization Underlying Natural Language", in Roger C. Schank and K. M. Colby, eds, *Computer Models of Thought and Language* (Freeman, 1973), p.187.

18. Goldschlager, Leslie A., *A Computational Theory of Higher Brain Function* (Computer Science Department, Standford University, Standford, CA, April 1984), p.1f.

19. Anderson, John A., *Language, Memory, and Thought* (Lawrence Erlbaum Associates, Hillsdale, NJ, 1976), p.21.

20. Kuczaj, Stan A., *Crib Speech and Language Play* (Springer-Verlag, New York, NY, 1983) p.162.

21. Narasimhan, A.R., *Modelling Language Behaviour* (Springer-Verlag, Berlin, 1981), p.27ff.

22. Pike, Kenneth L., and E. G. Pike, *Grammatical Analysis* (Summer Institute of Linguistics and University of Texas at Arlington, Dallas, Texas, 1977).

23. Cit. in Brown, Roger and Colin Fraser, "The Acquisition of Syntax", in C. N. Cofer and Barbara S. Musgrave, eds *Verbal Behavior and Learning: Problems and Processes* (McGraw-Hill, 1963), p.164.

24. Anderson, John R., *Language, Memory, and Thought* (Lawrence Erlbaum Associates, Hillsdale, NJ, 76), p.16.

25. Jacobson, M., *Developmental Neurobiology* (Plenum Press, New York NY, 1978), p.353.

26. Anderson, John R., *Language, Memory, and Thought* (Lawrence Erlbaum Associates, Hillsdale, NJ, 76), p.5.

27. Braine, Martin D.S., "On Two Types of Models of the Internalization of Grammars" in Dan I. Slobin, ed., *The Ontogenesis of Language* (Academic Press, 1971), p.153f; Kelley, K.L., *Early Syntactic Acquisition* (Rand Corporation, Santa Monica, CA, November 1967), p.53.

28. *Ibid.*, p.77f.

29, Brown, Roger, and Colin Fraser, "The Acquisition of Syntax", in C.N.Cofer and Barbara S. Musgrave, eds, *Verbal Behavior and Learning: Problems and Processes* (McGraw-Hill, 1963), p.185f.

30. Fillmore, C.J., "Scenes-and-frames semantics", in A. Zampolli, ed., *Linguistics Structures Processing* (North Holland, 1977), p.60.

31. Clark, Eve V., "What's in a Word? On the Child's Acquisition of Semantics in his First Language", in Timothy E. Moore, ed., *Cognitive Development and the Acquisition of Language* (Academic Press, New York, 1973); see also a similar point in Herbert H. Clark, "Space, Time, Semantics, and the Child", *Idem.*

32. Schank, Roger C., "Identification of Conceptualization Underlying Natural Language," in Roger C. Schank and K. M. Colby, eds., *Computer Models of Thought and Language* (Freeman, 1973), p.190.
33. Winograd, Terry, "A Procedural Model of Natural Language Understanding", in Roger C. Schank and K. M. Colby, eds, *Computer Models of Thought and Language* (Freeman, 1973), p.185.
34. Pike, Kenneth L., and E. G. Pike, *Grammatical Analysis* (Summer Institute of Linguistics, University of Texas at Arlington, Dallas, Texas, 1977), p.2.
35. Chomsky, Noam, *Syntactic Structures* (Mouton, The Hague, 1957).
36. See Clark, Eve V., "What's in a Word? On the Child's Acquisition of Semantics in his First Language", in Timothy E. Moore, ed., *Cognitive Development and the Acquisition of Language* (Academic Press, New York, 1973); Clark, Herbert H., "Space, Time, Semantics, and the Child", also in Timothy E. Moore, ed., *Cognitive Development and the Acquisition of Language* (Academic Press, New York, 1973); Clark, Eve V., "Building a Vocabulary: Words for Objects, Actions and Relations", in P. Fletcher and M. Garman, eds, *Language Acquisition: Studies in First Language Development* (Cambridge University Press, Cambridge, UK, 1979).
37. Clark, Eve V., "What's in a Word? On the Child's Acquisition of Semantics in his First Language", in Timothy E. Moore, ed., *Cognitive Development and the Acquisition of Language* (Academic Press, New York, 1973), p.33.
38. *Ibid.,* p.36.
39. *Ibid.,* p.38.
40. Pike, Kenneth L., and E. G. Pike, *Grammatical Analysis* (Summer Institute of Linguistics, University of Texas at Arlington, Dallas, Texas, 1977), p.4f.

Chapter Two

Metaphor as a Cognitive Process

Patterns: Metaphor, Analogy and Identity

Throughout this chapter the concept of metaphor is a constant theme, although the reader will find many diversions into discussion of related cognitive processes. In this first section, though, we look at the fundamental nature of metaphor, and the way this relates to the typically human classification systems and ontologies. Metaphor is possibly the most fundamental concept in the understanding of language and its acquisition, but is seldom regarded as more than a literary "device" used for illustrative or poetic ends. The common view is that some similarity between the present situation and something foreign to it is used to convey a "truth" about the situation. We hesitate to use the word "artificial" here, since the measure of a metaphor or analogy is its "aptness" or "naturalness". But these explicatory or literary "devices" or "artifices" imply conscious and deliberate construction.

Despite this suspicion of metaphor, there is, in fact, very little we can do or say which does not depend on analogy in some way. Even the very grammatical patterns used to express ideas are analogous to those we use to express a wide variety of other ideas. The very words we use have a breadth of meaning coming from extension by analogy of the basic meanings. Just think how difficult it would be, if not impossible, to avoid using such words as little, pattern, wide, breadth, extension, plebeian, and basic. Yet with perhaps one exception, a social analogy, all these words have their root meanings in the visual/geometric world of shapes and measures, and their common meanings in a type of metaphor.

Metaphor is fundamental not only to our language, but also to our science. Various philosophers have examined the nature, purpose, origin, function, and limitations of metaphor. Analogy between two systems or "worlds" or "kinds of experience" is similar to a model, or a theory. The basis of metaphor is a structural resemblance between two systems, such that certain details of the one suggest details of the other, and we are able to apply or project back to the original. This gives us an opportunity for prediction, and this in turn gives the "richness" of metaphor so beloved of the poet — since what is obscure in the phenomenon is focussed and evident in the well-chosen metaphor. Of course, one is in continual danger of reading more into a metaphor than is warranted, and analogy does not constitute proof.

This point leads us on to consider a particular class of metaphor, the myth. There are many metaphors which are fairly universally and uncritically employed. Indeed, some of the foundations of various sciences still have this character, although today they have been identified and formalized, and the correspondence qualified, if not quantified. The characteristic of the myth is that it is not recognized as metaphor. Turbayne[1] explores myth in detail, whilst Lakoff[2] focuses in particular on the "Myth of Objectivism" and the "Myth of Subjectivism". Yet metaphors are fundamental, arguably essential, tools for apprehending our environment, and indeed for human thought. There is little, if anything, which we do not see through myth-coloured glasses. However, no metaphor is perfect. Therefore to allow us to examine the world critically, we need to use a variety of mutually inconsistent metaphorical spectacles.

Metaphors can be grouped into families; there are metaphors which do not fit a single image, which are disparate alternatives, but which nonetheless have common implications. For example the metaphors of time moving towards us and past us, and that of us moving forward through time, have the common entailment of relative motion of time going past us from front to back (or equally of us moving forward relative to time). Although these metaphors are not absolutely consistent, they are relatively coherent, and "fit together".

In this chapter we continue our study of the nature of Language Learning by focussing in on the concept of metaphor. We see that Art and Science both make use of analogy in their attempts to capture reality. We claim that myth and model are both essential outcomes of the fundamental role of metaphor in our cognitive processes. One way or another we are perceiving and recognizing patterns and relationships, whether in some sense real, or merely apparent.

The processes of induction and hypothesis are based on recognition of similarity. The developed model or theory is then a fully fledged metaphor, carrying 'truths' by analogy, from one domain into another. But metaphor is also concerned with discarding the irrelevant and inconclusive - the details which do not map between the domains. This discarded information might attract attention as anomalous, might be ignored as noise, or might remain totally unperceived due to structural or perceptual restrictions. Some specific metaphors directly contribute to our understanding of the potential mechanism for NLL (Natural Language Learning). Some are scientific, some naïve; some reinforce each other, others are in apposition. But we do not have the right to reject any without coming to grips with the extent of their validity. So in this chapter, we present a wide spectrum.

The brain, in all its regions, is primarily a recognizer of patterns and a performer of transformations. The crowning achievement of intelligence is the ability to recognize similarities in patterns from disparate origins, and to identify them. This classification and identification process produces equivalence classes which become our concepts, rules, words, symbols, and objects. In some cases the myth is such that we realize that the word is not the object, but there are other cases where we do identify, say, the visual and tactile images with the object.

Some of these relationships are more direct — words and objects are relationships classified fairly directly from sensory input. Others are less direct — semantics, concepts and syntax involve different levels and different hierarchies. Some classes are basic but not usually specially significant — such as blobs or lines. Others are "built up" from more basic classes.

There is one metaphor, or class of metaphor, which is particularly interesting in the context of this study of language acquisition. This metaphor makes use of the analogy between language and various other processes. The language metaphor has typically been used of various other human processes (such as vision), other social processes (such as architecture), other natural processes (such as mechanics).[3] In mathematics, the language metaphor has been formally defined and studied in terms of the properties of language. In philosophy, the language metaphor has also been studied extensively in quite a different way, in terms of the implications of particular applications of the metaphor.

The language metaphor can be used to develop an understanding of language processes by looking at analogous processes; the study of vision is particularly appropriate. Language is more than a metaphor in these contexts. We suggest that the coherence of the language metaphor is no accident, but a fundamental manifestation of actual physiological commonality of mechanism. Such cognitive patterns are deep metaphors for processes which occur in all humans, and in particular, in human language acquisition and development. We regard them as models for the psycholinguistic processes, and we develop these models into a projected automatic acquisition system in Chapter Thirteen.

Conjecture and Refutation, Theories and Hypotheses

Anderson writes:

> One way to make progress in science is to discover the inadequacies of existing theories. This means that one must submit his theories and those of others to critical analysis ... It should be obvious that these analyses, if correct, are a contribution to cognitive psychology. However, this last "obvious" conclusion is not obvious to all. It has been argued that one should be positive and supportive of work similar to his own, that one should not try to find and point out faults because this disrupts an impression of consensus in the field and of continued pro-

gress in understanding of cognitive phenomena. Undoubtedly there is a role for praise in science, but to avoid criticism would seem to promote intellectual stagnation.[4]

Let us presume a simple model of theory. A theory, in this model, consists in a collection of axioms and hypotheses, lemmas and theorems. The axioms and hypotheses are conjectures which are assumed to be true; the lemmas and theorems are propositions for which there exist proofs from the conjectures by way of approved systems of reasoning, and are hence consequences of the conjectures. The proofs, which are not strictly part of the theory, support the theory. Those conjectures which are regarded as self-evident and not subject to rejection are the axioms; and those which are regarded as tentative and not directly evidenced are the hypotheses. Those propositions which follow more or less directly from the conjectures and will be useful in proofs of the theorems are the lemmas; and those which follow from the conjectures and the lemmas, are the theorems.

This model is extremely simplistic. For example, the difficulty in proving a theorem is often caused by the problem of recognizing which propositions are both sufficient to allow a straightforward proof of the theorem, and themselves capable of straightforward proof as lemmas. To simplify and clarify the model still further, we identify any derived proposition as a theorem while considering its derivation, but assume all proven theorems as lemmas from the viewpoint of their potential usefulness in subsequent proofs. For a conjecture to be axiomatic requires either a high degree of confidence, or an absence of concern for what basis it may have in reality. In empirical science, it is difficult to see how the axioms can include more than the previously mentioned "approved systems of reasoning". Furthermore, strictly speaking, even these "axioms of science" should be open to question and rejection. Hypotheses, by contrast, are intended to be provisional and open to revision. Moreover, one particular type of hypothesis, the supposition, is included amongst the conjectures specifically in the hope of obtaining a contradiction and being invalidated. This is the refutation proof procedure. Refutation proof captures the essential nature of empirical science: a theory is explored to maximize the number of predicted consequences which can be tested against the reality being modelled. If a prediction is invalidated, the hypotheses are *all* called into question, but the axioms are all assumed to be beyond question.

The more hypotheses there are, the more difficult it is to identify which one may be at fault. A major source of complaints about methodology is the researcher who treats various conjectures as axiomatic, and exempt from reconsideration even if the theory fails. A more fundamental objection to some research is when the theory cannot be refuted because its implications do not in fact extend beyond the currently accepted data anyway. Much of the empirical work of science lies in using a theory to suggest ideas for experiments which can support or refute it.

Model as Theory

We turn now to consider the question of what it could mean to test a *model*, as opposed to a theory. We can further specify this as a computational model. There is some difficulty with computational models, since in this case a mechanism will be viewed in the light of an hypothesis. Its status and appropriate testing then necessarily follow Popper's requirement that we attempt disproof, to test validity. An AI proof would thus consist of a working computational mechanism (program). "Proof" in AI, in this sense, is of course open to considerable debate. It is difficult to see how a working computational model could constitute "disproof". It is also difficult to see how failure to make a model run might constitute proof.

To the extent that the model is an accurate realization or projection of a theory, we can say that it is a "working computational model". But whilst this model realizes behaviour which is consistent with that observed empirically, it is impossible to fault it, because it is like a theory whose predictions are always borne out. On the other hand, such a model is testable and violable provided that it is capable of producing (that is the equivalent in a theory of predicting) non-trivial behaviour which falls outside the bounds of currently accepted data. We might also note that in order to refute the model it is only necessary to cause it to behave in a way which is inconsistent with the modelled system.

In practice, however, there are a number of other difficulties, not least of which is assuring that the model is an accurate "bug-free" realization of the theory. At another level, inaccuracies may be introduced deliberately into the model (and hence also into its underlying theory) in order to avoid the complexity of a full model and hence make the model practically realizable. In this case deficiencies in the working model could be attributable to the simplifying assumptions rather than to the hypotheses.

These principles also operate within the domain of language learning itself: the recognition that a grammar should be treated as a theory was an important element of Generative Grammar; the earlier approach to grammar as a "unified theory of human behaviour" dates from the late 1940s. Each class in our grammar is a formalization of a proposition that its members are somehow similar in function, and can fill a particular slot. Each formula in our grammar is also a formalization of a proposition that its subunits belong together in a certain relationship, and together comprise a unit of a particular class. Both formulae and classes thus have the character of hypotheses.

When we use the grammar, *viz.* the class and formula hypotheses, to "generate" a "sentence", we are making a prediction about our language: that that "sentence" is a legal grammatical sentence of the language. This then leads to us thinking about which predicted "sentences" are indeed legal; We consider experiments to decide whether a hearer of the language would judge the sentence grammatical, or a speaker of the language would produce such a sentence, in an appropriate context. The first of these experiments involves fairly direct testing, and the second less direct testing. Note that other experiments will be necessary to test for under-generality in the grammar, since there may be grammatical sentences which will not be "generated" or, more to the point, "recognized" by the grammar.

On the basis of our experiments and testing, if our grammar is found deficient in some respect, we should be able to identify which hypotheses participated in the "generation" of an ungrammatical "sentence", and thus these classes and formulae become candidates for revision. In the case where our grammar is insufficiently general, we may need to augment our hypotheses. Noting that parses correspond to theorems, and partial and alternate parses to lemmas, it is apparent that our grammar is a system which corresponds completely with our concept of a theory, although the hypotheses are of a restricted nature.

Learning as Theory

The scientific method captures the way science learns about the workings of the universe, its laws, relationships, logic, *etc.* Here we have a methodology that cannot necessarily "steer us" to an accurate understanding of the universe, but can at least help to ensure that we do not "get too far off course": an heuristic. We argue that a similar heuristic methodology is the essence of human learning. People, consciously and unconsciously, make hypotheses and construct models, and in various ways revise them according to experience. There is clear evidence as we look at the acquisition of language by babies that they make hypotheses, which are subsequently revised, again presumably as a result of experience. There is considerable controversy over just what a learning mechanism is capable of, but if identified with the methodology of theory, there is a wealth of attestation to its power. Many of the assumptions made in the course of theoretical consideration of language learning indicate a view of language learning which conforms well to this paradigm. For example, Gold writes:

> In the case of identifiability in the limit the learner does not necessarily know when his guess is correct. He must go on processing information forever because there is always the possibility that information will appear which will force him to change his guess. If the learner were re-

quired to know when his answer is correct ... then none of the classes of languages investigated in the next chapter would be learnable in any of the learnability models. My justification for studying identifiability in the limit is this: A person does not know when he is speaking a language correctly; there is always the possibility that he will find that his grammar contains an error. But we can guarantee that a child will eventually learn a natural language, even if it will not know when it is correct.[5]

There are a number of criticisms of such a model of language learning, and these centre on the question of negative information. On the one hand there has been a claim that children do not make use of negative information,[6] but that "hypothesis testing" is dependent on such information. On the other hand, there is theoretical work (*e.g.* Gold) which seems to show that negative information is needed in the learning of a language. But both Braine and Gold must be regarded as suspect and inconclusive in first language acquisition: in neither worker is there a consideration of semantics. We should also remember that the subjects in Braine's experiments were adults. There are, furthermore, results in Gold which suggest that sufficiently well ordered input actually allows the learning of a more general class of languages, even in the absence of negative information. Whilst it may be infeasible that the child's language input is sufficiently well ordered, it is not apparent that his environment is not. Piaget's thesis is that learning starts with the development of an ontology for our sensory-motor environment, which has often been recognised as having a formal linguistic nature. Kelley notes another possible problem with the theory model:

> Any hypothesis testing scheme [would be] muddled by the ungrammatical data ... Any grammatical sentence that was more complex than what the child was prepared to deal with would be just as bad ... The child wants ... data that will either serve to confirm (or infirm) previously acquired constructs or ... will bear on the next step.[7]

This would, however, be a problem in any learning paradigm. Kelley's solution is that the child somehow filters out such "unacceptable input data".

Deductive Processes and Specification

We now turn our attention to the "approved systems of reasoning", which we referred to earlier, and look at their wider application.[8] We can distinguish two reciprocal principles which may be broadly characterized as inductive and deductive. The simpler and more amenable of this pair of principles is deduction, which is basically intension. This is the primary form of reasoning used in the proof process and is typically a transformation from the more general to the more specific, from rules or principles to instances or cases. But there is also a more powerful form of deduction, which recombines propositions without losing generality. The use of the term deduction implies, in either case, a chain of reasoning achieved by the formal application of a small number of deductive rules.

One of the deductive processes that does involve a reduction of generality is specialization. This involves substitution for (instantiation of) some or all of the variables in a proposition allowing discovery of an instance (a special case) of that proposition (the general case). This is precisely what is involved when a grammar is used for "generation" or "recognition". Specialization is also usually the last step in making a prediction. Projection of a theory or proposition to a more limited domain is another typical application of specialization.

A derivative process is specification, which involves incomplete instantiation. Here the emphasis is on formulation of a specific case through a purposive top-down goal-oriented process. The purpose of specification, in this sense, is to completely determine a specific case or application of a theory or model, again limiting it to a subdomain. This is the primary language acquisition process proposed in Transformational Generative Grammar, where a completely general "grammar" or "theory of language" is refined to give the grammar of a specified language.

Specification is a process which is complementary to inductive learning, since it can be used to achieve as tight a model as possible, minimizing the possibility of over-generalization. In slight contrast to specialization, emphasis here is on the specific target, not so much the reduction in generality.

It is a commonplace that the usual logical deductive processes may be carried out at a conscious level. However it is equally obvious that they are carried out in a rather imperfect way at that level. What may be less obvious is the subconscious utilization of deduction. We hypothesize that subconscious deduction underlies the learning process, and gives rise to the powerful phenomena which are evident in the child's acquisition of language and ontology. As we will see in Chapter Seven, particularly impressive analogues arise in the neurophysiological study of vision.

Learning as Analysis: Abstraction, Induction and Generalization

The deductive processes are mainly used in making use of our "learned knowledge", or in the case of specification in restricting the application of general rules or processes. The complementary inductive processes seem to be much more fundamental to learning phenomena.

Inductive processes tend to move from specific cases to a general rule. A set of specific cases which appear to share some sort of commonality or relationship may suggest a set of rules capable of characterizing those cases, generating them, and testing for membership of the set. People find it quite easy to come up with a general rule to describe a set of objects; and conversely, to give an instance or make a judgement about a potential instance is just as easy. However, any deductive process other than instantiation is likely to give a little more trouble, to involve conscious effort, and to admit subsequent explanation.

There are logical and mathematical rules of induction complementary to those for deduction. These rules are usually applied without difficulty in an informal context, but are sometimes difficult to explain. The apparent naturalness of recursion for specific concepts contrasts with the equally apparent opaqueness of the paradigm to students. This observation, in particular, suggests that the inductive processes involved in learning are primarily unconscious.

Focussing first on inductive processes which involve an increase in generality, we want now to think about abstraction as a recognition of patterns. The point is that relationships which occur in one context often are similar to those that occur in another; there are features in common in any set of instances. Abstraction involves extracting such similar relationships and common features, and discarding insignificant features and unstable relationships.

The patterns of paradigm and abstraction are very similar, have a common basis, and presumably derive from a common human mechanism. In both cases a consistent framework is recognized and preserved, and the variability of the remainder is made explicit. We can thus characterize paradigm as a result of the process of abstraction which defines a set of variable slots and a set of filler classes which specify how the slots may be instantiated. The abstraction process also provides a basis for metaphor, which has a complementary relationship with paradigm.

Thus the inductive process of abstraction involves recognition of patterns. Taking a slight shift of perspective and emphasis, we can see that these patterns can be restated as, or generalized to, rules or formulae. Of course, the patterns observed need not fit into one complete overall pattern or hierarchy. It is to be expected that many different hierarchies of patterns will be observed, and that there will be patterns which transcend hierarchies. Metaphor and semantics are examples of inter-hierarchical relationships. Chomsky's "transformations" and Pike's "cohesion" are examples of trans-hierarchical patterns.

The essence of generalization as a cognitive process, we are arguing, is that the particular specific cases and the abstracted patterns are used to generate rules which cover every case and are presumed to denote only legitimate instances. It is when this assumption breaks down, that over-generalization can be said to have occurred. This is the primary problem with generalization as a learning mechanism. The relationship of generalization to abstraction is thus fundamental. In an earlier paper, we described the process of generalization a little differently as "forming more abstract concepts by the association of simpler objects".[9] In our present argument, we still have a link with abstraction but the process is correctly seen as more constructive than simple recognition. The way we view something is equivalent to the abstraction we have of it, or more colloquially, the construction we put on it. A model is a construction in this sense. Piaget sees the relationship between abstraction and generalization as even more complex:

> Abstraction and generalization are obviously interdependent, each founded on the other. It results from this that only inductive generalization, proceeding from "some" to "all" by simple extension, will correspond to empirical abstraction, whereas "constructive" and "completive" generalizations in particular will correspond to reflective and reflected abstractions.[10]

Here the prime distinction Piaget is making is between a process independent of observer, and a process involving the observer. This is quite a helpful contribution to our understanding of constructive abstraction. Piaget's secondary distinction, the obscure contrast of "constructive" with "completive", and "reflective" with "reflected", arises from his "sticky mirror" memory model. The distinction concerns the involvement of abstraction and generalization in the learning process: a novel concept is "reflecting" initially in a rather passive and temporary way, but with the participation of already "reflected" concepts. Eventually, though, through a process of reorganization, it itself becomes part of the "mirror", a permanent "reflection" or "abstraction". The point is actually quite an important one, that subsequent generalization must be built on the results of earlier consolidated generalizations. There are thus two phases: "constructive" building of the concept, and "completive" consolidation of the "mirror".

Recursive Processes, and Inductive Learning

The possibility of recursion is implicitly encompassed by the inductive processes. If the same paradigm fits at a number of levels, this is no problem. If the recursion is direct, the unit defined by the corresponding formula will be a member of the filler class of one of its own slots. If it is indirect, the appropriate relationship will still (by induction) naturally occur. A unit can be added to a filler class which it subtends just as easily as to any other.

It only now remains to consider how these inductive processes can be related to the learning process. There is a fairly good consensus that, as

Sinclair-deZwart says, "some kind of inductive [learning] procedure has to be supposed",[11] although Transformational Generative Grammar (TGG) rejects this viewpoint. The TGG usage of "hypothesis" and "hypothesis testing" does not conform to the paradigm of inductive learning, and indeed explicitly excludes induction as a learning mechanism.

It has been shown that the "inductive" process alone is not sufficient for learning of arbitrary languages, unless it happens to be fortuitously well ordered. The reason for this is that it is easy either to overgeneralize or to "imagine" patterns and rules where the cases generalized were extraordinary or coincidental. Goldschlager uses an example of how a superstition about spilling salt might arise.[12]

There are two primary mechanisms by which overgeneralization can be overcome. These are both used in AI in Concept Learning research. The first utilizes negative information, whether by "presentation" of negative examples, in some of the earlier work, or by yes-no "testing" of model generated examples, in some recent work. The second technique is specialization, and again this has two forms. An explicit form of specialization is the pseudo-parsimony espoused by Brown: subsequent to any generalization the model is shrunk to one which minimally covers the "given" examples and entails a minimum of additional cases.[13] Whilst this technique does operate in conjunction with parsimony, there is clearly a tension between specialization and parsimony: parsimony increases generality by decreasing the number of rules; but specialization decreases generality by decreasing the number of novel instances predicted. Such specialization is problematic and precludes incremental learning as it is necessary to maintain a sufficiently complete set of "given" examples.

An implicit form of specialization is also used. Whilst generalization and specialization may be seen as being in tension and are often applied alternately, conservative focussing limits generalization according to certain rules. In particular, generalization is performed tentatively, one variable at a time, and tested in one of the two ways outlined earlier. If necessary the step is undone, or re-specialized, to ensure that the current concept is kept a strict (but increasingly trivial) specialization of the target concept.

This leads to a third technique for avoidance of over-generality, one which derives from Neurolinguistics and Psycholinguistics rather than AI, although it overlaps with conservative focussing. This technique again involves restriction of the generalization process. It has been introduced in the context of the known limitations on human cognitive abilities. It is one of the main battlegrounds of the "innateness" debate. And it also arises in discussion of theoretical results concerning language.

The essence of the idea is that language is not completely arbitrary, and the restrictions imposed by the environment in combination with the limitations of human cognitive processes have determined a more restricted class of languages which humans learn. The nativist view is one extreme variant of such a hypothesis: it sees humans as endowed with a minimal generalization of all human languages, and generalization itself is completely obviated. A less extreme view supposes that general cognitive limitations in combination with general cognitive capabilities effectively determine the set of possible human languages, and avoid considerable effort in searching a wider space. There is little theoretical evidence that restrictions can be so used, other than the "anomalous text" case of Gold. However, some empirical evidence comes from a consideration of creoles.

A number of other heuristics have been proposed to explain various observations and to be consistent in the imposition of limitations on generalization. One of the more significant of these is Eve Clark's "complexity hypothesis", a linguistically motivated proposal that "the less complex is learned before the more complex".[14] This makes considerable sense, and fits in both with Piaget's idea that "the simple is involved in the construction of the complex" and with the AI lore that "you can"t learn anything unless you almost know it already".[15] Another significant linguistic hypothesis considered by Herbert Clark is "generalization ... from the concrete to the abstract". Abstract concepts are formed by removing the concrete from an idea, but can only be learned and understood by humans by using analogy with the concrete. This point, incidentally, is a major component in Piaget's ideas.

Rubbish, Noise, Skeletons and Partial Analyses

There is a certain amount of information which is necessarily, deliberately, and irretrievably discarded by devices such as abstraction and perspective. However, this is not everything we can expect a learning model to ignore: there may be data which is reluctantly discarded because the mechanisms do not (yet) exist either to store it or process it. There may also be data which is implicitly discarded because it is distorted by noise, and there may be data which ought to be discarded because it is incorrect or misleading.

In the case of language learning involving restricted generalization processes, there will be occasions when the "sentences" are simply too complex to be assimilated into the current framework of rules. We are well aware that much of what we hear is muddied by literal noise which distracts us from what is significant and can block out significant data. There is also the noise of free-variation, accents, dialects, colloquialisms etc. We also encounter the extreme noise of unmitigated ungrammatical "sentences". Kelley argues that to the child there is relatively little difference between these different types of noise: all must be regarded equally as "the abundant presence of unacceptable input data";[16] all of these must be discarded by the child. Telegraphic speech is one source of evidence of such discard. Thus Kelley reports evidence of "signalling mechanisms" mediating the discard process. For example:

Children tend not to listen to adult speech beginning with unfamiliar words.[17]

Insofar as we can recognize sequences which fit our classes and formulae, we parse them. Insofar as the unfamiliar portion is a fairly small proportion of the whole, we may be able to fit our data to our inductive rules. But as soon as some meagre limit of complexity or unfamiliarity is exceeded, we are at a loss. Kelley calls such enforced limitation "the mechanism of attempted comprehension".

One of the hardest things to do, especially in "Information Science", is to throw information away — but this is what science has always had to do. A learning system must be designed to "avoid biting off more than it can chew". It needs mechanisms which allow it to discover useful skeletons from which may be learned rough approximations and gross simplifications of eventual concepts, grammars and systems. Such a skeleton grammar may itself generate skeleton sentences which are not "grammatical" in the target "language". This contrasts, of course, with the way conservative focussing seeks to "generate" only interior specializations of the target "concept". Whilst it may be safer to approach the "concept" from within, skeletal successive approximation can quite usefully straggle both inside and outside the borders of a "concept". This is also currently one of the most significant contrasts between children learning a language and machines learning concepts. To remain totally within the realm of the "correct" is of major concern to the implementors of learning machines, but of little interest to children. Note the different responses to overgeneralization: the trainer always corrects the concept learner, the parent seldom corrects the child. The concept learner always immediately re-specializes, the child seldom abandons his generalizations.

We now turn to the notion of bootstrapping, which comes from computer science, describing the initial loading of an operating system. The image of the "bootstrap" is the somewhat unlikely one of "pulling yourself up by your bootstraps". The computing meaning is writing, loading, and executing a succession of programs, or tools, each of which makes it a little easier to write, load and execute more complex programs. This approach is also appropriate to the learning of languages,[18] and has been applied in the fields of "text analysis" and "higher criticism".

Siklossy learns language by relating it to a "functional language" (FL) which is essentially a parse tree representation of the world. FL presupposes a specific ontology allowing specific FL expressions to be given as the meanings for NL sentences. He recognizes that this approach to language learning merely "passes the buck" from under-standing the manifold "subtleties" of NL to mapping explicitly mani-fested "subtleties" of the FL. The problem is that the FL which sup-posedly represents the external environment is used as the internal rep-resentation. His proposed solution is that the internal representation should somehow "evolve", and once a given level of complexity has been achieved, this can be used as the base for further analysis and develop-ment:

> A much more powerful system may be able to bootstrap itself and use the natural language it has started to learn as its main representation, with possible references from time to time to the functional language. Semantic subtleties could then be described in the natural language it-self.[19]

This proposal is a little too simplistic. Whilst the phenomenon of sub-vocalization indicates some such role for language, a primary neural ontological representation must reflect more general sensory-motor functionality in addition to language.

One of the most intriguing metaphors derived from psychology is the "hologram" as a model of memory. The phenomena are quite extraordi-nary, whether we think of the recording as taking place on film, or in a brain. The hologram has four particularly interesting properties, of which only the first, and least interesting, is well-known. First, then, a hologram can store and project a three-dimensional image. The reason for this is an underlying second property, that every "point" on a holo-gram contains information about every "point" of the image. Thus if stereopsis gives us two perspectives on an object, holography stores mil-lions. The third property is that the size of a hologram correlates only with the sharpness of the image and a small portion of a hologram can project the entire image, with only loss of resolution and perspective. The fourth and most interesting property also follows from the second: a hologram may have a number of images stored on it, and if a portion of one image is projected through it, that image alone will be projected, in full. There are of course limitations to this associative property: there is a practical limit to the number of images which can be stored in the same hologram, and there is a decrease in resolution and increase in noise as the number increases.

Human memory seems to have properties analogous to each of these. The analogy with stereoptic and binaural perception is obvious. Destroying some small portions of the brain, both in experiments and in accidents, has no effects attributable to localization within an area of the brain. The effect rather relates only to the extent of the damage. The brain obviously stores many "images", and this evidence suggests that the memory traces are distributed throughout an area. It appears quite certain that the property of many "images" to one storage unit holds good, and correspondingly, so does the property of many "parts" of "images" per storage unit.

Evolution

The related concepts of evolution and development are recurring themes of this study which deserve a little explanation and clarification, particularly in relation to the biological "Theory of Evolution" which has become the prototype for the concept of evolution. The etymology of the two words is ultimately related to a pair of Latin words conveying the meanings of "roll" and "turn". The idea of development is an unrolling or exposing of a plan. The emphasis of evolution is a turning into something out of something else. Evolution exemplifies a particle perspective and development a wave perspective. Development is seen as a gradual change (emphasis continuity), while evolution is a series of apparently abrupt or independent changes (emphasis discontinuity).

Thus, not only can we talk about evolution in relation to species, we can talk about it in relation to culture, society, language, science, *etc.* What we are doing is emphasizing that there have been a series of transitions from one state or stage to another. Similarly we can talk about the "development" of any of these as a single entity, but by the nature of the particle perspective, we cannot de-focus the term "development" to a plurality or progression of individuals. Some writers do misuse the term "evolution" by application to a continuous process. However, for the most part, the general usage of the terms is consistent with this distinction. An interesting argument in this context is a recent book by Robert Young, *Darwin's Metaphor of Evolution* (1988) which sees evolution as a metaphor which assists the human cognitive process to grasp the complexity of change in the natural world.

In some cases the evolution of various systems is interrelated. For example, society includes culture which includes language. As society changes, so must the culture, and as these two change, so must the language, in order for it still to be relevant. Language is dependent on relationships with the environment, and thus is sensitive to any changes in the environment.

There is yet another important distinction between two classes of change which is made in relation to biological systems. There are the changes described variously as accommodation, assimilation or learning, which occur within an individual; and there are the genetic, mutation or selection changes which occur within a succession. The latter can only be called evolution, but are not real changes from one form into another. The former have different elements best considered from different perspectives but are essentially evolutionary in character, and are true reworkings of one physical form into another. The first form, individually environmentally determined change, is said to be phaenotypical, whilst the second, evolutionary genetically determined change, is said to be genotypical. This distinction is the crux of some of the arguments in Chapter Six about innateness. There is also a third sort of change – genetically determined development. This is not phaenotypical, but development of the capacity for such change is genotypical.

Siklossy describes the process used by ZBIE, his language learning system, as "Evolutionary Learning", being phaenotypical evolutionary change of the first type.[20] Similar considerations are evident in Piaget's "reflecting" versus "reflected" distinction – there is a distinction between the temporary and reversible "reflection" which is the result of current "reflecting" and the permanent and irreversible "reflection" which is the result of the "reflected" surface. Piaget's assimilation process may again be described as phaenotypical evolutionary change.

There are some problems with the second, genetic, type of evolution: there is no evidence of any effective relationship between phaenotype and genotype. There has been some controversial evidence of participation of genetic material in learning, and in some cases even of learning showing up in changes in the genes. In general even the simplest and most classical of the experiments of this nature which have been reported have been questioned, and have apparently not been successfully repeated. Note that the idea of a transfer from phaenotype to genotype is implicit in many views of language and "evolution". For example, Staats states unequivocally:

> The original acquisition of language by primitive man occurred on the basis of learning principles ... Languages evolve and change according to the same principles operating within one individual and over a number of individuals.[21]

He however fails to question how the language-learning mechanisms came to be genetically transmitted. This brings us to the question of Darwinian "evolution" and its progeny. We have never seen any even marginally convincing evidence for transmutation between species. On the other hand, there are many features of the neural and linguistic developmental process which evoke a strong "evolutionary" metaphor, and can indeed be accurately described in evolutionary terms since evolution denotes the progressive transformation of forms through stages. Descriptive usage in discussion of acquisition and development thus has no relationship to "evolution" in the "Darwinian" mould, which is the origin of the metaphorical usage.

The Importance of Errors: Successive Approximation

> In the natural situation of the child with his family the best evidence that he possesses construction rules is the occurrence of systematic errors. So long as a child speaks correctly, it is possible that he says only what he has heard. In general we cannot eliminate the possibility of an exact model for each sentence that is put out. However when a small boy says "I digged in the yard" ... it is unlikely that he is imitating. Furthermore, his mistake is not a random one. We can see how he might have made it by overgeneralizing certain existent regularities.[22]

It is easy for us to suppose that errors are totally bad, but here we argue that errors can be useful and helpful in language acquisition, and indeed at the heart of what learning is all about. The proverb about one "learning from his mistakes" illustrates the utility of errors, but we may make an even stronger claim that "to try to make errors" can be a useful learning heuristic.

The quotation above from Brown illustrates that errors provide us with evidence that learning can never be guaranteed to be complete. "Learning to criterion" is an approach used by psychologists and educationalists to counter this limitation. A criterion may be N correct responses in a row, or it may take the form of requiring 75% in an exam. "Criterion learning" can be distinguished from "norm learning" in that the learning process is continued until the "criterion" is reached, and the only grading is pass-fail.

Gold points out that in learning language we may never reach criterion, and even if we do, we have no way of knowing that we have.[23] The Brown quotation also illustrates that errors can provide us with evidence that something other than "rote learning" is taking place. In this case the error is evidence that the child is working with a system of rules. The existence of such a system of rules is evidence that generalization is taking place, and that the errors are over-generalizations. A recognition of such errors then affords the child the opportunity to correct his system of rules. Such errors may also prompt the parent to help the chid to correct his "grammar". Challenges to these interpretations are frequent, and are discussed in Chapters Four to Six.

Errors as Models

So far we have made the unfair assumption that the child is the one who makes all the errors. There is, however, a general recognition of "the inaccuracy of the child's input information". This creates another serious paradox—that the child can manage to learn so well given erroneous models. Braine did experiments which showed (to his disappointment) that learning of rules can proceed with no significant difference even when the error rate is 7% (which was originally to be the first and highest proportion of anomalies in a series of experiments).[24] We have already seen that over-complex "sentences" can be just as unhelpful and unacceptable to the child's learning system as overt erroneous models. The "signalling mechanism" and "mechanism of attempted comprehension" of Kelley[25] were proposed to show how the child could exclude all such incomprehensible data. The implicit assumption in these proposed exclusion mechanisms is that the true errors are not systematic. For if they were, the child could legitimately learn them as "grammatical rules", and there would be no reason why he shouldn't. We do see continual evidence of the phenomenon of the child picking up "bad grammar" (which could equally well be described as a dialectic difference).

We should also notice that the sentence is not the only significant unit, and that there may be useful segments in a sentence which is incomprehensible as a whole, although this possibility would be excluded by Kelley's "signalling mechanism". In considering both errors in the child's "input" and errors in the child's "output", we have seen positive as well as negative aspects. The fact that there are some advantages indicates that the deliberate courting of errors may be a useful heuristic at times, that "trial and error" strategies may be so directed as to guarantee that an incorrect "trial" generalization causes an "error" promptly. The conservative focussing strategy restricts the extension of a concept as much as possible, usually to a single dimension or variable. Each inductive step is then followed by a test example constructed to lie within the extension to the concept—in the new hypothesis, but not the original concept. If the test is positive, the generalization is permitted to stay. But the more useful case is where it is negative, the generalization is determined to be in "error", and it is discarded.

One concrete sense in which this stratagem is not ideal is that it presumes that there are no negative terms in the formulation of the concept. Thus if a concept is best expressed as a general rule with a relatively small number of exceptions, this optimal formulation of the concept cannot be learned and the procedure may not be able to do better than to list all the examples.

The Importance of Restrictions and Limitations

This project does have the ultimate goal of providing a faithful simulation of child language acquisition. One might question whether a system constructed just to succeed at language learning will have much in common with the child's acquisition system. I strongly suspect it will, provided we insist that the system have the same information-processing limitations as a child and provided its language-learning situation has the same information-processing demands as that of the child.[26]

All of us have experienced the overwhelming difficulty of some task which after a little time and thought produced a more restricted perspective, becoming a simpler problem. This can happen, perhaps by decomposition into subtasks, perhaps by analogy with a simpler domain, or perhaps by recognizing that only a restricted form of the problem actually need be solved. All of these possibilities involve the recognition of restrictions, of ourselves, of the domain, or of the problem itself.

The most obvious restrictions are those which derive from our general physical and mental limitations. The latter are discussed in Chapter Four and are what Anderson refers to above. If, as with Anderson, the object of the research is understanding child language acquisition, then the models proposed must take into account the cognitive limitations of mankind in general, and of babies in particular. The nativist view proposes that specifically linguistic restrictions on human capabilities constrain and determine the class of human language which can develop—implying that both the set of languages which may be learned and the subset of such languages which may have evolved are restricted.

Considering human restrictions has highlighted for us the probability that there are restrictions on human language, and on the class of human learnable languages as discussed above. This is an example of restriction of the problem.

Such restriction analysis is very common. It arises continually in computer science in terms of specification. The initial specification of the problem may be very general and open-ended: *e.g.* a system to solve equations, or an accounting package. The job of the analyst involves a tightening of these specifications by the discovery of more information about the requirements: *e.g.* the equations being solved, or the accounting systems being computerized. This results in the specification of a simpler problem or series of problems: *e.g.* a system of linear equations, or a payroll package for a hundred and a debtors system for ten thousand. This process continues until a cheapest adequate system has been specified. This corresponds to the mathematical concept of the necessary and sufficient.

In the case of language, it is helpful to have an accurate idea of the general class of language so that the relevance of theoretical studies may be determined, and the nature and specifics of the human limitations may be deduced or hypothesized less arbitrarily.

Domain Restrictions

A more general form of restriction involves changing the domain to be studied to one which is simpler or better understood. Human and problem restrictions can also be seen as special cases of domain restrictions where the full problem domain is the entire system of relevance. From this point, we will restrict the denotation of domain to that part of the total system which excludes the human and problem subsystems, namely their context, our sensory-motor environment.

The environment is a well-ordered system governed by consistent laws and exhibiting well-defined relationships. Our 'sensory-motor environment' is the external environment as viewed and affected by us, or more strictly, an ordered transformation of it which is mediated by some fairly consistent but incompletely-known mappings and processes. The term sensory-motor environment is used here to refer to the environment as it relates to the human, but again specifically excluding the human and problem subsystems, and the sensory-motor representations, mappings and processes, which are themselves part of the human and problem space.

Language is itself in a correspondence with the sensory-motor environment, mediated not only by the syntactic, semantic and phonological representations, mappings and processes, but by the sensory-motor representations, mappings and processes. The "better" this correspondence is, the closer to bijective the mapping is, but since the brain is a smaller domain, the correspondence is not injective. If we were referring to the universe, it would not be surjective either. But since we are referring to the sensory-motor environment, the correspondence is surjective by *fiat*, since it is part of the system of relevance defined by what is in direct relationship with the human and problem domains. This loose definition and concomitant surjection relationship is equivalent to the hypothesis that the relationships are generalizations. To the extent that the relationship is also injective, it is partly specialized, and partly restrictions in the sensory-motor environment which determine similar restrictions in language. This mapping of restrictions is at the heart of Piaget's constructivism.

These arguments seem to show that for these restrictions to take effect, the processes must be "sufficiently" injective. This is the essence of Piaget's "sticky mirror" model. Whilst the processes cannot be strictly injective, the existence of relationships between units of the sensory-motor environment determines a powerset of equivalence classes to which an individual learns an injective correspondence. For an injection to be a "sufficient" mapping of restrictions it must have a "good" choice of equivalence relationships. Since we observe, or assume, that we do individually have such a "good" choice, this argument leads us back to a consideration of heuristics for generalization, and obviates any need for specifically linguistic capabilities.

To give a simple example, there is a relationship between all "tables". In fact, we may actually find it hard to distinguish one table from another. Thus the visual system provides natural selection of relationships, being restricted in such a way that similar "tables" automatically go into the one equivalence class, presumably along with "benches", "desks", even "chairs", "stools", "coffee tables", *etc.* Physical considerations relating to the interrelated optics of size and distance help to commit this helpful confusion. Thus we have natural aggregations into classes, and we needn't spend much time devising purely semantic mechanisms for doing so.

Unhelpful Restrictions

Some authors see restrictions as totally unhelpful and indeed detrimental to learning. Their problem with restrictions may be attributed to three unhelpful restrictions on their own view of language and learning. These are that they may see humans as more restricted than they actually are, they may see the class of human languages as less restricted than it actually is, and, most generally, they may fail to conceive of a direct relationship between these human cognitive restrictions and human language restrictions. An example of these views is the following comment made by Wexler:

> As a description of a child constructing his grammar, this model clearly ignores the fact that at any one time only a little data is available to the child, who constructs his grammar over the course of time, using a little bit of data at a time. It might then be suggested that this cognitive constraint on the amount of data available might make the learning problem easier, thus vitiating the need for some formal constraints on grammars. But this conclusion is logically wrong; exactly the opposite holds. With all the data before the learner at one time, with no problems of loss of data because of memory limitations, with no restrictions on the complexity of computation based on large amounts of data, the learner has a relatively easy time. Allowing the learner only a bit of time, and not allowing him to remember past data, puts a severe cognitive restriction on the learner which will make his job more difficult. Thus, in general, stronger formal constraints will be needed.[27]

There is little argument against the existence of constraints on grammar: such constraints do exist and moreover ensure the fitness of a language for learning by humans within their limitations. However, these limitations are themselves well matched to the domain. Conversely, it is ridiculous to insist on "an absence of restrictions on the complexity of computations", since all mechanisms (especially Turing Machines) have such restrictions and subtend classes of learnable languages and unlearnable languages.[28] It is reasonable to suppose that restrictions on the living mechanism do restrict the class of learnable languages, and hence serve to limit the search space of valid generalizations and child grammars. A mechanism without some of these restrictions may well be able to take advantage of forms of presentation which the child cannot. But this has not been demonstrated, since no adequate artificial learning mechanism for NL (Natural Language) has yet been constructed. We are sure that understanding the human, problem and domain restrictions applicable will help to construct such a mechanism.

The Importance of Zero: Empty Sets and Zero Morphs

The invention of "zero", heralding the development of (fixed) radix arithmetic, was one of the foundations of mathematics. There is just as much importance attached to the knowledge that there is zero of something as there is in knowing that there is some other number. In fact there may be more information conveyed by zero, as negative information, than by the existence of some examples of something. This is also related to the central place of the empty set and the truth value *false* in mathematics and logic.

Another important truth pioneered in the invention of "zero" is the concept of a place keeper, the role it has in radix arithmetic. This concept is also important in linguistics and formal languages where it is useful to be able to specify that an element is optional or un-manifested in a rule. Thus the filler class for a slot in a formula may include the zero morph (or null morph). A simple example occurs in conjugation of the present tense of a regular verb, *e.g.* "to skip". The root is "skip", and only the third person singular requires the manifest suffix "-s", giving "skips". It is convenient to have this inflection correspond to a filler class, which therefore contains the zero morph.

The next section of this widely ranging chapter presents a group of fairly unrelated points, which have in common that they are all moving away from the concrete and scientific to the intangible, creative or artistic — the central domain of metaphor.

In our earlier discussion we distinguished two perspectives: a static or particle perspective, and a dynamic or wave perspective. This distinction is about alternatives for the perception of units. We can also distinguish alternatives for the achievement of goals. The first is a single complex process which is specific, deterministic, and reflects an external or global perspective: the process involves locating the initial and final states within the connecting state transition network, and analyzing the network to determine an effective path between. This is the normal cognitive analytic approach. A second way of achieving a goal is by a series of very general, very simple sub-processes operating on fairly local data which thus reflects an internal perspective: each sub-process transforms its own current input to become its output such that the total system accepts the initial state as input, generates the final state as output and is characteristically non-deterministic. We discuss the relative merits of these processes in Chapters Five and Nine.

The special case of parsing reduces perception to recognition, and achievement to generation or production. The usual distinction made for parsing processes is *top-down* versus *bottom-up* (based on the metaphor of part-whole hierarchies and upside-down trees) and reflects the direction of analysis rather than the nature of the mechanism. A top-down procedure is goal oriented, and characteristically backward. Its focus is on how to compose a specific unit from others which it will then have to consider as new goals. It will typically be implemented as an automaton exhibiting a degree of look-ahead sufficient to determine which choice to make. An equivalent alternative is that instead of a capability for look-ahead it has a capability for backtracking and undoing previous hypotheses. The bottom-up procedure starts from the data and works forward, constructing what units it can from those that are given, which are then the input data for the next stage or level of processing. It can be appropriately implemented by a network which recognizes groupings which form a unit at each level of the parse.

The first system is characteristically active, as choices are made according to the units found and the goal being pursued. Whilst the different choices can be explored in parallel and non-deterministically, it is inherently a sequential deterministic process and to exploit such possible parallelism requires an expensive "brute-force" approach involving duplicating the system for each choice. The second system is characteristically passive, since groupings of units are simultaneously recognized by distinct and independent processes. It is inherently parallel and non-deterministic as the parse or parses found are a function of independent processes at each level. Thresholds and internal contexts will determine priorities for alternate parses, and suppress potential parses. Expectations, external context and feedback will tend to produce more active effects.

The active or passive nature of language processing is implicit in many discussions of language acquisition and processing. It is also occasionally raised explicitly, and indeed Kelley characterizes the nativist "generative framework" by its:

> emphasis on the activeness of the evaluation as opposed to the passive establishment of associative networks.[29]

Kelley's comment is directed at the implications for the acquisition process: the development of active acquisition or parsing processes is very difficult to explain with current evolutionary and neurological theory.

Work and Play

When discussing the metaphoric use of language, we must recognize the all-too-common view that metaphor is a form of "play" — and therefore not a cognitive process for serious consideration. But here we would rather prefer to consider work and play as alternative structures in two orientations — practical *versus* pleasurable. Applied science and engineering are pre-eminently practical disciplines where achievement has some tangible benefit to society at large. On the other hand, we could argue that the main beneficiary of metaphor is art which, with pure mathematics, is primarily directed toward the intangible appreciation of an individual, and typically the process and achievement are equally a source of pleasure. Yet there is art in engineering (*e.g.* architecture) as there is engineering in art (*e.g.* sculpture). Furthermore, work-satisfaction is a primary source of pleasure, but the fulfillment of any obligation, even if self-imposed, can be work and is practical.

Sometimes the work/play distinction is made into too much of a dichotomy. This particularly affects views of the role of play in the development of a child. However, the recognition that play can be "educational" is an acknowledgement that practical and pleasurable achievement can be one, although the recognition that all natural play has practical value was historically slower to come. The sort of play we like to engage in is generally quite constructive, and this is particularly the case for children. One essential aspect of child's play is control:

> Typically, play is defined as those activities that are produced spontaneously and for which extrinsic rewards are either non-existent or secondary ... The intrinsic reward for play appears to be the control that the child possesses in play situations ... While playing, the child is in control of the situation, creating processes and results more or less at will.[30]

Kuczaj also relates the control attribute to various other aspects of play:

> Control ... seems to be one of the aspects of play that children most enjoy ... One of the aspects of the situation that children may particularly enjoy controlling is that of establishing the moderately discrepant event and attempting to resolve it in a situation for which there is no external consequence for failure. This hypothesis gains support from the fact that children seem most likely to play with (practice) those things that they are in the process of acquiring.[31]

This proposal has considerable merit and is complementary to, if not a sensory-motor analogue of, the process of consolidation we discuss in Chapter Five.

Intuition and Introspection

Before we move too much further into the theoretical examination of the processes involved in human cognitive activity, we should consider what humans *think* their methods of procedure are. Intuition describes an unconscious, if not sub-conscious, phenomenon, which is definitively not self-conscious. Introspection by contrast is completely conscious, and fundamentally self-conscious. Unfortunately, introspection has had a fairly bad press, and our intuitive ideas about things are negatively described as "naïve". However, although they fail us for scientific purposes at times, intuition is fundamental to all our scientific activity, and introspection to much of it.

The von-Neumann computer and the procedural programming methodology are supreme examples of introspection in practice. Every programmer approaches his problem with an idea of what has to be done, and how he would go about it if doing it by hand. Such introspection is the basis for the discovery of an algorithm, a "naïve" algorithm. Similarly our intuitions and expectations are involved in the processes of development, testing and understanding programs. As computer science has matured these processes have been formalized, with emphases on "program proving" and "declarative programming". The new formalisms are themselves based on "techniques" or "calculi" which originated in human intuition and introspection. Furthermore, when such methodology leads to the derivation of extraordinary results, we do not feel that we truly understand or believe them until we have an intuitive grasp of their truth.

Turning to language, we see both intuition and introspection as fundamental, and this is still the basis of most linguistic work, TGG notwithstanding. Schank is well aware of this and encourages us to use intuitions:

> We are not ... making all the possible human predictions.[32]

And in relation to learning in particular, and AI (Artificial Intelligence) in general, Hayes frequently appeals to and emphasizes the use of introspection:

> What it means, in introspective terms, is that learning a new fact or acquiring a new concept, is liable to have far-reaching consequences for the ways in which one understands the meaning of other concepts.

There is a tried and true way of getting knowledge out of people's heads and into a formalisation. Within AI, it has been called "knowledge engineering" ... but essentially the same technique is used by linguists ... In consultation with an "expert" ... one builds a preliminary formalisation, based on his introspective account of what the knowledge in his head is.[33]

Intuition is a unique human propensity. It can be a mysterious description for beliefs or conclusions to which we cannot directly attribute a logic. And scientifically we can relate it to some specific logical processes, such as association, creativity, or ingenuity:

Arthur Koestler (1965) argued that all creativity, including artistic creativity, scientific discovery and even humour, is the combination of concepts which are not usually combined. Thus original thinking does not involve creating something out of nothing; rather it is a novel combination of old ideas. [34]

In every case, the creative act involves some luck which is responsible for getting two previously un-associated ... concepts simultaneously active on the memory surface in conjunction with a degree of preparation on the part of the brain, consisting of having the appropriate features associated with the concepts and being able to recognize the AHA reaction *e.g.* Archimedes yelling eureka when it occurs ... Of course, there is no need for animals to just wait around until they are impressed by lucky inputs. Animals actively seek out varied inputs in order to increase the likelihood of forming useful associations. Thus animals are naturally inquisitive, children engage in play, newborn babies scan the environment with their eyes (Haith,1980) and techniques for encouraging lateral thinking (de Bono,1969) are indeed effective in promoting creative ideas.[35]

These comments illustrate the interplay of active and passive processes in human cognitive experience. On the one hand, creativity and abstraction are such passive processes, and notably primarily unconscious processes in the sense we are discussing here. By contrast animals are not passive, but active and, in particular, inquisitive and playful.

Notes to Chapter Two

1. Turbayne, E.M., *The Myth of Metaphor* (University of South Carolina Press, Columbia, South Carolina, 2nd Ed., 1971).
2. Lakoff, George, and Mark Johnson, *Metaphors we Live By* (University of Chicago Press, 1980).

3.   Pribram, K.H., *Languages of the Brain* (Prentice-Hall, Englewood Cliffs, NJ, 1971);
     Blakemore, C., and F. Cooper, "Development of the Brain depends on the Visual
     Environment", *Nature*, 1970, Vol. 228, pp.477-8.
4.   Anderson, John R., *Language, Memory, and Thought* (Lawrence Erlbaum Associates,
     Hillsdale, NJ, 1976), p. 23.
5.   Gold, E.M., "Language Identification in the Limit", *Information and Control*, 10
     (1967), p. 450.
6.   Braine, Martin D. S., "On Two Types of Models of the Internalization of Grammars",
     in Dan I. Slobin, ed., *The Ontogenesis of Language* (Academic Press, 1971).
7.   Kelley, K.L., *Early Syntactic Acquisition* (Rand Corporation, Santa Monica, CA,
     1967), p.83.
8.   See Powers, David M.W., "Natural Language the Natural Way", *DCS Report No 8404*,
     Department of Computer Science, University of New South Wales, Australia (May
     1984), Presented at the Australasian Association for Logic Annual Meeting, July
     4-8, 1984, p.2f.
9.   Turk, Christopher C. R., "A Correction NL Mechanism", *ECAI-84: Advances in
     Artificial Intelligence* (Elsevier Science Publishers, 1984), p.16.
10. Piaget, Jean, "The Psychogenesis of Knowledge and its Epistemological
     Significance", in M. Piatelli-Palmarini, ed., *Language and Learning: The Debate
     between Jean Piaget and Noam Chomsky* (Routledge and Kegan Paul, 1979), p.28.
11. Sinclair-deZwart, H., "Language Acquisition and Cognitive Development", in
     Timothy E. Moore, ed., *Cognitive Development and the Acquisition of Language*
     (Academic Press, New York, 1973), p.12.
12. Goldschlager, Leslie M., *A Computational Theory of Higher Brain Function*
     (Computer Science Department, Standford University, Standford, CA, April,
     1984), p.16f.
13. Brown, Roger, and Colin Fraser, "The Acquisition of Syntax", in C. N. Cofer and
     Barbara S. Musgrave, eds, *Verbal Behavior and Learning: Problems and Processes*
     (McGraw-Hill, 1963), p.185.
14. Clark, Eve W., "What's in a Word? On the Child's Acquisition of Semantics in his
     First Language", in Timothy E. Moore, ed., *Cognitive Development and the
     Acquisition of Language* (Academic Press, New York, 1973), p.55.
15. Winston, Patrick H., *Artificial Intelligence* (Addison-Wesley, Reading, MA, 1977, 2nd
     ed. 1984), p.396.
16. Kelley, K. L., *Early Syntactic Acquisition* (Rand Corporation, Santa Monica, CA,
     November 1967), p.83f.
17. *Op. cit.*, p.84f.
18. Siklossy, Laurent, "Natural Language Learning by Computer", in H. A. Simon and
     Laurent Siklossy, eds., *Representation and Meaning: Experiments with Information
     Processing Systems* (Prentice-Hall, 1972).
19. *Op. cit.*, p.323.
20. Siklossy, Laurent, "Natural Language Learning by Computer", in H. A. Simon and
     Laurent Siklossy, eds, *Representation and Meaning: Experiments with Information
     Processing Systems* (Prentice-Hall, 1972), p.323.

21. Staats, Arthur W., "Linguistic-Mentalistic Theory versus an Explanatory S-R Learning Theory of Language Development" in Dan I. Slobin, ed., *The Ontogenesis of Language* (Academic Press, 1971), p.141.

22. Brown, Roger Brown, and Colin Fraser, "The Acquisition of Syntax", in C. N. Cofer and Barbara S. Musgrave, *Verbal Behavior and Learning: Problems and Processes* (McGraw-Hill, 1963), p.160.

23. Gold, E. M., "Language Identification in the Limit", *Information and Control*, 10, 1967, p.450.

24. Braine, Martin D. S., "On Two Types of Models of the Internalization of Grammars", in Dan I. Slobin, ed., *The Ontogenesis of Language* (Academic Press, 1971).

25. Kelley, K. L., *Early Syntactic Acquisition* (Rand Corporation, Santa Monica, CA, November 1967), p.84.

26. Anderson, John R., "Computer Simulation of a Language Acquisition System: A First Report" in R. L. Solso, *Information Processing and Cognition: The Loyola Symposium* (Lawrence Erlbaum Associates, Hillsdale, 1975), p.301.

27. Wexler, Kenneth, and Peter W. Culicover, *Formal Principles of Language Acquisition* (MIT Press, Cambridge, MA, 1980), p.8f.

28. Gold, E. M., "Language Identification in the Limit", *Information and Control*, 10, 1967, p.450.

29. Kelley, K.L., *Early Syntactic Acquisition* (Rand Corporation, Santa Monica, CA, November 1967), p.78.

30. Kuczaj, Stan A., *Crib Speech and Language Play* (Springer-Verlag, New York, NY, 1983), p.13.

31. *Op. cit.*, p.166.

32. Schank, Roger C., "Identification of Conceptualization Underlying Natural Language", in Roger C. Schank and K. M. Colby, eds, *Computer Models of Thought and Language* (Freeman, 1973), p.241.

33. Hayes, P.J., "The Naive Physics Manifesto" in D. Michie, ed., *Expert Systems in the Micro-electronics Age* (Edinburgh U.P., Edinburgh, 1979), pp.251, 267.

34. Goldschlager, Leslie M., *A Computational Theory of Higher Brain Function* (Computer Science Department, Standford University, Standford, CA, April 1984), pp.20, 24.

35. *Op. cit.,*, pp.19–21.

Chapter Three

Psychology and Psycholinguistics

In this chapter we begin to consider the contribution of Psycholinguistics to our understanding of language. This subfield of Psychology concerned with language is indeed primarily concerned with language acquisition in the child, but also makes use of data from abnormal and artificial contexts, from foreign language learning and from the development of creoles and pidgins. We note that there is a spectrum of possible mixes of genetic and environmental determination of language facility. This chapter assumes a more acquisitive model and leaves discussion of the innate to a later chapter. Given that an acquisitive language facility involves a slow construction of language and ontology, we consider a step-by-step build-up. We see this in the learning of prosody, phonology and vocabulary, in a succession of increasingly complex production capabilities, and in overgeneralization as an indicator of generalized grammatical rules. At a single point of time in a child's development we can also see an instantaneous indicator of his relative capability in comprehension and production, and we note different apparent forms and roles of imitation and correction in this development.

It is often forgotten that there is a great difference in science between "discovery" and "verification". Verification has been the main concern of the philosophy of scientific method, and the conclusion some time ago, following the ideas of Karl Popper, seemed to be that verification, as such, was not possible. Only disproof was possible, and verification was the absence for the time being of disproof. A new kind of thinking about discovery, found in the work of Kuhn[1], suggests that discovery, as opposed to verification, will follow on what Kuhn calls a "paradigm shift". This is especially so in a new field such as Natural Language (NL) acquisition by automatic learning.

This point is well put by Langley, Simon, Bradshaw, and Zytkow when they write:

In the scientist's house are many mansions ... the progress of science calls for the most diverse repertoire of activities—activities so numerous and diverse that it would seem that any person could find one to his or her taste. Outsiders often regard science as a sober enterprise, but we who are inside see it as the most romantic of all callings. Both views are right. The romance adheres to the processes of scientific discovery, the sobriety to the responsibility for verification.[2]

NL acquisition by automatic learning, as we said on the first page of this book, is still at the stage of discovery. In any case, verification, itself a component of the scientific method is mediated by NL. Scientific verification in the field of NL may take a very different form from that appropriate to the physical sciences; after all it will have to be negotiated and understood through just the language and cognitive processes we are trying to acquire. So we make no apology for a great diversity of topics in this early sweep of the subject. As Langley, Simon, Bradshaw, and Zytkow observe "as in the recipe for rabbit stew, one must first catch the rabbit" (p.16). To catch this new and elusive "rabbit" one must beat a large area of bush and scrub to raise the prey, and there is no telling exactly where it may lurk. In the first two chapters we covered a large ground of cognitive processes, and in this chapter we focus more closely on psychology and psycholinguistics. By this method we hope to discover truths about language and its acquisition.

Artificial Intelligence is often recognized as having a special relationship to psychology as well as to computer science. In NL research, the overlap is even more obvious in areas such as *learning* and *memory*, as well as various less obvious areas such as *perception*, and *pattern recognition*.

There is also a close relationship between psychology and linguistics. The next chapters examine these areas, following a path from the patent and empirical to the latent and hypothetical. Our aim in this research is to come closer to an understanding of how we can give our machines language capabilities. Here we start by trying to get an insight into how we ourselves gained our language capacity.

Acquisition and Development: Characteristics and Models

Many workers recognize that the child's acquisition of language is a paradigm which will repay study for the computational theory of NL.[3] But in practice it has proved too complex a problem, and it is almost certainly true to say that no current NL system claims to reflect the *natural* way *natural* language is acquired. In effect, child language acquisition is the limiting case to which, at its simplest, a theory must be reducible. It is therefore the most promising basis for developing a NL mechanism. But we do not need to completely understand the child acquisition paradigm in order to discover useful hints for developing a NL system. We are not necessarily concerned with accurately modelling the child's learning of language any more than we are committed to building a machine out of flesh and blood—which is the logical extension of the *natu-*

ral approach. But if we do wish to be successful in modelling the adult's language, it is useful to understand enough to be able to approximate the child's learning process. The alternative would be to achieve comparable results by better means — means independent of these poorly understood *natural* processes.

The primary issue we consider here is the extent to which language is learned by means of an inductive generalization mechanism *versus* the extent to which the child's grammar and acquisition mechanism comprise "innate organs" where the acquisition "organ" is a deductive, specialization and specification mechanism for honing the grammar "organ". For the computer scientist, the simpler and less specific these "innate organs", the more there is which can be bootstrapped constructively. And so the study of the child's acquisition mechanism will be useful, and give a greater possibility of modelling language acquisition reasonably satisfactorily.

Such a point is made fairly strongly by Sinclair-de-Zwart who notes that, in contrast with Transformational Generative Grammar (TGG), Piaget's theory could actually be used in a (computational) model of language acquisition. The nativist assumptions, along with other imports from linguistics (especially exports of TGG), have had a considerable influence on the experimental work and theoretical models of psycholinguists. They provided, positively, a concrete set of hypotheses and proposals which could be used as a basis for investigation. But negatively, the tenets of TGG tended to be accepted as axiomatic rather than as hypothetical.

Notwithstanding this bias, we should notice that research founded on the implicit assumption of innate linguistic organs and structures has proven quite fruitful. However, in many cases the experimental data has required re-interpretation and many researchers have ended up abandoning TGG. This brings them more into line with the older sensory-motor traditions of psycholinguistics which are introduced in Chapter Five.

For now we will make the naïve assumption that all rules and relationships are acquired unless there is empirical evidence to the contrary. The child's language "learning" does appear to conform to the general learning paradigm despite its speed. Furthermore, there is no indication of linguistic genetic factors relating to race or ethnic background[4] — on the contrary, any child can learn any language with equal facility and little apparent effort.

The learning paradigm leads to a *constructivist* model. Sinclair-deZwart sees language acquisition as involving a "slow construction" utilizing the order of the "environment" of "internal laws".[5] Constructivism in psycholinguistics frequently assumes that:

the child knows all about space before he even begins to learn about language.

But this assumption is stronger than necessary. The constructivist view more properly allows that the learning of concepts and language proceed in parallel except that:

the learning of specific spatial terms must wait until the child knows the appropriate properties of [physical space (*P-space*)].[6]

This observation about parallel learning of language leads us to some of the fundamental theses of this work, and indeed allows for learning of language to be subsumed by learning of ontology — subject to appropriate partial ordering of domains. The principle of parsimony encourages us to make this hypothesis. This suggests that similar mechanisms are involved in the learning of *semantics, reference, syntax, phonology, prosody, etc.*

Having made such a hypothesis, Staats writes that "a credible theory of language must indicate ... the learning principles."[7] This focusses our attention on learning mechanisms which apply throughout linguistic and cognitive phenomena. Such a recognition has been the basis for Anderson's recent work:

Another major shift in my research concerns a renewed interest in the process of learning—not the learning of facts or lists, but rather the learning of procedures that underlie our ability to understand language, answer questions, make inference, *etc* ... Interest in the mechanisms of procedural learning seems to have died in cognitive psychology with the demise of stimulus-response theories. The lack of learning programs has long been acknowledged to be a serious gap in artificial intelligence ... It is important that cognitive psychologists who propose models of adult competence give attention to the question of how such systems might develop.[8]

Note that this more general emphasis on learning takes us further from the nativist proposals of a specifically linguistic language organ, and addresses the more general prior question of how we come to understand the world. The nativist would presumably have to postulate that we are genetically endowed, not only with a real linguistic organ embodying all the complexities of all learnable languages, but also a corresponding organ encompassing all the potential complexities of our environment.

Collection of Psycholinguistic Data

As we have said, errors and over-generalization are an important source of information (both to child and observer) about the nature, development, interaction and validity of the child's grammatical rules. We see plenty of such evidence relating to inflections and morphology; however we have to search hard to find evidence concerning more specifically syntactic rules.

We see interactions of syntactic rules whenever a child learns to use "real words" which are to him at first "new words". But the natural events are difficult to observe, and the history of contact and usage for individual words is difficult to verify. Brown has devised an artificial experimental situation in which useful data has been obtained for "twelve nonsense syllables [identified contextually as] belonging to one of six parts of speech."[9] In this case we can have some confidence in the validity of the experiment, because the natural process remains the same and the "new words" introduced could have been actual words. There is no reason to think that nonsense words have different properties from actual words since, providing certain phonological constraints are satisfied, they could become actual words.

Most evidence (indeed the most useful evidence) does come from direct observation of children. It will be apparent throughout this chapter that the most abundant data are corpora derived by researchers from their own children, or from families who have consented to be wired for sound, or to have the experimenter visit regularly. These "natural language in natural language situations" are the most reliable. The Brown experiment departed from the "natural" situation in using children older than the age group at which the most significant language acquisition occurs. It also departed from the norm in using an "artificial" education situation (school) rather than a "natural" parent-child situation (home).

Another source of evidence is the experimenter's, parent's, or (adult) subject's introspections about the language acquisition process. This can be related to second language acquisition (learning a foreign language) which is itself an area of psycholinguistic research. An especially interesting and significant observation is made by Brown about the experimenter's own position:

> The process of grammar discovery has two facets. It is, most immediately, the technique of the investigator who is trying to describe the grammatical apparatus of a particular child. The investigator induces from obtained utterances a probable generative mechanism. Since, however, the child is also presumed to have built this internal mechanism by processing obtained utterances, it follows that the investigator's procedure may be a good model of the child's learning. Of course the child has not induced his grammar from his own sentences but rather from the somewhat more varied and complex sentences heard from adult speakers. A comparison of the recorded speech of mother to child with the speech of child to mother shows that the grammars induced by the children from the adult speech are not identical with the adult grammars that produced the sentences. The investigator of a child's speech, on the

other hand, hopes to find the very grammar that produced the original utterances. Even so the similarity in the tasks of investigator and child is very great—to get from sentences to a grammar—and so while acting as investigators, we shall want to consider whether the child may have carried out operations similar to our own.[10]

The duality metaphor relating the experimental procedures and the learner's acquisition mechanism is often discussed in this book. Both the contrasts and the similarities which arise are potential sources of insight.

There is one final source of readily-available psycholinguistic data. This is a rather unusual and perhaps surprising one: the "new languages" which arise under various circumstances, and which we refer to collectively as *pidgins* and *creoles*. Pidgins are rudimentary subsets or impoverished derivatives of a colonial language. But with pidgin as the only common language in these polyglot situations, new languages, creoles, evolve amongst the children.

> [These newborn languages] exhibit the complexity, nuance and expressive power universally found in the more established languages of the world [and] a remarkable similarity of structure ... The finding suggests that what is common to creole languages may indeed form the basis of the acquisition of language by children everywhere.[11]

There are other naturally occurring, but abnormal or unusual cases, which can contribute to our data on language acquisition, notably language and hearing defects. For example, Moore reports that deaf children learn sign language at about the same time as normal children begin speaking, and there is evidence that they learn it faster, at least initially.[12] This is taken as evidence that motor control is one of the factors determining the onset of speech, since the child develops adequate motor control for gestures before adequate motor control of the speech organs.

Kelley provides a useful summary of:

> four more or less devious routes to obtain the information unavailable through direct experimentation ...

1. Experiments performed by nature. One might enquire whether the kind of experiment out of bounds to psychological investigators has not been performed by nature.
2. Indirect psychological experimentation. One can run very limited experiments with children, using artificially constructed languages ...
   Other non-linguistic experiments may be ... generalized to language acquisition.
3. Direct psychological study. One can attempt to study the course of language acquisition directly without, however, hoping to control for all possible relevant input variables.

4.   Modeling. One can attempt to model the mechanism and process of language acquisition in the hope that hypotheses and results will be more easily obtained by using the model than without it.[13]

Spontaneous Beginnings: Babbling and Crying, Play and Practice

We have already said that children appear to learn to speak, and to understand, fairly spontaneously. Whilst the first word is a momentous occasion, it is actually the culmination of a progression of sounds from birth. What relation do these sounds have to language? Are they independent? Are they practice? Are they imitation? Are they play?

Eisenson *et al* (1963) have suggested that there are five stages of prelinguistic vocalization ... Undifferentiated crying is said to be part of a total bodily response to any discomfort. This gives way to differentiated crying after the first month of life, when different stimulating conditions are capable of eliciting characteristic qualities of sound ... Around the sixth week ... cooing sounds may be noted. At first these seem to have the character of a reflex and may be elicited by specific stimuli, such as a nodding object that resembles a face ... After that the visual and social stimuli become increasingly differentiated ... By the third or fourth month of life the normal infant enters the babbling stage of pre-linguistic vocalization, but this does not seem to depend upon the auditory stimulation provided by others. ... There seems to be no evidence of any normal *speakers* of the model language who have not gone through a babbling stage ... Eisenson *et al.* (1963) characterize lallation, their fourth stage of pre-linguistic development, as involving the child's imitation of his own accidentally produced sounds, as against echolalia, the fifth and final stage, which is characterized by the imitation of the sounds produced by others. Lallation is said to occur during the second six months of life, while echolalia begins around the ninth or tenth month.[14]

This extensive summary gives a typical view of the stages of (pre)linguistic development prior to the first words. The intriguing aspect is that there is very little evidence for any connection between the major pre-linguistic stages and between pre-linguistic and linguistic stages. One indication that the early stages are linguistically relevant concerns the prosodic functions: intonation, stress and syllabification. From about five or six months there is a recognizable distinction between babies of certain nationalities (or primary model languages).[15] In particular it is extremely easy to distinguish by their utterances Chinese from Arabic, American or Russian babies and characteristic intonational features will be quite clear.

This form of language assimilation clearly does not involve correction, but must involve imitation with rewards or feedback of an indirect nature. This "babbling drift" is interesting to us because of some of the blanket comments made about the importance of negative information. The nativist explanation would be in terms of a reduction from an initially, and innately, larger repertoire, and at this level such a viewpoint is quite reasonable. However, it would appear to be quite feasible that the original repertoire was primarily a property of the speech motor systems (and also auditory systems), and does not require us to imagine an innate set of universal linguistic units. There is another noteworthy phenomenon observable from the late babbling stage and through into the "child grammar" stages. This is *crib speech*, the monologues in which children engage in bed before going to sleep.

> The available evidence suggests that speech plays an important role in the child's acquisition of language ... Britton concluded that crib speech ... was characterized by a freedom (due to lack of communicative intent) on the child's part to use free association to call to mind the next words in a sequence, the associations being either phonological, structural, or semantic. He also suggested that crib speech was the speech in which children first used language not tied to the here and now.[16]

It has been further proposed that crib speech, as a form of play, allows the child to experiment without having to worry about the consequences of his experiments or the interference or response of others. Such experiments may afford opportunity for practice, for comparison with recognition models, and for some form of implicit correction. One thing that must not be done is to make a dichotomy of the *play-practice* aspects. It is quite usual for play to have a useful "educational" function, and in a sense calling something play only highlights the motivations (*e.g.* that it is fun). This soft-pedalling of the work-play distinction is evident in Kuczaj:

> These two answers are not mutually exclusive. Children might find language practice pleasurable and might also use it to facilitate their acquisition of their native language.[17]

The role of play in language learning is one which is difficult to reconcile with a computer system, but it is sufficiently important in psycholinguistics to warrant some investigation of possible heuristics providing motivational equivalents.

The practice element, on the other hand, can be questioned on various grounds, particularly in the pre-linguistic stages. As pointed out above, there is little evidence of connection between the various stages, and some go further and challenge the existence of any developmental connection between babbling and language stages. Derrick addresses this extreme viewpoint.

They point to the discontinuity between babbling and true speech behaviour, the frequent period of silence that intervenes between babbling and the true onset of speech, and the low take-up in speech of the sounds which occur most frequently in babbling. This does not necessarily prove that the practice element in babbling is not significant for the acquisition of speech; indeed, the practice and control of intonation patterns may be of more significance than that of speech sounds.[18]

The concept of transfer of (prosodic) learning achieved in an earlier pre-linguistic stage ("toy" domain?) to the eventual linguistic behaviour ("real" domain?) again suggests intriguing possibilities and provides a conceptual challenge for the computer engineer. The discontinuity phenomena are themselves interesting, potentially significant, and controversial in their own right.

There are also other possible (intuitive) connections between the stages, and here it is best to take the viewpoint of the parent—who will be the first to seize upon the first word. For example, we may consider the relative semiotic function of the pre-linguistic and linguistic articulations in the context of the mother-baby relationship.

Mothers recognize the message conveyed by their baby's crying and respond accordingly. The difference between these cries can be described in terms of vowels and consonants (or approximations to consonants), the range of sounds gradually changing and being augmented. Some of these are clearly connected with sucking noises, *e.g.* lip movements which the baby makes in anticipation of sucking produce /m/ or /n/, from whence it is a short step to hunger cries that sound like *mama* or *nana*.[19]

Baby Talk and Child Grammars: Dialect *vs* Idiolect

We now turn to the linguistic development following that "first word". The first stage of significance is that period, typically from about twelve to eighteen months, in which the child uses isolated "words" with meaning. Of course:

Sounds resembling words such as *ma, mama, da, ba* are heard from six months onwards, emerging from and blending into the baby's babbling. But between nine and twelve months a small number of words undoubtedly begin to be used *with meaning.*[20]

The use the child makes of these few single words is quite remarkable. Again adopting a parental viewpoint, since mothers become highly adept at interpreting their children, these single words can be construed as standing in for an entire sentence. The one noun, to use the obvious example, can be used indicatively, imperatively, or even interrogatively.

We are not aware of any research which considers the child's use of intonation at this stage, but the child nevertheless does seem to get his point across for the most part. The mother's role in interpretation includes also the more specialist skill of being able to interpret words which can vary quite remarkably from the appropriate words of the model language — even to the extent of being relatively independent. In one study 83% of the vocabulary of a twelve month old child were deemed "approximations" and 5% of that of an eighteen month old child "inventions".

The one-word stage is important for the learning of words, although only a relatively small number (a couple of dozen or so) are typically produced prior to beginning to put two words together, and most of these are nouns. Again, the concept of a learning system which progresses through one- and two-word grammars is suggestive and challenging to the computer engineer. Moreover, the nature and usage of such single or paired words provide a useful opportunity for characterizing the effectiveness of a system and developing appropriate heuristics.

Studies confirm the intuition that a young child will hear a word in many situations before attempting to reproduce it, that he will probably attempt to reproduce it several times before it is understood, and that it will be some time before he will use it in the absence of the referenced object. The lack of feedback in the first stages of this process is a challenging anomaly. The usage of a word in the one-word stage is according to rules which are primarily contextual within the referential hierarchy, and thus semantic and very pragmatic. At this stage the word is fulfilling the grammatical function of both "word" and "sentence",[21] and this is being achieved through the charitable disposition of the mother (typically) and her understanding of the concerns and dispositions of the child. The single word can perform multiple roles: request, question, greeting, thanks, *etc.* And the linguistic function may be successfully supplemented and clarified by appropriate gestural accompaniment.

To the extent that words of different classes are evident through differences of role in the referential hierarchy, treatment of the single-word stage as evidencing a *holophrastic* grammar may be reasonable (*e.g.* compare "no", "go" and "dog"). There is also other evidence of distinct word classes in that certain classes of word appear later than others. Such a proposal reduces the sharpness of the gap between the one- and two-word stages despite the absence of direct evidence of syntactic rules.

Note that the intonation and stress features of babbling are evidence of rules within the phonological hierarchy. It should be emphasized that the distinguishing of different hierarchies is primarily a matter of perspective, and there is little reason to suppose that the child distinguishes the context of his rules at all. Although very different physical and mental processes may be involved, similar inductive processes must be at play. Such a distinction presumably arises gradually as the child compares his own sentences with others'. Note that the child at every stage appears to have a competence for comprehension in excess of that for production. This is to be expected if the learning takes place as outlined above, and is necessary to that learning.

As soon as the child begins to put words together, from the two-word stage onward, the existence of a grammar becomes evident, and in particular, word classes are differentiated. Indeed, it is the presence of such differentiation in even the earliest multi-word utterances that suggests that some form of grammar exists prior to this stage.

The step to the three-word stage (around 24 months) needs a more complex grammar than just the interaction of an open class of substantives, and a small closed class of pivotal words. Notice that what we are considering here is grammar quite independent of any formal "grammar", and only indirectly related to the "grammars" of the parent figures. The view that children speak their language poorly and have an incorrect grammar is, in our view, somewhat inaccurate, and very unhelpful. It is apparent to us that the child is developing his own grammar, and that he uses these grammars remarkably consistently and correctly.

These grammars comprise a "succession of approximations to the adult system".[22] We may go further and note that not only does each child have his own *idiolect*, but so does each adult, and there is thus no normative adult system, except as an average for a particular language. This itself allows for variety within a language, and on this view the child learns to approximate the local *dialect*. Note that the reality of *idiolect* can be seen by looking at almost any open class word, for which every individual has his own set of nuances and pronunciations.

The recognition that each child, at each stage, uses a unique grammar has implications for psycholinguistic research. It implies that child grammars need not exhibit the rules of adult grammar. Bowerman makes this point in relation to a number of specific rules at the three-word stage. She points out that no one has demonstrated that the verb "belongs with" the direct object. In fact, she says, the verb tends to be invariant, and nouns all tend to be in the nominative. The concept of subject would require in some cases that the child mistakenly identified the wrong noun as subject.[23] This leads to the conclusion that the concept of subject is "not required" in early child speech.

Brown gives an example which illustrates the difference between the child grammar and the adult grammar at a somewhat later stage:

> Adam ... produced one utterance for which no adult is ever likely to have provided an exact model: "No I see truck". His mother elects to expand it as "No, you didn't see it" and this expansion suggests that the child might have created the utterance by reducing an adult model containing the form *didn't*. However ... he did not say *no* as his mother said

it, with primary stress and final contour; Adam's *no* had secondary stress and no final contour ... It seems more likely that the utterance was created by Adam as part of a continuing effort to discover the general rules for constructing English negatives.[24]

The emphasis in analysis of child data should therefore be the determination of the child's grammar. Brown provides an excellent account of his experimental method in discovering the child's grammar.[25] He also compares his role as experimenter (*apropos* child grammar) with the child's role (*apropos* adult grammar according to the premise mentioned earlier).

Not only do children tend to have consistent grammar at a particular stage, but the sequence of grammars for one child seems to resemble those for any other child learning the same language. Furthermore, adult attempts at "baby talk" are remarkably uniform and similar to the child's. Brown's work is very important, and as far as we know a unique discussion of this uniformity, and the questions of reduction, telegraphic speech and span.

> When the analyzed records are ordered by mean utterance length, it becomes apparent that children all "reduce" English sentences in similar fashion ... We have checked all the records for progressive constructions (*e.g.* "I am going to town"). Without exception children whose mean utterance length is below 3.2 form this construction by omitting the forms of the verb *to be* (*e.g.* "I going"). We have checked sentences in which the verb would, for an adult, ordinarily require such a modal auxiliary as *will* or *can* (*e.g.* "I will park the car"). Children whose mean utterance length is below 3.5 invariably form these sentences by omitting modals ("I park the car"...) ... A basic factor causing the child's reduction of adult sentences is surely an upper limit of some kind of immediate memory span for the situation in which the child is imitating and a similar limit of programming span for the situation in which the child is constructing the sentences ... It is this limitation of span in children for which the work of the descriptive linguist provided no parallel, and our obsession with linguistic technique long diverted us from recognizing the systematically derivative nature of child speech.[26]

The evidence from child grammars about the inductive process has direct ramifications for computer modelling of the acquisition process. So does the possibility of a systematic transformation to reduce the complexity of model speech. This latter problem has been recognized by Kelley in his model. He describes the algorithm he uses, which in essence repeatedly attempts analysis (possibly employing previous partial analyses) of the sentence, allowing successively increasing numbers of words to be ignored, but is exhaustive rather than based on particular hypotheses or heuristics.[27]

Particular properties of child grammars can lead to insights into the learning process. But there is one area which is the most frequently remarked-on characteristic of child speech — over-generalization. This, of course, is also evidence for generalization, and since this occurs in a great many forms, we deal with it in a separate section. There is, however, another characteristic which is not often remarked on; where the readiness of the adults to accommodate is itself of significance — in the use of personal pronouns.

Tanz draws attention to the tendency of both child and parent to refer to themselves primarily in the third person using proper names or terms such as "mummy", and that furthermore references to self and to mother are amongst the most frequent "pivot" words used at the two-word stage. She suggests that the parents adopt this strategy to "simplify communication", and notes that "exclusion of the first and second persons also narrows the range of verb forms and keeps them more uniform".[28] Part of the explanation for this may be the importance the adults place on the child learning to say "Mummy", "Daddy", their own names, and derivatives. Perhaps parental speech is the major determiner, as "come to daddy" tends to occur rather than "come to me", and this long before the child starts to speak. The need for a common framework, the perceived difficulty of the child in sorting out the egocentric pronominal system, and the desire to assist the child in learning the names and concepts of significant elements of his environment, are likely to encourage use of such more easily resolvable forms.

Other insights into the child's grammar arise as children attempt to use pronouns, but in fact retain the pronoun used by their parent. This is described as "failure to shift" by Tanz (p.52) and has been attributed to the tendency to apply *you* and *I* specifically to self and mother as pairs of homonyms.

Overgeneralization of Syntax and Semantics

One method of gaining information about the development of grammatical rules is studying systematic errors. The most characteristic, and best-known, errors made by young children are errors which we can identify immediately as being the result of applying a regular rule (*e.g.* the "-ed" inflection) in an irregular context (*e.g.* the verb *dig* goes to *dug*, not *digged*). This is strong evidence that the child is doing more than imitating and expanding, but is in some sense analyzing language structure and inducing rules. These errors are thus described as over-generalization, and imply that the child's acquisition process includes generalization.[29]

The tendency for a rule to override an irregular form acts both retrospectively and prospectively. A freely used irregular form will be supplanted by the over-generalization, and the generalization will be applied indiscriminately, disrupting learning of new irregular forms. It is clear that this phenomenon illustrates not only the strength of the generalized rules, but also the power of generalization and the importance of generalization in the child's acquisition pattern.

The most common examples of over-generalization are, like those above, examples of inflection. Brown goes on to note that in English (unlike some other languages), "inflection is a rather trivial grammatical system, and knowledge of inflection cannot take a child very far beyond his corpus".[30]

The infamous uncorrectable "nobody don't like me" example illustrates more general syntactic generalization errors. Of particular interest are those in which the error concerns role, class and semantics. For example, the erroneous causative usage of verbs gives many insights into acquisition. Tanz quotes Bowerman's daughter, Christy, at 24 months: "I'm singing him" (making him sing) and "I come it closer so it won't fall" (... am making it come ...).

> Bowerman reasons that Christy must have discovered that verbs like the transitive *open*, *break*, and *melt* are related to their intransitive or adjectival forms and that she is producing novel causatives on analogy with these legitimate ones.[31]

Alternatively, it may be that causative use is made of arbitrary words and child "sentences", without consideration of grammatical or selection constraints. A younger child appears free to use the same two-word "sentence" to indicate indifferently a present, past, future, or desired situation. The interpretation of the telegraphic form is from context, and any particular gloss is of the listener's own construction, albeit constrained to conform to the word order of the child. Thus in this case, addition of a phrase involving "want" or "make" is always an option. When word order changes from (say) "door open" to "open door", what has been learned is imperative word order rather than the causative *versus* descriptive duality of "open". It is only when the child starts to fill out her own grammar that the "acceptable" form "No eat! Baby smelly!" becomes the "unacceptable" form "No, mommy, don"t eat her yet, she's smelly!".[32]

Note that the words occur in the same order (and that pronoun usage is assumed to have been learned in the interim). There is no clear evidence that causality is attributed only to specific verbs at one stage, and later over-generalized. It is probable that after a few causative usages have been recognized, a causative usage could be applied to any verb, and this long before any over-generalization error would be recognized by an observer. In this context, too, we should observe that the negatives "no" and "don"t" have extremely causative (imperative) connotations.

This question has implications for the methods used to learn word classes. On one view, particular words are either added as completely separate (but semantically and phonemically related) words to a new class (of causatives), or are borrowed from the existing word classes into a new class for which this class of use is acceptable. The over-generalization occurs when, through some process of consolidation, the subset property is recognized and generalization to the superset occurs. On the other view, as soon as the child is ready to use a new rule involving a known word, he or she will assume it applies to the entire class. In the computer models described in Chapter Eleven, both processes are simultaneously active, for better or worse. A new rule involving a known word will be considered for an hypothesis of a new class and corresponding rule, but a rule involving the known class will also be hypothesized and given the stronger weighting. This is because weighting of rules depends on the confidence levels for the component classes.

We should note that these over-generalization phenomena are a result of the application of parsimony in the simple sense (in contrast with the metric proposed by Brown[33]).

> Information about what is not a sentence [is] necessary ... to reject hypothetical grammars ... which are "overinclusive" ... The overinclusive grammar would clearly be simpler than the true grammar so that any ordinary simplicity would favour the wrong grammar.[34]

Discontinuity Between Stages

We can now highlight what seems to be a common thread of the discussions so far in this section. We have already considered stages, both generally and in relation to specific aspects of the acquisition process. In particular, there has been occasional reference to evidence of discontinuities providing a sharp distinction between pre-linguistic and early linguistic stages.

The phenomena of over-generalization and unresponsiveness to correction also indicate a fairly sharp transition between grammatical stages. A generalization is used pervasively, or not at all; a class of errors appears suddenly, and disappears just as suddenly. We can use the analogies of a bold stroke in a painting, and a new thread in a tapestry, to illustrate the idea that a grammatical rule is introduced suddenly, and complete, into the production grammar. The bold stroke may obliterate existing details, which need then to be reasserted. The new thread may actually need to be threaded around others which should have remained visible. This is in stark contrast to the gradual development illustrated by a photographic analogy. A language acquisition model should explain, predict and produce such discontinuities. Kelley incorporates staging quite explicitly:

There is a larger developmental time scale in which the model passes through acquisition stages. (In this model there are three distinct stages.) Each stage is characterized by the generation of a different set of grammatical hypotheses about the language. During a particular stage these hypotheses are tested against the sentences the model experiences, and those hypotheses which are accurate characterizations of the language will be confirmed in the usual manner, while those which are not simply atrophy and are discarded.[35]

In this model a thread, a hypothesis, is added, and if over a period of testing the resultant grammar fails to perform accurately, it will be discarded and another, possibly a variant, tried. In Kelley's work the gross stages are actually characterized by different classes of hypotheses which can be made.

So far, we tacitly accepted that language understanding precedes production. It is time to examine this proposition more carefully:

> Most writers agree that the child understands the language of others considerably before he actually uses language himself. This sentence is from Dorothea McCarthy's comprehensive review (1954, p.520) of research on the speech of children, and the sentence is certainly an accurate summary of what most have written. It is also an accurate summary of what parents believe that they have observed.[36]

Fraser and his colleagues go on to query just what is meant by this agreed observation. Is it that "*some* utterances are ordinarily understood before *any* utterances are produced", or "particular utterances or features of an utterance are ordinarily understood before the same utterance or features are produced"? The first is of less significance — a dog may be seen to respond to certain utterances "as a signal". The second, then, is the form which concerns us, but we have nonetheless highlighted the need to clarify just what we mean by "understanding" in this context. How may we gauge whether a child's language understanding is indeed ahead of his production, or whether in fact the child is being unduly credited with understanding features which he is simply treating as noise intervening in a "telegraphic" utterance such as he is himself capable of producing?

There is evidence that understanding comes before production from contexts other than normal child acquisition, including pet chimpanzees and anarthic (speechless) human subjects. Again, this highlights our tendency to charitable assumptions and raises the question of language in other animals. Fraser and his colleagues explore comprehension and production formally, by controlled experimental testing. We think it will be useful to give some of their experimental examples and results:

> Consider now a concrete problem drawn from those we have devised to test *Comprehension*, *Imitation*, and *Production* abbreviated sub-

sequently as *C, I* and *P*. We begin with a pair of sentences: "The sheep is jumping" and "The sheep are jumping" ... For each of the two sentences there is an appropriate picture ... In one picture a single sheep jumps while the other looks on; in the other picture both sheep jump ... The mean number of correct responses of *S*s on *I* was 15.83; on *C*, 10.08; and on *P*, 7.55. In short *I, C, P* ...this order holds with striking consistency for individual *S*s. For all 12, *C, P* and, for 9, *I, C* ... How stands the thesis that understanding precedes production in the development of child speech? The thesis is true if by production we mean task *P*, since *C* scores were higher than *P* scores. This outcome suggests that children learn a lot about referential patterning, the stimulus control of grammatical forms, before they can produce these forms.[37]

These results are both intriguing and informative, and lead to some interesting insights into the relationship of production to understanding. It seems that imitation may play quite an important role, despite a common belief to the contrary. The implication of this is that sentences (or parts of sentences) are likely to be imitated if they are a little beyond the range of full comprehension. Other evidence suggests that sentences which are more complex than can be understood completely, will not be imitated correctly. This imitation may come from an ability to comprehend which "parses" and "understands" most of the sentence, but leaves some semantic distinctions unlearned. The imitation presumably leads to further learning, since it gives the child the opportunity to process ("analyze" and "relate") the sentence. Similarly, we suggest that an ability to comprehend a sentence adequately will increase confidence in the rules guessed at so far. In turn, once a certain level of confidence has been reached, understanding will pass into production.

The results also suggest the hypothesis that imitation affects production *via* learning:

> Scollon (1976) suggested that imitation and repetition are two phases of one language-learning process. Imitation provides the means for children to practice contrasts that are not yet within their productive system in that the model utterance produced by another may exceed children's linguistic competence. Repetition provides the means for elaborating the system from within and testing it against the model system in that children provide the model and its reproduction.[38]

Notice that Kuczaj extends the scope of the evidence to the child's imitations (including repetitions, expansions, contractions and corrections) of his own sentences, and refers to:

> recent investigations by Reilly of children's "repairs", utterance sequences in which children spontaneously modify and typically improve the quality of their own utterances.

The first utterances in a repair sequence presumably reflect the child's present production competence, implying that he has access to more forms which are slightly beyond this competence.

> Reilly also noted that children make use of the utterances produced by others to help build more complex utterances ... She suggested that there are considerable functional (*i.e.* developmental) similarities between children's repairs and their use of others' utterances to help build more complex utterances.[39]

The observation supports the idea of a logical separation between production and comprehension grammars. It also suggests the "analysis by synthesis" technique, in which hypotheses made on the basis of the partial information immediately available, are used to generate sentences which are then compared with the original data. Kuczaj describes his own experiments on production and imitation, and concludes:

> Children ... consistently imitate the parts of model utterances that are either within or slightly beyond their current level of linguistic competence ... [This] suggests that children process more of the model utterance than they can reproduce, for otherwise we would expect the reduced imitations to be more random than systematic.[40]

This increases the importance of the idea that imitation mediates in the transfer between comprehension and production competence. Finally, we can note that there is a theoretical, or philosophical side to the question of recognition and generation. In considering the possibility of *testers* and *generators* for a language "L" (these being respectively procedures to test whether a sentence is in "L" and to generate the sentences of "L"), it is known that a *tester* exists when "L" is recursive, and a *generator* exists when "L" is recursively enumerable (a wider class). We also know that while it is simple to convert a *tester* into a *generator*, there is no effective way to develop a *tester* from a *generator*. Thus, it is theoretically and intuitively feasible that the child's understanding, testing or recognition capability is developed first and that his generation or production ability is derived from it.

This summary of psycholinguistics gives us interesting insights into the language acquisition process which we can aim to model on computational machinery. The TGG approach which was common some years ago has been increasingly replaced by an interest in learning as a stimulus-response activity which reverts to earlier theories of learning. The idea that language is acquired by a unique language "organ" now seems strange, since in theory a similar organ would be needed to acquire information about space and time as well as language. The most useful information about the learning process of language comes from errors. The kind of errors which are characteristic of children's language learning tell us a lot about the kind of mechanism which is being used. Typically children over-generalise, and apply deduced rules to situations where an idiosyncracy is the norm. There is also evidence that each individual child's rules are an idiolect, and what is acquired is an effective subset of the total rule system, adequate for communicative purposes. This feature of language acquisition can also be seen in the universal phenomenon of "babbling drift" where phonological rules are evidently being acquired. But perhaps the most telling feature of the natural acquisition process are the discontinuities introduced by the deduction of new rules into the process of understanding and producing language. All this seems to give evidence to support the idea that language acquisition proceeds by correction, rather than a single induction of production rule.

The next chapter moves on to look at the evidence about the brain structures which process language which we derive from accidental damage to the brain and its relation to language learning occurring naturally.

Notes to Chapter Three

1. Kuhn, T.S., *The Structure of Scientific Revolutions* (University of Chicago Press, 1978).
2. Langley, Pat, Herbert A. Simon, Gary L. Bradshaw, and Jan M. Zytkow, *Scientific Discovery: Computational Explorations of the Creative Processes* (MIT Press, 1987), p.3.
3. Selfridge, Mallory, *A Process Model of Language Acquisition, Yale University Computer Science Department Research Report, #172 (January, 1980); Anderson, John R., Language, Memory, and Thought* (Lawrence Erlbaum Associates, Hillsdale, NJ, 1976); Powers, David M.W., *Lateral Interaction Behaviour Derived from Neural Packing Considerations*, DCS Report No 8317, Department of Computer Science, University of New South Wales, Australia (April, 1983).
4. Kucera, Henry, "The Learning of Grammar", *Perspectives in Computing*, Vol. 1, No. 2 (1981), p.28.
5. Sinclair-deZwart, H., "Language Acquisition and Cognitive Development", in Timothy E. Moore, *Cognitive Development and the Acquisition of Language* (Academic Press, New York, 1973), p.11.
6. Clark, Eva V., "What's in a Word? On the Child's Acquisition of Semantics in his First Language", in Timothy E. Moore, *Cognitive Development and the Acquisition of Language* (Academic Press, New York, 1973), p.61.
7. Staats, Arthur W., "Linguistic-Mentalistic Theory versus an Explanatory S-R Learning Theory of Language Development", in Dan I. Slobin, *The Ontogenesis of Language* (Academic Press, 1971), p.108.
8. Anderson, John R., *Language, Memory, and Thought* (Lawrence Erlbaum Associates, Hillsdale, NJ, 1976), p.20.

9.   Brown, Roger, and Colin Fraser, "The Acquisition of Syntax", in C. N. Cofer and Barbara S. Musgrave, eds, *Verbal Behavior and Learning: Problems and Processes* (McGraw-Hill, 1963), p.162f.

10.   *Op. cit.,* p.160.

11.   Bickerton, Derek, "Creole Languages", *Scientific American*, Vol.219, No.1 (July, 1983), p.108.

12.   Moore, Timothy A., *Cognitive Development and the Acquisition of Language* (Academic Press, New York, 1973), p.4.

13.   Kelley, K.L., *Early Syntactic Acquisition* (Rand Corporation, Santa Monica, CA, November 1967), p.10f.

14.   Vetter, H.J., and R. W. Howell, "Theories of Language Acquisition", *Jnl of Psycholinguistic Res.*, Vol.1, No.1, (1971), pp.34ff.

15.   Slobin, Dan I., *The Ontogenesis of Language* (Academic Press, New York, 1971); Derwing, Bruce J., and William J. Baker, "Recent Research on the Acquisition of English Morphology", in P. Fletcher and M. Garman, eds, *Language Acquisition: Studies in First Language Development* (Cambridge University Press, Cambridge UK, 1979), pp.209-225.

16.   Kuczaj, Stan A., *Crib Speech and Language Play* (Springer-Verlag, New York, NY, 1983), pp.11-12.

17.   *Op. cit.,* p.162.

18.   Derrick, J., *The Child's Acquisition of Language* (National Foundation for Education Research, Windsor, Berkshire, UK, 1977), p.8.

19.   *Loc. cit.*

20.   *Op. cit.,* p.8f.

21.   Olson, Gary M., "Developmental Changes in Memory and the Acquisition of Language", in Timothy E. Moore, *Cognitive Development and the Acquisition of Language* (Academic Press, New York, 1973), p.154.

22.   Moore, Timothy E., "Introduction", in Timothy E. Moore, ed., *Cognitive Development and the Acquisition of Language* (Academic Press, New York, 1973), p.5.

23.   Bowerman, Melissa, *Early Syntactic Development: a cross-linguistic study with special reference to Finnish* (Cambridge University Press, Cambridge UK, 1973), p.207.

24.   Brown, Roger, and Ursula Bellugu, "Three Processes in the Child's Acquisition of Syntax" in E. Endler, L. Boulter, and H. Osser, eds, *Contemporary Issues in Developmental Psychology* (Holt, Rhinehart and Winston, New York, 1968), pp.419f.

25.   Brown, Roger, and Colin Fraser, "The Acquisition of Syntax", in C. N. Cofer and Barbara S. Musgrave, eds, *Verbal Behavior and Learning: Problems and Processes* (McGraw-Hill, 1963).

26.   *Op. cit.,* p.188f.

27.   Kelley, K.L., *Early Syntactic Acquisition* (Rand Corporation, Santa Monica, CA, November 1967), p.164ff.

28.   Tanz, Christine, *Studies in the Acquisition of Deictic Terms* (Cambridge, UK, Cambridge University Press, 1980), p.49ff.

29. Brown, Roger, and Ursula Bellugu, "Three Processes in the Child's Acquisition of Syntax" in E. Endler, L. Boulter, and H. Osser, eds, *Contemporary Issues in Developmental Psychology* (Holt, Rhinehart and Winston, New York, 1968), p.420.

30. Brown, Roger, and Colin Fraser, "The Acquisition of Syntax", in C. N. Cofer and Barbara S. Musgrave, eds, *Verbal Behavior and Learning: Problems and Processes* (McGraw-Hill, 1963), p.162.

31. Tanz, Christine, *Studies in the Acquisition of Deictic Terms* (Cambridge, UK, Cambridge University Press, 1980), p.138.

32. *Op.cit.,* p.137.

33. Brown, Roger, and Colin Fraser, "The Acquisition of Syntax", in C. N. Cofer and Barbara S. Musgrave, eds, *Verbal Behavior and Learning: Problems and Processes* (McGraw-Hill, 1963), p.185f.

34. Braine, Martin D. S., "On Two Types of Models of the Internalization of Grammars", in Dan I. Slobin, *The Ontogenesis of Language* (Academic Press, 1971), p.157.

35. Kelley, K.L., *Early Syntactic Acquisition* (Rand Corporation, Santa Monica, CA, November 1967), p.94.

36. Fraser, D., U. Bellugi, and R. Brown, "Control of Grammar in Imitation, Comprehension, and Production", *Journal of Verbal Learning and Verbal Behaviour*, Vol.2, No.1 (1963). p.121f.

37. *Op.cit.,* p.123ff.

38. Kelley, K.L., *Early Syntactic Acquisition* (Rand Corporation, Santa Monica, CA, November 1967), p.16.

39. Kuczaj, Stan A., *Crib Speech and Language Play* (Springer-Verlag, New York, NY, 1983), p.17f.

40. *Op.cit.,* p.164.

Chapter Four

Language Defects and Correction

In this chapter we deepen our study of Psycholinguistics with a particular focus on the 'negative' evidence from language deficiencies and errors. We note that damage to two particular areas of the brain, close respectively to the speech and auditory areas of the cortex, give rise to characteristic language deficiencies. These suggest localization of particular language functionality, and assymetries between recognition and production. More generally temporary language deficiencies characteristic of particular stages of development give insights into the mechanisms involved. Further the deficiencies in the language of the parents, and the corresponding insensitivity of the child to noise and unsystematic error, also place robustness constraints on the acquisition paradigm. On the other hand, some parental deviations from strict usage are evidently helpful to the child and appear to reflect an implicit understanding of the acquisition process and an ability to adjust and assist to the various stages. Yet, in contrast, explicit correction appears to evidence a dramatic failure to communicate and influence, but more closely constrained, delayed and self-generated corrections may be effective.

We now turn to consider more evidence on language use and acquisition. Firstly, we report investigations into patients with brain damage resulting in language defects. This necessarily partly preempts the discussion of neurolinguistics in Chapter Seven, although in that chapter we will mainly be concentrating on the microscopic aspects of neurology, rather than the macroscopic organization of the brain. The data in this chapter provides insights into the localization of brain function, and the partitions and subprocesses of the language mechanism.

Certain language defects seem to be caused by damage to two distinct areas of the brain—known as Broca's area and Wernicke's area after the workers who first identified them. Damage to each area produces its own characteristic forms of language deficiency.

In the case of Broca's area, the disturbance, known as Broca's aphasia, is characterized by slow speech, poor articulation and ungrammatical speech of a somewhat "telegraphic" character, leaving out the closed class words such as "if" and "and". The patient usually is unable to correctly interpret such words in the speech he hears.

In the case of Wernicke's area the problems are quite different, indeed almost the opposite. The aphasiac will speak faster than normal, easily, extensively, and with normal articulation, intonation and grammar. The problem is that he has difficulty finding the right word and is therefore forced to produce many circumlocutions.

The evidence points to a physiological basis for the distinctions between open and closed class words, and a separation between recognition and production in the speech processes. The evidence which has been reported does not so much suggest a division between hearer and speaker grammars. Rather, it suggests divisions between different aspects of language and, in particular, between syntax and semantics. But one particular case, used as an illustration in Gilling,[1] showed less correlation between understanding and production deficits than expected. The patient employed "the little words" (closed class), but could not understand their grammatical contrasts when he heard them.

Ervin-Tripp notes that the small "classes of affixes or function words"[2] occur with high frequency in normal language but are often not necessary to convey meaning, as with a child's "telegraphic" speech. She suggests that they have considerable functionality in comprehension, but are of little significance in production. It has been demonstrated that children understand normal sentences better than the "telegraphic" contractions, emphasizing both the importance of these words in comprehension and the lead of comprehension over production. However, adult communication is fundamentally symmetric, and these specialized particles must be added during production so as to reflect semantic relationships which have already been recognized and are now to be conveyed.

Wernicke's area is near the auditory cortex, and Broca's area is near the part of motor cortex concerned with the speech organs. Wernicke himself proposed that speech was first processed in the auditory cortex, the information was then passed to Wernicke's area and thence passed to Broca's area. It was then passed to the motor cortex and speech organs. This would suggest a close relationship between closed class words and production, and open class words to understanding – the reverse of the Ervin-Tripp proposal. Certainly, the high semantic content open class words are understood early; and the finer, less concrete, and more syntactically oriented facets are learned later. They also seem to be learnt by a successive approximation involving the production process, imitation, and possibly correction.

We have seen that the errors resulting from damage to Broca's area are reminiscent of those made by children. We will see later that the errors resulting from damage in Wernicke's area could be extreme versions of syndromes which occur in normal adult language usage.

Rate and Order of Learning

In the last chapter we referred to characteristic stages in the learning and developmental process. We have seen how various of these properties have implications for the generalization and learning processes, relating to both comprehension and production. We now look at the order and rate of learning.

The question of the rate of learning is fundamental. It is so difficult to explain learning at all, yet children succeed in learning an arbitrary language in an extraordinarily short time. And this feat is one which adults cannot in general compete with. "The basic fact which faces investigators ... is the speed of language acquisition."[3] This fact has often been used in support of arguments against learning, and in favour of an innatist TGG viewpoint, with comments such as:

> We can now understand why the speed of language acquisition seems
> so great.[4]

The rate of learning is an important aspect against which the predictions of theories and models should be tested. This includes, in particular, explanations of the deceleration of language learning, and the abysmal performance of adults. We saw in the last chapter that the order of learning is significant from the point of view of being able to build on what has already been learned. But "ease of learning" is a more general factor, which we would expect to affect both rate and order of learning. And what is easy to learn will depend both on the model of learning and the language been learned. Conversely, examination of rate and order of learning will tend to show what is easy to learn.

Schlesinger presents an interesting analysis in the comparative linguistics of the order and ease of learning, along with hypotheses about the underlying reasons.[5] He proposes that it is easier to learn position rules than those involving inflection — it is only a matter of distinguishing two possibilities in the case of position rules. But in the case of inflection there are a great many more (the learner needs also to learn a position rule, in any case). Even in languages which depend more on inflection than word order, position rules seem to be learned first, inflections later. Similar considerations apply to the learning of auxiliaries in English. Redundancy of some inflections, such as the possessive -'s and the third person singular -s, is thought to retard the learning of these relative to others, such as the plural -s and the past -ed, which are not also indicated by position.

These ideas are instructive and appealing, but they do, of course, beg the question of why inflections ever arose. In the case of the possessive and personal inflections, there is a morphophonemic explanation involving contraction of particles which were originally separate words.

In both cases the inflection derives from a pronoun, but this is certainly not the case for the plural and past suffixes.

Another interesting point for us is that it is assumed that the number cohesion originates with the noun and extends to the verb. We think that this assumption is correct, and that plurality does have intrinsically closer ties to the noun subject than to the verb. This is evidenced by the asymmetry of subject and object, and by the presumption that the number inflection originated as a number clitic rather than as a pronoun.

In any case, these examples will have illustrated the relevance of the rate and order of learning to the development of a learning model.

Parents and Teachers: Good and Bad Examples

We now want to consider how the child's acquisition process is influenced by the external environment, partly because any computer learning system must also learn through external interactions. Here we are particularly concerned with the effect of both the purposive and unconscious roles played by the learner, and those who provide his language models. We start by considering the parents' and teacher's roles, and the child's reinforcement and feedback system. We are then going to look at the evidence as to the supposed irrelevance of these factors. We shall look also at the actual function of the child's and the parent's imitation and repetition propensities. Finally, we move on to the semantic effects of the environment, although we will look at these more thoroughly in Chapter Eight.

Much is made of the fact that a large proportion of adult speech, and in particular of speech to and around children, does not always conform strictly to grammatical conventions. Not only does adult speech include ungrammatical sentences as such, but it also includes unfinished sentences, sentences which are aborted or whose framework is changed midstream, and deliberate and unconscious modifications of speech for the benefit of children. Such accommodation can take a number of forms. Sometimes it is the vocabulary and syntactic complexity used, but it can also be the parent's use of baby language, or a child grammar.

We should also consider parental accommodation in any language model, both for its effect on the learning process, and for its implications for the design of the model. On the other hand, we could argue that the ungrammaticality of parental speech to children may not be particularly significant and problematic at all. It has been noted that:

> any grammatical sentence that was more complex than what the child was prepared to deal with would be just as bad for him.[6]

Kelley further proposed some specific mechanisms by means of which the child would be able to vet his input, and ignore unhelpful speech. Remember that our consideration of imitation in relation to recognition and production grammars implied such selectivity.

The notion of the unhelpfulness of parental speech has also been challenged by Ervin-Tripp:

> The argument that input is degenerate, confusing, that the surface orders in English are displayed in so many permutations that simple order heuristics relating surface orders to meanings would be impossible must be produced from observations of speech styles at conferences, not in family kitchens. Input simplicity and grammaticality do not remove the problem of later learning of complex orders, but they do make the discovery of the first structures much less a problem.[7]

More positively still, it is apparent that various patterns of parental speech are oriented to help comprehension and learning by the child. Presumably this help is real and the parental modifications are warranted. Such potentially helpful features include:

- structural simplicity "… in the sense of brevity, few subordinations, few passives, lack of false starts and intercalated material";
- repetitiveness: "contrary to linguists' belief that phrases are not repeated, in speech to children they are repeated *ad nauseam*";
- paradigmatic styles such as discourse modelling: "… "Where's the doggy? There's the doggy" types of sentences in which replacement or discourse agreement is instructed";
- parental imitation: "Children who were fast language learners had mothers who were more likely to provide an input of build-ups, completions, and breakdowns".[8]

As Kuczaj says, "parents may facilitate children's language development by providing children with models of language learning strategies".[9] This brings us to the other side of the parent's role: his or her understanding, acceptance, feedback and correction of the child's utterances. Whilst there has been a movement against the behaviourist view, spearheaded by Chomsky's criticism of Skinner,[10] and recognizable in a moderate form throughout recent linguistics and psycholinguistics, we still think that a behaviourist view is viable. Indeed, it is difficult to envisage a language learning process in which feedback, positive or negative, played no part. Specifically, Palermo makes the reasonable proposal:

> that the acquisition of language may be much like the process which Skinner has called shaping, in the sense that initially the parent will accept any efforts the child makes and, as the child shows progress, the requirements for communication become more and more stringent … It is not a matter of the adult dropping pellets for each correct utterance, but it is a matter of achieving a goal of mutual intelligibility.[11]

Reinforcement: Punishment and Reward

The question of reinforcement has become controversial. The complete exclusion of *correction* as a part of language acquisition, by many workers, has tended to steer them to exclude reinforcement. Nonetheless, there is still considerable support for reinforcement paradigms. We have proposed the idea of less direct forms of positive or negative feedback (*e.g.* "anticipated correction") elsewhere.[12] Interestingly, despite the nativist's reminder that learning is computationally infeasible, those who have produced computational models have always adopted a generalization learning paradigm, involving some sort of reward and punishment protocol (including negative as well as positive information). Thus the earliest such work, which was already post-Chomsky, and aware of his work, is based on a recognition that data·must "either serve to confirm (or infirm) previously acquired constructs or ... bear on the next step".[13] These views about feedback fit in with recent work:

> The very role of some reinforcement (simulated in our programs ...) is controversial. Clearly, mothers do not often say to their children anything like: "Yes, my boy, that is a grammatical sentence". ... That mothers do ... repeat a child's simplified sentences in fuller form ... or ... that a child may not be understood when speaking, would certainly seem to play a [reinforcing] role in this complex learning process".[14]

What we have to do, then, is not to deny that reinforcement and feedback exist, but rather to consider how the child uses such feedback. So we turn our attention to the "imitation and correction game". We also look at the problem of reconciling the belief that parents give reinforcement and children use this feedback, with the well-documented evidence of the unresponsiveness of children to negative feedback in the form of explicit correction. As Derrick says, "the game of imitation and correction may be just that — a game which has very little to do with the processes of either comprehension or production".[15]

This unwillingness, or inability, of the child to accept correction and modify his production is the primary, but most naïvely interpreted, evidence available on the place of negative feedback in the child's acquisition process. In this "game" the child will not imitate correctly. We suggest that the correction is processed with the recognition grammar, the semantics extracted, and the sentence built up again using the production grammar. On the other hand, when imitation does occur (and this is supported by a more sophisticated combination of experimentation, observation and reasoning) it has been suggested that imitation bypasses the semantic levels.

> Consider, for example, the Indirect object/Direct object contrast in such a pair as: "The woman gives the bunny the teddy" and "The woman gives the teddy the bunny". In five cases when *S*s were given the

problem, with appropriate pictures for the *P* task, they transformed the original sentences so as to express the indirect object with a preposi- tional phrase ... If on the *I* task, these *S*s had decoded the sentences into meanings, as they do on the *P* task, the same transformations ought to have occurred. It never did occur ... It seems reasonable to conclude that the imitation performance did not work through the meaning sys- tem.[16]

The tenor of this proposal is that if semantics are unavailable, imita- tion purely involves recognition, without necessarily complete under- standing, and without semantic processing, or production. However where semantics are involved, imitation *per se* is not, and the progres- sion comprises recognition using the recognition grammar, comprehen- sion of the semantics, and production using the production grammar. This suggests separation between the recognition and production gram- mars, but while the evidence is quite strong that imitation does not re- quire complete understanding, it is not completely independent of the meaning system. The claim that it is could perhaps be tested by examin- ing sentences in which the open class words are replaced by nonsense syllables — complete independence would imply that imitation perfor- mance should not be reduced in this modified experiment (subject to controls for unfamiliarity of the new words).

Although correction is a form of negative feedback, the usage we are discussing has the flavour of a positive model. In particular, "the imi- tation and correction game" can only help if the child can make use of the new model, or if it helps the child to realize that his production grammar is faulty. These are two different functions, which are respec- tively a positive model, and negative feedback. Moreover, the problems with this "game" relate to the ability to make use of a model immediate- ly. The most which could be achieved with solely negative information is the abandonment of a rule, but "nature abhors a vacuum". This is an im- portant point, which seems to have been missed by many researchers. It is not surprising, therefore, if an effect must wait until the child has de- veloped an alternative rule, or perhaps "patches", to supplant, or sup- port, the faulty rule.

There is another factor, neither positive nor negative in itself. Pres- umably the repetition involved in the game is useful in strengthening both positive model and negative feedback. Repetition is a feature of child speech in its own right, and worth looking at in relation to models and predictions. But we want now to look at imitation further, as repeti- tion, or one individual repeating the utterance of another. Equally, repe- tition can be a form of imitation, one individual imitating his own utter- ances.

Whatever their relationship, imitation and repetition are specific examples of a wider class of relationships, which we can call *variations*. We have already encountered the concept of variation, along with an example of the use of the indirect object, in the passage we have just quoted from Fraser. This illustrated the transformations at the heart of Transformational Generative Grammar, and provides some evidence for a transformational approach. But there are classes of variation which are much more important from the perspective of parent-child interactions and modifications of their own or the other's speech.

Telegraphic speech is separately treated, but the other modification, *expansion*, is considered now. We should recognize that expansion reflects an important facet of "the imitation and correction game", and more generally of parent-child interactions. Expansion typically involves the "correction" of a child's utterance to, or towards, the supposed adult model. If correct and successfully imitated, such expansion permits one of the following three results. As the worst case, there may be, firstly, no long term effect as the child did not recognise the significance of the correction (and the expansion was not fully comprehended). There may, secondly be no long term effect because the child did not see the difference (although the expansion was fully comprehended). Thirdly and best, there may be a reinforcing or focussing effect (if expansion is taking place at the "noise" threshold):

> When the child has already produced part of the sentence, his storage capacities may be freed for attention to and storage of additional components [which had been] just "noisy" to him.[17]

> One often has the impression that the young child has a severely limited span in speaking—that he can make only so many decisions per sentence—and that an expansion ... can stretch this span slightly ... The sentence-programming span ... is not so much a matter of length as a matter of the number of operations involved in generating a sentence.[18]

Expansion provides a perfect opportunity for a child to see the additional step beyond what he has been able to achieve himself. Imitation in such a circumstance must at least serve as a form of rehearsal to reinforce latent rules. Lenneberg suggests that imitation does play a significant, if catalytic, role in language learning.[19] It is also possible that "grammatical" rules and capabilities are being developed at first to help in understanding, and that until reaching a level of confidence, an utterance of that level of complexity will not occur in spontaneous or elicited production. Where a model exists this may boost the child's confidence in his own latent production (whether voiced or not). This will reduce the load on the production process, thus allowing processing below the normal production threshold, and resulting in imitations of greater complexity than could be produced without the help of the model. If there is too big a gap between the complexity of the model and the child's current production capability, this load/threshold reduction phenomena will not serve to affect the complexity of the imitation produced. Presumably the strength with which a below-threshold construct might be reinforced would depend on the certainty of the surrounding context. Thus, models just slightly above the child's own level should produce maximal learning effect, and those overly above this level could not be expected to produce any learning effect.

There are further variations on the theme of imitation. In a sense, the parent is imitating the child when correcting him or her, and similarly the parent is imitating the child when reflecting back the child's sentences. This is perhaps to establish that he or she has understood the child correctly, perhaps to help the child, and perhaps not consciously for either of these reasons. But the most characteristic forms of imitation are the child's variations, and in particular the reduction modification. Frequently this is what is referred to as "imitation" in the literature, although it is actually a reduction from a sentence of a more mature grammar into the "telegraphic" form of a child grammar.

We can now consider some recent research by Kuczaj[20] on the variety of modifications available in imitation, and their significance. In this case the data area under consideration is not only parent-child interaction, but also language play, particularly the crib speech in which children engage before they go to sleep. There is thus a distinction between other-imitation ("imitation") and self-imitation ("repetition"). These are all examples of useful language learning strategies, but here we will consider only the child's usage of these paradigms in language play. Kuczaj clarifies the distinguished forms of modifications which occur:

> Buildups constitute an utterance sequence of two or more parts, each successive part including the words of the previous utterance and additional linguistics units ... Breakdowns are the opposite of buildups. In a breakdown, the first utterance is the longest and most complete. Successive utterances involve the reproduction of parts of the original utterance ... A third type of modification is the completion. Completions are not always modifications in the true sense of the term in that the original utterance is not necessarily modified. A completion sequence involves two or more utterances that are separated by a pause (or pauses) but which form a more complex utterance when considered as a combined utterance. Parts of the original utterance may or may not be repeated in the successive utterance ... The final type of linguistic practice sequence is the substitution. This consists of a substitution in the second or third utterance of a different word of the same form class in a sentence grammatically parallel to the original utterance.[21]

All of these forms of modification are highly paradigmatic, and thus suggestive of the existence of rule based child-grammars for recognition and production. There is also an overlap between modifications and the spectrum of exact, reduced and expanded imitations and repetitions, the modification terminology emphasizing the supposed purposive function of the sequences. There is overlap, finally, with the concept of "repairs" where a child modifies his own utterance in an (often successful) attempt to improve it.

In general, imitation seems to allow a child to identify and practice contrasts slightly beyond his production competence by use of another's model, whilst repetition allows testing of his production competence against his own recognition competence. This seems like a very tangible manifestation of an *anticipated correction* paradigm which we proposed in an earlier paper.[22]

The evidence we have been discussing suggests that imitation and repetition, particularly if it involves expansion, can be helpful. But the evidence does not prove that it is essential to the language acquisition process. Imitation certainly increases the rate of exposure to negative information, and slightly challenging models. That overt spoken imitation and repetition is not requisite is demonstrated by Lenneberg's anarthic case.[23] This evidence would seem to put paid to both imitation and correction as a primary mechanism for acquisition of a recognition grammar and of speech comprehension ability. It seems, on this evidence, to be unnecessary even for development of a production grammar and speech communication capability. Despite this evidence, we would argue that the importance of correction is supported by the research into repetitions. Our hypothesis suggests that child language acquisition takes place partly as a result of correction. There can be two ways in which this correction takes place: explicit, where the child makes an error and is reprimanded more or less forcibly by an adult, and the "correct" string for the purpose given. Secondly, there is the *anticipated correction* case, where the child infers that in certain circumstances the acceptable string should use a certain syntagm already learned. How the child knows which tokens form paradigms in which syntagms is not clarified, although it is likely that *memories* of what has been noticed in strings used by adults are the prime mechanism. The main motive in these acts is the desire to imitate, and the desire to please.

The outline hypothesis here would be that learners make inferences about what is likely to be corrected, from listening to the speech addressed to them. They then supply their own corrections in the form of anticipated correction. Anticipated correction is not simply self-correction, it is a form of *avoidance*.

There is evidently some difficulty in reconciling this hypothesis with evidence such as Lenneberg's. Of course, the absence of production precludes the role of *implicit correction*, but not necessarily that of *anticipated correction*. But this still leaves this theory open to the criticism of Jenkins and Palermo's *covert imitation*.

This suggests that, at best, anticipated correction is a useful metaphor, and that there ought to be alternative ways of explaining the effects of anticipated correction. This is further suggested by the observation that the explicit "imitation and correction game" includes both negative feedback, and a positive model. So anticipated correction needs to use either old (*viz* remembered), or new (*viz* synthesized) positive models to provide negative feedback, which is one of the primary roles we see for the proposed phenomenon.

The advantages of an anticipated correction hypothesis, rather than a pure imitation theory are that it explains the "feedback" character of learning, shown by over-extension of new rules, and their correction in a series of oscillations. It also explains why child learners do not pay attention to structures they are not yet ready to produce themselves. Only when the speech of others uses structures and words already recognized does it affect the child, because he is then able to use this data for anticipated correction. It can also explain why later stages of learning proceed with relatively little explicit correction, apart from marking by teachers, and correction of gross errors by parents.

Lenneberg's anarthic case does not in fact negate the utility of this hypothesis, since it is quite reasonable that the dumb child should still be capable of sub-vocalization. This would, as in normal children, be the basis and primary medium of thought. Moreover, we suggest that this anticipated correction hypothesis can be thought of as an intriguing analogy to the formal mathematical construction of a *generator* from a *tester*. It also corresponds to the recognition grammar forming the framework from which the production grammar is developed. But this is quite a distinct mechanism from the threshold paradigm described in our experiments in later chapters. It would be required, however, if it were not possible directly to transfer rules from the recognition grammar to the production grammar.

A recognition grammar *tester* could provide a form of negative feedback, although there would not be the accompanying positive model which is expected in a correction paradigm. Positive models would be generated when the feedback from the *tester* was positive, and these would presumably be the spontaneous utterances produced or sub-vocalized. Implementing this hypothesis would require a pre-existing generator of a more general language, which is then filtered by the tester. This might be innate and specifically linguistic (*cf* Chomsky proposals), or a more general function of the learning of ontology and semantics. Futhermore, a threshold model may allow generation and utterance of a faulty sentence (*e.g.* through utilisation of a high weight generalisation). But once generated, as with puns *etc.*, alternate possibilities, for example from rote learned forms, may be generated. These can be with or without utterance if they achieve higher acceptability; they can provide both the negative feedback and the positive model.

On the question of correction generally, it should further be noted that it is not fair to dispose of the evidence for correction on the basis of an anecdote from Lenneberg which does not include any attempt to qualify, let alone quantify, the rate, ease or difficulty of learning. But such evidence must be borne in mind.

The position on imitation and correction which has been adopted in this research is as follows. The solution to the apparent anomaly of correction being necessary for learning, but not used by children, comes from the hypothesis of separate recognition and production grammars. The surprising fact that children do not appear to be able to make use of the correction paradigm is an indication that the *productio grammar* is lagging behind the *recognitio grammar*. Only once there is a certain degree of confidence in the "grammar" being recognition-tested, will the hypothesis pass into use in the *productio grammar*. Conversely, only once the threshold of recognition confidence has been passed, does the over-generalization ever become available for production testing. The recognition testing and production testing paradigm is reminiscent of the commercial alpha-test and beta-test paradigm. Only once a degree of confidence has been achieved through in-house testing is a product made tentatively available for independent testing. Since it is trivial to transfer rules directly between recognition and production grammars, there is no practical reason for adopting the generate-and-test paradigm suggested by anticipated correction, although in neurological terms the separation between sensory and motor functions might well make it expedient.

The explanation of the role of imitation relates to this transfer between partitioned grammars. Children will only imitate what they comprehend fairly closely, which indicates that the rules in the recognition partition of their grammar are almost at the threshold where they will be available to participate in the production grammar. Thus, the reinforcement of the rules may be enough to take a rule over the production threshold. A second possibility is that general motivational and attentional confidence factors result in an effective lowering of the threshold. This might result in a local or global raising of neuronal (rule) firing rates. And a third factor may be that the cognitive computational load is reduced in the imitation paradigm, and hence more effort can be expended on the more difficult, and less well-established, portions of the analysis.   We must finally consider Lenneberg's case. This is quite consonant with imitation and repetition acting as catalysts, or acting in the transfer from recognition to production grammar. There is scope for further research into the rate and extent of learning of such handicapped children, and control of other factors which may allow similar effects (*e.g.* sign language, written language, perhaps).

The correction hypothesis is that this is available to all children in many ways, but that it cannot be reflected directly in production. The Lenneberg case thus poses no problem here. In the experiments of Chapter Fourteen there is no direct use of negative information, and as expected these have severe limitations. Kelley's model also has similar limitations: whilst it is more complex, it too uses no overt negative information and no semantics, but employs a time decay property which is a questionable substitute for negative information.

Telegraphic Speech

We earlier discussed various paradigms apparent in the speech of children and their interlocutors. These were examined primarily in terms of the possible advantage the child could gain from them, and the type of learning which the child is involved in. Discussion of the particular form of reduced imitations and spontaneous two to four word (morpheme) production has largely been deferred until now. This is known as *telegraphic* speech, since it has some characteristics we are familiar with when we are paying by the word in telegrams. As mentioned earlier, adults are startlingly competent at producing telegraphic speech which corresponds closely with that of a child. It has even been observed that older children are capable of modifying their speech to the level appropriate to a younger child.[24]

The evidence also indicates that this ability is not merely one of the parent learning his or her child's language, but that apparently any individual is capable of quite reasonable performance. This suggests many possibilities: is this because the capability is innate in some sense; is it because we still retain the rules of our own child grammars in some form; is it because the telegraphic speech is an important part of the framework for our normal speech; is it that the categories of words to retain are well recognized or even syntactically indicated; is it because the prosody of the language highlights these words anyway? Whilst no answers are available yet, we tend to feel there is some truth in all of these suggestions.

Another battery of questions is raised by the use of telegraphic speech by adults (or older children) when talking to young children. The main question is why: is this some sort of natural response; is it some sort of conditioning; is it that it is supposed to be helpful to the child; or is it helpful to the child? Again, we are sure there is an element of truth in each suggestion, but the last is the crux. It is helpful to the extent that it helps the child to handle the gross word order functions, but it does not give the child some of the additional cues, and it does nothing to help them to use the omitted words. The evidence suggests that the most helpful forms will be those which are just a little beyond the child's present production capability, but probably within their comprehension capability. This is possibly achieved by our tendency to a somewhat generous or charitable assessment of the child's capabilities.

Brown and his group have been responsible for a number of useful analyses of telegraphic speech, which as we have seen arose from a comparison of their role as experimenters in learning child grammar with the child's own learning of adult grammar. Brown notes the preservation of word order of the obvious models, and the fact that (in English especially) order is so important. This allows comprehension by the adult, and suggests meaning intention by the child. He also shows that the length of an utterance is a function only of developmental stage, not of the length of the model. He attributes this to span limitations. The span/length limitation forces the dropping of words, and leads to a study of the particular forms retained and omitted.

It turns out that children are remarkably consistent, and the selection of words is highly systematic, both in development and in uniformity across individuals. The forms retained are open class words ("contentives"), and the words omitted the small functional words ("functors"). Thus telegraphic child speech is much more than superficially similar to telegraphic aphasic speech. The contentives are mostly words which have been useful to the child singly at an earlier stage. The functors are only useful in terms of relationships between other words or their referents, and have a smaller information content. In fact, Brown has shown an exceptional correlation between the omission of particular forms or classes of forms, and the mean utterance length. For example, the verb *to be* is omitted in progressive constructions (*I am going*) below 3.2 morphemes; the modals *will* and *can* are omitted below 3.5 morphemes.

There are two main factors which might explain this highly systematic and quantifiable ordering of words. It may be a matter of information content, as suggested by Brown's terminology. Or it might be a function of sensory-motor relevance. It is likely not to be a matter of the extent to which practice of the forms has been possible, since children will retain contentives that are relatively unfamiliar. However, we can note that the classes of words retained are those which have been practised in simpler contexts. The function words can only be practised effectively in a relatively complex context.

We can also note that, while information content is important in telegraphic speech, it is hard to see how a child could analyze sentences in order to choose those with optimal information content. There are overt cues which point to the contentives, including stress and intonation. Brown emphasizes differential stress as a determinant of telegraphic retention and rejection. Pragmatically, though, marked stress would be a tiresome addition to the written forms used in computer models, and we prefer to emphasize the sensory-motor relevance of words, and the attentional role of difference and contrast. It is also difficult to see that stress provides the consistent gradation observed in the appearance of word classes during language development. This seems more consistent with a complexity factor, involving learning of functional relationships and grammatical rules.

We have made no attempt in our experiments to implement an explicit deletion scheme. But we do expect that the proposed frequency, utility and span related heuristics we discuss in Chapter Thirteen will implicitly favour contentives in the early stages. By contrast, Kelley has implemented a complex system based on deletion coefficients, in order to achieve reduction prior to other analysis.

Deixis and Ostension: Pointing and Indicating

We now follow through a particular example in which one aspect of language is traced through the phenomena of the errors of the child or the accomodation of the parent.

> Deixis is the Greek word for indicating or pointing. It has been taken over as a technical term in linguistics to refer to those terms or expressions which serve this linguistic function. Thus the category of deictic expressions includes, typically, pronouns, demonstratives, some verbs of motion like *come* and *go*, adverbs of place, definite articles, *etc.* ... What these expressions do when grouped as "deictic", is to introduce an explicitly subjective orientation into linguistic classification.[25]

We have already looked at various aspects of deixis, without explicit reference. We have also, in discussing child grammar, imitation and telegraphic speech, come across the notion of closed class words. Deictics mainly fall into this category. The deictics contrast with the functors — remember that this subclass of the closed class words proved significant in telegraphic and aphasic speech. We should note, too, that some deictics, the verbs *come* and *go* for example, are actually contentives and often easiest categorized as open class. These examples are difficult to discriminate, and the precise classes seldom carry over exactly into other languages. Even if they do, they are very difficult to learn in a monolingual context, as Brown reported of his monolingual learning of Japanese. The distinction is largely one of movement toward or with, as opposed to away from, either speaker or addressee, but it is somewhat more complex than that (*e.g.* reference is his home). The base meaning is the same, and the penalty for missing the subtle distinction is usually slight. While the words may seem virtual synonyms, they will be learned and will tend to be used only in appropriate contexts.

The personal pronouns are more straightforward to define, but are perversely difficult for children to learn to use or understand correctly. McNeill[26] sees the problem with first and second person as stemming from the fact we previously noted that in identical context the words *I* and *you* are virtually synonymous. This is not so much with each other as with *mummy* and the child's own name. They are expected to be reversed in his own speech. This then results in two pairs of homonyms—one of each pair used by himself, the other by his mother. It is difficult to see how this shift of reference can be learned other than by correction by the mother, or eavesdropping on third party conversations. The child should never hear *I* used of himself, for example. The problem of "failure to shift" is illustrated in the following dialogue:

Adam: Fell down mommy.

Mother: You fell down?

M: Did you hurt yourself? *M:* What did you hurt?

Adam: Hurt your elbow.[27]

We take this problem of "failure to shift" to indicate the difficulty the child has in shifting between his viewpoint (and self-relative pronomial system), and that of a second person (the speaker/addressee) or a third person (the referent). First, he has the enormous problem of recognizing the concepts of speaker and addressee at all—these being the correct first and second person referents. Then there is considerable complexity involved in the proper use of these words by the child.

The general function of deictic forms is indexical, that is they are used to show and direct focus of attention. This function, it is proposed, is "primitive and ontogenically prior to other referring expressions"[28]. One of the first pivots used by children is usually a derivative of *this* or *that*—initially purely deictic, accompanied by gesture, and neutral with respect to gender, proximity and speech role. Separation of the distinct deictics, and indeed deictic classes is a gradual process. Its complexity is well known to any who have studied non-European languages. There are many dimensions along which one or more distinctions may or may not be made: dimensions including distance, direction, speaker, male/female/mixed, inclusive/exclusive we/you, single/dual/plural, *etc.*

Often the distinctions seem to be made unnecessarily difficult for the language learner. We have already noted the difficulty involved in making the first/second person singular distinction. Parent/child dialogue tends not to use these pronouns, but as we have said relies solely on the third person forms with specific appellations. This presumably makes it easier for communication and identification to take place in the earlier stages, but does not help with regard to person deixis. It also saves confusion with alternate verb forms for first and second person, but does not help learning of conjugations or cohesion.

Surprisingly, correct third person deictic usage seems to arrive after first and second person, despite the speaker distinction problems with those. This is also despite assistance with use of third person forms, and the similarity of third person deixis with the primitive demonstrative deixis described above.

Wales describes experiments which suggest that "only the announced interlocutors were considered"[29] by half the subjects, and notes that the hardest sentences were those involving accusative or possessive third person forms. One small point of unknown significance about the four problem pronouns is the asymmetric overloading which may be seen by contrasting: "Look at *her*", "Look at *him*", "Look at *her* dog", "Look at *his* dog", "Look at *hers*" and "Look at *his*". Wales' reference to the need for gestural support with demonstratives and third person pronouns is not really surprising. Another observation indicates that the child uses what is essentially a surrogate nominal deixis in his early stages:

> Some of the indexical terms of nomination (*this, that, there*) first occur alone in early speech and then gradually with "referential" terms. But in early speech the distinction between deixis and full symbolic reference is in effect neutralized. Many observers have reported that at first children only talk about the contemporaneous situation. Under these circumstances nouns are used, as demonstratives or deictic personal pronouns must be, only in the presence of the objects to which they refer.[30]

It should also be noted that the prime characteristic of the third person pronouns is their non-deictic cohesive relationships.

In summary, the closed class deictics are amongst the earliest closed class words to be learned. There are two likely reasons for this: they are directly reflected in the environment; and they have clear functionality. The closed class words whose function is primarily cohesive (or solely paradigmatic) are naturally harder to learn. The significance of the deictics arises from, and demonstrates, the importance for language learning of the relationships between the child and his sensory-motor environment.

Rote Learning

Finally, we complete this chapter with an alternative view on imitation. It has been suggested by Kuczaj that children use imitation for rote learning. This is potentially useful in that such holistic processing allows storage and use of unanalyzed units plagiarized from the model. He also emphasized that these forms may be reproduced later—giving rise to delayed or deferred imitation. It has been shown that infants initially produce inflections and irregular forms by rote, and it is apparent that in the final analysis all morphemes are in a sense learned by rote. The essence of rote is, however, that forms capable of analysis into elements are learned without analysis and without reference to the elemental de-composition. Another role for rote memorized forms is as "prefabri-cated routines" and "prefabricated patterns". These phrases refer to paradigmatic use of phrases or templates, emphasizing respectively the functional usage of what is memorized, and the substitution of alterna-tives for a variable part in an otherwise constant whole.

> Eventually, routines and other un-analyzed and under-analyzed seg-ments come to be analyzed by the child and so become more productive and less routine-like. This occurs because syntactic development de-pends on the comparison and relation of known forms, rules, and struc-tures (including rote forms and structures with new input".[31]

Throughout this section (and indeed throughout the entire book) we have outlined and espoused other explanations of the role of imitation and the learning of particular classes of morphemes and paradigms. We cannot see rote as being essential at any level. Even at the morphemic level, learning is primarily of relationships, and even morphemes are composed as relations from syllables. They are themselves composed of phonemes, which are themselves equivalence classes (a relational term) of phones *etc.*

Notes to Chapter Four

1. Gilling, Dick, and Robin Brightwell, *The Human Brain* (Orbis, London, UK, 1982), p.48f.
2. Ervin-Tripp, Susan, "Some Strategies for the First Years", in Timothy E. Moore, ed., *Cognitive Development and the Acquisition of Language* (Academic Press, New York, 1973), p.283.
3. Slobin, Dan I., *The Ontogenesis of Language* (Academic Press, New York, 1971), p.3.
4. McNeill, David, "The Capacity for the Ontogenesis of Grammar", in Dan I. Slobin, *The Ontogenesis of Language* (Academic Press, New York, 1971), p.21.
5. Schlesinger, I.M., "Production of Utterances and Language Acquisition" in Dan I. Slobin, *The Ontogenesis of Language* (Academic Press, 1971), p.81f.
6. Kelley, K.L., *Early Syntactic Acquisition* (Rand Corporation, Santa Monica, CA, November 1967), p.83.
7. Ervin-Tripp, Susan, "Some Strategies for the First Years", in Timothy E. Moore, ed., *Cognitive Development and the Acquisition of Language* (Academic Press, New York, 1973), p.264.
8. *Op. cit.,* p.263-264.
9. Kuczaj, Stan A., *Crib Speech and Language Play* (Springer-Verlag, New York, NY, 1983), p.159.

10. M. Piatelli-Palmarini, ed., *Language and Learning: The Debate between Jean Piaget and Noam Chomsky* (Routledge and Kegan Paul, 1979).

11. Palermo, David S., "On Learning to Talk: Are Principles Derived from the Learning Laboratory Applicable?" in Dan I. Slobin, ed., *The Ontogenesis of Language* (Academic Press, 1971), p.7f.

12. Turk, Christopher C. R., "A Correction NL Mechanism", *ECAI-84: Advances in Artificial Intelligence* (Elsevier Science Publishers, 1984), pp.225-226.

13. Kelley, K.L., *Early Syntactic Acquisition* (Rand Corporation, Santa Monica, CA, November 1967), p.83.

14. Kucera, Henry, "The Learning of Grammar", *Perspectives in Computing*, Vol 1, No. 2 (1981), p.35.

15. Derrick, J., *The Child's Acquisition of Language* (National Foundation for Education Research, Windsor, Berkshire, UK, 1977), p.10.

16. Fraser, D., U. Bellugi, and R. Brown, "Control of Grammar in Imitation, Comprehension, and Production", *Journal of Verbal Learning and Verbal Behaviour*, Vol.2, No.1 (1963). p.133.

17. Ervin-Tripp, Susan, "Some Strategies for the First Years", in Timothy E. Moore, ed., *Cognitive Development and the Acquisition of Language* (Academic Press, New York, 1973), p.264.

18. Slobin, Dan I., "Imitation and Grammatical Development in Children", in Endler, L. Boulter, and H. Osser, *Contemporary Issues in Developmental Psychology* (Holt, Rhinehart and Winston, New York, 1968), p.439f.

19. Lenneberg, Eric H., "The Natural History of Language", in F. L. Smith and George A. Miller, eds, *The Genesis of Language* (MIT Press, 1966), pp.219-252.

20. Kuczaj, Stan A., *Crib Speech and Language Play* (Springer-Verlag, New York, NY, 1983), p.3f.

21. *Loc. cit.*

22. Turk, Christopher C. R., "A Correction NL Mechanism", *ECAI-84: Advances in Artificial Intelligence* (Elsevier Science Publishers, 1984), pp.225-226.

23. Lenneberg, Eric H., "The Natural History of Language", in F. L. Smith and George A. Miller, eds, *The Genesis of Language* (MIT Press, 1966), p.410f.

24. Brown, Roger, and Colin Fraser, "The Acquisition of Syntax", in C. N. Cofer and Barbara S. Musgrave, eds, *Verbal Behavior and Learning: Problems and Processes* (McGraw-Hill, 1963).

25. Wales, Roger, "Deixis", in P. Fletcher and M. Garman, eds, *Language Acquisition: Studies in First Language Development* (Cambridge University Press, Cambridge, UK, 1979), p.241.

26. Tanz, Christine, *Studies in the Acquisition of Deictic Terms* (Cambridge, UK, Cambridge University Press, 1980), p.55.

27. *Op. cit.*, p.52.

28. *Ibid.*, p.2.

29. Wales, Roger, "Deixis", in P. Fletcher and M. Garman, eds, *Language Acquisition: Studies in First Language Development* (Cambridge University Press, Cambridge, UK, 1979), p.255.

30. Tanz, Christine, *Studies in the Acquisition of Deictic Terms* (Cambridge, UK, Cambridge University Press, 1980), p.3f.

Chapter Five

Cognition and Restriction

Cognitive Processes

In this chapter we look again at the constraints and restrictions on language, language users and language processes. We are looking again at the fine contextual balance needed to communicate information. We consider the gradual refinement of associations in the formation of concepts. Expectation provides both the metric for judging the relevance, novelty and value of content and context, and the impetus for refining the scope, generality and focus of perceptions and associations. We further consider transformation and consolidation as processes which mediate the effective and efficient use of learned associations, and forgetting as a positive correlate of the existence of multiple associations acting as alternate hypotheses or levels of generality. Finally, we turn to the impact of the sensory motor mechanisms on the conditions for and restrictions on cognitive processing and learning. We review the respective spans of absolute judgement and immediate memory, including the ubiquitous magical number seven, along with the traditional behaviourist approach to conditioning. And we compare characteristics of man and animal, native and foreigner, speaker and hearer, oral error and aural error, to refine our concepts of both comprehension and production processes.

The thesis we are putting forward, by contrast with those of the nativists, sets language in a context of general cognitive principles and mechanisms in common with other cognitive functions. On this view, to discover what is unique about human language, with dual emphasis on *human* and *language*, we had first to explore the potential of the more general cognitive processes. In this chapter we are going to look at cognition at the neural level. We are now moving to what we think of as a slightly deeper level of analysis, considering from a psychological and neural perspective the basics of cognitive processes, and their relation to language.

We are not going to use the concept of consciousness in a technical sense, but it does provide some useful distinctions. In general, the processes we will be talking about here are not conscious. Most will be *unconscious*. That is, we usually have no awareness of the process, let alone of the mechanisms of the process, and even deliberate introspection is of little direct help. These are the kinds of processes which may be argued to be innate.

We, as language users, are usually unaware of the mechanisms of the language process, although we may be aware of the process as a whole. By focussing our attention on the process, we may even be able to become aware of some of the mechanisms, or perhaps supplant and even take over conscious control of the process. This take-over by the conscious may indeed be an unavoidable part of the focussing of attention, *i.e.* consciousness. In general these processes are learned, and so they are initially conscious, but become *subconscious* "reflexes".

Other processes are fully conscious, and we have no direct interest in these here. Once we have shown that a process may be conscious, we will cease to try to explain it. We are not trying to frame a theory of consciousness as such, although Goldschlager, for example, takes it as within his charter.[1] But we are going to take it as a fundamental empirical psychological building block, and are not concerned to explain it at a physiological level — although any neurological theory would eventually have to cope with the phenomenon. Examples of the role of the distinction are puns and garden-path sentences (*e.g.* respectively "In a blackout, many hands make light work"; "The horse raced past the barn fell"). Such examples are often cited as evidence for backtracking in our basic language parsing process. But we differ from this view, and take them as evidence against backtracking. When it encounters such a sentence, the unconscious or subconscious process refers the sentence or parts of it to the conscious mind.

At this point it is useful to consider the universally held, and widely ignored, "charitable assumption". This phrase is borrowed from metaphysics and is employed *inter alia* in psychology and theology. It refers to our tendency to treat people as if they had the same basic intelligence, understanding, and beliefs as ourselves. This is a fundamental hypothesis underlying all cognitive psychology, although we have already suggested that there may be different ways in which language may be learned by different people, and individual differences in the learning process. For example, for some children imitation may be helpful, whilst for others it was not.

Hayes addresses the charitable assumption in its usual habitat, the realm of communication:

> However, in order that communication be possible at all, it should obviously be that people's cognitive structures are *similar*: and, as a working hypothesis, we will make such an assumption in developing naive physics.[2]

An elementary tenet of information theory is that we only communicate what is not shared. And equally important (and this is Hayes' point), we can only communicate with reference to an agreed context. This is where the charitable assumption comes in. We assume that we and our interlocutors are agreed on the rules, context and meanings of language, our fundamental beliefs, presuppositions and perceptions, and our intentions and motivations in communicating.

At a general and superficial level, this assumption is true, and therefore adequate. But at a deeper level there is a tension between the requirements of assumed shared context and (unexpected) unshared information. Thus a certain amount of protocol and redundancy is required to ensure that an adequate shared context is maintained (lest we "lose" our audience). On the other hand, a certain novelty and information value must mark our communication (less we bore our audience). Furthermore we also maintain and conform with a model of cognitive capability (less we swamp our audience). Fundamentally, at the deepest level, the charitable assumption is false, since no two people share an identical lifetime of previous experience, and there are innumerable individual differences of genetic origin.

Association

We now turn to another concept where again we do not want to be tied too closely to the traditional psychological definitions, although the general concept is fundamental in a number of ways. This concept is closely allied to that of relationships, and in particular the recognition and construction of relationships. The concept is *association*, and is fundamental to the learning process as well as being the essence of semantics.

There are a number of macroscopic empirical phenomena which go by this name, expressed by idioms such as "free association" and "association of ideas". These phenomena reflect the underlying process of association which is fundamental to memory and language. It is the essence of our human cognitive processes. The traditional way of considering association is in behaviouristic terms. So in considering the acquisition of semiotics and semantics, one would "assume that the child is capable of learning relationships between stimuli and responses",[3] and also the relationships of "response equivalence [between say the] pivot word "want" and an open class of items which a child may want".[4]

The common view of concept formation is that association is made between common features of the visual scene — those that occur together are grouped together. The existence of a distinct input stream of speech allows a word to become associated with the concept, and probably helps the distinction and specification of the concept. This must be true at some level, but it is important not to be overly simplistic — it needs to be extended to be functional and multimodal:

Nelson gives as an illustration the concept "ball" which may have the following kind of core functional-relationship set:

activity-locale:living room, porch, playground
actor: mother, I, boy, ball
action: throw, pick up, hold, catch
object motion:roll, bounce
object locale: on floor, under couch, under fence.[5]

The functional and motor aspects of association are emphasized in Piaget. There is also evidence that the popularly recognized phenomenon of "association of ideas" has a place in the fundamental associative and learning processes. Thus:

> Britton concluded that crib speech … was characterized by a freedom (due to lack of communicative intent) on the child's part to use free association to call to mind the next words in a sequence, the associations being either phonological, structural, or semantic.[6]

Let us consider the possible role of association in concept formation. A child first labels whole situations and only subsequently refines these to specify individual objects, *etc.* Initially, he or she cannot associate a word more specifically than to the entire context, and initial attempts to be more specific are often wrong. He or she furthermore needs to be able to distinguish meaningful components of the scene before they can even consider labels.

Fillmore suggests that *scenes* invoke linguistic frames by means of association, and that frames must also be activated by language and other frames. Such scenes must encompass entire, functionally rich sensory-motor situations. The active frames then provide the context and supplementary information necessary for the determination of meaning.[7] This illustrates the wider scope of association in the everyday processes of language and shared context.

Thus *association* must be recognized as a fundamental process in language which gives rise to empirical phenomena needing explanation. This should then be reflected in a model of language or memory.

Expectation

One of the most fundamental properties of human cognitive and memory processes is our propensity to form "expectations". At a conscious level, we may predict what will happen in a given set of circumstances; negatively, we may be surprised at what does happen. But expectation is a far more basic and ubiquitous property than our conscious experience suggests.

We have already encountered expectation in several other guises. The essence of information theory is that information is conveyed when data fails to confirm our expectations, or at the very least when it enables us to select or specify from our expectations. The essence of the scientific method is that predictions are made on the basis of what we know, and can deduce from such knowledge. If these predictions are confirmed, our theory is shown to conform to reality. If our expectations are denied by experiment, this shows that our theory requires replacement or modification.

The essence of the active, top-down parsing process is that the parser tries to use the grammar to construe the raw data in terms of the higher level classes it expects. If an expectation fails, backtracking occurs and alternate expectations or rules are tried. The phenomenon of positive and negative reinforcement is also about expectation. The learning effect is presumed to occur because of the motivational (and perhaps activational) value of the reinforcement. But it is the development, and continued confirmation of expectation in a particular environment which is the crux of the learning process.

Expectation is thus fundamental to any linguistic model, and has been employed in many natural language systems by, for instance, Winograd and Schank.[8] The concept of expectation is also implicit in anticipated correction. In our experiments, in which no explicit correction is used, an effect resembling anticipated correction is available since the production grammar may be tested according to whether sentences produced accord with the expectations of the recognition grammar. The job of the recognition grammar is thus twofold: to allow the extraction of meaning from "sentences", and to reject those "sentences" which sound "funny". The expectation of the model is a fundamental property of the neural network model, which tries to reproduce the "holographic" property. This is that superposition of images (*e.g.* concepts) forms a composite which is capable of accepting (and completing) a pattern similar to those stored, and rejecting a pattern dissimilar to those it has been exposed to (producing an incoherent image).

Consolidation, Dreaming and Rationalization

We now consider the role of dreaming in relation to learning. Dreaming is an important, but still poorly-understood, part of sleep which is somehow essential to our normal functioning. This has been studied through disturbance of the REM (Rapid Eye Movement) state of sleep during which dreaming occurs. Investigators have tried to characterize the nature of the dreams, and the disfunction caused by disruption of dreaming. Interspersed with this active sleep are periods of quiet sleep during which daydream-like drifting by association of idea is reported.

There are two hypothesized phenomena which have been associated with sleep. The first is "consolidation" and the second "random stimulation", and these may variously be associated with active and quiet sleep. Goldschlager points to the reduced level of awareness of the environment during sleep and proposes that the reduction of the onslaught of the senses has some important effects:

> The role of quiet sleep may be to give some reinforcement to those less immediately important patterns ... Associations between patterns which are more distant from input patterns will be reinforced during quiet sleep.[9]

Our tentative proposal can be seen as consolidation. Somehow useless, or apparently useless, associations are discarded, and related ideas become associated. There is presumed to be some residue of activation in the associations of the preceding waking period. Such a proposal is modelled, in a very simplistic way, on our experiments, where it is an essential process whose purpose is to free-up the system for further learning.

Goldschlager also proposes a role for active sleep, which he sees as characterized by random stimulation, presumably suggested by the regular three-hour cycles of quiet and active sleep.

> Each burst of random stimulation will cause a random set of patterns to become active, and these active patterns will then lead to a flow of activation from pattern to pattern in the normal manner until the next burst of random stimulation arrives. Hence possibly unusual chains of associations and unusual combinations of concepts will be activated. Indeed, dreams seem to be the playing out of unusual combinations of concepts, with periodic jumps (or additions of new dream material) as the random bursts of activation occur (Crick and Mitchison,1983) ... In general, active sleep helps the memory surface to retain events, concepts and skills which are not necessarily used regularly or frequently by the animal.[10]

We do not know of any model which incorporates any analogous process. One problem with any model is the probable impossibility of correlating "on-line" each association against each other to determine the higher level associations. A consolidatory process such as this would allow "off-line" correlation attempts, after some vetting of the useful and the useless has taken place. It is certainly worthy of further consideration and elucidation.

Transformations

The influence of TGG (Transformational Generative Grammar) has prompted some psycholinguists to seek to view psycholinguistic data in terms of TGG transformations. However, as Slobin observes "growth of grammatical transformations has, as yet, been little investigated".[11] We have never seen any particular need to view psycholinguistic data in such gross transformational terms, and recently psycholinguistics has started to free itself once more of the TGG constraints, and to concentrate on observing what is actually taking place.

Although we do see language and cognitive processes as highly transformational, we have great difficulty with the specific doctrines of TGG as contrasting with traditional Phrase Structure Grammar (PSG). While there may be a case for viewing certain grammatical forms as more basic than others, we see no reason to construe the others as being transformational derivatives of these. Nor, indeed, that such a relationship exists between their underlying structures. Moreover, TGG ignores the semantic content of the form, and thus suffers from the myopia, whence it loses sight of all but the elementary word meanings and relationships, and cannot see beyond the syntactic role within a single sentence. Thus TGG appears to us arbitrary in its view of transformation.

Having set out these qualifications, let us note that it is apparent that transformations are fundamental to both language and other cognitive processes. The nature of the neural mechanisms is evidently highly transformational, and the nature of the linguistic process is obviously that of a transformation between language and meaning in some sense. The successive grammars of children can also be described in terms of transformations; each child grammar can be seen as a transformation of adult grammar. The various modifications involved in imitation and repetition are transformations, whether by parent or by child, of the others' sentences.

The parsing process of, say, production is clearly transformational, with each rule of a PSG transforming from a non-terminal symbol to terminal symbol or a series of terminal and/or non-terminal symbols. The relationships between parse trees, or other representations of the linguistic domain, and those corresponding structures of the sensory-motor domain, can also be seen as defining transformations. Either parse tree suggests the other, by means of semantic and semiotic rules. These are the senses in which we see cognitive and linguistic processes as being transformational.

That cognitive and perceptual processes are transformational is perhaps nowhere more evident than in the transformations which take place in the visual system. Here we can literally *see* a transformational parsing process in action, as the visual data is organized through a sequence of cortical layers which have been mapped by neurophysiologists.

Forgetting

We now turn to a phenomenon of some ambivalence. Usually we regard forgetfulness in a rather negative light, but forgetting may also be fundamental to our memory and cognitive processes. It may also be that forgetting includes, or derives, from a number of quite independent memory effects.

The first distinction we make is the existence of both Long and Short Term Memory (LTM and STM). STM does not last for long – this is a necessary part of its operation. STM has particular properties and limitations which enable it to function as an I/O buffer. The process of forgetting in STM is apparently directly related to a neural correlate of forgetting – adaptation or habituation.[12]

LTM is apparently mediated primarily by changes in synapses, and possibly neurons. Hence forgetting may take place as a result of a natural decay in synaptic strength in synapses which are not used. This is apparently also essential to the operation of LTM, as there must be a mechanism by which random associations and incorrect associations may be rendered ineffectual and the total activity of a region of the memory kept within reasonable bounds, but there are many models and theories of the modification of synapses.

Motivation, Activation and Attention

Traditionally, several factors are recognized which are distinct from learning, but which do have an effect on learning or the speed of learning. These can be understood in very simple terms. It is obvious that motivation is a factor which will affect the learning response. In behaviourist psychology, this is extended to drives and needs of various sorts. Since the effect on the organism is primarily to increase the general level of activity, such phenomena are grouped together under the term "activation".

A different phenomenon which contrasts with activation is "attention". Attention can also have obvious positive effects on a learning process. Note that activation and attention need not operate in harmony. Thus for example, hunger may increase activation but decrease attention. Both activation and attention appear to have direct physical and neural correlates. For example, the overall level of activity of a neural network on the one hand, and the physical reflex activity of saccade on the other.

There is however a problem in the design of computational models of cognitive processes in that machines don't normally have properties which correspond with motivation, activation or attention, whereas these seem fundamental to the language learning process.

The relevance of motivation to language learning is self-evident, since both child and parent wish to communicate better. The role of attention is also straightforward, and we have already seen that the child is selective about what he attends to (*e.g.* he will ignore unfamiliar words, or words whose semantics or function are beyond him).[13]

So what of the computational model? Specific heuristics such as Kelley's signalling mechanisms can be incorporated into the program, but the more general problem of motivation is not so simply handled. Some have attempted to simulate such human characteristics by random perturbation, but such expedients seem pointless, if not theoretically shameful.

The obvious answer to the need for motivation is to simulate various needs or drives directly. It is also possible to provide a machine with drives of a somewhat different nature from human drives. Thus, it is possible to give a machine "curiosity" or "play" drives in which it "aims" to discover novel properties, and is rewarded by doing so. It is also possible to give it an artificial drive involving the keeping of certain variables within limits. (This may be practical, *e.g.* disk space management.)

In general, any positive or negative reinforcing variable provides motivation in this sense. But it does not necessarily provide the activational effect, and it is not clear exactly what effect the changes in activational level should have. Part of its importance may relate to the consolidation function. The basic function of the activation level is to determine the appropriate speed and extent of learning (a role which we may also attribute to "relevance").

The matter may be summed up by observing that internal and external stimuli may not only produce polarized positive or negative reinforcing effects, but may affect the learning process in a general manner irrespective of polarity by increasing or decreasing some general variables representing activation and attention. It is certainly possible to take into account a relevance metric in some of the neural network models we discuss.

Concept Formation

We now take an overview of the psychological limitations and their role in cognitive processes. One of the most unique and intriguing papers of psychology begins:

My problem is that I have been persecuted by an integer.[14]

This is, of course, Miller's paper "The Magical Number Seven, Plus or Minus Two: Some Limits on Our Capacity for Processing Information". Miller opens his discussion with an introduction to the theory of information and communication in which he relates them to the statistical concepts of variance. The higher the degree of variability in our predictions, the more information is conveyed by a particular event. The greater the dependence of the output upon the input of a communication, the more information has been communicated. He then proceeds to introduce the concepts of *channel capacity* and the *bit*. Without repeating all his arguments, we will outline his results and conclusions on this ubiquitous integer.

He first describes experiments with absolute judgments of tones, testing the ability to discern between two to fourteen tones, ranging between 100 and 8000 Hz in equal logarithmic steps. The amount of information transmitted approaches an asymptote of 2.5 bits—that is we are capable of accurately distinguishing only about six alternatives, or of narrowing down N alternative stimuli to one out of $N/6$. Those with musical training can do considerably better, but what do they do? In identifying the notes of a sequence played on a piano, a musician is identifying one of seven notes of a scale, in one of seven octaves, from one of only a few different scales, recognized holistically.

Similar experiments with other classes of stimuli yield similar results: for loudness over a 15 to 110db range the result is 2.3 bits, for salinity over 3 to 347g/l it is 1.9 bits, and for points on a line between nominal bounds of 0 and 100 it is 3.2 to 3.9 bits depending on the length of exposure.

> The channel capacity for judging size of squares is 2.2 bits ... In a separate experiment ... 2.8 bits for size, 3.1 bits for hue, and 2.3 bits for brightness ... The channel capacity for the skin [was measured] by placing vibrators on the chest region. A good observer can identify about four intensities, about five durations, and about seven locations.[15]

Thus we seem to have a built-in channel capacity of on average 2.6 bits, or 6.5 categories. The importance of this discrimination and classification has already been discussed in general terms. The more general classification problem is multi-dimensional, giving us potential "channel capacities" equal to the sum of the individual one-dimensional judgments. This is a number of discriminable categories equal to the product of those applicable to the individual one-dimensional discriminations. In practice, what humans can distinguish falls short of that predicted on this simple basis. It may, of course, be overheads incurred by the added complexity of handling the multi-dimensional input:

> The point seems to be that, as we add more variables to the display, we increase the total capacity, but we decrease the accuracy for any particular variable. In other words, we can make relatively crude judgments of several things simultaneously.[16]

Linguistic analysis admits eight to ten distinctive features each either binary or ternary. Miller reports 6.9 bits or 120 categories of sound were distinguished using tonal stimuli that varied in eight binary dimensions.

Spans of Attention and Immediate Memory

We can now leave the area of discriminating judgments, and look at our ability to "count" objects and semantic sequences.

> Dots were flashed on a screen for one fifth of a second ... The first point to note is that on patterns containing up to five or six dots the subjects simply did not make errors. The performance on these small numbers of dots was so different from the performance with more dots that it was given a special name. Below seven the subjects were said to *subitize*; above seven they were said to estimate ... This discontinuity at seven is, of course, suggestive. Is this the same basic process that limits our unidimensional judgments to about seven categories? The generalization is tempting, but not sound in my opinion ... In any event, the comparison is not so simple as it might seem at first thought ... This is one of the ways in which the magical number seven has persecuted me.[17]

The best known limitation we experience is our immediate memory. We all know that we can easily remember and recite back a seven-digit phone number, but not a longer one. This does not, however, represent a fixed constant limitation of short-term memory capacity. Experimental results show an almost linear, but *gradual*, decrease in the number of items in the memory span with increasing information content per item. Similarly "the amount of information transmitted is not a constant, but increases almost linearly as the amount of information per item in the input is increased".[18]

And so, as Miller writes, the long arm of the coincidence reaches out:

> In spite of the coincidence that the magical number seven appears in both places, the span of absolute judgement and the span of immediate memory are quite different kinds of limitations that are imposed on our ability to process information. Absolute judgement is limited by the amount of information. Immediate memory is limited by the number of items. In order to capture this distinction in somewhat picturesque terms, I have fallen into the custom of distinguishing between *bits* of information and *chunks* of information. Then I can say that the number of bits of information is constant for absolute judgement and the number of chunks of information is constant for immediate memory.[19]

On the "coincidence" of the magic number seven in attention subitizing and absolute judgement, note that there is a considerable difference between discrete and continuous phenomena.

Span in Language and Recoding

> A man just beginning to learn radio-telegraphic code hears each *dit* and
> *dah* as a separate chunk. Soon he is able to organize these sounds into
> letters and then he can deal with the letters as chunks. Then the letters
> organize themselves as words, which are still larger chunks, and he be-
> gins to hear whole phrases ... In the terms I am proposing to use, the
> operator learns to increase the bits per chunk.[20]

This process of recoding is fundamental to phonology. What are discrete units at one level form one continuous unit at another level. In experiments, with only a few minutes to understand the coding scheme,
subjects showed less improvement than theoretically possible. Careful
and protracted drilling however did allow results very close to those predicted. We have discussed span in the child's language, imitation, and
telegraphic speech. Telegraphic speech is reminiscent of Miller's Morse
analogy. As Brown writes:

> A basic factor causing the child's reduction of adult sentences is surely
> an upper limit of some kind of immediate memory span for the situ-
> ation in which the child is imitating and a similar limit of programming
> span for the situation in which the child is constructing the sentences. A
> comparison of the mean lengths of utterances produced as imitations ...
> with the mean length of spontaneously produced utterances from the
> same children ... shows that the paired values are very close and that
> neither is consistently higher. An increasing span for random digits is so
> reliably related to increasing age that it is a part of the Stanford-Binet
> test (*e.g.* a span of two digits at 30 months, three at 36, and four at 54
> are the norms).[21]

The first deliberate attempt to take account of the magical memory
span in linguistic theory and modelling was Yngve's.[22] His depth hypothesis essentially provided a restriction of the generality of human languages (in terms of various classes of embedding or recursion). The attempt was only marginally successful, and never either generally accepted or further developed.

We have already considered the immediate memory span of STM,
the amount of information which may be stored, and how information
may be encoded and recoded. But this leaves questions of temporal span
(how long information is stored), rehearsal (subvocalic recitation or re-
cycling of information), age factors ("digit-span memory ... age and IQ
are so systematically related"[23]), motivation and attention, the nature of
the information, classes of unit, redundancy, and other aspects of the
process. These considerations are all known to be important and ought
not to be neglected, although they must be left aside here.

LTM also gives us some fascinating insights into cognitive processes.
How and what does LTM store? We are particularly interested in lan-

guage and concept storage. There is direct and indirect research using tools as different as probes and hypnosis, subjects as different as amnesiacs and students, operations as different as surgery and quizzes. Again, this is an area of universally recognized importance.

Habits, Norms and Skills

Pascal (1670) [commented] "Habit ... is a second nature which destroys the first. But what is this nature? Why is habit not natural? I am very much afraid that nature is itself only first habit as habit is second nature".[24]

The sort of learning which takes place by rote, or through training or routine, is very different from the acquisition process we have been considering. It is much less powerful, but may still be involved in the higher level learning paradigms. We should particularly note the highly motor-centred and directly functional aspect of this form of learning.

Throughout his or her early life, the child who is learning language is embedded in rituals, such as feeding, bathing, dressing, *etc*. These provide the scenes for his earliest linguistic frames since they are typically accompanied by a commentary on the activity which is the focus of the child's attention. This provides highly repetitive conjunctions of phrases and activities, giving the child the opportunity to make the associations. The child's eventual participation in the conversation, and especially his errors, provides a further impetus and focus for the commentary.[25]

Repeated routines will obviously lead to habits in both the child and the parent, and these may therefore be essential ingredients of the language learning protocol. In a fundamental sense, habits and skills are a form of LTM, but it is not completely clear what their relation is to the traditional concept of LTM. Not all of this learning takes place in the brain. Most *physical* skills are interned by local reflex arcs which largely act independently of, and faster than control by the brain. Such learning is still neural, and presumably related to some of the brain's learning processes.

Any cognitive model of higher brain function must also take into account apparently lowly habits and skills, and also the routines which engender them. There are two levels at which sensory-processing or motor-control can be performed, an initial general processing level in terms of more basic units, and an "interned" specialized processing level in terms of an indivisible unit. This "interiorization" process is highly significant, as it allows for "interned" responses to become building blocks used within more complex operations.

It is conceivable that recognition is basically a habituation, a learning not to respond to repeated stimuli sequences—with only departures from the norm triggering a response. This then would allow a recognition grammar to perform anticipated correction during production. Consolidation of the production grammar may also involve "interiorization".

Conditioning: Classical, Instrumental and Operant

> It has been suggested ... that the individual's language is actually composed of repertoires of skills that he must learn ... The repertoire of speech responses ... is learned on the basis of instrumental conditioning. On the other hand, classical conditioning is the principle by which large numbers of words come to elicit emotional responses, another important aspect of language.[26]

Behaviourism has been in the doldrums since Chomsky's critical review of Skinner. But there is no workable empirical cognitive model other than some sort of mechanism, and the psychological consequences of a mechanistic viewpoint must be some form of behaviourism.

Notwithstanding these remarks, classical behaviourism has severe limitations. A reductionist approach must lead to some set of basic learning or conditioning processes, although not necessarily naïve S-R (Stimulus-Response) theory. And we should remember that valid criticism of one particular theory does not automatically extend to others. Staats and others have their own criticisms of Skinner, but still maintain a behaviourist approach providing insights into at least some of the data.[27]

We, somewhat unconventionally, characterize conditioning in contrast with learning in general. We argue that learning is a specialized response, which uses the temporal relation of approximate simultaneity as evidence of causality. In an experiment, workers can distinguish between the stimuli and responses of the various conditioning paradigms. In the arbitrary camp are the trial and error, instrumental and operant paradigms. In each case there is no overt stimulus to prompt the response, which becomes a major source of difficulty in characterizing these paradigms in the S-R framework. This difficulty shows an inadequacy of the S-R framework, since the hypothesis of a covert stimulus is perhaps unwarranted, or at least inadequately justified. Whilst we argue that there is relatively little of an arbitrary character amongst the array of sensory-motor experiences of the child, there is a degree of undirectedness or randomness about the child's early behaviour. A stimulus may not be necessary, but there is plenty of evidence that there are motivational factors which affect both activation and reinforcement.

In classical conditioning stimuli are paired as unconditioned and conditioned, and the association is learned. In the case of child language acquisition, the difficulty in this theory is the existence of a response. In children's development there is usually a multiplicity of stimuli, but, particularly in the early stages, there may be no identifiable response. The problem is then that the choice of response may still be arbitrary, since there may be no unconditioned response to a particular stimulus.

Another issue is who is initiating a trial—the subject or the experimenter (operant *vs* instrumental). This is not a problem in a natural context, but there is a distinction as to whether the child or the environment has the initiative in a given situation. A further distinction concerns whether the responses are voluntary or involuntary, somatic or autonomic.

Given that the classical conditioning paradigm comes closest to the child acquisition paradigm, we should think about what is actually learned. Is a CS—(U)CR relationship learned? Or is a CS—UCS relationship learned? This has been investigated by varying the temporal relationship of the three conditions. The CS may be before (forward conditioning), between (false backward conditioning), or after (true backward conditioning) the UCS and UCR. The results have been inconclusive.

An association between stimuli probably occurs, but for CR to be learned which are not innate UCR to any UCS, there must be an association formed between CR and CS. Generally, behaviourism assumes the latter and then excludes the former by parsimony. Any relationship between stimuli would therefore be mediated by overt or covert responses. This is the basic viewpoint reflected in recent models of human (linguistic/referential) learning.[28] Anderson avoids a mistake made by Chomsky and others, who ascribe to covert responses the same properties as are observed in overt responses. Kelley criticizes "Jenkins and Palermo" for this error when they propose that "the child's speech ... served as the response in terms of which s-r relations are acquired".[29]

Focus, Saccade, and Reading

A special case of attention is "focus of attention". We have already considered possible linguistic mechanisms which babies might use to focus on the "telegraphic", functional, open class words which are most important in what they are hearing. We considered that other, "little", closed class words may act to direct attention to this focus.

Clearly, every one of our senses is assaulted with more information than is useful at a given time. Even speech must be filtered out from an abundance of other auditory material. In general, we have little idea how such filtering of the senses is done, but in the case of vision, we have a literal focus onto an area of the retina known as the *fovea*. When peripheral vision detects motion or objects this leads to eye movements and a new fixation allowing more detailed analysis.

When we examine the movements of the eyes, we also find that they are continually making small, sharp, possibly random movements, changes of focal point. The frequent involuntary motions assist with maintaining the retinal image and apparently for binocular fusion.[30] The motions may also play a part in the recognition of relationships in the visual image. This is a physical effect, from which we get an insight into the focussing which takes place in all our senses. Note that our usage of "focus" here is not related to focussing of the lens, but refers rather to fixation.

Other involuntary eye movements compensate for movements of the object and ensure a stable image. This ballistic effect is a function of signals from both the eye muscles and the middle ear. It is useful to distinguish four classes of eye movement: *saccade* (which are rapid, voluntary motions appropriate to bring a peripheral target onto the fovea), *foveal pursuit* (or tracking motions which are slower involuntary motions which keep a target on the fovea), *slow drift movements* (which are involuntary motions about a focal point), and *rapid tremor* (which is rapid motion about the fixation point).[31] One interesting aspect of saccade is the effect of "visual suppression during a saccade",[32] again to maintain the integrity, sharpness and stability of the image. There is also apparently a preemptive effect, "selective presaccadic enhancement" involving "increased rates of response just before a saccade is made to the particular location in the visual field", as well as an analogous "post-saccadic enhancement".[33] Rogers presents an interesting computational model of vision in which saccade plays a significant part.

By observing eye motions during reading, we can learn more about the linguistic processes involved, as has been demonstrated in the classical work of Huey.[34] There is no physical correlate of fixation in sensory processing in general, and to determine what is being processed is much more difficult. Yet subjectively, consciously and unconsciously, we are able to focus our attention on a small part of what we are perceiving and ignore the rest. These focussing phenomena seem to be related not only to attention, but also to expectation and feedback. That mental visual scanning is real and effective has been demonstrated experimentally with quantifiable results by Inui *et al.*[35]

Grammar *vis-à-vis* Speaker and Hearer Sequence

The quest for grammar, which has traditionally been the focal point of linguistics, runs into problems as soon as we start to compare our ideas of grammaticality with our practice in using the language. Our ideas of grammaticality are somehow normative, yet in general not strictly adhered to except in an edited written form. Thus the "grammar" that traditional linguistics has been working so hard to discover is in fact the grammar of some presentation language which is very different from "English as she is spoke".

Thus, in developing a grammar we really need to consider both what our speaker should have said, or intended to say, and what he did say. We should perhaps even consider what he might have said, and what errors he would be likely to make. We have in fact already considered this in relation to the use that children make of adult speech, and the filtering they must employ.

What we really require is not just a model of the language in the "grammar", but a model of the "speaker" and a model of the "hearer" as well. A speaker has information which he is trying to communicate in real time, in response to particular factors in the sensory-motor environment and with particular effects on it. Moreover he may simultaneously be assembling and associating this information, as well as encoding it for transmission as speech. The nature of his or her thought processes are such that they can see a need to revise, augment or correct information that is already partially coded for transmission. They can therefore change track mid-sentence, or introduce so much parenthetic material that it is impossible to complete or continue the original grammatical construct. The speaker is not like the engineer who draws up a complete blueprint of the structure before starting to build. On the contrary, grammatical constructs are started in the expectation that other material may be encoded into suitable building blocks. This assumption is frequently not valid. The speaker may miss a word (*e.g. tompt*, the "tip of the tongue" phenomenon), or simply be unable to adequately express the complexity of a concept within the bounds of the class of constructs permitted.

The hearer has a similar problem. Unlike the grammarian, he or she is not in the position of a doctor performing an autopsy on a cadaver laid out before them to dissect at leisure. On the contrary, they are faced with a continuous succession of speech input which they must process in sequence, within severe memory and cognitive limitations. They not only have to be able to unravel the presentation "grammar", but also the comedy of errors which generated the speaker" eventual utterance.

There is thus no direct correspondence between "grammar" and "the grammar of the hearer" or "the grammar of the speaker". The speaker and the hearer themselves have different problems, and the similarity may not be sufficient even to allow equation of "the grammar of the speaker" with "the grammar of the hearer". The functions are quite separate; it is only the language which is the same.

Animal Language Acquisition Characteristics

> It used to be believed that what distinguishes human beings from other animals is their ability to fabricate and use tools ... But ethological studies in the last few decades have convincingly established that human beings are not unique in this respect ... Medwar (1976) has persuasively argued that it is not the tool fabrication know-how that sets apart human beings from other animals but their ability to *communicate* this know-how from one generation to the next.[36]

We can use the difference between human language and animal communication to gain insight into language and the restrictions which would constrain it. It is difficult to come up with a good reason why animals cannot use some comparable form of language. Narasimhan appears to be making the presupposition that we are the only animals with a language capability. To investigate this supposition, work has been done on the ability of apes to learn human language or sign language. This work tries to answer the question "can apes learn language?" by trying to teach apes language, and changes the question to "have these chimps demonstrated a capacity for language?"[37] Notice the similarity of this issue with the Turing question "can machines think?" Once again the answer becomes very much a matter of definition, unless one can devise a suitable empirical demonstration, such as the Turing test. In this case, however, the Turing test is much too strong, since the contrary claims about ape language capacity have been phrased in the strongest terms. These workers deny even a weak capacity in animals to acquire "its barest rudiments" and "the most primitive stages" of language.[38]

On the other hand, the Turing test itself, as a test of "thought", concentrates on language as the epitome of human intelligence. To demonstrate that the machine can think, the machine is tested on its language capability. This implies that language is the essence of thought, and the essence of language is thought.

The two most extensively documented studies of apes learning language was the chimps Washoe and Sarah, who learnt sign language.[39] Washoe was a wild chimpanzee about a year old when caught, and was immediately placed in a rich human-style environment. She was taught American Sign Language by ritualising all her daily routines, accompanying them with the appropriate signs, playing games, using pictures and scrap books, and ensuring that there were people present who were communicating in ASL. Sarah was about six years old when her training programme began. This programme was designed to train systematically in the sentences appropriate to particular language situations and behaviour. Washoe was able to put together "sentences" of two or three "words", and to use signs appropriately (*e.g.* the sign for "dog" for either the picture of a dog, or the sound of a dog barking). Sarah, on the other hand, learned to perform tests of her understanding of symbols and relationships between symbols.

One significant difference between the two chimps proved to be in their tendency to initiate communication. Whilst Washoe used sign language to ask for things or make comments, Sarah did not. Sarah's behaviour was quite unlike that of human children in this respect. Although initiating communication is not normally enumerated as a universal of human language, "when it is absent we notice how unhuman the performance is".[40]

Other attempts have been made to teach a chimp to speak, not just to sign.[41] A notable example is Viki, who was brought up for six years exactly as if she were a human child. She learned to pronounce four words reasonably: *mama, papa, cup, up*. Of course, the chimp does not have the articulatory organs to produce human speech, and such evidence is thus of limited value.

The primary distinguishing characteristic of human language is that it is a *second signalling system*. It allows for a level of removal from direct relationships. This mediation allows reference to sensory or motor events using names, and expressions, which are essentially arbitrary and based on convention.

Another important aspect of language is *displacement* – the ability to refer to events or objects which are displaced from us in space and/or time. Whilst the signalling aspects have been demonstrated in most experiments, displaced signalling, initiation, and the use of novel "sentences" are far more rarely observed.

The generalised characteristic we propose here is our ability to manipulate relationships at arbitrary levels of abstraction. Considering this modified Turing question enriches and focusses our understanding of language. Narasimhan also makes the further comparison with human language learning, using the autobiographical account of Helen Keller. Despite her disability, Helen succeeded in developing her language capability, and had propensities to imitate, tell her experiences and role-play. These are features absent, or virtually so, in the chimps.

Another feature which some behaviourists claim to be significant is the affective role of language – its ability to influence emotional states. Narasimhan and others claim this is absent in animals, and there is no convincing evidence for a directly affective role. But a calming affect can be achieved in man and animal by voice or music independent of meaning, and hence of language. The ability to communicate can be therapeutic. These phenomena seem to involve a wide variety of effects, and at best simply indicate the breadth of the mediating role of language.

There is also neurophysiological evidence of differences between man and animal which correlate with proposed mechanisms of language. Thus Narasimhan notes that even in the primates, "primary association areas are not present (or are only poorly developed), and the sensory and motor areas are linked only to the limbic area".[42] The significance of this arises from the high place accorded association in the more useful theories of language.

Foreign Language Learning and Bilingualism

As Brown points out, there are similarities between the task of the child, as first language learner, and that of the descriptive linguist in the field, as he seeks to analyze an unfamiliar language. And there is the question of possible interference between the languages known to a bilingual, and the possible effects of when and how first, second and subsequent languages were learned.

Consider first the linguist seeking to describe a new language. He develops a *corpus* of utterances and seeks to induce rules. He then seeks to test them in novel contexts – to use his theory to predict new utterances or contrastive distinctions. Unfortunately, the testing of prediction other than by silent observation can be problematic. First, the informant may misunderstand your intention and judge the statement on its truth, his or her comprehension of it, or other criteria. Second, his or her main desire may be to please employer or guest by giving the answer they think you want. And third, not having had the benefit of a "grammar" school education, he or she may be genuinely unable to give you a precise indication of which "sentences" are wrong. He or she will certainly be unable to be precise as to where and why, and even their corrected version may be overly influenced by your model, and thus may represent a departure from the natural spontaneous expression of the idea.

The child, similarly, is quite likely to be reinforced on the basis of content, or cuteness, by dint of parental indifference to or ignorance of the correct form. Second language teaching traditionally emphasizes grammatical rules, vocabulary and "correct" if not particularly idiomatic "sentence" construction using those rules. More modern techniques emphasize "sentence" rehearsal with "automatic" construction of "sentences" implied by those rehearsed. This latter approach has features of a "text" language learning situation rather than a "teacher" language learning situation. Unless the examples chosen meet various stringent conditions, the paradigm fails the theoretical learnability restriction presented in Chapter Eleven. Of course, in this situation teachers can provide far more accurate feedback than is usual in the first language or monolingual field learning contexts.

We now come to the contrasts between the first-language and second-language learning processes. To see why the differences may be so important, compare the difference in both efficiency and efficacy of the child's first-language acquisition process with his parents' capability in second-language learning. This is particularly stark in the monolingual field situation, where an untrained baby will far outstrip his or her linguistically trained parent in learning the language. In fact, it can be useful to the researcher to have a baby with him or her, since it develops quickly into a bilingual informant. Elizabeth Elliot, who, accompanied solely by her baby daughter, went back to work amongst the Ecuador tribe who killed her husband (the baby's father) and four other missionaries, reports the child's relative speed in picking up the language. She also reports the child's speed in understanding the social and cultural codes – on a number of occasions she found her daughter's explanations, advice and assistance invaluable.[43]

As a preliminary to Brown's consolidatory work "A First Language" he sought to discover insights into a child's acquisition of a first language by examining the process of an adult learning another language. In this case he was introspecting on his own learning of Japanese in a monolingual context, a Berlitz "total immersion" course. He felt that some of his experiences were akin to those of a child, whilst others were unrelated. In particular, he seemed to spend a lot of time worrying about relatively fine distinctions (such as whether a word means *book, magazine, pad* or even *cover,* or distinguishing *come, go* and *return*).

One of us also spent time learning a language, the Solomon Island language *Maringi,* in a monolingual context as part of an SIL course. In our case the problems centred around the pronouns and deictics – but even when we tried to cheat and find out the distinctions from our informant, we could not because he did not adequately understand the English distinctions! The child just doesn't worry, since he or she learns both concepts and words together and doesn't have a collection of predefined categories to cause confusion. The process of learning is an integrated process of successive refinement.

So where does this leave the relationship between first and second language learning? And how does it relate to computer natural language learning?

> It may be of course that the fastest method of acquiring a second language need not be one that replicates the conditions existing under *natural* language acquisition. In fact various claims for highly intensive language courses followed by individuals with high foreign language aptitude put the time requirement for the acquisition of a foreign language at between 250 and 500 hours of study (Carroll, 1966). Compare this figure with a minimum estimate of 3000 hours for first language acquisition.[44]

The traditional approach to developing computer natural language capabilities (programming "grammars") has some points of similarity with the classical language teaching methods (the Latin and Greek "grammars"). But our work is based on the proposition that a "natural" language learning approach has more potential. Of course, there are some difficulties with this proposal. The natural language learning paradigm is largely restricted to first-language learning in a particularly pliant period of the child's life. If the machine can be made to reflect the child's change in pliability, this learning approach would then be appropriate.

Jakobson's comprehensive treatment of second-language learning from a psycholinguistic viewpoint considers second-language learning in relation to the psycholinguistic framework for first-language learning. He is wary, however, of prematurely taking over "empirical generalizations" in the absence of "theoretically derived principles". He quotes "five *facts*" (italics indicating his reservations) arising from research in adult verbal learning. The first "fact" is that frequency of practice is not so important as frequency of contrast. The second is that the more meaningful the material, the greater the retention. The third is that visual material is more easily learned than aural material (tertiary signalling is not considered). Fourth, conscious attention to features facilitates learning, and fifth the more numerous the associations the better the retention.[45]

There are two special cases of language learning which do not fit neatly into the first–second, mother–foreign classifications. These are the quite intriguing characteristics of creoles and pidgins, and the phenomenon of bilingualism.

In considering bilingualism, we can note that people regard good accent, fluency and pronunciation of a few phrases as marking a bilingual, whilst breadth and depth of knowledge of the language, accompanied by strong accent or lack of fluency does not.[46] Similarly, formal style is often rated higher than appropriate idiom. Even linguists may look for "balance" of ability in the two languages, or conversely for "interference", as evidence of bilingualism, rather than objective competence.

Of particular interest are "interlanguage" and "interculture", the tendency for each language and culture to be distorted from the norm of monolingual native speakers. Jakobson characterizes the bilingual in terms of various significant factors: the "dominance relation" between two languages (as he speaks them), the "interlanguage" relation between his second language and the respective ideal, and the "backlash interference" on his native language in relation to the respective ideal.[47] He further proposes some contributing factors, the degree of ethnocentricity, and the orientation, which may be "instrumental" (doing a job), or "integrative" (getting to know the people better). There are two remarkably dissimilar classes of bilingual, the "coordinate" and the "compound". The coordinate is a virtual "bilingual schizophrenic" who switches personality and culture when he switches language, whilst the compound bilingual displays considerable interlingual and intercultural interference characteristics. The former, according to Jakobson, are those who have moderate attitudes to the cultures, whilst the latter are at one or other extreme of ethnocentrism, either oriented strongly to their native or the foreign culture.

This relationship between language and culture also emphasizes that language is learned in the context of a sensory-motor environment, and that language and ontology are learned contemporaneously and interdependently. The final question about foreign language learning concerns the teaching methods used for foreign languages. If we are going to produce a machine capable of learning language, how then do we teach it language? Siklossy's answer is to use picture-books:

> The design of Zbie has been influenced by the *Language-through-Pictures* series ... Booklets in the series have been used to teach foreign languages to humans. The learning of a second language is not the task considered by Zbie. Nevertheless, the technique used by Richards helps one to understand the design of Zbie ... The pictures are to act as a general representation for all human beings ... Furthermore they are intended as means of bypassing the student's main or mother tongue, thereby avoiding problems of translation from one tongue to another. It is intended that the student learn to express situations directly in the NL.[48]

"Picture book learning" approach is a useful initial approach, but as described by Siklossy it is inadequate in at least three respects. First, the pictures in a book are static, second the visual "language" ought to be learned too, and third the importance of the child's own motor responses is not allowed for. The systems which follow such an approach tend to learn a language which is close to a built-in representational language.

Pidgins and Creoles

Throughout the millenia emperors, dictators, linguists, and scientists have tried to find the original source language from which all others derive. In more modern times, they have tried to find the characteristics which are fundamental to language, or in TGG terms what is the innate language, mechanism, or deep structure which underlies all language. In the past, the experiments have involved isolating one or more children from external linguistic influence — their nurses or guardians were not allowed to speak to them. The results, needless to say, were inconclusive. Many did not survive the experiments, none learned to communicate richly at all. The experiments were so ill-conceived that we would not expect full language development under the experimental conditions. The particular array of first "words" of an individual or group would be made to correspond with the first concepts they became aware of in their environment. Even in the simplest and most standard of environments there is plenty of room for individual differences to result in different associations — unless, of course, one is expecting to prove that there is some innate language which has somehow become universally perverted.

One obvious common element amongst languages is the similarity of the familiar words, like "mama", "papa", "baba", "dada", "tata", amongst the different languages of the world. The meanings interchange, but these easiest possible words for the baby to say are fairly constant, being the ones which are most eagerly awaited and avidly reinforced. In these experimental situations, we would also expect these to be amongst the words to be consistently applied, if any, but we would not expect consistency across distinct experiments.

There have been other, accidental experiments (natural experiments to the extent that imperialism, colonization, transplantation and transportation can be considered natural phenomena) which give us insight into this question. One of the earliest examples comes from the conquests of Alexander the Great. In this case, two processes were at work. The first process occurred in his army. When Alexander set out to conquer the ancient world from Greece to India and Egypt, his army consisted of men speaking the dialects of the various Greek city states. The exigencies of life in the army during their campaigns ironed out many of the dialectical differences and forged a new Greek form, common Greek. The second process was a consequence of Alexander's policy of colonization, in which Greek people, culture and language were exported to the territories he conquered. The resulting polyglot communities came to use a Greek shorn as far as possible of dialectical differences.

More recent is European colonization of the Americas, India, Australasia and the Pacific. These same two processes were at work, in the navies (leading to *e.g.* "Ship's Jargon" or "Maritime English") and in the colonies (leading to *e.g.* the related forms of pidgin English). This period was also marked by transplantation of slave labour. Again two factors have given rise to polyglot communities:

> Under more salutary conditions of immigration the workers or their children would eventually have learned the language of the local colonial power, but two factors combined to keep them from doing so. First, the number of speakers of the colonial languages rarely exceeded 20 percent of the local population, and it was often less than 10 percent. In other words, there were relatively few people from whom the dominant language could have been learned. Second, the colonial societies were small, autocratic and rigidly stratified. There were few chances for prolonged linguistic contact between field laborers and speakers of the dominant language.[49]

A traditional distinction is that pidgins developed to allow contact between social groups, whilst creoles arose among the children of the workers as an expansion of pidgin:

Pidgin languages provide a natural experiment in the creation and preservation of fundamental features. Under the social conditions in which pidgins arise, formalisms which mark social status are of minimal importance; concrete substantive communication and ease of acquisition for adults are the primary factors. What we might call transitory pidgins arise in many contact situations between monolinguals. The pidgins which have become conventionalized tend to share certain features, such as morphological simplicity and the use of optional syntactic devices relying on order rather than inflection. But it is the more surprising that in such languages entirely new derivational affixes are sometimes created.[50]

Pidgins and creoles give us various insights into the acquisition process, and the nature of language. Presumably the effects apply to children in normal society as well. What then stops them adopting such simplifying features? Is it purely the additional examples they experience? Or is it to do with the availability of some sort of negative information or correction? By comparing the properties of creoles with properties of child speech, we see that children do attempt to adopt such simplifying features.[51] The question is then how these features have come to drop out of our evolving languages.

There is now evidence which calls into question the traditional view of creoles as expansions of pidgins, and addresses the question of the surprising novelties noted by Ervin-Tripp.

The historical evidence is consistent with the view that the structure of Creole arose without significant borrowing from other languages. Bilingual or trilingual children of school age need not (and usually do not) mix up the structural features of the languages they speak, and there is no reason to suppose that such crossovers were common in Hawaii. The most compelling argument for the autonomous emergence of Creole, however, is its observed uniformity. How, within a single generation, did such a consistent and uniform language develop out of the linguistic free-for-all that was pidgin in Hawaii? ... Fifty years of contact among pidgin-speaking adults were not enough to erase the differences among the national language groups; the homogeneity must have resulted from the difference between adults and children.[52]

One of the most telling properties of creoles is their verb and tense systems, which are based around particles which act as clitics or affixes. They include (with examples from Hawaiian Creole) an anterior (past) tense marker (e.g. "bin"), a non-punctiliar (continuous, recurrent, incomplete) aspect marker (e.g. "stay") and an irreal (future, conditional) modality marker (e.g. "go"). There is also a distinction between singular,

plural and neutral number, and a prefix marker for third person verbs
("i-").

This evidence is used to support the TGG idea of an innate universal
grammar. It can equally well support the idea that these concepts are at
a deeper level fundamental to human ontology and epistemological development. The universality of the *anterior + irreal + non-punctiliar verb*
ordering of markers and verb in creoles, suggests that the aspect of the
action is bound tightest to the verbalized concept, the modal property
(actual or proposed) less tightly, and the tense (past or present) least
tightly. It is moreover not possible to change this natural order without
inviting an unnatural concurrence (*e.g.* intending today to do something
yesterday, rather than observing today the intention to do something
yesterday). What is not at issue is that the creole environment allows the
natural grammar to survive, in the absence of strong competition from
another.

This then brings us to the question of why children do not all end up
speaking creoles, and the more complex question as to why other languages have developed. This latter question of historical linguistics has
itself a long and interesting history, but it is not particularly relevant to
the child acquisition issue. The former question most definitely is:

> How is it, then, that not all children grow up speaking a creole lan-
> guage? The answer is they do their best to do just that. People around
> them, however, persist in speaking English or French or some other
> language, and so the child must modify the grammar of the native cre-
> ole until it conforms to that of the local language.[53]

This hypothesis predicts that where the local and creole structures
differ, children will have difficulty and make systematic errors, but
where they are similar, they will learn rapidly and without error. One
example is the grammar of negatives. We continually meet examples
like McNeill's "nobody don't like me" and Brown's "no I see truck" (or
better, "I no see truck"), which illustrate features found in creoles (such
as the double negative). Brown's concern was that his example does not
look like a reduction from any adult model, least of all the mother's interpretation and expansion of it to "no, you didn't see it", which has different stress and contour.

The creole evidence holds out another possibility, that there is a
natural order to which children's sentences tend to conform, a natural
order by which grammars are tested.   Bickerton dissects another
example and finds six points of similarity between a sentence "spoken by
the three-year-old daughter of an English-speaking linguist" and an
equivalent sentence in a creole:

> Consider the sentence "A gon' full Angela bucket". Although such a
> sentence is unacceptable in English, it is perfectly acceptable in Ha-
> waiian Creole, Guyanese Creole or any of several other creoles related

to English ... First, the first-person pronoun "I" is reduced to "A"; second, the auxiliary verb "am" is omitted; third, the forms "go" or "gon" are used to mark the future tense; fourth, the word "to" in the infinitive is omitted; fifth, the adjective "full" is employed as if it were a transitive verb, and sixth, the possessive marker "-s" is omitted. All these features are characteristic of creoles.[54]

Slips and Tips of Tongues

A final source of psycholinguistic evidence on the nature of our cognitive limitations is that of errors in adult speech. We have already discussed the normalities of child speech, creole languages, the abnormalities of brain damage, and socio-linguistic deprivation. We now consider errors in normal adults in normal environments.

One very common phenomenon which people encounter is the "tip-of-my-tongue" syndrome (the TOT state, the *tomt* or *tompt* phenomenon). This shows itself when we are in conversation, when writing, or even when simply thinking. It is especially common when trying to put into words thoughts or ideas which we had some time earlier, or if we are thinking faster than we can talk, type or write, or when trying to remember material which we have read or been taught. Names, technical terms and other more erudite words are particularly vulnerable.

Here we clearly have the concept — in fact we may moments earlier have had even the word — but the associations have weakened to the extent that it cannot be recalled, though we will recognize the tompted word if prompted. Note that again the recognition task appears to be easier than the production task. Frequently we will also think that we know the first letter (or even syllable) of the word, sometimes we may even have an idea of the ending. These intuitions are more often than not correct, and when not, they often differ only in one phonemic feature (*e.g.* voicing: /d/ for /t/ or vice-versa). Intuitions about the number of syllables are also correct about half the time, and in this case there is some evidence that they also have some idea of the stress pattern.

Such results are evidence for how we store words, and can be used to suggest and test models of such storage. The phenomenon also gives us insights into the associative properties of the brain. The type of model pointed to is one in which associations bring features to mind which eventually come to retrieve the entire word. The presence of other associations is likely to reduce the precision with which the correct word is associated, and hence may result in a Freudian slip.

This leads on to a related class of errors, "malapropisms", in which similar sounding words are used instead of the word which should have been employed. This is an example of the "slip-of-the-tongue" phenomenon. Others include "Spoonerisms", "slips-of-the-ear" (when the phonemic stream is improperly perceived or segmented and again associates to an incorrect concept), "blends", (of two candidate fillers for the one slot *e.g. biled* for boiled/wild, *everybun* for everybody/everyone) and multitudinous other transpositions of phonemes, features or syllables.

Note that blends do not occur at a grammatically meaningful place in the words. This would indicate that this form of error arises in the process of translation to phonological/articulatory form, and that associations which are fairly evenly weighted towards the two words have caused an attempt to pronounce both simultaneously, possibly even with a shift in weighting from one to the other.

Three distinct sources of interference have been proposed to account for speech errors: "plan internal errors", "alternative plan errors" and "competing plan errors". Respective examples would be Spoonerisms, blends, and Freudian slips, depending on whether there were no extraneous associations involved, those that were involved were alternative formulations of the same thought, or the associations involved stemmed from unintended thoughts.

It is difficult to do justice to the wealth of evidence, but such research leads to a greater appreciation of the processes involved. Data from normal speech errors seems particularly to have served to emphasize the associative nature of memory and language, the distributed and transformational nature of the processing, and the complex "separateness" yet "interrelatedness" of the various functional "organs" and "hierarchies" involved in the language process.

Notes to Chapter Five

1. Goldschlager, Leslie M., *A Computational Theory of Higher Brain Function*
    (Computer Science Department, Standford University, Standford, CA, April
    1984), p.1, p.23ff.
2. Hayes, P.J., "The Naive Physics Manifesto", in D. Michie, ed., *Expert Systems in the
    Micro-electronics Age* (Edinburgh U.P., Edinburgh, Scotland, 1979), p.252.
3. Palermo, David S., "On Learning to Talk: Are Principles Derived from the Learning
    Laboratory Applicable?" in Dan I. Slobin, ed., *The Ontogenesis of Language*
    (Academic Press, 1971), p.47.
4. *Op. cit.*, p.48f.
5. Narasimhan, R., *Modelling Language Behaviour* (Springer-Verlag, Berlin, 1981),
    p.296f.
6. Kuczaj, Stan A., *Crib Speech and Language Play* (Springer-Verlag, New York, NY,
    1983), p.12.
7. Fillmore, C. J., "Scenes-and-frames semantics", in A. Zampolli, ed., *Linguistics
    Structures Processing* (North Holland, 1977), p.63ff.

8. Winograd, Terry, "A Procedural Model of Natural Language Understanding", in Roger C. Schank and K. M. Colby, eds, *Computer Models of Thought and Language* (Freeman, 1973), p.179; Schank, Roger C., "Identification of Conceptualization Underlying Natural Language", in Roger C. Schank and K. M. Colby, eds, *Computer Models of Thought and Language* (Freeman, 1973), p.189.

9. Goldschlager, Leslie M., *A Computational Theory of Higher Brain Function* (Computer Science Department, Standford University, Standford, CA, April 1984), p.22.

10. *Ibid.*

11. Slobin, Dan I., *The Ontogenesis of Language* (Academic Press, New York, 1971), pp,10ff.

12. Goldschlager, Leslie M., *A Computational Theory of Higher Brain Function* (Computer Science Department, Standford University, Standford, CA, April 1984), p.17.

13. Kelley, K.L., *Early Syntactic Acquisition* (Rand Corporation, Santa Monica, CA, November 1967), p.84.

14. Miller, George A., "The magical number seven, plus or minus two: Some limits on our capacity for processing information", *Psychol. Rev.*, vol. 63/1 (1956), p.14.

15. *Op. cit.,* p.23f.

16. *Op. cit.,* p.29.

17. *Op. cit.,* p.31f.

18. *Op. cit.,* p.35.

19. *Ibid.*

20. *Ibid.*

21. Brown, Roger, and Colin Fraser, "The Acquisition of Syntax", in C. N. Cofer and Barbara S. Musgrave, eds, *Verbal Behavior and Learning: Problems and Processes* (McGraw-Hill, 1963), p.193.

22. Yngve, Victor H., "A Model and an Hypothesis for Language Structure", *Proc. Amer. Phil. Soc.*, Vol. 104, No. 5 (1960), pp.444 - 466; Yngve, Victor H., "Random Generation of English Sentences", in A. M. Uttley and L. E. Dostert, eds, *Intnl Conf. on Machine Translation and App. Lang. Analysis* (London, Her Majesty's Stationery Office, 1961), pp.66 - 80; Yngve, Victor H., "The Depth Hypothesis", *Proc. Symposia in App. Math.*, XII (Amer. Mathl Soc., 1961), pp.130 - 138.

23. Olson, Gary M., "Developmental Changes in Memory and the Acquisition of Language", in Timothy E. Moore, *Cognitive Development and the Acquisition of Language* (Academic Press, New York, 1973), p.148.

24. Skinner, B.F., "The Phylogeny and Ontogeny of Behaviour", in E. Endler, L. Boulter, and H. Osser, eds, *Contemporary Issues in Developmental Psychology* (Holt, Rhinehart and Winston, New York, 1968), p.66; Reprinted from *Science,* (1966), Vol 153, pp 1205-1213.

25. Wells, Gordon, *Learning through interaction: The study of language development* (Cambridge University Press, Cambridge, UK, 1981), p.98ff.

26. Goldschlager, Leslie M., *A Computational Theory of Higher Brain Function* (Computer Science Department, Standford University, Standford, CA, April 1984), p.16.

27. Staats, Arthur W., "Linguistic-Mentalistic Theory versus an Explanatory S-R Learning Theory of Language Development", in Dan I. Slobin, *The Ontogenesis of Language* (Academic Press, 1971), p.108.
28. Anderson, John R., *Language, Memory, and Thought* (Lawrence Erlbaum Associates, Hillsdale, NJ, 1976), p.122.
29. Kelley, K.L., *Early Syntactic Acquisition* (Rand Corporation, Santa Monica, CA, November 1967), p.57.
30. Rogers, T.J., *TRIPS — A Computer Model of Primate Vision* (Department of Computer Science, University of Melbourne, 1983), p.26; cf Zuidema, P., J. J. Koenderink, and M. A. Bouman, "A Mechanistic Approach to Threshold Behavior of the Visual System", *IEEE Trans Sys. Man. Cyb.*, Vol. SMC-13, Pt. 1 (September, 1983), pp.923-934.
31. Murch, Gerald M., *Visual and Auditory Perception* (Bobbs-Merril, Indianapolis, IN, 1973), p.73ff; Eckmiller, R., "Neural Control of Foveal Pursuit Versus Saccadic Eye Movements in Primates — Single-Unit Data and Models", *IEEE Trans Sys. Man. Cyb.*, Vol. SMC-13, Pt. 1 (September 1983), pp.908-989.
32. Rogers, T.J., *TRIPS — A Computer Model of Primate Vision* (Department of Computer Science, University of Melbourne, 1983), p.27.
33. *Op. cit.*, pp.35-38.
34. Huey, E. B., *The Psychology and Pedagogy of Reading* (MIT Press, Cambridge, MA, 1908, 1968).
35. Inui, T., M. Kawato, and R. Suzuki, "The Mechanism of Mental Scanning in Foveal Vision", *Biol. Cyb.*, Vol. 30, Pt. 1 (1978), pp.147-155.
36. Narasimhan, R., *Modelling Language Behaviour* (Springer-Verlag, Berlin, 1981), p.17.
37. Brown, Roger, *A First Language: the early stages* (London, UK, Allen and Unwin, 1973).
38. *Op. cit.*, p.33.
39. Narasimhan, R., *Modelling Language Behaviour* (Springer-Verlag, Berlin, 1981).
40. Brown, Roger, *A First Language: the early stages* (London, UK, Allen and Unwin, 1973), p.44.
41. Narasimhan, R., *Modelling Language Behaviour* (Springer-Verlag, Berlin, 1981).
42. *Op. cit.*, p.69f.
43. Elliot, Elizabeth, Personal Communication (1984).
44. Jakobson, A. L., and J. M. Schlecter, "Chemical Transfer of Training: Three Years Later", in K. H. Pribram and D. E. Broadbent, eds, *Biology of Memory* (Academic Press, 1970), p.23.
45. *Ibid.*
46. *Op. cit.*, p.85.
47. *Op. cit.*, p.88f.
48. Siklossy, Laurent, "A Language-Learning Heuristic Program", *Cognitive Psychology*, Vol.2, Pt.1 (1971), p.481ff.
49. Bickerton, Derek, "Creole Languages", *Scientific American*, Vol.219, No.1 (July, 1983), p.108.
50. Ervin-Tripp, Susan, "Some Strategies for the First Years", in Timothy E. Moore, ed., *Cognitive Development and the Acquisition of Language* (Academic Press, New York, 1973), p.283f.

51. Bickerton, Derek, "Creole Languages", *Scientific American*, Vol.219, No.1 (July, 1983), p.110; Brown, Roger, and Ursula Bellugu, "Three Processes in the Child's Acquisition of Syntax" in E. Endler, L. Boulter, and H. Osser, eds, *Contemporary Issues in Developmental Psychology* (Holt, Rhinehart and Winston, New York, 1968), pp.411-422.
52. Bickerton, Derek, "Creole Languages", *Scientific American*, Vol.219, No.1 (July, 1983), p.111.
53. *Op. cit.,* p.113f.
54. *Ibid.*

Chapter Six

Nativism and Constructivism

We now enter the heart of the hottest debate in the history of psycholinguistics. This is the question of just what processes are innate, and how they explain language behaviour, and acquisition.

One would think it basic that meaning is embodied in the relationships between the sensory-motor environment and the language. But much psycholinguistics research loses sight of this. Even when it is conceded, as eventually it must be, there is a tendency for researchers to act as if it is irrelevant. The school of psycholinguistics originated by Piaget is, however, based on this proposition. But the current tendency is to overemphasise syntax, and import into psycholinguistics Chomsky's TGG (Transformational Generative Grammar) with its intrinsic independence of other human functions, and its emphasis on language as an "organ".

So we start, now, to draw the threads together and consider the totality of the interactions and relationships in language. First, it is helpful to consider the individual and environment as a system, and hence to see the relationships which must be learnable and expressible in language. Then we consider the individual as a system, and concentrate on the nature of the language and learning processes. This systems approach leads us to extend our definition of "sensory-motor" to include sensing and influencing of internal as well as external events.[1] Thus as we take our systems view of individual and environment, we are really including the physiological aspects of the organism as part of the environment. Of course, this reflects the paradox of the object we are considering. The individual is actually part of his or her environment, part of what they sense, part of what they affect.

The system also includes the language community with which the child interacts, and his or her functioning within the system includes not only general sensory-motor functioning in their environment, but their functioning in the language of their community. Thus, language development reflects both the general and the specifically linguistic development of the child.

The basic feature of language is that it mirrors the world in some sense. What can we learn about these relationships at the level of linguistic observation? We have already seen something of the work of Clark concerning the isomorphism of P-space ("perceptual space" or "space as it is cognitively structured") and L-space ("the language of spatial relations").

Whilst this is still largely a matter of controversy, it is generally agreed that ontology must precede language. But Wells points out that unwarranted assumptions are often made about the nature of this temporal connection, and gives three reasons why language is not simply an extension of pre-linguistic cognitive development.[2] The first merely expresses the principle that some sort of "bootstrapping" must be involved. The second is a restatement of the fact that the process must be "dynamic". And the third rightly observes that language must be functional and relational. These underlying principles are basic to the theories of Piaget, which are both theoretically plausible and empirically practical, but are obscure because of terminological distinctions which are difficult to follow. Piaget addresses all three of these points directly. He tries to show how language is essentially a part of sensory-motor intelligence. In particular his proposals have the dynamic bootstrapping nature suggested by the first two criteria, and he has always emphasized the effective side of sensory-motor intelligence, functionality and interactive experience:

> In fact, no knowledge is based on perceptions alone, for these are always directed and accompanied by schemas of action, and all action that is repeated or generalized through application to new objects engenders by this very fact a "scheme", that is, a kind of practical concept. The fundamental relationship that constitutes all knowledge is not, therefore, a mere "association" between objects, for this notion neglects the active role of the subject, but rather the "assimilation" of objects to the schemes of that subject. This process, moreover, prolongs the various forms of biological "assimilations", of which cognitive association is a particular case as a functional process of integration. Conversely, when objects are assimilated to schemes of action, there is a necessary "adaption" to the particularities of these objects (compare the phenotypic "adaptions" in biology), and this adaption results from external data, hence from experience.[3]

We will look at Piaget's process of "assimilation" in terms of arbitrary relationships of sensory-motor intelligence, rather than from a linguistic perspective. Note, in particular, the role of the "schemes" of action available to the child:

> The fundamental phenomenon at the level of this logic of actions is the phenomenon of assimilation, and I will define assimilation as *the integration of new objects or new situations and events into previous schemes* ... These schemes of assimilation are somewhat like concepts, but of a practical kind ... They are concepts of comprehension, they bear on qualities and predicates, but there is no extension yet ... And if there is no extension, it is for lack of evocation, for in order to be able to represent to oneself the totality of objects with the same quality, one must

naturally have a capacity of evocation, in other words, representation. This will be the role of the symbolic or semiotic function.[4]

Thus actions and their consequences if repeated constitute "schemes" into which new analogous preconditions may be "assimilated". This constitutes an intensional recognition of instances, but does not initially allow an extensional generation of examples. This thus reiterates the principle that recognition precedes production. However, Piaget has added to the concept of production that of "representation to oneself" as a form of implicit production—in this case "evocation" of the total "scheme" by the instance or the symbol. He therefore proceeds from the "scheme" to the "concept" by examining the development of extension *via* the phenomenon of coordination. This is the empirical recognition of observable spatio-temporal laws and relationships which must derive either from consequence or coincidence:

> If there is not yet any extension, there are coordinations of schemes, and it is these coordinations that are going to constitute all of sensori-motor logic ... One finds in this sensori-motor logic all sorts of correspondences or practical morphisms ... one finds relationships of order ... one finds interdependencies ... In short, one finds a structure that announces the structure of logic.[5]

To this point, Piaget has allowed sensory recognition of objects amenable to a motor action scheme, and recognition of coordinations amenable to a motor action scheme. In each case the action leads (for correct instances) to a desired consequence. He now pursues the course toward extension by generalizing the concept of "assimilation":

> Up to now, assimilation was the integration of an object to a scheme of action; for example, this object can be grasped, that other object can be grasped, and so on—all the objects to be grasped are assimilated, incorporated into a scheme of action which is the action of grasping. Whereas the new form of assimilation that is going to develop and allow conceptual logic is an assimilation between objects, and no longer only between objects and a scheme of action; in other words, the objects will be directly assimilated to each other, which will permit extension. But this presupposes evocation, of course; for this, there must be a necessity to evoke, that is to think of something that is not actually and perceptibly present. Now where does this evocation come from? It is here at this stage of development that we see the formation of the symbolic function.[6]

If there is to be any significance to a concept, it must stand apart from the presence of the objects or conditions it relates—if not it is explicable in terms of recognition of a coordination amenable to a scheme of action. A symbol provides a surrogate object for a condition or a scheme of action. Piaget points out that the semiotic function appears during the second year, and is first seen in gestural imitation of an object or condition, or in symbolic play evoking an action. An example is the opening and closing of the mouth symbolizing the desire to open a door:

> You can see my hypothesis: that the conditions of language are part of a vaster context, a context prepared by the various stages of sensori-motor intelligence. Six of these stages can be distinguished ... It is at this moment that language appears, and it can profit from all that was acquired by sensori-motor logic and by the symbolic function ... I think, therefore, that there is a reason for this synchrony, and that there is a link between sensori-motor intelligence and language formation. I further believe that the formation of the symbolic function, which is a necessary derivative of sensori-motor intelligence, allows the acquisition, and this is the reason why, for my part, I do not see the necessity of attributing innateness to those structures (subject, predicate, relationships, and so on) which Chomsky calls the "fixed nucleus" ... This synchrony is meaningful as a synchronization because in the hypothesis of innateness, one does not see why language would not appear six months earlier or a year earlier or later. Why this synchronization? It does not appear to me to be the result of chance.[7]

Our formulation distinguishes two "grammars" of a different sort: labelled as "recognition" and "production". This is clearly comprehensible at a macroscopic behavioural level, but at any level it seeks to capture the idea that once a certain threshold of confidence is surpassed, a concept can be used as a building block for other purposes, and indeed the relationships may be used in the reverse direction.

At this stage, we will skirt the nativist issues in the last two quotations. We continue with Piaget's explanation of the formation of semiotics, which illustrates the two-stage theory. We can then elaborate this distinction in terms of the "sticky mirror" reflecting analogy, and through discussion of assimilation in relation to accommodation:

> Sensorimotor signifiers already exist in the form of cues or signals, but they constitute only one aspect or a part of the signified objects; on the contrary, the semiotic function commences when signifiers are differentiated from what is thereby signified and when signifiers can correspond to a multiplicity of things signified. It is clear, then, that between the conceptual assimilation of objects between themselves and semiotization, there is a mutual dependence and that both proceed from a completive generalization of sensorimotor assimilation. This generalization embeds a reflective abstraction bearing on elements directly borrowed from sensorimotor assimilation.[8]

An earlier (1954) distinction between assimilation and accommodation may help us see the force of his distinction between the passive recognition and the active generalization processes:

In their initial directions, assimilation and accommodation are obviously opposed to one another, since assimilation is conservative and tends to subordinate the environment to the organism as it is, whereas accommodation is the source of changes and bends the organism to the successive constraints of the environment. But if in their rudiments these two functions are antagonistic, it is precisely the role of mental life in general and of intelligence in particular to intercoordinate them.[9]

Interlingua: Deep Structure and Language Acquisition

The word "interlingua" has been used by different researchers with quite different meanings, a situation further confused with the coming of TGG (Transformational Generative Grammar). The oldest meaning of "Interlingua", in the work of the traditionalist linguists and psycholinguists (*e.g.* Jakobson and Lenneberg), is of the common element of all languages. This is the language *defined by* the *intersection* of all possible human languages.

Chomsky introduced "Interlingua" to refer to the internal representation of language, which was then supplanted by the term "Deep Structure". As TGG developed, these terms came to mean the language *defining* the *union* of all possible human languages. The term "Deep Structure" indicated that the representational "Interlingua" was in essence still a language or a grammar of a language in some conventional sense — it was explicitly not a prelinguistic or conceptual base. "Deep Structure" is contrasted with the "Surface Structure" of the generated language. The proposal is that "Surface Structure" is transformed into "Deep Structure", on the one hand, and on the other, that language is learned by eliminating those aspects of the "Interlingua" which are not present in the language being learned.

The third meaning of "Interlingua", also suggested by Chomsky, is that of a Language Acquisition Device (LAD) or System (LAS).[10] TGG often fails to distinguish the language, grammar, representation and mechanism meanings of "Interlingua". "Deep Structure" is used strictly of an "innate language" but is used interchangeably with the grammar of that language. It is also not always distinguished adequately from the "innate organ" which is responsible for translating and learning to translate between "Surface Structure" and "Deep Structure". "Interlingua" is much more reasonably used to describe this whole bundle of nativist hypotheses, but as a term has dropped out of use.

We propose that "Interlingua" should mean that there exists some sort of common language of basically conventional kind. This can be defined as a subset or superset of empirical languages, or as a representation, grammar or device involving such a language. But we want to reject almost every aspect of the notion.

If such a system existed, it would need to be considerably more complex. It would need some sort of sensory-motor semantics and representation, related by *transformation* to "Deep Structure", and in turn related by TGG "Transformation" to "Surface Structure". The former transformations would certainly be no more trivial than the latter. But in any case, the TGG "Transformations" are sufficiently trivial that the functional product of the conceptual transformations and the TGG transformations need not be complex. They would increase more in number than in complexity. But both number and complexity would remain of much the same order. This alternative configuration is actually quite consistent with the apparent redundancy of the brain. But it should be emphasized that this is a fictive construct, intended only to show that parsimony should not allow a literal Interlingua. In later discussion, we will explain that we do not see a place for even a fictitious interlingua in linguistics, psycholinguistics or neurolinguistics.

Let us think about two alternative proposals. A fundamental problem with TGG is its over-concern for grammar, and its neglect of semantics, representation and intention. They are merely linked by simple "Transformations" to language's "Surface Structure". We have already discussed Piaget's proposals, but there are two other proposals:

> Geschwind (1964) conjectures that the ability to develop language among human beings is very likely the outcome of two features: (1) that the major part of the human brain consists of association areas directly linked to the primary sensory and motor areas, and (2) that these association areas are themselves richly interconnected through a centralized association area of association areas.[11]

Note that the two features of Geschwind's proposal are similar to the two stages of assimilation proposed by Piaget. Other evidence Geschwind gives indicates a binary separation of various functions respectively associated with "recognition" and "production". The essence of this type of evidence and viewpoint is that language is only the "tip of the iceberg" in a sea of sensory-motor, cognitive and conceptual complexity.

Schlesinger partly opposes, partly develops, TGG with an emphasis on the intentionality of language:

> the term *input marker*, or *I marker*, for the formalized representation of those of the speaker's intentions which are expressed in the linguistic output ... How do our I markers differ from underlying P markers (phrase markers)? The latter are the "deep structures" discussed by McNeill (1971), and contain grammatical categories such as: verb, verb phrase, noun, and noun phrase. It is well known that there is no one-to-one correspondence between these grammatical categories and semantic categories: not all nouns designate "things" and not all verbs desig-

nate actions. Hence, the I marker should not be taken to specify such categories.[12]

This approach tries to stay within the TGG fold, but makes proposals similar to ours above, arguing that transformations may as well operate directly on the "I markers" without the mediation of "P markers". However, Bowerman who is aware of Schlesinger's rejection of "Deep Structure", wishes to reject the nativist view without rejecting "Deep Structure":

As Ervin-Tripp (1971) observes, "the weakest argument" of all is the notion that if we cannot think of a way to teach something *viz* "Deep Structure", it must not be learned or learnable (p.190) ... If we accept this [weak argument] we must agree that all aspects of deep structure are unlearnable for the same reason. But many aspects of deep structure are language-specific, such as the underlying order of constituents.[13]

This attempt to reject nativism and retain "Deep Structure" (DS) seems doomed. The nature of DS has to be changed to include non-language-independent aspects to make such arguments valid. Including a language-specific order within DS is rejected by most TGGs.[14] Moreover, several of the psycholinguists writing within the TGG framework in 1971 have since abandoned it.

The Debate on the Innateness of Language

Have you heard of Chomsky? I believe he ...

In this section we will try to justify our position on the innateness issues which is the fundamental difference between our approach and the Chomskian tradition. Like many workers, we accepted that Chomsky had some important insights, and was bringing a new level of discipline to linguistics. Recently, however, he and others have been considering his view a valid psycholinguistic model, and in some eyes it has come to be received as the *de facto* truth. This acceptance has never been unopposed; a useful collection of papers documents an organized debate, on *innatism vs learning*, between Chomsky and Piaget.[15] The debate clarified the *learning* position, but did not demonstrate either validity or utility in the *nativist* positions. Our position is based on pragmatics, because we do not expect success from the traditional "grammar programming" approach of computational linguistics.

What indications are there that the language faculty may be an "innate organ"? Would this require language acquisition to be primarily a "maturational process"?[16] Some of the indicators proposed are:

- consistency of appearance and chronology of language developmental stages[17]
- innate structural differences[18]
- language being species-specific[19]
- language being characterized by universal categories and hierarchies[20]
- language being characterized by universal basic functional relations[21]

Although various proponents and opponents are cited, none of these properties really addresses the significant question. Even if we accept all of these points, there is nothing to say that the innate properties are linguistic properties, or that the empirical universals ultimately derive from innate linguistic properties distinct from other conceptual or sensory-motor properties of general aspect and applicability.

Suppose there is a specific innate organ, the Language Acquisition Device (LAD). How would it work? Nobody is claiming that language is acquired without any sort of learning, that language acquisition is solely language maturation, but neither can LAD "learning" be learning in the conventional inductive sense. LAD "learning" is typically envisaged as a maturational process combined with a process of atrophy or degeneration of those parts (corresponding to TGG transformations) of the linguistic organ which are not appropriate to the language being learned.

We have never seen anyone address the question of how this would affect later learning of a second language. It may be that atrophied parts can recover, or that somehow the function is simply taken over as best it can by the remainder of the linguistic and general cognitive facility.

Acquisition Models

So far, there have been no totally successful linguistic models or computer simulations. The models developed to date seem to have been either of the traditional static grammar-driven (or even semantics-driven) sort, or have been acquisition models well down the learning track. The concept of "naïvety" is important. It is usually *not* claimed that the theory represents exactly the way in which human infants acquire language. Many mechanisms may have been evolved to truncate or by-pass learning stages. This is not thought significant, because firstly, it appears to be an empirical fact that *no* regularities are true of every known NL. For many workers it therefore seems sensible to model the NL mechanism by a mechanism which has *no* prior tendency to prefer some syntagms over others. "Naïvety" is used in these systems in the sense that only simple features of the natural mechanism which can be modelled on automatic mechanisms are considered.

This raises three questions: Is the bypass suggestion a reasonable proposal? Is there any evidence of intermediate forms of language capability? Is this laudable pragmatism really "naïvety" or is it actually seriously indicated by the depth of the computational metaphor? Anderson writes, "LAS only induces the network grammars; the interpretative SPEAK and UNDERSTAND programs represent innate linguistic competences".[22] Is this support of nativism? Or is it mere acquiescence, owing to the problems dismissed being outside the model and their nature irrelevant? Block writes:

> We present a model of language acquisition which demonstrates that considerable language competence can be acquired without presupposing innate linguistic factors. Vague or magical properties are avoided by describing the model as a design for a robot using clearly defined algorithms and mechanisms which can be simulated or constructed ... For the project described here, we deliberately avoid the use of innate grammatical categories, especially categories which are assigned on the basis of *a priori* ontological classifications. The Syntax Crystal Learning Algorithm assigns words to grammatical categories on the basis of their relationship to other words on a string. The category distinctions are developed only as needed and none are available before the acquisition process begins.[23]

There are no concessions to innateness for either linguistic or ontological relationships. Staats writes that "Criticism of a particular learning theory of language does not disqualify learning approaches in general".[24]

Block goes further and identifies the learning techniques which provided the ammunition for the nativist onslaught: attempts which employ "association frequencies" but "ignore the underlying structure of syntax"; and attempts which tackle "grammatical features" but "without paying attention to meaning".[25] Others attack the innatist position whilst presenting their own:

> Some researchers have hypothesized that humans possess some species-specific ... language acquisition device ... separate from the general information-processing capabilities possessed by man. In the present research, we examine the hypothesis that language-learning is an information processing task, and that general information-techniques are sufficient for the task.[26]

> Some Linguists have argued that language learning must be considered separately from other kinds of learning and that it requires the assumption of a distinct mechanism in humans that is specialized for language acquisition ... This kind of acquisition model assumes that the child internalizes a grammar ... which ... is essentially an adaption or realization of some pre-programmed principles of a "universal grammar"

with which humans are born and which they apply to the particular language to which they are exposed ... As it is, the "universal grammar" proposed by this school of thought turns out to be not a set of positive requirements of what properties all languages *must* have, but rather a set of abstract *constraints* which no language supposedly violates.[27]

All these language acquisition models adopt a fairly consistent middle ground on the innatist debate, but do not consider the situation in much more detail.

Chomsky's Charter

Much has been written on the conflict surrounding this question of innateness *vs* conditioning and learning. There are several collections of papers which include considerable coverage of innatism, as well as the Piatelli-Palmarini volume we mentioned earlier.[28] To complete the background to the debate, let us look at an "authorized" summary of Chomsky's claims assembled and criticized by Hockett:

C1.   The vast majority of the sentences encountered throughout life by any user of a language are encountered only once.

C2.   Any user of a language has access, in principle, to an infinite set of sentences.

C3.   The user knows the grammar of his language, though not in a sense of "know" that would imply that he can explicitly tell others of his knowledge ... This body of knowledge constitutes the user's *competence*.

C4.   A user's *performance*—what he actually says and hears—reflects his competence, but is also conditioned by many other factors.

C5.   A convenient device ... is to imagine an ideal speaker-listener, in a perfectly homogeneous speech-community, who ... is unaffected by such grammatically irrelevant conditions as memory limitations, distractions, shifts of attention and interest, and errors (random or characteristic).

C6.   Since the user's competence is a *mental* reality, linguistics is necessarily mentalistic.

C7.   Probabilistic considerations pertain to performance, not to competence.

C8.   The distinction between grammatical and non-grammatical sentences (whether absolute or a matter of degree) applies to competence, not performance. The degree of *acceptability* of an actually performed utterance is a different matter.

C9.   Meaningfulness, like grammaticality, pertains to competence. But these two are distinct.[29]

We have already countered C5. Not only must our language faculty be able to cope with such "problems", but they may actually be functional or be evidence of the nature of underlying processes. C7 runs counter to any theory of neurolinguistic activity. We have explicitly compared direct probability based acquisition with more neurophysiologically motivated acquisition. Let us continue to look through Hockett's summary of Chomsky's claims:

C10. The grammar of a language is a finite system that characterizes an infinite set of (well-formed) sentences [and is] by definition not more powerful than an universal Turing machine.

C11. At present there is no known algorithm for computing or "discovering" the grammar of a language ... knowledge of grammatical structure cannot arise by application of step-by-step inductive operations ... of any sort that have yet been developed within linguistics, psychology, or philosophy.

C12. It must be, therefore, that the infant brings to this task at least the following: an *innate* system for the production of an indefinitely large set of grammars of "possible" human languages; and the *innate* ability to select, from this set, the (or a) correct grammar for the language of his community ... the infant's innate system must include much more, *e.g.* an algorithm for determining the structural description of an arbitrary sentence given an arbitrary grammar.

C13. An explicit formulation of the innate grammar-producing system just mentioned would constitute a *general grammar* (or *general linguistic theory*).

C14. The innate grammar-producing system is a well-defined system in the sense of C10.

C15. It is at least plausible that the grammar of a language consists of three components: (a) The *syntactic* component ... (b) The *phonological* component ... (c) The *semantic* component (which possibly is the same for all languages).

As well as being dependent on the rejected C1, C10 embodies a very serious problem which Hockett has identified: Chomsky has assumed "that only a well-defined system can give rise to a well-defined system", that is "a sort of "Law of Conservation of Well-Definition". The problem with this is one common to every nativist argument. If one says something cannot be achieved at a high level, this means it must be achieved at a lower level, if it is indeed an empirical fact. Continued repetition of the argument leads to either a *reductio ad absurdum*, or a teleological "proof" that "this additional mechanism cannot be physical ... and this non-physical system, or its antecedents, must be as old as the universe".[30]

We agree that environment plus organism provide *innate* systems, but would not limit these mechanisms to being specifically linguistic. Continuing Hockett's summary:

C16. In searching for the grammar *of* a language, one may propose various explicitly formulated grammars ... *for* the language ... A grammar proposed *for* a language is descriptively adequate "to the extent that it correctly describes the intrinsic competence of the idealized native speaker". A descriptively adequate grammar for a language is principled to the extent that it conforms to a general linguistic theory of the type mentioned in C13.

C17. [A proposed general linguistic theory (C13)] is *descriptively adequate* "if it makes a descriptively adequate grammar available for each natural language". A descriptively adequate general theory is explanatorily adequate to the extent that it approximates the innate grammar-producing system, and other innate capacities, of the infant (C12).

C18. The proposal in C15 ... says nothing about how the user *employs* his grammar in either the production or the reception of sentences.

C19. A linguistic *change* is a shift from one grammar to another (presumably similar) one. It is essential to distinguish between *system-conforming* and *system-changing* events. It is important not to mistake an awkward or inaccurate performance for one that is really symptomatic of a change in underlying competence.

Most of the other propositions are founded on propositions which have already been rejected. This is particularly unfortunate in the case of C16 and C17, because these suggest a very attractive methodology for evaluating grammars and theories.

Non-Linguistic Innateness

So let us consider the various positions in the innateness debate. What are the evidence and interpretations available when dealing with the "organs" and functions which are more directly accessible than the linguistic ones. The remainder of this section is an appendix or extended footnote, intended to set out in one place an overview of this issue.

First of all, note some perceptive comments of Skinner:

Parts of the behaviour of an organism concerned with the internal economy, as in respiration or digestion, have always been accepted as "inherited", and there is no reason why some responses to the external environment should not also come ready-made in the same sense. It is widely believed that many students of behaviour disagree ... And it is a myth. No reputable student of animal behaviour has ever taken the position "that the animal comes to the laboratory as a virtual *tabula rasa*, that species' differences are insignificant, and that all responses are about equally conditionable to all stimuli (Breland, 1961) ... But what does it mean to say that behaviour is inherited? ... Insofar as the behaviour of an organism is simply the physiology of an anatomy, the inheritance of behaviour is the inheritance of certain bodily features ... If the anatomical features underlying behaviour were as conspicuous as the wings of *Drosophila*, we should describe them directly and deal with their inheritance in the same way, but at the moment we must be content with so-called behavioral manifestations.[31]

The recognition that all observable behaviour is at least in part a consequence of anatomical features is significant, and leads to the question of how direct the link is, and whether it derives from specific or general features. Skinner makes this point using a number of landmark examples:

> Licurgus, a Spartan, demonstrated the importance of environment by raising two puppies from the same litter so that one became a good hunter while the other preferred food from a plate ... Stenddahl refers to an experiment in which two birds taken from the nest after hatching and raised by hand exhibited their genetic endowment by eventually mating and building a nest two weeks before the female laid eggs. Behaviour exhibited by most of the members of a species is often accepted as inherited if it is unlikely that all the members could have been exposed to relevant ontogenic contingencies ... When contingencies are not obvious, it is unwise to call any behaviour either inherited or acquired. Field observations, in particular, will often not permit a distinction. Friedmann (1956) has described the behaviour of the African honey guide ... saying that the behaviour is "purely instinctive", but it is possible to explain almost all of it in other ways.[32]

The explanations of this behaviour in Skinner are particularly instructive. They demonstrate that the question must be left open until various possibilities are closed off by empirical investigation. Skinner concludes with these general observations:

> Ontogenic and phylogenic behaviors are not distinguished by any essence or character ... Behaviour is behaviour whether learned or unlearned; it is only the controlling variables which make a difference. The difference is not always important ... Nevertheless the distinction is important if we are to undertake to predict or control the behaviour. Implications for human affairs have often affected the design of research and the conclusions drawn from it.[33]

There have been well engineered experiments to explore the balance between learning and hereditry in various non-linguistic fields. One example is the research of Melzack. He introduces his experiments by citing various amplifications of the complexity of this balance:

> Until recently the argument was often stated in "either-or" terms ... Tinbern (1957b) has noted that "we tend to say, or tended to say, that this type of behaviour is innate and that type is learned; now we have learned from experimental biology that this is an improper use of words ... As far as we can see nowadays, most behaviour in the course of its development depends on a very complicated interaction between inherent properties and environmental influences" (p.2). This is in good agreement with the position taken by Hebb (1958) that "heredity, by it-

self, can produce no behaviour whatever ... Similarly, learning can produce no behaviour by itself, without the heredity and prenatal environment that produce the structures in which learning can occur. The two
collaborate. Further, it seems highly probable that heredity makes some
kinds of learning easy or inevitable, others hard, and thus guides learning" (p.120).[34]

Having outlined the dangers of insisting on a learning/innateness dichotomy, Melzack presents the methods and results of a series of experiments performed to clarify the role of learned and innate factors in one
particular behavioural phenomenon:

> In the present experiment an attempt has been made to study the gen-
> esis of the behaviour elicited by the "hawk" and "goose" shapes in mal-
> lard ducks which were raised in a carefully controlled environment.

1. Mallard ducks were reared in a highly restricted environment from
    hatching until testing began at 25 days of age; the stimuli presented
    were moving cardboard models resembling a "hawk" or a "goose" in
    flight.
2. Those ducks which had earlier experience with "flying" models showed
    no fear when the same models were presented in a series of tests.
    Ducks that had no early experience with the models showed marked
    fear of the models initially, regardless of shape.
3. There was significantly more fear of the hawk than of the goose model
    in the second series of presentations [both models moving three
    times faster]. But habituation to both models occurred quickly, and
    fear responses to the cardboard models "flying overhead" were not
    elicited after the third day of testing.
4. The results indicate that both inherited and environmental factors colla-
    borate in the genesis of fear of visual patterns presented by preda-
    tory birds.[35]

Another, now classical, experiment involved pairs of kittens whose
entire visual experience was virtually identical, but one in a harness had
locomotor control, and the other in a sling could not affect his position.
He used a counter-balanced horizontally-linked pivot arrangement to
move in the same way as his partner. The active kitten consistently chose
the safe, shallow side in a depth test, whilst the passive kitten chose
either side as would be expected due to chance without any account of
depth cues:

> The results are consistent with our thesis that self-produced movement
> with its concurrent visual feedback is necessary for the development of
> visually-guided behaviour. Equivalent, and even greatly increased, vari-
> ation in visual stimulation produced by other means is not sufficient ...
> These findings provide convincing evidence for a developmental pro-

cess ... which requires for its operation stimulus variation concurrent with and systematically dependent on self-produced movement.[36]

This last experiment is very significant. Piaget and others emphasize the importance of the motor aspects of sensory-motor assimilation. The validity of the results in supporting the stated thesis depends on there being no significance in the depth cues to the active cat during pre-training. The experiment does not preclude the possibility that degeneration occurred in the restricted animal, rather than lack of normal development.

A significant problem encountered by researchers in robotics and pattern recognition is that of orientation. It is one thing to recognize something in one particular orientation, but it is rather more difficult to recognize it in an arbitrary position. Simple template techniques, for example, not only have problems with angle, but also precise location in the visual field. It might be expected that infants would find it hard to recognize things when presented in orientations different from the norm. Held has tested orientation preferences for faces, stylized faces, and other patterns with infants of various ages. Showing similar characteristics at each age would indicate an absence of learning, and an innate orientation handling capability. Similar conclusions might be reached if for some reason the older infants showed greater differentiation. Interestingly, the experiments were performed with a different rationale, acknowledging the possibility that orientation invariance may be followed by orientation discrimination:

> Does an infant first see form as form and then slowly learn to note object orientation, or is orientation initially of prime salience, followed later by the capacity to recognize object form independent of its orientation? ... It is interesting to note here that while 0° shows a peak at the 14-week period, the 90° presentation shows a peak efficacy at the 20-week period.[37]

The conclusion was that perception of orientation may be innate. The data is not clear, but suggests that at first orientation is innate, but has less effect in delaying recognition after 14–20 weeks. It seems to us that orientation invariance is learned.

Piaget's Position

We now leave the non-linguistic context and its suggestive, but somewhat inconclusive, results for the specifically psycholinguistic debate. We look first at the two principal exponents:

> Piaget began his professional career as a biologist. By a circuitous route ... Piaget was stimulated to investigate the origins of knowledge in in-

fancy and the stages through which children pass *en route* to acquiring an adult level of logical thought. Although at one time he considered his days with children merely a detour in his effort to devise a biological account of the nature of knowledge, Piaget remained a student of children's thought for nearly sixty years and eventually founded a new field—genetic epistemology—which probes the origins of intellectual structures in children. It studies also the evolution of knowledge within specific scientific disciplines, and the parallels between these two ... Although Piaget criticized his old nemeses, the behaviorists and the nativists, for the most part he remained eager to convert others to his general picture of universal human development—a portrait attractive and convincing in its overall outlines but difficult to formulate in terms sufficiently precise for ready confirmation or disconfirmation.[38]

Piaget's precise formulations lead to large numbers of specialized definitions, and a lack of accessibility in his writings. But now the computer makes it possible to model pragmatically many aspects of his proposals. Piaget's position paper for the Royaumont debate makes a strong stand against any innate cognitive structures:

> Fifty years of experience have taught us that knowledge does not result from a mere recording of observations without a structuring activity on the part of the subject. Nor do any *a priori* or innate cognitive structures exist in man; the functioning of intelligence alone is hereditary and creates structures only through an organization of successive actions performed on objects. Consequently, an epistemology conforming to the data of psychogenesis could be neither empiricist nor preformationist, but could consist only of a constructivist, with a continual elaboration of new operations and structures. The central problem, then, is to understand how such operations come about, and why, even though they result from non-predetermined constructions, they eventually become logically necessary.[39]

This is uncompromising, but he is more flexible in the subsequent debate. He continues to make his position clear by defending the generality of his proposed mechanisms in terms of the "scientific metaphor" which shaped our thinking in Chapter One:

> [The mechanisms] of "assimilation" and "adaption", which are visible from birth, are completely general and are found in the various levels of scientific thought. The role of assimilation is recognized in the fact that an "observable" or a "fact" is always interpreted from the moment of its observation, for this observation always and from the beginning requires the utilization of logico-mathematical frameworks ... in short, a whole conceptualization on the part of the subject that excludes the existence of pure "facts" as completely external to the activities of this subject, all the more as the subject must make the phenomena vary in order to assimilate them.[40]

Having given the rationale behind his proposals, he defends his "naïve" constructional view by comparing it with the nativist view. This starts with characterizing the opposing positions, but is followed by an overkill of often specious arguments to show how unattainable the nativist position is:

> If one considers the facts of psychogenesis, one notes first the existence of stages that seem to bear witness to a continual construction ... However, these beautiful successive and sequential constructions (where each one is necessary to the following one) could be interpreted as the progressive actualization (related to factors such as neurological maturity) of a set of preformations, similar to the way in which genetic programming regulates organic "epigenesis" even though the latter continues to interact with the environment and its objects. The problem is therefore to choose between two hypotheses: authentic constructions with stepwise disclosures to new possibilities, or successive actualization of a set of possibilities *existing from the beginning*.[41]

Piaget's subsequent arguments focus on that last phrase — not only must the function *exist from the beginning* in the individual, but also in the species. For, since the mechanisms which might allow a function to develop in an individual are excluded, this only leaves random mutation to explain development in a species. This negative argument is meant to show the implausibility of the nativist position. He also argues for constructivism on the basis of autoregulation, and that innateness is unnecessarily restrictive:

> While fully sympathizing with the transformational aspects of Chomsky's doctrine, I cannot accept the hypothesis of his "innate fixed nucleus". There are two reasons for this. The first one is that this mutation particular to the human species would be biologically inexplicable; it is already very difficult to see why the randomness of mutations renders a human being able to "learn" an articulate language, and if in addition one had to attribute to it the innateness of a rational linguistic structure, then this structure would itself be subject to a random origin and would make of reason a collection of mere "working hypotheses" ... My second reason is that the "innate fixed nucleus" would retain all its properties of a "fixed nucleus" if it were not innate but constituted the "necessary" result of the constructions of sensorimotor intelligence, which is prior to language and results from those joint organic and behavioral autoregulations that determine this epigenesis. It is indeed this explanation of a non-innate fixed nucleus, produced by sensorimotor intelligence, that has finally been admitted by authors such as Brown, Lenneberg, and McNeill. This is enough to indicate that the hypothesis of innateness is not mandatory in order to secure the coherence of Chomsky's beautiful system.[42]

The primary point is not that it is impossible to have such innate mechanisms, but Piaget's second reason, which is that it is possible to do without innate mechanisms. We believe the "probability" that such mechanisms *do not* exist, or equivalently, the "probability" that more general yet sufficient mechanisms *do* exist. Our proposal is that not only is language acquired through some general mechanism, but so is reason. The order and structure comes from, and parallels, the sensory-motor environment. Piaget argues that whilst this is feasible for the individual, for the phaenotype, it surely is not for the species, the genotype. Furthermore it is easier to explain in terms of learning than in terms of mutation. The term he uses for this "interlocking" process of coming into a correspondence or "equilibrium" with the environment is "equilibration".

The final pragmatic thread of Piaget's arguments is his delight that several prominent psycholinguists have initially embraced an innate fixed nucleus, but have since become converted to explanations in terms of sensorimotor intelligence. This mechanism makes the innateness restriction unnecessary.

Chomsky's Position

Noam Chomsky began his academic career as a student of language whose approach was rooted in rigorous philosophical analysis and in formal logical-mathematical methods. Convinced early on of the inadequacy of previous attempts to explain language, Chomsky introduced into linguistics a set of revolutionary concerns. He formulated an agenda for scientific linguistics: to find a set of grammatical rules that would generate syntactic descriptions for all of the permissible and none of the non-permissible in any given language ... Chomsky then put forward a specific set of proposals articulating the formal nature of the grammatical system that could fulfil these goals. In a series of influential writings, he posited a set of extremely abstract linguistic structures that do not have to be taught because they are part of the child's innate knowledge system.[43]

These two antagonists in the psycholinguistic debate have diverse backgrounds from which each is striking out in unusual directions. Thus the biologist is concerned with reason and language and proposes general logical mechanisms to explain their development within the individual. But the linguist is concerned with supposed anatomical organs and proposes specific linguistic mechanisms leaving explanation of their development to evolutionary theory. There are further marked contrasts in their approach to tradition, demonstration and application:

Chomsky's break with the linguistic past was perhaps more radical than Piaget's rupture with earlier psychology, and his influence on the next generation of researchers spread even more quickly ... Chomsky ... offered a number of intriguing specific examples to support his point of view, but his overall approach was markedly different. Unlike Piaget's, his examples were not of dramatic behavioral phenomena; rather he pointed to abstract internal rules ... These rules are discovered by examining the features of correct linguistic utterances and of certain incorrect but "possible" syntactic constructions that seem never to appear. Once pointed out, such regularities (though not necessarily Chomsky's specific explanations) are evident, and further experimentation to demonstrate their validity seems superfluous. Accordingly, Chomsky relied heavily on such examples and on artful *reductio ad absurdum* to discount alternative rules and rival points of view. Disenchanted with empiricist accounts, he displayed little patience with the version of genetic-environmental contact that stands at the core of Piaget's interactionism.[44]

So we now examine Chomsky's position as he sets it out for the Royaumont debate.

Specifically, investigation of human language has led me to believe that a genetically determined language faculty, one component of the human mind, specifies a certain class of "humanly accessible grammars". The child acquires one of the grammars (actually, a system of such grammars ...) on the basis of the limited evidence available to him. Within a given speech-community, children with vastly different experience acquire comparable grammars, vastly underdetermined by the available evidence. We may think of a grammar, represented somehow in the mind, as a system that specifies the phonetic, syntactic, and semantic properties of an infinite class of potential sentences. The child knows the language so determined by the grammar he has acquired.[45]

We find the claims of "vastly different" and "vastly underdetermined" quite unwarranted. Chomsky has never sought to adduce rigorous experimental research to support these claims. Instead, he has taken these as agreed and obvious "facts", "facts" which we dispute as naïve and exaggerated interpretations. Chomsky not only make his innateness claims for linguistic mechanisms, but speculates "that other cognitive structures developed by humans might profitably be analyzed along similar lines."

Chomsky addresses two of Piaget's principal arguments; the first answer is well taken, but Chomsky's second seems to fall into the same trap as Piaget's first: the difference between *unexplained* and *inexplicable*, or *undemonstrated* and *indemonstrable*:

Against this conception Piaget offers two basic arguments: (1) the mutations, specific to humans, that might have given rise to the postulated innate structures are "biologically inexplicable"; (2) what can be explained on the assumption of fixed innate structures can be explained as well as "the *necessary* result of constructions of sensorimotor intelligence". Neither argument seems to me compelling. As for the first, I agree only in part. The evolutionary development is, no doubt, "biologically unexplained". However, I know of no reason to believe the stronger contention that it is "biologically inexplicable" ... The second argument seems to me a more important one. However, I see no basis for Piaget's conclusion. There are, to my knowledge, no substantive proposals involving "constructions of sensorimotor intelligence" that offer any hope of accounting for the phenomena of language that demand explanation. Nor is there any initial plausibility to the suggestion, as far as I can see. I might add that although some have argued that the assumption of a genetically determined language faculty is "begging the question", this contention is certainly unwarranted. The assumption is no more "question-begging" in the case of mental structures than is the analogous assumption in the case of growth of physical organs.[46]

This is the cruellest cut of all. Several researchers are working on precisely such "implausible" proposals. The point is an *a priori* belief that some specific language acquisition mechanism exists. The consequence is the stifling of research. It is really precisely the difference between "unexplained" and "inexplicable". We *can* conceive a distinction between organs which are physical, and observed directly from birth, and "organs" which are intangible, and have never been observed. But the analogy can have no firm empirical basis since the mechanism is itself only an "unwarranted contention". It is possible that an entity hypothesized from observable effects will eventually be discovered, but it is foolish to assume that it will not, in time, be explained in terms of other, fewer and more general, principles and components.

Arbiters

The Royaumont debate sparked off a number of attempts to strike a balance, many of them criticizing both extremes of the debate, and seeking some sort of compromise. We now consider some of these. It has already been observed that Piaget has been willing to make concessions. So too has Chomsky, who has ostensibly agreed that the dichotomy is unfortunate, but it is not clear that he is willing to move from his fairly extreme nativist stance:

> When Chomsky ... asserts that "the two strategies ... pose the issue in a way which it would be well to get away from", I am in full agreement with him, as I believe that *the full power of both evolutionary theory and genetic psychology will be necessary to account for the interactive development of the innate and acquired features of language*. However, when Chomsky goes on to say that the right strategy is to "treat the question of ... the nature of language without prejudice and exactly as one would treat the question of some physical organ of the body", such as the heart, I can only conclude either that he does not believe the development of the heart to be innately determined, or that he does, and is thereby reverting to one of the two strategies he has just declared "it

would be well to get away from", which is a contradiction. Both terms of the alternative introduce an inconsistency in Chomsky's defence of innatism.[47]

Chomsky's comparison of the supposed linguistic organ with the heart, as if they are comparable, is unreasonable, and Chomsky's innatist attacks are unfair in another respect. He is guilty of "misrepresenting by extension"[48] the constructivist position in that he attacks the latter as if they admit of no innate mechanisms involved in language acquisition. Cellerier writes:

> The notion that "the mental equipment utilized by the child to learn a language possesses a certain number of genetically determined properties" ... is in fact Piaget's, whereas in Chomsky's version "a certain number" is replaced by "all", since the environment provides no equipment, but only content for it to process. This basic misconception clearly weakens his indictment against constructivism.[49]

The Artificial Intelligence (AI) perspective is more positive. Here are some comments of Papert's on how AI relates specifically to this debate on innateness. This is especially appropriate as his work in conjunction with Minsky has been misconstrued, and has triggered another major debate:

> AI has thrusts in three directions which relate to controversies in psychology and linguistics about the property of innateness. Two of these are easy to state. The first tends to reduce the set of structures considered innate by showing how they could be acquired through the operation of more powerful developmental mechanisms. The second thrust goes in the opposite direction; paradoxically, by understanding very powerful developmental mechanisms one is able to see how certain structures totally unsuspected by traditional psychology could, if they were innately present, play the role of seeds for the growth of mental functioning ... These two thrusts find a direct translation in terms of the present debate. I believe that Chomsky is biased towards perceiving certain syntactic structures as "unlearnable" because his underlying paradigm of the process of learning is too simple, too restricted ... But I will argue that a stronger learning shifts the balance of plausibility towards conjecturing that syntactic structures are "learned", and so toward adopting a research strategy that looks for how this could happen rather than following a strategy of assuming "innateness" ... The highly metaphorical flavor of these last remarks [on supposed "mental organs"] leads to the third, and more subtle, thrust of AI: to prune psychological language of prescientific metaphors by developing a more precise terminology, conceptual framework, and indeed, a new set of "metaphors" in the form of well-understood situations against which general ideas can be tested for intellectual coherence.[50]

Papert offers "hints" about specifically computational mechanisms and structures which are "almost certainly necessary" to brain function, and it is the power and generality of these which has contrasted sharply with the "organicist" tendency of Chomsky:

> These structures are not specifically linguistic ... The contribution of AI to this area is to show how computational primitives are fundamentally important to all the mental functions: by seeing all the "mental organs" as computational processes, we are inclined to see them as less fundamentally different from one another than are hearts and livers.[51]

Ironically, the idea of learning automata which Minsky and Papert are supposed to have laid to rest, is used by Papert to support a position which denies Chomsky's characterization of innate linguistic mechanisms, in favour of a far more general "learning mechanism":

> The first of some more technical comments, to which I now turn, is intended mainly to illustrate more sharply the need for greater clarity about what it means to be innate. I will do this by describing an automaton, a machine that we understand quite thoroughly, and asking questions about what is and what is not innate in the machine ... The machine in question is called a perceptron.[52]

Given his claim that Chomsky "is in an absurd position", Papert provides a "theory of Chomsky" to explain how the misconceptions could have arisen!

> Despite his well-known criticism of Skinner ... Chomsky seems to be tacitly committed to a very Skinnerian kind of GDM (General Developmental Mechanism) which has the following characteristics of typical behaviorist models: the emphasis on teaching, either explicitly or by correction of mistakes; the apparent rejection of "experiment" as applicable to the child's learning of language; and the assumption that what is being learned is the thing itself (the adult structure) rather than some developmentally deep structural precursor ... Of course the child does not learn SSC (Specified Subject Condition) by being taught in any direct sense; this is not the way any fundamental structures or skills are ever acquired. And of course the child does not learn the SSC by passive observation. Piaget has removed any lingering tendencies people might have had to see the child as *ever* engaging in "passive observation". So I would have thought that the "only rational conclusion" from Chomsky's set of statements is that the child discovered the SSC through "experiments" ... We certainly know that recognizable precursors of components of the complex activities involved in experimenting are visible in very young babies.[53]

Piaget's continual emphasis is that language, and indeed reason, take their form from the order of the sensory-motor environment—this is what he means by "constructivism". As a balance to Piaget's extreme argument from genetics, I include the following remarks of Fodor:

The nativist isn't committed to saying that viruses know about set theory any more than he is committed to saying that viruses have legs; it hardly follows from the fact that viruses dont have legs that legs aren't innately specified. It is true ... that in any theory of the modification of concepts available to us, there is no such thing as a concept being invented. It is obviously also true that there must be *some* sense in which our conceptual repertoire is responsive to our experiences, including the experiences of the species in doing things like inventing mathematics. What that implies, it seems to me, is that a theory of the conceptual plasticity of organisms must be a theory of how the environment selects among the innately specified concepts. It is not a theory of how you acquire concepts, but a theory of how the environment determines which parts of the conceptual mechanism in principle available to you are in fact exploited. I don't know whether or not such a theory can be made to stick, but I simply don't see that it is an incoherent notion in principle, and whether it can be made to stick is something that we can find out by trying (as we tried to do for several hundred years with the alternative theory, and to utterly bankrupt consequences, it seems to me).[54]

The main problem with this is that whatever is innate cannot be "concepts" or "ideas". It brings to mind Piaget's reflection metaphor. There is a sense in which the available conceptual *mechanism* is a "sticky mirror". The environment impinges and is reflected dimly. However, what strikes frequently, makes an impression—it starts to stick. And these "stuck" features then make it easier to reflect concepts having similar features. The observation that each part of the surface appears to have some information about each feature or concept, all of them being overlaid, leads us to the holographic principle.

Fodor's argument hinges on the proposition that one system may never give rise to a more powerful one. Thus, given that we do have a system more powerful than a child, or a protozoan, how is the more powerful system generated?

What I was arguing against was the position according to which you start at [one place] and by some computational procedure you get to [a higher one]. If you grant that you can't do it, then there are various possibilities: God does it for you on Tuesdays, or you do it by falling on your head, or it is innate.[55]

Now of course the last alternative *is* preferable if we are considering only phaenotypical development within a genotype. But if we are considering development across genomes, we are left with only the first two choices:

Now the question is: how did the organism get to [the point]? Various things might have happened: maturational events might have occurred which have nothing to do with any learning process or any computational procedure. It is simply that its brain rewires itself, as I said, "on

Tuesdays". This is perfectly possible. Indeed, I think that this must be
what happens in some cases of "cognitive development". But another
possibility is this: some learning process takes place—this is the classic
story—and this learning process essentially involves hypothesis formation and confirmation.[56]

This answer is still not satisfactory. The solution to the problem is to
throw away the hypothesis concerning "impossibility of acquiring a more
powerful structure", and to consider organism plus environment as a
single system, since the hypothesis that one cognitive system can never
give rise to the more powerful one could only apply to a closed system.

Fodor's proposal is actually that the individual *does* have an innate
propensity for such "novelties". And his logical grounds do seem to ignore the points made by Papert about the innatist's limited view of
learning. Fodor also seems to misunderstand Piaget's point that he is describing a discovery process: a discovery of natural and extant relationships. (Note that "extant" is more general than "innate".) This particular
argument of Piaget's is intended to focus on the analogy between child
language acquisition and the history of science, which arises from this
"learning as analysis" paradigm.

The focus of Fodor's critique is "learning as analysis" and such "analysis" represents the full spectrum of techniques known to, and employed by, science. If these processes are excluded "on logical grounds",
what unscientific unknown, and unknowable, processes are capable of
and responsible for innovation? The innateness and power of a system
are well defined concepts, but the innateness and power of a concept are
meaningless terms unless the concept is embedded in a system. This is
consistent with Piaget's general mechanisms, rather than the overly specific "organs" of Chomsky which Fodor is seeking to support. There is
moreover no logical reason why the new concept should supplant the old
in any circumstances if it isn't more powerful or more parsimonious.
Concepts are simply a recognition of ontological coincidences or laws,
and this is the starting point for Piaget's proposals.

The Royaumont debate also included presentations from a biological viewpoint. Chang's interesting contribution to the debate points out
that both Chomsky's and Piaget's arguments are superficial (his term
would be "exploitative") in their relation to neurobiology:

> The human nervous system is rarely regarded by the linguist or the psy-
> chologist with any more curiosity that he would give to a *black box* ... In
> fact, there exists an underlying organization ... in (1) the anatomy of
> the relevant neuronal circuits, (2) the activity of these circuits, and (3)
> the signals that the organism receives by its sense organs. A satisfactory
> description, and therefore an explanation, of any behavioral act should
> by obligation include these three underlying levels of organization ...
> This is indeed a formidable task in practice, but *a priori* possible in the-

ory, and it is actually becoming successful with some simple (or simplified) systems.[57]

The powerful and inescapable constraints imposed by anatomy on behaviour make hazardous any attempt to infer the underlying organization — anatomy, activity, and genetic determinism — of behaviour. As pointed out by Chomsky, "part of the intellectual fascination of the study of language is that it is necessary to devise complex arguments to overcome the fact that direct experimentation is rarely possible"; fascination for some, deception for others. Is this why the words "infer" and "inference" occur frequently in Chomsky?

Chang refers briefly to evidence supporting Piaget's reflections, but puts considerable effort into explaining some of the improbabilities of the nativist view:

> Anatomical or functional alterations, sometimes very discrete, underlie the hereditary variations of behavior ... The connectional organization of the nervous system down to the synaptic level is thus subjected to the omnipotence of the genes ... IF the functional organization of the nervous system, down to its slightest details, is subject to such a strict genetic determinism, is there a sufficient number of genes in the chromosomal apparatus to account for it? ... The human body has about 200 different cell types: neurons, muscle cells, gland cells, and so on ... Each ... neuron or synapse is engaged in a characteristic function. A high degree of cross-linking exists between cell bodies organized in well-defined patterns. To this extreme complexity ... one classically opposes the small amount of genetic material information available ... In fact, a large fraction of chromosomal DNA, about 40 percent, exhibits repeated sequences (that is, seems to be redundant), and the number of "true" structural genes coding for proteins is estimated to be in the range of 10,000 to 30,000 ... How, from such a limited number of genes, can one generate the complexity of the brain?[58]

In answer to this question, he points to the extensive initial redundancy of the brain, and its progressive developmental reduction:

> The existence of a transient redundancy in the development of neuronal networks is now well documented. The problem still remains of determining to what extent the activity of the developing network contributes to the observed decrease of redundancy.

Toulmin is also critical of the extremity of the views of both Piaget and Chomsky. Each takes a simplistic viewpoint, in the case of Chomsky, about the necessity of the supposed innate language mechanism, and in the case of Piaget, about the sufficiency of the supposed innate intelligence mechanism. In both cases, they equate the logical structures of their systems with the empirical structures of biology:

In a way that raises grave and difficult issues which they do not adequately deal with ... Secondly, in regard to the biological and other empirical reasons for taking a middle way: both writers seem to me to play fast and loose with the available evidence, such as it is. Piaget's claim ... is far too sweeping in one direction. Many species with complex neural networks are known to display highly specific perceptual/cognitive responses and skills that are evidently "hereditary" ... Chomsky's arguments, on the other hand, are too sweeping in the opposite direction ... There are some very real problems in regard to reconciling his theories of the human "language capacity" with general biology, including evolutionary theory ... Certainly, as against Piaget's claim, we must suppose that the ability to learn language depends on the human infant possessing some quite specific "capacities" that are "innate" in the sense of being "wired into the central nervous system"; there is, of course, independent neurological evidence of such "innate" capacities. But the particular capacities Chomsky attributes to the child appear *far too* specific to be plausible, quite aside from the difficulty of conceiving what sort of neurological counterparts they might have.[59]

Computer Programs as Psychological Models

We start with a fairly standard statement of the operation of the computational metaphor:

> A computer is a psychological model if it is intended to perform some psychological task in the way the organism being modeled [does] ... Correspondence between a program and a behavioral mechanism ... is determined not by the program but by the model builder.[60]

The model used depends on the abstraction employed by the model builder, including the paradigm and metaphor which embody its relationship to the modelled system. The goals will include success in both an absolute and a relative sense:

> This project does have the ultimate goal of providing a faithful simulation of child language acquisition. One might question whether a system constructed just to succeed at language learning will have much in common with the child's acquisition system. I strongly suspect it will, provided we insist that the system have the same information-processing limitations as a child and provided its language-learning situation has the same information-processing demands as that of the child ... In many ways the task faced by LAS.1 is overly simplistic, and its algorithms are probably too efficient and free from information-processing limitations. Therefore, the acquisition behavior of LAS.1 does not mirror in most respects that of the child. Later versions of this program will attempt a more realistic simulation.[61]

Validity depends not only on the correspondence in the positive aspects of the morphism, but is also necessarily dependent on the preservation of the restrictions and limitations of the archetype. From an engineering viewpoint, we would want, presumably, the programmed system to be as efficient as possible, but where we are wanting to maintain psychological validity and testability, we must maintain the restrictions. This is because we want a model which builds our confidence through prediction of, for example, the timing of the human's performance. Discovering, and modelling, restrictions and limitations is thus necessary.

Even from an engineering perspective, it may be that the unrestricted problem is insoluble, and that the human restrictions are thus useful heuristics in building the model so as to solve the problem effectively. The "copycat" approach to Engineering is ancient, but the explicit and deliberate derivation of insights from biological systems is in its infancy. Thus, because of the problems now being attempted in AI (Artificial Intelligence), AI researchers must learn how to borrow from the biological sciences:

> In perception, learning and motivation when we try to model these aspects of organismic behaviour in a computationally exact manner ... our current knowledge of the processes that underlie behaviour is pitiably inadequate. This means that we cannot at present attempt modelling anything more than fragmentary aspects of behaviour ... Computer simulation of complex information activities ... has attained a high level of sophistication in the past two decades or more. Unfortunately, very little of all this work has real relevance to modelling organismic behaviour ... The designs of these systems have been motivated by practical considerations of their potential utility. Because of this the principles incorporated in these systems tend to be ... quite *ad-hoc* ... Problems of perception, learning, and motivation, which are central to the computational modelling of organisms, do not figure in these AI studies in any relevant sense.[62]

Psychology can probably learn from the advances of computer science. We can argue that psychology cannot afford to believe that it is fundamentally different from Engineering, and its subjects totally different from computer or machine:

> If we believe that a science of psychology is possible at all—that is, if we believe that it is worth pursuing and finally cornering and confronting with a clear-cut test the hypothesis that the brain's procedures are in some way describable, then we believe that the brain's procedures can also be described on the computer ... If we take the attitude that the brain is ineffable, partaking of something completely inscrutable and unknowable, the computer cannot get around that—but then it follows that there is no hope of a science of the mind, and if we are honest, there is no point in trying to be psychologists ... But unless we are willing to assert that we *know* the brain is unknowable, then the best way to

pursue and test out this assumption is, as in a *reductio ad absurdum* proof, to assume the opposite, provisionally, in the hope of finally proving the impossibility of this pursuit.[63]

Note that the "unknowability" assumption stems from a very common and most ancient view in philosophy that no system is capable of comprehending itself. We have already encountered a form of this put particularly strongly by Fodor. The argument that "computers can only do what they are told" is in the same category. The level of "understanding" that *is* impossible is "prediction", and this is impossible precisely because the system must be sufficiently powerful to admit (personifying) "perversity". This is "the halting problem", in essence. The prediction becomes a new part of the environment and hence can logically invalidate the basis for the prediction. What I call the "Delphic" phenomenon was a favourite motif for Greek Tragedy, such as *Oedipus Rex*, in which the fate predicted by the Delphic oracle could never be thwarted — but this is demonstrably unachievable, in general, at the level of a system applied to itself.

This does not say anything about a person's ability to understand a completely independent system, his observation of which was completely passive and in no way affected the operation of that system.

The components of any model proposing psychological validity should themselves constitute models of psychological phenomena. They can either be models of known phenomena, or predictions about yet-to-be-discovered phenomena for which evidence should then be sought. Some of the top level details of Anderson's LAS (Language Acquisition System) serve to illustrate this principle:

> Central to LAS is an augmented transition network grammar similar to that of Woods (1970). In response to the command *Listen*, LAS evokes the program UNDERSTAND. The input to UNDERSTAND is a sentence. LAS uses the information in the network grammar to parse the sentence and obtain a representation of the sentence's meaning. In response to the command *Speak*, LAS evokes the program SPEAK. SPEAK receives a picture encoding and uses the information in the network grammar to generate a sentence to describe the encoding. Note that LAS is using the same network formalism both to speak and understand ... The philosophy behind the LEARNMORE program is to provide LAS with the same information that a child has when he is learning a language through ostension. It is assumed that in this learning mode the adult can both direct the child's attention to what is being described and focus the child's attention on that aspect of the situation being described ... The SPEAKTEST program constructs a parsing network adequate to handle all the sentences it was presented with. Also it makes many low-level generalizations about phrase structures and word classes ... However, many essential grammatical generalizations are left to be made by the program GENERALIZE. Principally, GENER-

ALIZE must recognize that networks and words occurring at various points in the grammar are identical. Recognition of identical grammars is essential to identifying the recursive structure of the language.[64]

In summary, LAS is a useful, but still far from ideal model. An ideal comprehensive model would start from scratch: learning sensory-motor, grammatical and semantical relationships independently of a directive teacher. Furthermore, Anderson's HAM (Human Associative Memory) is not an ontological model but a propositional model. Thus, LAS cannot directly make use of real or simulated sensory-motor peripheral devices. The preprocessing needed for both the HAM representation and the LAS learner is considerable. Anderson also notes that ATN's are needlessly powerful: it is better to avoid complexity by restricting the power of the computational tools, processors and preprocessors. As we shall see in the following chapters, our model takes account of this and other issues raised so far.

Notes to Chapter Six

1. Narasimhan, R., *Modelling Language Behaviour* (Springer-Verlag, Berlin, 1981).
2. Wells, Gordon, *Learning through interaction: The study of language development* (Cambridge University Press, Cambridge, UK, 1981), p.86f.
3. Piaget, Jean, "The Psychogenesis of Knowledge and Its Epistemological Significance", in M. Piatelli-Palmarini, ed., *Language and Learning: The Debate between Jean Piaget and Noam Chomsky* (Routledge and Kegan Paul, 1979), p.23f.
4. Piaget, Jean, "Language within Cognition", in M. Piatelli-Palmarini, ed., *Language and Learning: The Debate between Jean Piaget and Noam Chomsky* (Routledge and Kegan Paul, 1979), p.164f.
5. *Op. cit.*, p.165.
6. *Ibid.*
7. *Op. cit.*, p.167.
8. Piaget, Jean, "The Psychogenesis of Knowledge and Its Epistemological Significance", in M. Piatelli-Palmarini, ed., *Language and Learning: The Debate between Jean Piaget and Noam Chomsky* (Routledge and Kegan Paul, 1979), p.28f.
9. Piaget, Jean, *The Construction of Reality in the Child*, Original Title: *La Construction du Reel chez l'Enfant* (New York, Basic Books, 1954).
10. McNeill, David, "The Capacity for the Ontogenesis of Grammar", in Dan I. Slobin, *The Ontogenesis of Language* (Academic Press, 1971), p.19f; Ervin-Tripp, Susan, "Some Strategies for the First Years", in Timothy E. Moore, ed., *Cognitive Development and the Acquisition of Language* (Academic Press, New York, 1973), p.285f.
11. Narasimhan, R., *Modelling Language Behaviour* (Springer-Verlag, Berlin, 1981), p.69.
12. Schlesinger, I.M., "Production of Utterances and Language Acquisition" in Dan I. Slobin, *The Ontogenesis of Language* (Academic Press, 1971), p.6.

13. Bowerman, Melissa, *Early Syntactic Development: a cross-linguistic study with special reference to Finnish* (Cambridge University Press, Cambridge UK, 1973), p.211f.

14. See McNeill, David, "The Capacity for the Ontogenesis of Grammar", in Dan I. Slobin, *The Ontogenesis of Language* (Academic Press, 1971), p.21; Schlesinger, I.M., "Production of Utterances and Language Acquisition" in Dan I. Slobin, *The Ontogenesis of Language* (Academic Press, 1971), p.67; Roeper, Thomas, "Connecting Children's Language and Linguistic Theory", in Timothy E. Moore, ed., *Cognitive Development and the Acquisition of Language* (Academic Press, New York, 1973), p.188.

15. Piatelli-Palmarini, M., ed., *Language and Learning: The Debate between Jean Piaget and Noam Chomsky* (Routledge and Kegan Paul, London, England, 1979).

16. Uhr, Leonard, *Pattern Recognition, Learning, and Thought: Computer-Programmed Models of Higher Mental Processes* (Prentice-Hall, Englewood Cliffs, NJ, 1973), p.285.

17. Moore, Timothy A., *Cognitive Development and the Acquisition of Language* (Academic Press, New York, 1973), p.4.

18. Palermo, David S., "On Learning to Talk: Are Principles Derived from the Learning Laboratory Applicable?" in Dan I. Slobin, ed., *The Ontogenesis of Language* (Academic Press, 1971), p.61.

19. *Ibid.*

20. McNeill, David, "The Capacity for the Ontogenesis of Grammar", in Dan I. Slobin, *The Ontogenesis of Language* (Academic Press, 1971), p.21; cp Pike, Kenneth L., *Language in Relation to a Unified Theory of the Structure of Human Behavior* (Mouton, The Hague, Holland, 1954/1967); Kelley, K.L., *Early Syntactic Acquisition* (Rand Corporation, Santa Monica, CA, November 1967), pp. 64f.

21. *Op. cit.,* pp. 71, 82.

22. Anderson, John R., "Computer Simulation of a Language Acquisition System: A First Report", in R. L. Solso, ed., *Information Processing and Cognition: The Loyola Symposium* (Lawrence Erlbaum Associates, Hillsdale, 1975), p.311.

23. Block, H.D., J. Moulton, and G. M. Robinson, "Natural Language Acquisition by a Robot", *Int. J. Man-Mach, Stud.*, Vol. 7 (1975), pp.571-7.

24. Staats, Arthur W., "Linguistic-Mentalistic Theory versus an Explanatory S-R Learning Theory of Language Development", in Dan I. Slobin, *The Ontogenesis of Language* (Academic Press, 1971), p.103.

25. Block, H.D., J. Moulton, and G. M. Robinson, "Natural Language Acquisition by a Robot", *Int. J. Man-Mach, Stud.*, Vol. 7 (1975), p.578f.

26. Siklossy, Laurent, "A Language-Learning Heuristic Program", *Cognitive Psychology*, Vol.2, Pt.1 (1971), p.479.

27. Kucera, Henry, "The Learning of Grammar", *Perspectives in Computing*, Vol 1, No. 2 (1981), p.29.

28. Skinner, B.F., "The Phylogeny and Ontogeny of Behaviour" (Reprinted from *Science,* (1966), Vol. 153); Melzack, R., E. Penick, and A. Beckett, "The problem of "Innate Fear" of the Hawk Shape: an Experimental Study with Mallard Ducks" (Reprinted from *Journal of Comparative and Physiological Psychology,* 1959, Vol 52, pp 694-698); Epstein, William, "Experimental Investigations of the Genesis of Visual Space Perception" (Reprinted from *Psychological Bulletin,* 1964, Vol 64, pp

115-128); Held, Richard, and Alan Hein, "Movement-Produced Stimulation in the Development of Visually Guided Behaviour" (Reprinted from *Journal of Comparative and Physiological Psychology,* 1963, Vol 56, pp 872-876); Watson, John S., "Perception of Object Orientation in Infants" (Reprinted from the *Merrill-Palmer Quarterly of Behavior and Development,* 1966, Vol 12, pp 73-94); all in E. Endler, L. Boulter, and H. Osser, eds, *Contemporary Issues in Developmental Psychology* (Holt, Rhinehart and Winston, New York, 1968), pp.370-385.

29. Hockett, Charles F., "Grammar for the Hearer", *Proc. Symposia in App. Math.,* Vol. XII (Amer. Mathl Soc., 1961), p.3ff.

30. *Op. cit.,* p.58.

31. Skinner, B.F., "The Phylogeny and Ontogeny of Behaviour", in E. Endler, L. Boulter, and H. Osser, eds, *Contemporary Issues in Developmental Psychology* (Holt, Rhinehart and Winston, New York, 1968), p.62.

32. *Ibid.*

33. *Op. cit.,* p.70f.

34. Melzack, R., E. Penick, and A. Beckett, "The problem of "Innate Fear" of the Hawk Shape: an Experimental Study with Mallard Ducks" (Reprinted from *Journal of Comparative and Physiological Psychology,* 1959, Vol 52, pp 694-698), in E. Endler, L. Boulter, and H. Osser, eds, *Contemporary Issues in Developmental Psychology* (Holt, Rhinehart and Winston, New York, 1968), p.333.

35. *Op. cit.,* p.338.

36. Held, Richard, and Alan Hein, "Movement-Produced Stimulation in the Development of Visually Guided Behaviour" (Reprinted from *Journal of Comparative and Physiological Psychology,* 1963, Vol 56, pp 872-876), in E. Endler, L. Boulter, and H. Osser, eds, *Contemporary Issues in Developmental Psychology* (Holt, Rhinehart and Winston, New York, 1968), p.368.

37. Watson, John S., "Perception of Object Orientation in Infants" (Reprinted from the *Merrill-Palmer Quarterly of Behavior and Development,* 1966, Vol 12, pp 73-94), in E. Endler, L. Boulter, and H. Osser, eds, *Contemporary Issues in Developmental Psychology* (Holt, Rhinehart and Winston, New York, 1968), p.379.

38. Gardner, Howard, "Cognition Comes of Age", pp.xixff, in M. Piatelli-Palmarini, *Language and Learning: The Debate between Jean Piaget and Noam Chomsky* (Routledge and Kegan Paul, 1979), pxxif.

39. Piaget, Jean, "The Psychogenesis of Knowledge and Its Epistemological Significance", in M. Piatelli-Palmarini, ed., *Language and Learning: The Debate between Jean Piaget and Noam Chomsky* (Routledge and Kegan Paul, 1979), p.23.

40. *Op. cit.,* p.24.

41. *Op. cit.,* p.25.

42. *Op. cit.,* p.30.

43. Gardner, Howard, "Cognition Comes of Age", in M. Piatelli-Palmarini, *Language and Learning: The Debate between Jean Piaget and Noam Chomsky* (Routledge and Kegan Paul, 1979), p.xxif.

44. *Op. cit.,* p.xxii.

45. Chomsky, Noam A., "On Cognitive Structures and Their Development: A Reply to Piaget", in M. Piatelli-Palmarini, ed., *Language and Learning: The Debate between Jean Piaget and Noam Chomsky* (Routledge and Kegan Paul, 1979), p.35.

46. *Ibid.*

47. Cellerier, Guy, "Some Clarifications on Innatism and Constructivism", in M. Piatelli-Palmarini, ed., *Language and Learning: The Debate between Jean Piaget and Noam Chomsky* (Routledge and Kegan Paul, 1979), p.83.

48. Thouless, Robert H., *Straight and Crooked Thinking* (Pan, London, UK, 1930/1953).

49. Cellerier, Guy, "Some Clarifications on Innatism and Constructivism", in M. Piatelli-Palmarini, ed., *Language and Learning: The Debate between Jean Piaget and Noam Chomsky* (Routledge and Kegan Paul, 1979), p.85.

50. Papert, Seymour, "The Role of Artificial Intelligence in Psychology", in M. Piatelli-Palmarini, ed., *Language and Learning: The Debate between Jean Piaget and Noam Chomsky* (Routledge and Kegan Paul, 1979), p.91f.

51. *Ibid.*

52. *Op. cit.,* p.93f.

53. *Op. cit.,* p.96.

54. Fodor, Jerry, "Fixation of Belief and Concept Acquisition", in M. Piatelli-Palmarini, ed., *Language and Learning: The Debate between Jean Piaget and Noam Chomsky* (Routledge and Kegan Paul, 1969), p.151.

55. *Op. cit.,* p.155.

56. *Op. cit.,* p.156f.

57. Chang, C. L., and R. C. Lee, *Symbolic Logic and Mechanical Theorem Proving* (Academic Press, 1973).

58. *Op. cit.,* p.189f.

59. *Op. cit.,* p.197.

60. Kelley, K.L., *Early Syntactic Acquisition* (Rand Corporation, Santa Monica, CA, November 1967), p.5.

61. Anderson, John R., "Computer Simulation of a Language Acquisition System: A First Report", in R. L. Solso, ed., *Information Processing and Cognition: The Loyola Symposium* (Lawrence Erlbaum Associates, Hillsdale, 1975), p.334.

62. Narasimhan, R., *Modelling Language Behaviour* (Springer-Verlag, Berlin, 1981), p.53f.

63. Uhr, Leonard, *Pattern Recognition, Learning, and Thought: Computer-Programmed Models of Higher Mental Processes* (Prentice-Hall, Englewood Cliffs, NJ, 1973), p.10f.

64. Anderson, John R., "Computer Simulation of a Language Acquisition System: A First Report", in R. L. Solso, ed., *Information Processing and Cognition: The Loyola Symposium* (Lawrence Erlbaum Associates, Hillsdale, 1975), p.302ff.

Chapter Seven

Neurology and Neurolinguistics

We come now to an overview of the anatomical and physiological evidence, and the neurological models which underlie and motivate the research we described earlier. We start with the brain, its organization and connection. The most accessible parts of the brain for physiological investigation are those which are directly sensory-motor related. These therefore form the focus of our brief neuroanatomical tour.

The brain, in common with the rest of the Central Nervous System (CNS), is functionally composed of neurons, of the order of 10^{11} of them. There are many physically recognizably different types of neuron, and there are also many classes of support cells which we will ignore in this discussion. Neurons make connections with each other, called synapses. The remote sensory-motor receptors and effectors are special classes of neuron which will not be considered separately. Similarly, although sensory-motor processing generally starts and finishes outside the brain proper (*e.g.* in the retina), we will not usually try to identify such processing.

In this subsection we identify the major subsections of the brain, with only brief comments on likely function. Logically in the computer science sense, as a simplification, the brain mediates between sensory and motor functions. Generally the outer layers of the brain (the cortex) are directly involved in the transformation of sensory-motor signals, and the other regions have less specifically sensory-motor functions. Useful introductions to the gross organization and structure of the brain are Nauta and Geschwind.[1]

The brain has three main physical subdivisions (vesicles) corresponding to "swellings" labelled *hindbrain*, *midbrain* and *forebrain*, which curl forward from spinal cord to retina. The hindbrain has a much-studied appendage, the *cerebellum*, which is like a small self-contained brain with its own *(cerebellar) cortex*. But it is the forebrain which is most complex and of most interest here. The three major divisions of the forebrain are its *(cerebral) cortex*, the *thalamus*, and below that (and connected to the pituitary gland) the *hypothalamus*. The cerebral cortex contains some 70% of the neurons of the CNS, including the *hippocampus* which is folded underneath the main *neocortex*.

Bundles of neuronal fibres, called axons, from the somatic sensory system travel up the spinal cord towards the thalamus. Some of them terminate earlier in the hindbrain, including the cerebellum, and in the midbrain. The thalamus then projects to the somatic sensory area of the cortex. The visual and auditory sensoria also project to their respective cortical areas *via* the thalamus, some pathways being routed through the midbrain. Interestingly, most of the neurons in the heart of the hindbrain and midbrain are multimodal (nonspecific) and the thalamus thus receives many signals of this nonspecific nature. These multimodal neurons towards the mid and back of the brain (the reticular formation) possibly include functions relating to general arousal and regulation of activity states such as sleep and wakefulness.

The thalamus is an important relay for almost all the sensoria, including especially the auditory and visual modalities, which project coherently to the medial and lateral geniculate nuclei of the thalamus, and thence to the corresponding cortical areas.

Note that the relaying process is actually a transformational process. Furthermore the thalamocortical projections are reciprocated and evidently this feedback from the cortex influences the nature of the transformation of the sensory-information in the thalamus. The various sensory cortices also project to other areas of the cortex, thence to still others. These are called association areas; the directly-fed areas are called primary sensory fields and represent only about a quarter of the total. The final destination of the succession of association areas is one or both of the hippocampus and the amygdala (forward of the hypothalamus).

Adjacent to, and forward of, the sensory areas (the sensory cortex) are primarily motor areas (the motor cortex). But the sensory-motor integration and interdependence is considerable and no sharp separating line can be drawn. Tracing the motor system backwards from effectors and the spine, we once again find a fairly non-specific source of projections in the reticular formation. There are also coherent projections from the cerebellum and cerebral cortex, *inter alia*. There are also corticospinal fibres which project directly from the cortex to the spinal cord. These functions are also primarily somatic (*i.e.* voluntary).

The autonomic (*i.e.* involuntary) nervous system (*e.g.* controlling internal organs) seems to have its control centred on the hypothalamus. Fibres from the hypothalamus passing directly to the autonomic motor neurons have been found but constitute a relatively small proportion of those it projects. Most apparently project to the reticular formation. This activation-regulating and mood-sensing structure seems an important source of autonomic control, and projects to the hypothalamus. However, the most important influences on the hypothalamus appear to be the hippocampus and amygdala, which are the principal components of the limbic system and which we have already seen are the ultimate target of the sensory association areas of the cortex.

Geschwind shows how both the somatic sensory and motor cortices are specialized into regions into which the body can be mapped, yielding "two distorted homunculi"[2] — distorted because both the sensory and motor areas devoted to particular parts of the body are proportional to the amount of information and the degree of precision requisite for it. Thus the homunculi have greatly exaggerated face and hands.

Broca's and Wernicke's areas of the cortex of the left hemisphere are located respectively adjacent to (and forward of) the facial areas of the motor cortex, and adjacent to (and behind) the primary auditory cortex. They are connected by a bundle of neuronal fibres called the *arcuate fasciculus*. Adjacent to Wernicke's area, slightly above and further back towards the primary visual cortex, is the angular gyrus. Damage to this region causes dyslexia — whilst spoken language is undisturbed, the written language cannot be employed. Damage to the hippocampus (folded under the neocortex) in the temporal lobe produces an inability to learn (into LTM) new material without affecting pre-existing knowledge or STM.

In contrast with the claim of Nauta that about 70% of the neurons of the CNS lie in the cerebral cortex, Eccles suggests that the cerebellum may contain more than the rest of the CNS. The cerebellum is evidently involved in the learning of skills and in the fine control of movement and provides "corrective information that keeps the movement on target".[3]

The Neuron and the Synapse

Neurons, or nerve cells, are the building blocks of the brain ... Their forms generally fall into only a few broad categories, and most neurons share certain structural features that make it possible to distinguish three regions of the cell: the cell body, the dendrites and the axon ... The dendrites are delicate tube-like extensions that tend to branch repeatedly and form a bushy tree around the cell body. They provide the main physical surface on which the neuron receives incoming signals. The axon extends away from the cell body and provides the pathway over which signals can travel from the cell body for long distances to other parts of the brain and the nervous system.[4]

The function of a neuron is dependent on the properties of various proteins, the membranes, and the concentrations of particular ions, specifically those of sodium, potassium and calcium. Certain proteins act as pumps, exchanging ions of one element for those of another across the cell membrane, creating a potential difference (an ion gradient). Other proteins act as channels which can open to admit, selectively, particular ions. These proteins act to change, and react to changes in, membrane potential, and in combination are responsible for the firing of the neuron and the propagation of the nerve impulse (an *action potential*):

> Information is transferred from one cell to another at specialized points of contact: the synapses. A typical neuron may have anywhere from 1,000 to 10,000 synapses and may receive information from something like 1,000 other neurons. Although synapses are most often made between the axon of one cell and the dendrite of another, there are other kinds of synaptic junction ... The "firing" of a neuron ... reflects the activation of hundreds of synapses by impinging neurons. Some synapses are excitatory in that they tend to promote firing, whereas others are inhibitory and so capable of canceling signals that otherwise would excite a neuron to fire".[5]

On arrival of the action potential at a terminal button, synaptic vesicles attach to the presynaptic membrane, discharge their transmitter into the synaptic cleft, are reclaimed and refilled. The transmitter opens chemical gates in the postsynaptic membrane which allow loss of membrane potential (changes called postsynaptic potentials). Specific gates are sensitive to specific transmitters which are specific to various terminal buttons. Whether the synapse is excitatory or inhibitory is a function of the type of transmitter in the vesicles "although some transmitters are excitatory in one part of the brain and inhibitory in another".[6]

Layer and Columnar Arrangements of Neurons

Several of the major neuroanatomical structures consist of layers. In some cases these layers are differentiated by the type and shape of their neurons, and this is nowhere so evident as in the cerebellum. Layers need not be distinguished by cell type, so much as by function. Physically they may merely be recognized as fairly uniform layers, some of which are characterized by the impinging of afferents (incoming long-distance axons) or as efferents (with outgoing axons). In the visual cortex six layers are distinguished, of which the fourth is subdivided into three. This thus gives rise to the designations I, II, III, IVa, IVb, IVc, V and VI (outer to inner). Investigation of the visual system involves identifying the best stimulus for many representative cells, recorded individually by microelectrode, in each layer of each structure; first the retina, then the Lateral Geniculate Nucleus (LGN) of the thalamus, and finally the visual cortex.

The retinal ganglion and geniculate cells exhibit the well-known "on-centre/off-surround" property (or its converse). They respond optimally to roughly circular spots of light of critical size and position in the visual field. The LGN cells project largely to layer IVc whose cells show the same property. Cells outside this layer respond best to lines of specific orientation. As the distance from layer IVc increases, so does the generality or complexity of the recognized property. Thus they become less position dependent and more sensitive to motion and thickness:

> These differences from layer to layer take on added interest in view of the important discovery that fibers projecting from particular layers of the cortex have particular destinations. For example, in the visual cortex the deepest layer, layer VI, projects mainly (perhaps only) to the lateral geniculate body; layer V projects to the superior colliculus, a visual station in the mid brain; layers II and III send their projections to other parts of the cortex.[7]

There are also several other levels of phenomena in the cortex, *e.g.* size of receptive fields (the largest tend to be in layers II, V and VI) and binocular vision (layer IV is solely monocular).

Even more interesting than the evidence for horizontal structuring is that for vertical structuring of the cortex. In this case there are not quite the same anatomical cues, since the physical differences between neurons and cortical texture occur only in a vertical dimension.

Considering again the visual cortex, and comparing the results of vertical and near horizontal penetrations on preferences first for a particular eye, secondly for a particular receptive field, and thirdly for a particular orientation, we find some interesting results. The vertical penetrations produce little change in these variables; but the horizontal penetrations produce very consistent changes. We find that ocular dominance changes every 0.4mm, receptive field changes every one or two millimetres by a shift corresponding with the size of the receptive field, and the preferred orientation changes by on average about 10 degrees each 25 or 50$^{\mu m}$ (the direction of rotation occasionally reversing suddenly).[8]

The existence of intriguing columns is not limited to the visual system. For example Jacobson discusses columnar arrangement of spinal motorneurons and Hubel describes similar size columns in the somatic sensory area alternating between pressure and touch sensitivity:

> In the somatic sensory area ... the basic topography is a map of the opposite half of the body, but superimposed on that there is a twofold system of subdivisions, with some areas where neurons respond to the movement of the joints or pressure on the skin and other areas where they respond to touch or the bending of hairs. As is the case of the visual columns, a complete set here (one area for each kind of neuron) occupies a distance of about a millimetre. These subdivisions are analogous to ocular-dominance columns in that they are determined in the first instance by inputs to the cortex ... rather than by connections in the cortex, such as those that determine orientation selectivity and the associated system of orientation regions.[9]

This then raises the question of how these columns are formed, and to what extent they are innate or learned, self-organized or genetically determined.

Neighbourhoods

The processing which takes place in the cortex is largely local, confined to one or two cubic millimetres. This is the idea of a neighbourhood. Nowhere is it clearer than in the basic retinal, LGN and layer IV on-centre/off-surround cells in which local inhibitory processing produces a very sharply defined response.

We should note that connectivity, which is the problem highlighted by Minsky and Papert[10] is not a recognized property of the cortex. A simple experiment, such as bringing two fingers or pencils slowly together about 3 or 4cm in front of one eye, shows that loss of disconnectivity (with accompanying distortion) occurs prematurely at a gross level.

Anatomical studies show clear evidence that the interaction between neurons in the brain is always fairly localized, and that interneurons operate within a neighbourhood of the expected order. This is the basis of the distinguishing of afferents and efferents which mediate non-local communication between different areas of the brain.

So far we have looked at the gross structural anatomical side of neurology. We turn now to consider the physiology of the neuron itself, and the threshold and refractory effects.

An important property of the firing of a neuron is that the neuron is essentially a binary device which detects if the aggregate of excitatory over inhibitory stimulus strength exceeds a certain threshold. If the neuron has not fired recently, it will be in the resting state and exhibit its characteristic resting threshold. Thus it acts as a yes/no binary decision function on the question of whether the aggregate stimulus exceeds its current "firing" threshold.

For a brief period after a neuron fires, the absolute refractory period, the axon cannot transmit another action potential, *viz.* the threshold is essentially infinite. However this period is followed by another interval, the relative refractory period, during which the firing threshold is greater than the resting threshold, and decreasing. This in turn is followed by the supernormal period during which the threshold sinks below the resting threshold and rises again. This is followed by another subnormal period during which the threshold is somewhat greater than normal but settles down eventually into the resting state.

A maintained level of stimulus activity will result in refiring at a frequency directly related to the aggregate level of stimulus, whose inter-spike period lies between the absolute refractory period and the total refractory period. Even if the aggregate stimulus level is below the resting threshold, it is possible for firing to be retriggered in the subnormal period and sustained at a still lower frequency. The neuron thus acts as an analogue device whose output is a certain firing rate. This property is frequently appealed to, to argue for hypotheses of higher level systems of neurons, which exhibit a degree of sophistication unwarranted in relation to a single neuron.

In the computational neurolinguistic model of Gigley, however, the refractory state plays the specific binary role of blocking "accidental misfiring of information".[11]

Habituation and Sensitization *vs* Fatigue and Adaption

Continued stimulation of a neuron or a receptor results in cell fatigue: its activity will drop towards zero, and for a time its sensitivity is reduced. This effect is automatically and quickly reversed once the fatiguing stimulus is withdrawn. This has been demonstrated most remarkably in the visual system by preventing eye movements, thus fixing the image on a particular set of retinal cells. The image is recognized instantly, but disappears almost immediately.

A related phenomenon is sensory adaption. Cells tend to respond to any increase or decrease in the strength of a stimulus, and thus to operate relative to the immediate stimulation history. The best known demonstrations of this use heat and cold adaption, whereby warm water is sensed as hot or cold depending on whether the hands have been exposed to cold or hot water beforehand.

There are other phenomena which have been confused with these, namely habituation and sensitization. But these represent longer term effects and are mediated by the presynapses, rather than receptors or postsynapses. They are in fact forms of learning, unlike fatigue or adaption, and appear to be correlates of behaviouristic learning, involving absence or presence of activating stimuli.

There appear to be long-term and short-term habituation effects, of which at least the latter are mediated by a decrease in the inflow of calcium ions.[12] Both are strongly correlated with a change in synaptic effectiveness. The synaptic mechanisms proposed for sensory-motor habituation are facets of a more generally applicable paradigm of synaptic plasticity.

We know that synapses may be either inhibitory or excitatory. This corresponds to the transmitter having a hyperpolarizing or a depolarizing effect on the postsynaptic cell. There are different classes of neuron with different characteristic shapes which can occupy characteristic layers of a region. This is seen clearly in the cerebellar cortex where we can identify a class of inhibitory neuron which selectively avoids synapse with its closest neighbour, but inhibits half a dozen further afield.[13]

We saw earlier that certain visual processing neurons in the retina, the LGN and the cerebral cortex layer IVc, have a specific on-centre/off-surround characteristic. This is a picturesque example of the effect of having the peak of inhibition at a greater radius from a cluster of cells than the peak of excitation. We also saw that we could regard any square millimetre of a layer of the cortex as, in a sense, a unit, which is one layer of a larger unit. This is a slab of the cortex with all these layers, and a cubic millimetre or two in volume. The distinct cells in such a unit appear to have characteristic connection functions.

First, we will assume that each cell is basically excitatory or inhibitory, as in the cerebellar cortex. Second, we will note that neurons tend to function as a distributor of connectivity probability over distance. Third, there may also be an average efficacy distribution function on the same domain. The net interaction function for a given cell type typically falls off fairly quickly as a function of distance. The resultant interplay of different excitatory and inhibitory functions produces an annulus effect, where excitation prevails over a certain range, but inhibitory effects prevail further afield. Even further away, the result is once more (weakly) excitatory.

We show this diagrammatically as a simplistic model in a recent paper.[14] The model shows that the interaction functions are extremely natural, and close to what would be expected from purely geometric considerations.

One particularly interesting feature is that the interaction function for some spot or line detector cells closely resembles a cosine Gaussian, or even a symmetric Gabor function. That of the edge detector or motion sensitive cells also resemble the sine Gaussian, or a symmetric Gabor function. Such functions provide the best tradeoff for frequency against localization, that is to say they minimize the product of the errors. They also form a complete mathematical basis for approximation of an arbitrary function. Furthermore, there is evidence of pairing of cells with odd and even profiles in the optimum 90Æ phase shift.[15] The interaction function is important to the consideration of self-organization, and to some of our experiments.

Plasticity and Engram

The idea that memory is concerned with synaptic connections, and that learning involves changes in synaptic strength, has a history of well over 60 years.[16] The specific proposal that the change was associated with a correlation between presynaptic and postsynaptic firing, was first made by Hebb in 1949.[17]

The hypothesis that the synapse is reinforced if the firing of the afferent fibre leads to firing of the postsynaptic neuron has come to be known as synaptic plasticity, although in fact it is only one of several possible explanations of how synaptic plasticity works. At least in the short-term, synaptic plasticity seems to have a neurophysiological basis, mainly in the presynaptic terminal. But there is no clear indication of a correlation mechanism operating implicitly there.

The earliest form of plasticity which had been advocated seems to have been specifically synaptic. It was supposedly characterized by a reduction of synaptic resistance by the passage of an action potential – a function of frequency and intermittance of firing. These proposals were severely criticized by Lashley, mainly on the basis that it was a psychologically motivated hypothesis, and that in fact there was no direct evidence of synaptic plasticity. There was also evidence against a drop in synaptic resistance.

Recently there has been a move against the Hebbian conception of correlation plasticity, and a return to something approaching a utilization activated increase in synaptic strength. Nonetheless Hebbian plasticity is still one of the main hypotheses in neuroscience today. The habituation evidence seems to suggest a reverse relationship, since the strength of the synaptic connection apparently reduces the more the connection is used. But the sensitization evidence indicates that under activation use does produce a positive effect.

Another possible form of learning and memory mediated by plasticity is the plasticity of the neuron itself – in particular the cell body (the soma). This proposal has as long a pedigree as synaptic plasticity and it has frequently been identified with Long Term Memory (LTM). Recent experiments suggest that certain neurons do have such an endoneural (somatic locus) memory property.[18] These experiments have, incidentally, also been performed on a snail, the edible *Helix pomatia* – on neurons which have been isolated and subjected *in vitro* to a classical conditioning regime.

Such plasticity is a type of modification mediated by use. But it is not the transmittance which is increased but the firing threshold of the (presynaptic) cell that is decreased.

The role of RNA in synaptic plasticity and memory has been shown by Matthies and Kandel.[19] They demonstrated that during learning, RNA and related products are formed, since radioactive precursors are incorporated. Earlier work showed that stimulation by learning significantly increases the amount of RNA per neuron. No other cell produces nearly so much RNA as do neurons.[20]

The specificity of the RNA produced is controversial. Although these results have been with us now for over two decades (and the most controversial ones were duplicated within three years in at least fourteen independent laboratories) they remain controversial. They have not been taken seriously in many quarters, and have confused rather than clarified the problem of the mechanism and localization of memory. McConnell demonstrated in 1960 that "transfer of acquired behaviour tendencies"[21] was possible, through untrained flatworms (*Planaria*) being given mashed trained flatworms. More intriguing still, if a flatworm was cut in half it would regenerate so that both resultant animals would retain the learned response. The results have also been achieved by injecting the flatworms with RNA extracted from trained animals.

An undergraduate student in Los Angeles, who had covered this in a course, surprised his lecturer by claiming to have repeated the experiment with rats, by injecting an untrained rat with a brain extract derived from a trained rat. They then collaborated to reproduce the experiment.[22] In 1965 this was independently demonstrated in half a dozen laboratories. Following disbelief, the experiments were refined and repeated on other animals, including experiments in which rats were injected with extracts from trained mice or hamsters or guinea pigs. Other factors were eliminated, including experiments with differential learning, and the injection of RNA from untrained controls.

How do these RNA transfer characteristics relate to plasticity? How can global introduction of trained RNA affect the responses of many individual neurons? It has been proposed that there may be some common mechanism with genetic memory. It is also conceivable that there is some sort of labelling mechanism responsible for these effects.[23] The evidence does not prove that RNA incorporates the memory; it may also be that locally (intraneurally) it is involved in neural or synaptic plasticity.

Eventually, the mediation of RNA will be incorporated into a neurological model, but no specific hypotheses have yet appeared.

Taxonomy of Plasticity

Most models of association, or conditioning do not depend on whether the site of plasticity is endoneural, presynaptic, postsynaptic or some combination of these. Some authors try to show that particular physiological processes fit their particular mathematical models. In many instances, though, the theorists are not even willing to commit themselves to a one synapse, or even one neuron model. Nonetheless, it is usual to assume a synaptic locale. This need not reduce the generality of the consequent discussion, despite the fact that many proposals clearly do not fit known processes.

The basic concept of synaptic plasticity is extremely simple: somehow the synaptic strengths come to represent the "desired" connections or correlations between neurons. This still leaves plenty of scope for different models of how the synaptic efficacies change with respect to the firing and timing relationships between the presynaptic and postsynaptic neurons. The first distinction in our model of plasticity is whether we have a Hebbian correlation model, or an utilization model. In the Hebbian model both cells must fire for reinforcement to occur (S-R association), whereas in utilization plasticity the reinforcement occurs in relation to just one cell firing. The extent in this model is determined either specifically by other reinforcing afferents, or generally by activational level (allowing S-S association). This distinction is blurred in the classical conditioning paradigm, where the UCS plays multiple roles as stimulus, reinforcer and activator. The strict Hebbian model has a distinguished input with an unmodifiable "synapse" acting as a reinforcing control signal.[24] But usually the Hebbian postulate is taken to involve just the simple pairing. In this case the UCS is taken to be strong enough to have the reinforcing effect, simply because it causes the cell to fire strongly.[25]

In the *Aplysia* study, repeated firing of the cell decreased efficacy. Evidently the occasional noxious stimulus is necessary to prevent habituation to the recurrent stimulus. Clearly, either the stimuli or their effects must overlap temporally to effect habituation. Examples are found in transmitter residue, refractive state or activation. Such transmitter/mediator mechanisms have been identified empirically by several workers.[26] The majority of theoretical accounts and models of plasticity have also proposed such a mechanism.[27]

Note that Marr[28] and many other early theorists use the strict Hebbian model with the specialized "teacher" inputs, which gives rise to the perceptron family of models. Kupfermann's earlier research on *Aplysia* was done using these distinctions, and supported both synaptic and endoneural plasticity, proposing both specific and non-specific reinforcement models.[29]

However, the usual formulations of the Hebbian proposals are founded on the proposition that synaptic learning occurs as a strengthening whenever the presynaptic firing results in a postsynaptic firing. This may be characterized more pragmatically as a condition of "coincidence of activity"[30] which does not depend on any particular theory of how the synaptic modification occurs. It would have to be mediated by some sort of direct feedback from the postsynaptic cell. Reduction of synaptic strength is then seen as being a function of disuse or reallocation of resources. Increase of synaptic strength is independent of whether the postsynaptic firing was "useful".

This discussion leads us not only to consider whether the synaptic change was a direct function of postsynaptic firing or not, but whether it was a function of activational level or explicit positive reinforcement. It also raises the questions about the relative timings of the various firings and/or states, of whether the fundamental plastic change involves strengthening or weakening, of whether the converse change is possible at all.

The models of Barto, Sutton and Klopf[31] and that of Matthies[32] are specifically related to the classical conditioning paradigm. They specify the modification of the input weights of those inputs which fired, providing the postsynaptic cell fired. Sutton compares a spectrum of different models in relation to classical conditioning. His eventual preference is a correlative model which can be strengthened or weakened. Sutton acknowledges three possible temporal interrelationships: the usual simple simultaneity condition involving instantaneous values, the delay factor used by some to explain classical conditioning timings, and a trace or history based on the assumption that there are effects of firing which subside gradually and may accumulate.

There is also a question about the quantitative extent of the modification. Is it a constant increment, a function of the synaptic input trace, or both? Sutton and Malsburg both make it a linear function of both the traces or signals. Many of the older theories make use of binary functions acting as threshold elements.

Klopf makes another general distinction concerning the unit as a system. Is it seeking *homeostasis*: to maintain an equilibrium of some set of variables; or *heterostasis*: to achieve some other, better state of some variable? This latter proposal, which he advocates, is directly related to reinforcement. In particular Klopf regards depolarization (movement toward a firing state) as positively reinforcing. By contrast with the perceptron-like specific reinforcement signals of what he calls "restricted reinforcement models", the heterostate is a "generalized reinforcement model".[33]

The advantage of Klopf's model is that it gives a very simple condition for reinforcement. If after a cell fires it is further depolarized, the synaptic strengths needed for excitation increase (positive reinforcement). On the other hand, if it is then inhibited (hyperpolarized) the eligible excitatory synapses are weakened. Thus repeated firing without any other form of external affectation will increase its tendency to fire. This leads at face value to predictions contrary to what Kandel reports, but consistent with what Sinz reports.[34]

Klopf considers the interplay of the various distinctions relating to synaptic plasticity in the course of developing his model: of 256 possible combinations he eliminates all but 12 as being blatantly unbalanced. On the remaining freedoms, he concludes that one can assume, without loss of generality, that all synaptic strengths may increase and can only increase, irrespective of cell or synapse type.

Normalization

One essential element of any theory of plasticity and neural organization is the question of normalization. There is a danger that a neuron or a network model will oversaturate or undersaturate. There is an intrinsic problem with the monotonic plasticity adopted arbitrarily by Klopf; the model allows synaptic strengths to rise but not to fall.

Some models have dealt with the problem arbitrarily by determining that the total of the synaptic strengths, thresholds and/or firing levels of a neuron or local network must remain constant. Therefore the model simply includes a final step which determines the unnormalized total activity or strength and reduces all activity or strengths proportionately to bring it back to the canonical level. An example of such an arbitrary approach is Malsburg's original self-organizing network.[35] The approach is quite reasonable, but explicit global normalization is computationally horrendous.

Goldschlager's model provides and explains normalization as a natural consequence of the model:

> The net effect of each column continuously adjusting its level of habituation to the background noise is to tend to keep the overall level of activity over the entire memory surface within reasonable bounds.[36]

The most detailed implicit formulation and analysis of normalization is that of Grossberg and his colleagues mediated through the recurrent inhibitory network.[37]

An important principle in normalization is *competition*: many modern neural network theories are founded on this concept. Since there is sometimes interference in learning, especially where concepts are closely related, competition may result in some direct reallocation of resources, similar to that modelled by Malsburg.[38]

Decay *vs* Atrophy

Another explanation for normalization is the natural tendency for synaptic strengths to decay. This explicitly provides that correlative synaptic changes are monotonic, but that forgetting occurs unless continuously reinforced. To stabilize the network, the decay must depend on at least three factors: activation, competition and age. This approach is the basis of our models. But decay does not necessarily explain habituation: decay is a result of disuse of a path but habituation results from misuse of a path.

An extreme form of disabling of a neural pathway is by degeneration of neurons or synapses. There is well known evidence of atrophy of neurons in the face of disruption of the nervous system (*e.g.* removal of a kitten's whiskers resulting in degeneration of related neurons).[39] But there is little evidence of atrophy as a result of learning. There is rather evidence of reorganization as a result of experience.[40]

Our discussion of plasticity made the traditional assumption that there were changes in the existing synapsing connections, but no degeneration, sprouting or shifting of synapses in learning. Since a widespread phenomenon called *sprouting* is now recognized, the scope of the term *plasticity* has been extended to this phenomenon.

> This "plasticity" is thought to be the neural basis for adaptive behaviours. In other words, the "plasticity" and "rigidity" of the neural networks may relate to the environmental versus genetic factors which underlie behaviour.[41]

A particular form of sprouting is that which is artificially lesion induced and is hence regenerative. Such sprouting is difficult to find in adults. Hence renervation following denervation in the neonate may be a residue of the ontogenetic process, and not an instance of plasticity. Nerve (*e.g.* axon or dendrite) growth has been well documented, and growth cones have been identified which appear to use some kind of search, and a protein, nerve-growth factor. These cones are both *tropic* (direction-determining) and *trophic* (growth-promoting). Interestingly nerve-growth factor is essential even in adult animals.[42]

One controversial ontogenetic hypothesis is the Gaze "shifting hypothesis" that connections can shift around, sampling sites, until the final connection has been made.[43] Other proposals have suggested that markers or labels are involved in ensuring that neurons synapse in the correct pattern, and that self-organization occurs within the constraints of specific genetic markers.[44] Jacobson argues strongly that neither labelling nor self-organization on its own is capable of explaining the evidence.

Neural Communication; Languages of the Brain

Our discussion has largely been about the processing and transmission of information from one part of the brain to another. There are considerable similarities between the signal paths, processes and processors of the different sensory-motor modalities. The sense of smell, though, is uniquely "primitive": the actual sensors are exposed neurons, and the olfactory bulb connects directly with the cortex rather than via the Geniculate Nuclei of the thalamus.

In the cortex, the projections of all modalities show similar units, layers and columns. All sensory-motor modalities have a direct spatial correspondence with an area of the cortex, giving rise to a spatio-temporal receptive field. In the case of the auditory sensorium (the organ of Corti, with its active dual bandpass spectro-spatial transducer) this represents a spectro-temporal receptive field.[45] This similarity is the reason for considering other modalities which can be studied more easily.

Natural Language is a second-signalling system: it depends on a set of symbols rather than on observation of the primary information source. Once we leave the actual sensoria, all information in the brain is recoded in a logically, and perhaps genetically, determined way. In each layer of neurons, at each level of processing, the sensory input is transformed into yet another signalling system. The language analogy suggests that parsing may be an appropriate way to describe any sensory-motor modality, and may correspond in some way to the processing within the brain. This proposition underpins our experimental programme. We propose that the processes interrelating the different modalities, and hence semantics, may be treated similarly.

The various levels of processing in the brain transform between signalling systems or languages. This suggests to us that conversely we may be able to characterize parsing in terms of transformations. This also suggests, but by no means confirms, Chomsky's theory of Transformational Generative Grammar (TGG). From a more static perspective, the transformations define mappings. In particular the cortical homunculi are, at the simplest level, topologically accurate maps of the sensory-motor interface, distorted according to the respectively requisite degrees of resolution.

Our discussion so far has been in terms of a succession of transforming levels, performing a succession of mappings and recognition processing. But this succession may not be quite so straightforward: the neural networks appear to make extensive use of recurrence. In general, the hierarchy of processing is not strictly tree structured, nor even "partially ordered" (in the mathematical sense). We saw that cells interact with their neighbours, and from this it follows that the network is cyclic: local negative feedback is an essential ingredient of the network, as is local positive feedback. It has also been proposed that resonance is at the heart of Short Term Memory (STM). Some mathematical models have focussed quite profitably on this possibility.[46]

There is also evidence of less local forms of feedback. In particular, it appears that the way-stations in the thalamus (LGN and MGN) filter information on the basis of processed information fed back from the cortex. It also appears that feedback is integral to the arousal and activity regulation function attributed to that locus. One very interesting feedback phenomenon is the greater than unity gain due to feedback to the basilar membrane of the cochlea. More sound leaves the ear than enters. This extraordinary effect is so far completely unexplained.

Templates, Demons and Sprites

Psychologists, computer scientists and other philosophers have adopted yet another group of metaphors to explain the association and pattern matching processing of the brain. The traditional formulation has been in terms of templates and their corresponding homunculi: the "demon" and "sprite". The various complex and hypercomplex cells which recognized particular patterns correspond to these active counterparts: *e.g.* one little demon shrieks when he sees a line at a particular angle moving in a particular direction.

More sophisticated "demon neurons" have been identified in some animals (*e.g.* fly and predator detectors in the frog).[47] They have also been simulated in some computational neural network models (*e.g.* the recognizers for individual letters of the alphabet[48]). Linguistic correlates of these have also been proposed in language understanding models (*e.g.* "TEMPLATES bound together by PARAPLATES ..."[49]

Various activational factors are involved in learning, and the thalamus mediates activation. It is, however, difficult to conceive how to provide motivation and activation in a computational model — the traditional behaviourist drive reduction paradigm does not seem applicable. This leaves us with the psychological phenomenon of reinforcement and its apparent difficulties, with the metaphor of the hedonistic neuron and its self-activational properties, and with the poorly understood sensory-motor synthesis performed by the thalamus.

In our experiments we have used no explicit reinforcement, nor have we separately synthesized any activational signal. Thus the motivation of the system corresponds closest either to curiosity, or to hedonism, since it is success in finding possible matches that provides the sole drive for the systems. In the future, models will need to provide reinforcing, activational and/or motivational input.

Neural Nets

We now look at some neural network models with memory, association and temporal sequence properties. We start by considering the holographic analogy and the abstract, temporal and spatial association models. Abstracting the associative properties of a hologram, the system is a function of two or three spaces. We can simply distinguish input space from storage space, but it is more useful to divide the input into separate spaces for the patterns which will act as key and the patterns which will be associated. If we consider the spaces (respectively *BA*, *BB* and *BC*) as linear and finite, consisting of N consecutively numbered points, we may use any binary linear surjection from *BA/BB* to *BC*, such as the mean, sum or difference *modulo N*, or absolute difference. In each case there will exist a unique inverse binary linear surjection from *BB/BC* to *BA*, and from *BC/BA* to *BB*. The "digital correlograph" of Willshaw uses this model with the *modulo* difference (or constant cyclic displacement) function.[50] If each pattern consists of M points, and R pairs of pattern are stored, we can be sure that a particular stored pattern will give rise to M mappings to each of the M points of the associated pattern. The probability of spurious points exceeding this threshold of M can be calculated on the basis that the recorded patterns are uncorrelated.

With Willshaw's modulo difference function, shifting of the patterns does not affect retrieval. This is known as *displacement invariance*. This model may be physically (digitally) realized with BC as a set of switches which are latched on when selected by an active mapping from BA/BB, with BA and BB outputs mediated by threshold detectors. The number of pattern pairs that can be stored in such a system is rather small (for $N = 256$, $M = 8$, the theoretical expected maximum number of pairs which may be stored for accurate retrieval is given by R = 2). But we can sacrifice "the displacement invariance of the correlograph for a much greater storage capacity".[51]

The structure proposed is a two dimensional associative net in which the size of BC is increased to N-$4P$. The function can now be any bijection, but the natural matrix labelling is the most straight forward. This net has the same threshold M as the correlograph, but a more relaxed capacity limitation. We could also pursue the different invariance properties and arrive at a range and surjection appropriate to any rotation, expansion, translation, reflection or combination of these. There is some evidence for the brain having banks of ranges insensitive to diverse combinations of the basic transformations.

In general, the actual cognitive tasks consist in recalling the appropriate context given an actual portion of input from one domain. In this respect, auto-correlation is indicated rather than some artificial division between input domains. However there is a natural division of the sensory-motor domain into the individual somatic and sensory-motor modalities.

Similar effects can be achieved in the temporal and acoustic domains. The holophone of Longuet-Higgins and Willshaw uses a bank of frequency filters with equal spacing and bandwidth.[52] These are integrators which store the energy at the respective bandwidth, and amplifiers whose gain is increased proportional to the stored reading. An excerpt from any one of several stored signals will evoke the remainder of the signal. This is analogous to Fourier analysis: whilst the hologram stores the square of the Fourier transform, the holophone stores the square of the Laplace transform, and the cortex utilizes Gaussian-like interaction functions which have similar properties.

A similar spectro-temporal neural model has been developed by Spinelli.[53] Also, spatio-temporal models have been proposed involving synaptic plasticity or coupling which produces autoassociation through recurrence in an associative network.[54] Such models have been taught to display a portion of the alphabet (typically A to H) starting from an association of an input pattern.

Cells: Neurons and Clusters

We have seen the basic principles which underlie the physiology of the neuron, the synapse and the brain. But we do not yet sufficiently understand the connections between individual neurons, so as to be able to produce a theory of the operation of any part of the brain, based on the anatomy and physiology of the brain. But we do have an idea about individual classes of neuron, can characterize them by layer, and group them into columns. Whilst we can deduce the interaction functions between neurons within a given column (or between adjacent columns), we cannot be sure that they can be attributed to interactions solely of the neurons of a given class. On the other hand, we can be almost certain that the interaction functions cannot be attributed to the connectivity of individual neurons.They are the product of interaction between different classes of neuron which comprise or transcend a unit. Indeed it seems that no neuron has both a direct excitatory, and a direct inhibitory action, on other neurons.

The function of the inhibitory interneurons is far from being understood; and we do not know the extent and purpose of the recurrence in the interaction functions. For these reasons, many models assume a unit intermediate to the neural cell and the layer/hypercolumn intersections. The layer/column intersection itself is a candidate for such a unit. For this reason, the word "cell" should be seen as an abstraction which is more likely to refer to a cluster of cells than to a single cell. Sometimes, as in Malsburg, the unit is thought of as separate excitatory and inhibitory components.[55]

There are known clusters of neurons which act as a unit, and whose internal structure is very inadequately understood. These cells are called ganglia. For example, the processing in the retina is completed in the retinal ganglia which project to the Lateral Geniculate Nucleus (LGN).

We are now going to return specifically to the question of memory. Where is memory located? Where is the memory trace, the engram? Lashley concluded his 1950 paper "In Search of the Engram" with this comment:

> This series of experiments has yielded a good bit of information about what and where the memory trace is not. It has discovered nothing directly of the real nature of the engram. I sometimes feel, in reviewing the evidence on the localization of the memory trace, that the necessary conclusion is that learning just is not possible. Nevertheless, in spite of such evidence against, learning does sometimes occur.[56]

This comment reflects a specifically locationist viewpoint. It wants to be able to say "this cluster of neurons is responsible for storing this particular memory." The contrary viewpoint, fundamental to the holographic and self-organizing network paradigms, is that memory, the engram, is somehow spread throughout a network, in the plasticity of the connections, and in concept recognition memory. This focus avoids the question of the engram as such, but concentrates on the explanation of the properties of the brain that we have discovered, such as the layers and columns. As far as the engram is concerned, we still have no direct evidence of the method or locus of storage of higher concepts, and our models have not been able to approach the complexity where they might be explained. The research described later is a step toward showing how natural language phenomena can be fitted into the connectionist framework.

Self-Organization vs Genetic Determination

"Learning" has in recent years become mistakenly associated with weak "self-organizing" systems that often start out in a random manner, and usually end up having learned only the most trivial things. This is *not* the kind of learning examined here ... We need to examine the middle ground, between the extremes of the self-organizing and the pre-programmed systems. The limits of each are becoming more and more apparent. Self-organizing systems often *sound* intriguing, but they just don't *do* anything interesting—their performance is usually abominable. Pre-programmed systems bear a small amount of fruit for an enormous amount of effort at analysis and programming, but they show virtually no generalization; and increasing effort gives diminishing returns.[57]

Self-organizing systems have a surprising power, of which Uhr would have been aware, although the first effective demonstration by Malsburg was published in the same year (1973). Malsburg simply specified a unit cell with inhibitory and excitatory components (in sub-layers) which resulted in an excitatory centre, and inhibitory surround lateral interaction function. A small piece of simulated retina was then projected onto a small piece of cortex so that every cell of the retina was in the receptive field of each unit of the cortex. A plasticity function was defined so that afferent (retinal input) synapses were strengthened if the cell and its afferent fired together, using a conservation of total synaptic strength requirement to maintain normalization. The initial values of the synapses were assumed to be random within the feasible range. A simulation for one hundred presentations of nine different retinal images representing lines at nine different angles then resulted in almost every cortical unit developing a sharp preference for one particular angle. Furthermore, the gradual shift of preferred angle corresponded with the columnar arrangement within the visual cortex.

Hirai produced a similar simulation: with five levels and recurrence from the fifth back to the first, using precisely specified excitatory and inhibitory strengths between levels. Again, the only modifiable synapses were the afferents. After twenty presentations of 26 letters, the system had successfully learned to distinguish the letters of the alphabet. In this case there was no formation of columns, and no redundancy, but exactly one cell learned to respond to each letter. The effect of the recurrence was to act as a competitive maximizer or threshold to ensure that only the strongest response to any given letter in the first level actually gave rise to an output in the fourth level.

On the other hand, there is evidence of tropic substances, markers and labels, which directly guide, allow or disallow the formation of connections. For example:

> It is of considerable importance that several antibodies were isolated that label the mechanosensory cells mediating the motor responses to the environmental stimuli touch, pressure and noxious mechanical.[58]

There is still considerable debate about the role of self-organization, with adherence to totally innate specific genetic specification on the one hand, and proposals for actual physical self-organization at the other extreme:

> According to one interpretation, interaction with the external world does not enrich the system in any significant way; its action would be limited to triggering preestablished programs. It would stabilize a synaptic organization that had already been genetically specified. This is the attitude adopted by Hubel and Wiesel, Chomsky, and Fodor. On the other hand, the "empiricists" postulate that to a large extent, the activity of the system specifies the connectivity, for example by orienting the growth of the nerve terminals or by tracing pathways in more or less random networks.[59]

There is a dichotomy between innately specified and learned structure, but there are quite separate dichotomies between self-organization and genetic specification, and between changes in physical structure and development of logical organization. The first diatribe hinges on the question of experience, and would be decided if (as indicated by some evidence presented), the columns are present without any experience, and hence without learning. This obviously would discount the models we have just discussed. However, self-organization is not limited to experientially guided development, and so the second spectrum turns out to be relevant. For example:

> Turing (1952) has proposed a "chemical theory of morphogenesis" which can account for the development of patterns consisting of stripes or discrete patches or spots. He showed how cells that are coupled through permeable junctions—plastic synapses—or are able to interact by diffusion, starting with uniform chemical conditions in all cells, can develop marked nonuniform conditions that are initiated by small fluctuations that are always present in the system ... Turing's model and other similar models in which more than one morphogen interact or in

which there are inhibitory as well as excitatory interactions between cells ... can result in the formation of repeating patterns such as bands (*e.g.* cerebral cortical ocular dominance columns) or peaks and valleys (*e.g.* cerebral cortical barrels or columns) ... Although the maximum wavelength that can be generated by Turing systems is about 1mm, or about 60 cells $15^{\mu m}$ in diameter, the wave can be repeated, so that the size of the system is unlimited.[60]

It is likely that labels are involved in the genetic determination of connections, but they are few, and distinguished at a gross level of modality, rather than more specifically. This level of evidence would point to the labelling being inadequate to determine cortical columns without the mediation of self-organizing processes, whether experientially or randomly initiated. Thus it would be parsimonious to suppose that direct innate specification would specify the gross formation of the homuncular mappings and general development of the nervous system, and that self-organization constrained by these boundary conditions would be responsible for the final finer structural detail. This may or may not always be influenced by environmental factors.

Willshaw and Malsburg, whose models we considered above, have developed a variant of the Malsburg scheme which is given genetically determined boundary conditions of the form of a trace of spatial ordering of the afferents. This weak ordering then allows self-organization to determine columns on the basis of random firings and the ranges of the interactions of the interaction functions.

Some of the latest reports of contemporary research focus on olfaction (the sense of smell) and provide additional support for connectivism and self-organization. Two such projects are those of Walter Freemen at the University of California, Berkeley and Gary Lynch at the University of California, Irvine.

> Vision, the best understood of the brain's capabilities, is organized in a much more regular and less creative way, at least at the lower levels ... The main difference between vision and smell is topographical—you use your eyes to locate the position of things and to identify them, while smell only identifies things ... Several independent lines of evidence point to the fact that the pyriform cortex contains circuits with special characteristics ... The design is "iterative combinatorial", and ... includes feedback loops ... Each nerve cell sends out long connections which instead of contacting just one other cell, contact a series of different cells ... with the result that a grid is built up ... Its critical feature was that the strengths of the connections could be tuned ... The activity of an enzyme called calpain is thought to increase if a synapse ... is used frequently with the result that the junction is restructured to open up a new channel of communication between the neurons.[61]

Redundancy

The connectionist viewpoint carries with it the concept of a highly redundant system. This may very well be true. There appears quite frequently to be a large overlap between the functions of various neurons.
Moreover it is known that it is possible to destroy 10 percent of certain
areas of the brain without causing much disfunction, and to continue to
do so until all of it has been destroyed, yet still retain the function. However if the whole area is destroyed in one go, the function is lost. Thus it
appears that other areas are, given time, able to take over the functions
of nearby regions. This has also been observed in terms of the gradual
development of lesions caused by brain tumour.

One of the essential properties of holographic memory and related
associative systems is their remarkable tolerance to ablation. In the case
of the hologram it is known that what is sacrificed as the effective area of
the hologram is reduced is essentially resolution. If one considers the
self-organizational paradigm, the interpolation of waves of distinct but
repeated detectors is quite likely to produce apparently redundant cells.
But what appears to be redundancy may hide subtle differences, as in
the hologram, or may become discriminatory by learning of subtle differences.

New research published in 1988[62] gives substantial evidence that individual clusters of nerve cells in the brain learn to respond to individual
letter patterns. Researchers probed single cells in an area of the brain
known as the medial temporal lobe. They found that particular neuron
groups seemed to respond strongly to preferred word patterns. The associated contextual information is probably stored elsewhere in the
brain than the hippocampus where cells respond strongly to individual
words with no evidence of change during repetition. Only thirty-nine
cells were recorded, but about seventy per cent showed a strong preference for a particular word. The explanation seems to be that particular words set off a particular sequence of events in the brain, specific to
that word, though recent experiments happen to have probed one of the
many thousands of cells probably associated with the recognition of an
individual word. This result confirms the growing conviction amongst
workers in this field that networks of cells form the basis for much of the
brain's processing. The attempt to reproduce the acquisition patterns of
the brain in artificial learning mechanisms must, eventually, be based
firmly on such work in the neurosciences.

Notes to Chapter Seven

1. Nauta, W. J. H., and M. Feirtag, "The Organization of the Brain", *Sci. Amer.*, Vol.241 (September, 1979), pp.78-105; Geschwind, N., "Specializations of the Human Brain", *Sci. Amer.*, Vol.241 (September, 1979), pp.158-171.
2. *Op. cit.*, p.160.
3. Eccles, J.C., M. Ito, and J. Szentagothai, *The Cerebellum as a Neuronal Machine* (Springer-Verlag, 1967), p.314.
4. Stevens, C.F., "The Neuron", *Sci. Amer.* Vol. 241 (September, 1979), p.49.
5. *Op. cit.*, p.49ff.
6. Iversen, L.L., "The Chemistry of the Brain", *Sci. Amer.* Vol.241 (September, 1979), pp.112-3.
7. Hubel, D.H., "The Brain (Introduction)", *Sci. Amer.* Vol.241 (September, 1979), p.136.
8. *Op. cit.*, p.36ff.
9. *Op. cit.*, p.144; also Jacobson, M., *Developmental Neurobiology* (Plenum Press, New York, NY, 1978), p.359.
10. Minsky, M., and S. Papert, *Perceptrons* (MIT Press, 1969).
11. Gigley, H.M., "Artificial Intelligence meets Brain Theory: An Integrated Approach to Simulation Modelling of Natural Language Processing", in R. Trappl, ed., *Proceedings of the Sixth European Meeting on Cybernetics and Systems Research (North Holland, 1982)*, p.127.
12. Kandel, E. R., "Small Systems of Neurons", *Sci. Amer..* Vol. 241 (September, 1979), pp.60-77.
13. Eccles, J.C., M. Ito, and J. Szentagothai, *The Cerebellum as a Neuronal Machine* (Springer-Verlag, 1967).
14. Powers, David M. W., "Lateral Interaction Behaviour Derived from Neural Packing Considerations", *DCS Report No 8317, Department of Computer Science* (University of New South Wales, Australia, April, 1983).
15. Pollen, D. A., and S. F. Ronner, *IEEE Trans Sys. Man. Cyb.*, Vol. SMC-13 (September, 1983), p.909; Sakitt, B., and H. B. Barlow, "A Model for the Economical Encoding of the Visual Image in the Cerebral Cortex", *Biol. Cyb.*, Vol. 43 (1982), pp.97-108.
16. Kupfermann, I., and H. Pinsker, "Cellular Models of Learning and Cellular Mechanisms of Plasticity in Aplysia", in K. H. Pribram and D. E. Broadbent, eds, *Biology of Memory* (Academic Press, 1970), pp.163-174; Lashley, K.S., "Studies of Cerebral Function in Learning, VI, The Theory that Synaptic Resistance is Reduced by the Passage of the Nerve Impulse" (Reprinted from *Psychol. Rev.*, 1924, 31, 369-375), in F. A. Beach, D. O. Hebb, C. T. Morgan and H. W. Nissen, eds, *The Neurophysiology of Lashley* (McGraw-Hill, 1960), pp.136-141.
17. Hebb, D.O., *Organization and Behaviour* (Wiley, New York, 1949).
18. Sinz, Rainer, and Mark R. Rosenzweig, *Psychophysiology: Memory, Motivation and Event-related Potentials in Mental Operations* (VEB Gustav Fischer Verlag, Jena and Berlin, GDR, 1983); Grechenko, T.N., Rainer Sinz, and E. N. Sokolov, "Neuronal Memory: Localization and Stimulus Discrimination", in *Psychophysiology: Memory, Motivation and Event-related Potentials in Mental*

Operations, ed. Rainer Sinz and Mark R. Rosenzweig (VEB Gustav Fischer, 1983), pp.131-135.

19. Matthies, H., "Memory Formation: A Model of Corresponding Neuronal Processes", in *Psychophysiology: Memory, Motivation and Event-related Potentials* in Mental Operations, Rainer Sinz and Mark R. Rosenzweig, eds. (VEB Gustav Fischer, 1983), pp.31-38; Kandel, E. R., "Small Systems of Neurons", *Sci. Amer..* Vol. 241 (September, 1979), pp.60-77.

20. Hyden, H., "The Question of a Molecular Basis for the Memory Trace", in K. H. Pribram and D. E. Broadbent, eds, *Biology of Memory* (Academic Press, 1970), pp.101-119.

21. McConnell, James V., T. Shigehisa, and H. Salive, "Attempts to Transfer Approach and Avoidance Responses by RNA Injections in Rats", in K. H. Pribram and D. E. Broadbent, eds, *Biology of Memory* (Academic Press, 1970), pp.129-159.

22. Jakobson, A. L., and J. M. Schlecter, "Chemical Transfer of Training: Three Years Later", in K. H. Pribram and D. E. Broadbent, eds, *Biology of Memory* (Academic Press, 1970), pp.123-128.

23. Sinz, Rainer, and Mark R. Rosenzweig, *Psychophysiology: Memory, Motivation and Event-related Potentials in Mental Operations* (VEB Gustav Fischer Verlag, Jena and Berlin, GDR, 1983), p.119.

24. Fukushima, K., "Cognitron: A Self-organizing Multilayered Neural Network", *Biol. Cyb.*, Vol. 20 (1975), p.122.

25. Sutton, R.S., and A. G. Barto, "Towards a Modern Theory of Adaptive Networks: Expectation and Prediction", *Psych. Rev.*, Vol. 88 (1981), p.138f.

26. Matthies, H., "Memory Formation: A Model of Corresponding Neuronal Processes", in *Psychophysiology: Memory, Motivation and Event-related Potentials in Mental Operations*, Rainer Sinz and Mark R. Rosenzweig, eds. (VEB Gustav Fischer, 1983), pp.31-38; Kandel, E. R., "Small Systems of Neurons", *Sci. Amer..* Vol. 241 (September, 1979), pp.60-77; Tsukahara, N., "Synaptic Plasticity in the Mammalian Central Nervous System", *Ann. Rev. Neurosci.*, Vol. 4 (1981), pp.351-379.

27. Melkonian, D.S., H. H. Mkrtchian, and V. V. Fanardjian, "Simulation of Learning Processes in Neuronal Networks of the Cerebellum", *Biol. Cyb.*, Vol.45, (1982), p.80.

28. Marr, D., "A Theory of Cerebellar Cortex", *J. Physiol.*, Vol.202 (1969), pp.437-470.

29. Kupfermann, I., and H. Pinsker, "Cellular Models of Learning and Cellular Mechanisms of Plasticity in Aplysia", in K. H. Pribram and D. E. Broadbent, eds, *Biology of Memory* (Academic Press, 1970), pp.163-174.

30. Malsburg, C. von der, "Self-Organization of Orientation Selective Cells in the Striate Cortex", *Kybernetik*, Vol. 14 (1973), p.88.

31. Barto, A. G., and R. S. Sutton, "Landmark Learning: An Illustration of Associative Learning", *Technical Report #81-12* (Dept of Comp. and Inf. Sci., U. of Massachusetts, 1981); Barto, A. G., R. S. Sutton, and P. S. Brower, "Associative Search Network: A Reinforcement Learning Associative Memory", *Biol. Cyb.*, Vol. 40 (1981), pp.201-211; Sutton, R.S., and A. G. Barto, "Towards a Modern Theory of Adaptive Networks: Expectation and Prediction", *Psych. Rev.*, Vol. 88

(1981), pp.135-170; Klopf, Harry, *The Hedonistic Neuron: A Theory of Memory, Learning and Intelligence* (Hemisphere, Washington DC, 1982).

32. Matthies, H., "Memory Formation: A Model of Corresponding Neuronal Processes", in *Psychophysiology: Memory, Motivation and Event-related Potentials in Mental Operations*, Rainer Sinz and Mark R. Rosenzweig, eds. (VEB Gustav Fischer, 1983), pp.31-38.

33. Klopf, Harry, *The Hedonistic Neuron: A Theory of Memory, Learning and Intelligence* (Hemisphere, Washington DC, 1982), pp.9-16.

34. Kandel, E. R., "Small Systems of Neurons", *Sci. Amer.*. Vol. 241 (September, 1979), pp.60-77; Sinz, Rainer, and Mark R. Rosenzweig, *Psychophysiology: Memory, Motivation and Event-related Potentials in Mental Operations* (VEB Gustav Fischer Verlag, Jena and Berlin, GDR, 1983).

35. Malsburg, C. von der, "Self-Organization of Orientation Selective Cells in the Striate Cortex", *Kybernetik*, Vol. 14 (1973), pp.85-100.

36. Goldschlager, Leslie M., *A Computational Theory of Higher Brain Function* (Computer Science Department, Standford University, Standford, CA, April 1984).

37. Grossberg, S., "Associative and Competitive Principles of Learning and Development", in *Competition and Cooperation in Neural Nets*, S. Amari and M. A. Arbib, eds (Springer-Verlag, 1982), pp.295-341; Ellias, S.A., and S. Grossberg, "Pattern Formation, Contrast Control and Oscillations in the Short Term Memory of Shunting On-Centre Off-Surround Networks", *Biol. Cyb.*, Vol. 20 (1975), pp.69-98.

38. Malsburg, C. von der, and J. D. Cowan, "Outline of a Theory for the Ontogenesis of Iso-Orientation Domains in the Visual Cortex", *Biol. Cyb.*, Vol. 45 (1982), pp.49-56.

39. Cowan, W.M., "The Development of the Brain", *Sci. Amer.*, Vol.241 (September, 1979), p.116.

40. Pettigrew, J. D., C. Olson, and H. V. B. Hirsch, "Cortical Effect of Selective Visual Experience: Degeneration or Reorganization?", *Brain Research*, Vol. 51 (1973), pp.345-351.

41. Tsukahara, N., "Synaptic Plasticity in the Mammalian Central Nervous System", *Ann. Rev. Neurosci.*, Vol. 4 (1981), p.430.

42. Cowan, W.M., "The Development of the Brain", *Sci. Amer.*, Vol.241 (September, 1979), p.116.

43. Jacobson, M., *Developmental Neurobiology* (Plenum Press, New York, NY, 1978), p.399ff.

44. Willshaw, David J., and C. von der Malsburg, "How patterned neural connections can be set up by self-organization", *Proc R. Soc. Lond. B*, Vol. 194 (1976), pp.431-445; Willshaw, David J., and C. von der Malsburg, "A Marker Induction Mechanism for the Establishment of Ordered Neural Mappings: Its Application to the Retinotectal Problem", *Phil. Trans. Roy. Soc. Lond. B*, Vol. 287 (1979), pp.203-243.

45. Aertsen, A. M. H. J., and P. I. M. Johannesma, "The Spectro-Temporal Receptive: A Functional Characteristic of Auditory Neurons", *Biol. Cyb.*, Vol. 42 (1981), pp.133-143; Aertsen, A. M. H. J., and P. I. M. Johannesma, "A Comparison of the

Spectro-Temporal Sensitivity of Auditory Neurons to Tonal and Natural Stimuli", *Biol. Cyb.*, Vol. 42 (1981), pp.145-156.

46. Grossberg, S., "Associative and Competitive Principles of Learning and Development", in *Competition and Cooperation in Neural Nets,* S. Amari and M. A. Arbib, eds (Springer-Verlag, 1982), pp.295-341.

47. Lettvin, J.Y., H. R. Maturana, W. S. McCulloch, and W. H. Pitts, "What the Frog's Eye Tells the Frog's Brain", *Proceedings of the Institute of Radio Engineers,* Vol.47 (November, 1959), pp.1940-1951.

48. Hirai, Y., "A Template Matching Model for Pattern Recognition: Self-Organization of Templates and Template Matching by a Disinhibitory Neural Network", *Biol. Cyb.*, Vol. 38 (1980), pp.91-101.

49. Wilks, Y., "An Artificial Intelligence Approach to Machine Translation", in Roger C. Schank and K. M. Colby, eds, *Computer Models of Thought and Language* (Freeman, 1973), p.115.

50. Willshaw, David J., and H. C. Longuet-Higgins, "The Holophone - Recent Developments", in D. Michie, ed., *Machine Intelligence 4* (Edinburgh UP, Edinburgh UK, 1969), p.353f.

51. *Op. cit.,* p.355.

52. Longuet-Higgins, H. C., "Holographic Model of Temporal Recall", *Nature*, Vol. 217 (6th Jan 1968), p.104; Willshaw, David J., O. P. Buneman, and H. C. Longuet-Higgins, "Non-Holographic Associative Memory", *Nature*, Vol. 222 (7th June 1969), pp.960-962.

53. Spinelli, D.N., "OCCAM: A Computer Model for a Content Addressable Memory in the Central Nervous System", in K. H. Pribram and D. E. Broadbent, *Biology of Memory* (Academic Press, 1970), pp.293-306.

54. Hirai, Y., "A Model of Human Associative Processor (HASP)", *IEEE Trans Sys. Man. Cyb.*, Vol. SMC-13 (September, 1983), pp.851-856; Willwacher, G., "Storage of a Temporal Pattern Sequence in a Network", *Biol. Cyb.*, Vol. 43 (1982), pp.115-126.

55. Malsburg, C. von der, "Self-Organization of Orientation Selective Cells in the Striate Cortex", *Kybernetik*, Vol. 14 (1973), pp.85-100.

56. Lashley, K.S., "Studies of Cerebral Function in Learning, VI, The Theory that Synaptic Resistance is Reduced by the Passage of the Nerve Impulse" (Reprinted from *Psychol. Rev.,* 1924, 31, 369-375), in F. A. Beach, D. O. Hebb, C. T. Morgan and H. W. Nissen, eds, *The Neurophysiology of Lashley* (McGraw-Hill, 1960), p.500f.

57. Uhr, Leonard, *Pattern Recognition, Learning, and Thought: Computer-Programmed Models of Higher Mental Processes* (Prentice-Hall, Englewood Cliffs, NJ, 1973), p.xix.

58. Zipser, Birgit, and Ronald McKay, "Monoclonal antibodies distinguish identifiable neurones in the leech", *Nature*, Vol. 289 (12 February 1981), p.554.

59. Chang, C. L., and R. C. Lee, *Symbolic Logic and Mechanical Theorem Proving* (Academic Press, 1973), p.193.

60. Jacobson, M., *Developmental Neurobiology* (Plenum Press, New York, NY, 1978), p375.

Chapter Eight

The Nature of Language

Our approach throughout this book presupposes that psycholinguistically-inspired analytic models should be used to discover linguistic truths. On the other hand we think it is also necessary and helpful to consider the huge range of linguistic ideas accumulated in the history of linguistics and philosophy. The starting point of such discussions is the nature of language, its uniqueness to man and its role in his pre-eminence in the animal kingdom. It then moves to the function, role and mechanism of language. This takes us to consideration of our language representation and processes, to the universals of language, its structure, components and features. Finally, we must consider the models of language, the traditional and the novel, and of course, the computational.

These facets of philosophy and linguistics will be our concern in this chapter and the next, although we cannot give more than a brief indication of the importance of many of the points.

The Quintessence of Language

A language is a relation between sound and meaning, expression and content, outer and inner form.[1]

This is at the heart of TGG, which suggests that there is a similarity between the inner and outer forms of language. But this is too simplistic, and focuses on only one of the primary points. Language is not only its outer form:

The deaf ... learn sign language at about the same time as normal children ... begin speaking.[2]

Is sign language a true example of language? Writing is perhaps a better example, and is often treated as the purest form of a language. Reading and writing are learned at around the same time as, and in parallel with, the spoken language. The fine ordering of signing, speaking and writing has to be explained in terms of development of motor skills.

This view of language is rather passive. In fact language is much more active than these definitions suggest.[3] In particular language is a repertoire of skills and capabilities, the most notable of which is the ability to evoke absent and even unexperienced scenes. Narasimhan notes that this leads directly to the ability to "talk about the "talking-about aspect" itself",[4] leading to meta-language functionality (and opening the door to semantic paradox).

Since language is an evident primary distinctive between man and animal this leads to definitions of language which may make it a solely human prerogative:

> The definition of language begins with the notion that any language will be or will have been the major medium of communication in some human social group, the members of which are not afflicted with any major sensory or motor impairment. This makes the various sign languages of the world borderline cases ... [The chimps] Sarah and Washoe are disbarred from full linguistic participation by the very first requirement: vocal production and aural reception ... Both the Gardners and Premack seem to have thought that previous experiments in the linguistic-chimpanzee tradition might have failed not because of an incapacity that was essentially linguistic but because of a motoric ineptitude that was only incidentally linguistic. And I think we must all agree that vocal production cannot be the essence of linguistic capacity, since writing systems are certainly languages, and sign systems used by human communicators very likely are.[5]

Brown continues by considering Chomsky's two essential properties: the existence of an infinite range of sound-meaning correspondences, and the existence of a surface/deep structure distinction:

> In various ways Chomsky's position on this question is unsatisfying. The properties defined as essential are abstract structural properties ... They are a long way from behaviour either human or animal. Even among linguists there is controversy over the proper form of notation and the necessity of postulating deep structure ... Chomsky's "essentials" will certainly keep the animals "out", but what is the use of that if it is not clear that we ourselves are "in"? Chomsky's "barest rudiments" have the further interesting property that, allowing ourselves to draw structural conclusions from the data of spontaneous speech, children are not clearly producing what must be called language in Stages I, II, and III ... This conclusion about child speech is not necessarily the wrong conclusion; it is just novel.[6]

Brown finally espouses a third approach which focuses explicitly on the human/animal differences, emphasizing the relative importance of "cultural evolution as opposed to biological evolution". This leads naturally to an emphasis on writing since the communication of knowledge stretches indefinitely across time and distance by this means.

Once we have a feel for what language is, we can discuss specific languages and classes of languages. In particular, we become interested in the class of actual and possible human languages. Wexler sees this as the requisite starting point for linguistics.[7] But, why *must* we begin here with the class of possible human languages? Why not consider the process of acquisition with respect to the class of known natural languages (and child languages)? Such a theory of natural language acquisition will have as a corollary a theory of possible natural languages.

The language is the observable fact, but it is the acquisition process which determines the class of possible natural languages. Hence the psycholinguistic approach.

Language as Association

The pivotal concept of McNeill's definition of language is that it is a *relation*. Whatever we may argue concerning just what is related to what, it is incontrovertible that relationships are at the heart of language. A relation points out a correspondence construed or constructed between two or more sets of structures. From a more active and concrete viewpoint, a relationship involves a mapping of entities from one domain to another. Each sensory-motor modality is such a domain. The first order relationships constitute a further domain, as do successively higher order relationships. Such relationships must underlie any representation we may introduce, and provide the basis for semantics.

Thus language admits of a translation process from one domain to another. The sensory-motor domains themselves have the character of language, communicating useful information about relationships between physical entities. Similarly, the processes of the brain have the character of language: operating on the symbolic perceptions of our sensory modalities to produce a new semiotics and meta-language. Relationships themselves become a new set of symbols, having some form of neural representation probably similar to that into which our senses of vision and sound are translated at retina and cochlea.

The essence of a language relationship is that there is an active and in some sense meaningful association. The operation of language requires the ability to associate the structures of one domain (or language or meta-language) with those of another. Moreover the process of language learning needs the ability to form new associations. These may be more or less directly associated with the sensory-motor modalities, according to whether they are more or less concrete, as opposed to abstract.

One distinguishing prerogative of the human species is the ability to conceive of, and communicate about, something not currently present in the sensory-motor field. At its simplest, this is simply a *second-signalling system*. A particular cry or whistle can cause a reaction to danger, as if the danger was directly realized. In essence, the ability to learn such a *second-signal* is what is explored in the classical conditioning paradigm. What is unique, it seems, is that we can convey information about *detached* events. We can hear the phrase "man-eating tiger" without immediately panicking. We can distinguish between past, present and future; anticipated, certain, improbable and conditional; complete, incomplete, repeated, continuous and intermittent; command, query and statement; self and other; actor, undergoer, and bystander. We can of course even label these attributes, as I have just done, and we can further classify them by tense, aspect, mood, person, *etc.*

Not only can we convey *detached* information but the evidence from creoles indicates that the marking of these features reflects the way we view the world and wish to describe it. This is shown by the fact that these groupings develop their novel languages in a consistent way.

This is not just a linguistic trait, but a considerable cognitive advance over simple association. The different types of detached association must be distinguishable as cognitive entities, and hence capable of semiotic association. Detached events have not been handled adequately in computer natural language systems. For example, Winograd notes that SHRDLU "does not attempt to handle hypothetical or counterfactual statements".[8] But such statements are implicit in the planning paradigm which is being investigated within Artificial Intelligence (AI).

Semiotics: Intension and Extension

The basis of language, as a form of communication, is the mediation of agreed signs or symbols. We should think about the basis of these symbols and the concepts they relate to. We saw earlier that Piaget proposed that assimilation first gave rise to a precursor of a concept which had *intension* ("comprehension") without *extension*. Unfortunately, these terms are overloaded in both philosophy and linguistics. First, there is confusion with the related term *intention*, with its specific popular meaning of "purpose", or more generally (in the Philosophy of Husserl) in relation to conscious experience.

Then there is the specific meaning of *intension* which contrasts with *extension* in relation to truth values, referents, the unreal, and the subjective. The *extension* (*e.g.* truth) of a "sentence" may or may not be a function of the *extension* of its components (*e.g.* referents or truth). Thus "I think that ..." is an *intensional context* since its truth is actually not dependent on the truth of the statement which is substituted into the paradigm. *Intensional* theory is also intended to cope with the fact that not all names for an entity need be in the shared context (*e.g.* I may not know that my boss is my long-lost uncle, and I may say "I last saw my boss twenty minutes ago and my uncle twenty years ago").

The common basis of meaning for these terms comes from a distinction between simple association with a set of instances, and association with a generalization from instances, namely a concept. Strictly, the *in-*

tention is the meaning intended, and the *extension* is the truth value, true meaning, or true referent.

The concept of *extension* is evident in that of *overextension* in which children give symbols (*e.g.* words) extensions that are broader than those of the adult language. But there is also another child error phenomenon relating to extension:

> "Word realism" describes children's tendency to treat names as inherent properties of objects. When questioned, children reveal a belief that if the name is changed, the object is also changed, and that the name is held by virtue of the object possessing various others of its properties. Could the sun have been called "moon", and the moon "sun"?—No. Why not? —Because the sun shines brighter than the moon.[9]

> Stated in a different way, children who display word realism speak as if referential words were icons and indices rather than symbols. Although word realism is a meta-linguistic orientation that is incorrect from our point of view, it could be regarded as having a certain amount of validity—as a description of children's own initial language performance. In children's early output, names are indexical. They do not occur without their referents, and hence behave *like* attributes of the referents.[10]

The sun is not known only by means of a single sensorium. It is both visually and tactually experienced: it is both bright and warm. How is the child to know that the diverse properties of colour, brightness and warmth are intrinsic properties in a way that the word "sun" is not? Generalization is needed to establish any concept, and the particular complex relationships associated with sun and moon—rising, setting, fullness and obscurity—involve different subsets of their properties. Thus *word realism* is an overgeneralization of *object constancy*, and indeed the word may be a most significant feature in the development of discrimination for a particular object. There is a sense in which the word is naming not the object, but a set of attributes pertaining to the object, and therefore naming the object only by extension.

Concrete and Abstract

In our discussion of relations and associations, we considered a layered system of (meta-)languages moving away from the concreteness of the sensory-motor to the abstractness of the higher cognitive levels. The problem of abstract concepts is one of those most frequently used to challenge the proponents of natural language understanding systems: *e.g.* "how can a computer understand the meaning of "love"?". But it is possible to conceive a plausible method, involving development from the sensory-motor level and the use of analogy and generalization, of teaching the computer a reasonable working definition of any abstract concept.

We have already discussed the role of norms: there are certain words, notably adjectives and other forms of description, which are relative. Thus the objective meaning (or sensory range) of "white" in "a white man" differs substantially from that for "a white tablecloth". There is a similar objective difference between "big" in "a big ant" and "a big elephant". The meaning of the word is thus dependent on the norms of the described class in the contextual domain.

An example of the complexity of the operation of this normalization can be found in speech to a child ("Aren't you a big boy!") in which the norm may be autocorrelative in the temporal domain (*i.e.* he is bigger than he was a month ago). Another example can be found in the child's own speech ("Big elephant" referring to a baby elephant) in which the norm is also autocorrelative (i.e. it is bigger than he is).

The development of norms is probably related to, in Piaget's schedule of development, the learning of properties such as conservation of volume (*e.g.* you have to allow for one glass being narrower than the other before assuming a higher level equates to more water). In this case the norm has to be sensitive to multiple dimensions of the concept in question. Children reach the point of being able to make this correction at quite a well-defined stage of their development.

There is a tendency to associate linguistics with grammar and the analysis of syntax. This view pervades the traditional AI approach to Natural Language which originated in computer science. But it is also an error that has crept into Linguistics rather recently, while the pendulum swung to an extreme following the reintroduction and emphasis by Chomsky of the laudable principle that grammars must be testable. Sometimes it is even declared that sentences which don't make semantic sense are in some way less grammatical than those that do. This is a pointless observation, which only confuses theory, because language is dynamic. Of course, there are other extremes which make semantics, functionality, or logic supreme at the expense of other facets of language.

Epistemology and Ontology: Knowledge, Belief and Reference

In this section we discuss the analysis of language in its wider framework, looking particularly at the three hierarchies recognized by Pike. The first is the *referential hierarchy*: somehow language exists in relation to the contextual environment. We have said that the essence of language is relationship, and that relations start in, and take their form from, the environment. Words are symbols for relationships. Some, like concrete nouns and verbs, refer directly to relationships in the environment, or are derived from it by metaphor.

So our study of language must directly lead to a study of the total environmental system and the way we have knowledge of it. In its turn this leads to the distinction between what we know and what we believe. Upon consideration it becomes readily apparent that we know nothing with absolute (as opposed to contingent) certainty. Hence in essence our referential structure consists in our sensory-motor perceptual structures and our belief systems.

This raises a range of philosophical problems. The concept of "belief" relates to the conscious part of our referential processing, although we do not distinguish conscious knowledge, except in terms of expectation probabilities. The concept of perceptual structures relates to our unconscious processing. We do not really yet understand much about consciousness. There must be an interface, the unconscious perceptual field being the referential system for some species of conscious homunculus. But physiologically, we can find no evidence of any such sharp transition.

Since the referenced relationships are external, and only reflected in our belief system, language is really based around our belief system rather than reality. Thus the first stage of any linguistic consideration must be ontology: a language learning system must develop and employ an ontology, a conception of reality, a model of the world.

The importance of an ontology as a framework for all AI research has been emphasized by Hayes. He decried the plethora of half-hearted toy-worlds in which AI programs were exercised, and proposed:

> to construct a formalisation of a large part of ordinary everyday knowledge of the physical world. Such a formalisation could, for example, be a collection of assertions in a first-order logical formalism ... Although it is important to bear control and search issues—in short, *computational issues*—in mind, we propose to deliberately postpone detailed consideration of implementation. All too often, serious work on representational issues in AI has been diverted or totally thwarted by premature concern for computational issues.[11]

Our research has assumed a logical formalism for both language and visual/motor world. In accord with Hayes' approach, these experiments proceeded with hand-simulated sets of logical assertions in PROLOG which represented the modalities and their inter-relationships, and the parsers and learning programs were applied to these. However, the formalism has also taken form in the robot world graphical simulation, Magrathea.[12]

We can now discuss our sensory-motor interface with the world and the ontology that it determines. First let us consider the function of our sensory-motor organs. Whilst the sensory organs, particularly vision, give us a highly accurate and metric model of the world, they are already interpreted. Frequencies are interpreted as colours or tones, visual and acoustic gradations are interpreted as cues of various kinds. The sensoria are highly functional, and integrated with motor functions especially in the lower-organisms (*e.g.* the frog[13]). Our consciousness is again the source of some enigma.

In fact our relationship with the world depends far more on the way the world affects us or is affected by us, than on patterns of light or sound. These, along with the more basic sense of smell, are less directly concerned with important events, and are thus in reality attached to these events only as second-signals. To take an example from the lower orders of the animal kingdom again, the smell or sight or sound of a predator is not intrinsically related to undesirable events in the way that the senses of touch and pain are. Similarly the sight or sound of food is divorced from the essence of food, since "the proof of the pudding is in the eating".

For the ultimate in direct effect, we must turn to motor functions, and our feedback systems relating to motor function. As muscles respond to flee or pursue, they change the environment perceived. This can give us a straightforward sense of the innateness of ontology. Clark reviews a number of proposals about the properties or primitives represented by semantic features. The hypothesis of some set of semantic primitives is assumed by a diverse range of authors in both linguistics and AI. Very few provide any reasonable basis for the actual existence of such a universal semantics, and indeed Chomsky's proposed innate organ appears quite unreasonable. What is reasonable is that the common physiological sensory-motor and higher brain functions lead to a common core of ontology which does allow some common semantic basis:

> This view of universal semantics has been spelled out in more detail by Bierwisch, who pointed out (1967) that "the idea of innate basic elements of semantic structure does not entail a biological determination of concepts or meanings in a given language, but only of their ultimate components (1967, p4)" ... It seems natural to assume that these [semantic] components represent categories or principles according to which real and fictitious, perceived and imagined situations and objects are structured and classified. The semantic features do not represent, however, external physical properties, but rather the psychological conditions according to which human beings process their physical and social environment. Thus they are not symbols for physical properties and relations outside the human organism, but rather for the internal mechanisms by means of which such phenomena are perceived and conceptualized.[14]

This point is worth emphasizing. It is a gross oversimplification to assume that there is a more direct relationship between language and sensory-motor function, although this can give rise to an interesting computational model used by Harris (1977) and eschewed by Block:

> Harris (1972) successfully simulated some aspects of language acquisition. His [simulated] robot was able to build up a lexicon by correlating the names of several objects and activities with "built-in concepts" (p89) defined in terms of the robots' sensory and motor apparatus. Each piece of apparatus was "wired to" a grammatical category, *e.g.* its motors were wired to the "verb's category. The robot inferred a simple ... phrase-structure grammar by operating on the sequence of grammatical categories assigned to incoming strings according to the maxim: "The parts of speech are the parts of the robot" (p87). For the project described here, we deliberately avoid the use of innate grammatical categories, especially categories which are assigned on the basis of *a priori* ontological classifications.[15]

So far our discussions are mainly about concrete open class words. The closed class units tend to act in terms of selection from a limited number of possible relationships amongst the more concrete units. These functions may be limited to a single hierarchy, and so be mainly cohesive (*e.g.* inflections). Others may express specific concrete relationships in another hierarchy (*e.g.* prepositions), Yet others have a more complex role in terms of a grammatical function which crosses hierarchical contexts (*e.g.* pronouns, articles and demonstratives). These mediate such functions as specificity of reference, continuity of reference and self-other reference. This makes these words a class which is far more complex and difficult to understand than the traditional higher concepts which are thrown the way of computational linguistics as test cases.

Tanz's study of the acquisition of deictics, and her accounts of the demonstratives *this* and *that* and the adverbs *here* and *there*, show the extraordinary complexity of such spatial deictics. They emphasize how essential the sensory-motor environment and self-awareness of the child are to his learning of these terms:

> The deictic terms appeared as a recalcitrant class of terms to linguists because their meanings could not be specified without introducing the extra-linguistic context. But contextual determination of meaning does not seem inherently problematical for children. Numerous studies done from quite different perspectives indicate that for young children, meaning is more profoundly embedded in context than it is for adults ... This orientation toward the contextual determination of meaning is adaptive. How can pre-linguistic children come to understand language at all if they don't constantly try to interpret it in relation to context? Part of their problem in learning to talk lies in having progressively to *de*contextualize meaning. In adult language use (production and comprehension), meaning emerges out of the integration of language and context. In child language, acquisition meanings are *discovered* through the interpretation of integrations between language and contexts.[16]

Phonology: Phonetics, Phonemics and Morphophonemics

Every language has a sound system ... of some 15 distinctive features.[17]

A language analysis model should go to the level of speech, or at least to a phonologically-motivated level. However, in preliminary experiments the phonological hierarchy may be replaced by the standard orthography and need not extend below the word level. Eventually, though, the model must move towards the true speech level.

To illustrate this necessity, consider words like "a" and "an" which involve morphophonemic cohesion. This is but one example of a far wider class of quite well understood interactions between the phonological and grammatical hierarchies. The basic rule is that things change so as to be easier to say.

Recall also that we are considering the acquisition paradigm: how language is learned. The child's first sounds defy grammatical analysis, and the first words contain systematic phonological errors. Does the child produce units of sound, some combinations of which are reinforced? Does he test his capacity for making sounds, and then put units together to imitate adult words? The answer is probably "yes" to one or both of these questions, but there is not much evidence yet. If the answer to either is "yes", what then are the units?

The simplest recognized units in the phonological hierarchy are the roughly fifteen *features* or types of articulatory distinction which can be made. Particular tuples of values along these dimensions (actually points or arcs in feature space) constitute unique *phones*, or single sounds. Considering these significant differences leads to the development of equivalence classes of which the *phones* are interchangeable, whose differences are deemed insignificant in a given language. Pike, for instance, developed techniques for this analysis. The classes produced in the phonological hierarchy, forming the level above the *phones*, are called *phonemes*. These are the units of which the given language is composed, and into which it is transcribed. An orthography is usually the written correlate of the set of *phonemes* — English is, of course, probably the language with the most obscure correspondence between sound and writing. Other classes of orthography, however, are based upon the word or syllable (Chinese and Japanese are the classic examples).

The next level up is the syllable, and in our given language, there will be a limited number of syllable patterns. These are, basically, binary subclassification of the feature space, and hence the *phonemes* set, into vowel (V) and consonant (C). Particular CV, VC, CVC *etc.* patterns are typically limited to particular parts of a word (*e.g.* initial or medial).

Above this we might expect to have the word level. This is almost true, but it is sometimes necessary to distinguish between a phonological word and a grammatical word. The definition of what is a grammatical word in a given language is in general a non-trivial operation, and the natural phonological segments pronounced as a single unit are very often quite independent, being neither supersets nor subsets of the grammatical words.

The question is,which is the practical starting point for child acquisition? Our models deal only with words, but further experiments must look at the learning of words in terms of lower hierarchical levels. The best approach seems to be by composition starting at the syllable level. One reason for not going to the phoneme level is that phonemes are not pronounceable on their own—virtually by definition—since if they are they are really syllables. This model would make random syllabic combinations of sounds, moulding them to the CV syllable structures (since the vowel consonant contrast is fairly dominant) and restricting the feature combinations (*phones*) to the appropriate phonemes. It then reacts to reactions to its syllabic constructs.

This brief overview has completely left out pitch and stress, which we discussed earlier in terms of their sentence level "grammatical" function. But we should note that they are features which can be phonemic. The languages where pitch is phonemic at or below the word level (it causes otherwise identical words to have different meanings) are called tone languages (*e.g.* Vietnamese, Chinese). English is actually a language in which stress is phonemic at the word level (*e.g.* consider the difference between stressing the first and second syllables of "content"— giving either the noun or the adjective).

Prosody: Intonation and Stress

Four binary features—accent, emphasis, cadence, and endglide—plus a feature discriminating strong and weak syllables, account satisfactorily for all the grammatically relevant prosodic patterns of American English.[18]

We now look at these features of intonation and stress as they apply above the word level, nominally at the sentence level. The role of prosody in phonology is very much like the role of punctuation in orthography: phrasing contours correspond to commas, parentheses, colons and semicolons; rising and falling intonation correspond to questions and statements.

Whilst it is traditional not to regard punctuation and prosody as having an essential grammatical function, it can be useful in experimental models to treat them as phonemic. In our experiments punctuation marks are in fact treated as words. Moreover, prosody clearly plays an important part in the child's linguistic development. We have already seen that at the babbling stage a baby's prosody is sufficiently characteristic of his mother tongue to allow partial identification of his ethnic background from his babbling alone, and some time before he produces his first recognizable words.

Whilst Pike takes prosody into account in Tagmemics, Chomsky and Halle have deliberately omitted it from consideration. Vanderslice does something to rectify this omission, however. His main contribution is to point out that there are systematic rules governing stress, whilst on the other hand ambiguities are not always resolved as decisively by stress as some have claimed:

> We have seen first that some of the prosodic variation dismissed by Chomsky, Halle, and Lukoff (1956) as expressive deviation is in fact perfectly regular and expounds grammatical ... referential relationships in ways closely analogous with pronominalization, definitization, ellipsis, *etc.* Accent deletion in fact offers an especially fruitful area for study because the structural residue is usually identifiable. Failure to account for such prosodic phenomena constitutes a major gap in transformational theory.[19]

Expressive stress plays a valuable part in focussing the child's attention accurately. This can be used as another tool to aid the computational model in analyzing language input, although it may well be inessential. It certainly does not seem appropriate to employ such an overt mechanism as stress marks in the natural language systems working with orthography since they are not used by human readers and writers. On the other hand, the forms which are used in text, such as capitalization, underlining and font changes, do help the reader if properly used, particularly to read sentences aloud correctly.

In speech, the stressed words may be those which are heard and received most clearly, and are subject to least elision. On the other hand, the unstressed words are subject to more noise and elision, and may need to be partially reconstructed on the basis of the contextual evidence from the stressed words. Thus stress has a function here which is not required in text.

Another interesting property, discussed by Vanderslice under the heading of "Accent Deletion", concerns the use of contrastive stress to indicate the focus of information or surprise. Such contrastive stress is deleted (this is a TGG motivated discussion) if a nonce-equivalence or nonce-synonymy relation holds — *i.e.* contextual equivalence or synonymy. It can also be deleted if there is a relation of inclusion or subsumption (although presumably not reverse subsumption). This should help in the acquisition paradigm by helping the process of contrast.

Representation: Logic *vs* Meaning and Syntax

One of the hardest questions which faces anyone who is trying to produce a Natural Language system or model is the question of representation. The problem first arose in relation to machine translation, once it became apparent that some form of intermediate representation was required. And this then posed the question of whether it should be "logical or linguistic in form".[20] Many recent language understanding systems are still meandering around in the translation arena, although the key word is now "paraphrase" rather than "translation". Schank's approach tries to find a representation which has psychological validity through capturing the significant relationships, functions and procedures which a human might employ. To the extent that this representation may be translated into an "effective language" used to affect the environment, it does hold some promise.

Other representations are based on pure logic. Thus "Montague analyzes John as denoting ... John's properties",[21] and translates language into a representation which is an extension of first order logic. This approach also has considerable merit. Indeed, the brain never gets to act on "John" in any sense. It does not even directly act on the light and sound waves which emanate from him. Thus what we come to perceive as "John" is a set of transformations of sensory-motor properties which correlate with the language stimulus "John" and is unique to each individual. The approach taken in our experiments involves a similar approach in that PROLOG, itself a derivative of first order logic, is used as the representation language.

However no representation, whether expressed as semantic primitives or logical relations, can actually solve the fundamental problem:

> Sentences are just concatenations of arbitrary symbols and so have no meaning in and of themselves. The important thing to realize, however, is that abstract structures, like the above, are also just concatenations of symbols and so have no meaning in and of themselves. Thus, translating from one symbol structure to another will never expose the meaning of either symbol structure.[22]

A common complaint is that these representations are arbitrary. They may by chance have some logical relation to our actual representation (assuming there is any such thing). To the extent that they do, it is possible to derive some insights from these representations. The alternative adopted here, however, is to begin with the properties the model should have, and in particular the sensory-motor foundation, and use this as the starting point for a representation. The actual notation and formal manipulation are governed by expediency, and should not be an object of great commitment. As Anderson notes:

> There is little for choice among the four propositional theories reviewed in this chapter ... The general psychological community is being forced to absorb an apparently endless parade of formalisms without really gaining anything from the new additions.[23]

The question of representation extends also to the area of procedural versus declarative knowledge—a distinction emphasized by Anderson. The logic programming paradigm is more general than that of production systems, and hence its adoption tends to bypass the question by allowing the distinction to become blurred once more.

A propositional theory of knowledge provides some set of definitions and notations with which representations of sentences can be expressed in terms of propositions about entities. As Anderson points out, transformation into such a representation is largely vacuous.[24] The approach taken in our program has expressly avoided introducing propositions or entities. Relations are expressed directly between input tokens, whether linguistic, visual or relational. PROLOG is used to express these relationships, which are exemplified using specific recognized units of child language and a toy world. The visual toy world notation is in a sense similar to some of these theories, but is fundamentally different in that it is only standing in for the real world—it is not intended to be an internal representation for language: a "deep structure", "semantic net" or "interlingua". However, since there is a function which must be performed and which these theories seek to model, there is a degree of correspondence between these PROLOG parse trees and relationships and the propositional theories. The notation is however the standard PROLOG-style parse tree.

Rules: Semantics and Meaning *vs* Syntax

It is fairly clear that languages follow rules of some sort; those we call grammar. It is not so clear what these rules are which are used in speaking and understanding a language. It is apparent that in speaking we must be employing rules of construction in order to be able to produce speech which largely conforms to the formal rules of syntax. There is a distinction here between the linguist's grammar of a language and the speaker's production "grammar".

There is also a sense in which no grammar rules are adequate to specify the meaningful expressions of a natural language, and this leads us to make the distinction between syntax and semantics. Wilks emphasizes the semantic role and downplays the syntactic role, whilst Chomsky reverses this emphasis.

Rules must be important not only to a speaker, but to a hearer. When learning a language, rules must first be recognized in heard speech before they can be incorporated into spoken speech. Hence we must distinguish also, in the abstract at least, the hearer's recognition "grammar".

It is clearly not sufficient to have rules which describe the syntax, but it is necessary to have something which relates the meaning to the sentential form. Such semantic "rules" or "cues" may either complement the grammar, or subsume the syntactic rules. Wilks claims that such semantic rules are adequate to the domain of machine translation with which he is concerned. Even if this is true, it does not necessarily extend to language understanding. Understanding seems to consist, objectively, in the capability of translating from sensory and linguistic input to appropriate motor and linguistic output. The Schank school evidences understanding through paraphrase, which is a form of translation. Subjectively, of course, we see it as something more.

Once again, we must consider the philosophical tradition in semantics:

> While linguists have had little of interest to say about semantics, there is a deep and conceptually rich tradition in logic and philosophy that can be used for the semantical analysis of children's speech and that can provide a body of methods and concepts appropriate to the task ... The tradition of model-theoretic semantics that originated with Frege (1879) in the nineteenth century is *the* serious intellectual tradition of semantical analysis, and the recent offshoots by linguists, to a large extent conceived in ignorance of this long tradition, have little to offer in comparison ... No doubt the preponderance of emphasis on formal languages has put off deeper perusal of these matters by psycholinguists who might otherwise be attracted to the theoretical developments. What has come to be called the theory of models in logic, which is really the semantical theory of formal languages, has been relatively inaccessible to outsiders until fairly recently.[25]

To illustrate how a logic of semantics can interrelate with syntax, an example or two will be useful:

> Let us look at the subject noun phrase "black cats". Our grammar for noun phrases contains the production rule NP - Adj + N ... The denotation of *black* is the set B of black things, and the denotation of *cats* is the set C of cats. Using the semantic rule of intersection, we see that the denotation of NP ... is simply B C ... I have found that in many cases, but perhaps not all, it is useful to let the definite article *the* ... denote a set C that is the union of the set of objects in the perceptual surround with the set of objects denoted by phrases in immediately prior sentences in the conversation, and in some cases, also the set of objects denoted by images or symbolic storage in long-term memory. Thus, when Nina said, "I want the lion", the set C denoted by *the* is in-

tersected with the set of lions both real and toy, and if everything is in good order, the set intersection consists of a unique object.[26]

Leaving aside the simplistic and incomplete nature of these examples, this approach has a lot to offer, and is essentially quite simple. However it begs the question of how the child learns whether a particular grammatical collocation represents intersection (as above) or union (*e.g.* "black or white cats"), and how it might fit into a neurally motivated model.

There is also experimental evidence that semantics can improve syntactic learning, but this experimentation uses subjects older than the age group we are really concerned with:

> The importance of semantics has been very forcefully brought home to psychologists by a pair of experiments by Moeser and Bregman (1972, 1973) on the induction of artificial languages. They compared language learning in the situation where their subjects only saw well-formed strings of the language versus the situation where they saw well-formed strings plus pictures of the semantic referent to these strings. In either case, the criterion test was for the subject to be able to detect which strings of the language were well formed—without the aid of any referent pictures. After 3000 training trials, subjects in the no-referent condition were at chance in the criterion test, whereas subjects in the referent condition were essentially perfect ... How does this semantic referent facilitate grammar induction? There are at least three ways. First, rules of natural language are not formulated with respect to single words but with respect to word classes like noun or transitive verb which have a common semantic core. Therefore, semantics can help determine the word classes. This is much more efficient than learning the syntactic rules for each word separately. Second, semantics is of considerable aid in generalizing rules. A general heuristic employed by LAS (Language Acquisition System) is: if two syntactically similar rules function to create the same semantic structure, then they can be merged into a single rule. Third, there is a nonarbitrary correspondence between the structure of the semantic referent and the structure of the sentence that permits one to punctuate the sentence with surface-structure information.[27]

Our experiments do not make use of multimodal information in learning word classes and grammar rules, and it is expected that modifications which allow such correspondences to be exploited will considerably aid the learning in all hierarchies.

Functionality *vis-a-vis* Meaning

Semantics is not just concerned with relationships between structures as they are perceived, but also with relationships with structures as they affect or are affected by the individual. This is to say that both sensory and motor modalities are fundamental to ontology. Piaget emphasizes the importance of the motor side in his discussion.

An amusing anecdote which illustrates this concerns a class of children who were shown a grapefruit. They all agreed it was a grapefruit. But when they saw it peeled, segmented and eaten like an orange, they thought that it must instead be an orange.[28] This clearly demonstrates that the meaning of the names for these two fruit is allied not only to their appearance (and presumably smell and taste), but to their use.

There has been a recent craze for "procedural representation of knowledge in Artificial Intelligence". Part of the meaning of a word is about what the named object or event is doing, how it does it, and how and what the hearer does to it. In fact, it must be associated with a set of functional, descriptive, and contextual (*e.g.* when, where) properties. In short, Kipling's true friends, the interrogative pronouns, all define essential properties integral to the full meaning of a word.

We now turn to consider further universals of language. To do this we take a quick look at a number of very general points, some of which have already been discussed in a more general context in Chapter One. Language is a personal characteristic in each individual and each society. In an earlier discussion of coordinate bilingualism, we saw that the individual's culture, and even his or her personality, is bound up in their language. The set of contrasts made, the framework for thought and behaviour, even the degree of introversion or extroversion, are all influenced by the culture of a language.

In a very real sense, language is just an extension of our culture, a happy convention for the purpose of mutual communication. This shared context is essential for communication, it enriches it, and it limits it. Language is not merely an outgrowth of our culture, a convention for living in that culture. It is a fundamental determiner of our perspective. Our thinking is linguistic. We subvocalize everything. Language is not only a medium for external communication, but for internal communication, planning, decision making and problem solving at the conscious level. Language appears to be deeply tied to the intangible property of consciousness.

Since language is primarily a complex network of learned relationships, it is a collection of metaphors, propositions that one situation is to a greater or lesser degree similar to another. Our battery of pragmatic metaphors is essential for our outlook on the world; and the ability to view the world from multiple perspectives, using multiple metaphors, is essential to our developing a more comprehensive appreciation of it. Employing too few and too limited a range of metaphors is dangerous; some common metaphor-based perspectives or myths are misleading. Lakoff's study is a most valuable contribution to an understanding of language and ourselves.[29]

Overloading: Generalization of Class or Context

The mechanisms involved in the development of meaning are intimately related to those of homonymity, perspective, and metaphor. These are crucial to an analysis and generation process whereby a sequence of sound segments (let us suppose it is a word) come to be associated with certain features. At first, according to Piaget's view, the association is intensive or comprehensive. It consists of one or possibly more sets of undifferentiated features which occur in temporal and/or spatial association. Subsequently, by generalization, the concept is extended to similar situations.

The latter step seems to be more basic and easier to explain or model, since the differentiation and association of features would appear to occur both together and consecutively. Clearly, the etic distinctions must be learned separately first. The association paradigm has the hologram-like property that it depends for its selectivity on the simultaneous presence of a number of features, or "bits" of information. Thus parallel, partially but not completely redundant, associations must form for the various scenes associated with a given word. Indeed the same processes are occurring in the association of different feature sets of that word.

Generalization probably occurs as scene *allos* and word *allos* (*i.e. allomorphs*) interassociate. It also occurs as templates, which wrongly use non-contrastive features, decay or are taken over for other concepts. As this binding of *allos* and reduction of features occurs, the result is an increase in the generality of what will match this concept. When the templates of the concept don't use contrastive features, there can be overgeneralization. When there is differentiation based on the presence or absence of contextual features, there will be no overgeneralization.

Such processes are not limited to static sensory-data, but extend to dynamic relational, functional and internal processes and states. An example of this is the overgeneralization of word function. Some verbs and nouns share the same form, *e.g.* "cough"; some can be negated by prefix, *e.g.* "undo"; some can be used actively and passively or transitively and intransitively, *e.g.* "open". Others can't. It is not clear whether erroneous over-generalizations of function are natural attempts to expand the range of what the child can express, or are actually modelled on the legitimate overloading of various words. It has been suggested that there is an influence, and some evidence has been cited, but it is not a convincing case. Braine illustrates the sort of errors children make:

> "They just cough me" ... "You can only ride a young child" ... "I can't unscotch it" ... "Why doesn't it wind your hair, this big wind?".[30]

Metaphor, Simile and Etymology

> Metaphor consists in using, in connection with one scene, a word—or
> perhaps a whole frame—that is known by both speaker and hearer to
> be more fundamentally associated with a different frame. The require-
> ment for a true metaphor is that the interpreter is simultaneously aware
> of both the new scene and the original scene.[31]

This definition is particularly helpful in explaining why we don't
think of our normal use of extended meanings in language as metaphor.
We may or may not be aware that the meanings are fundamentally related, but in our normal usage in a derived context we are simply unconscious of its root meaning. In other words the metaphor has become a
homonym.

But since analogy, and hence metaphor, seems to be fundamental, it
is worth looking at it a little more closely as a universal characteristic of
the language acquisition process. We quote from Lakoff, particularly his
observation that spatial metaphors seem to provide the basis for the remainder of language, the visual ontology for the less directly perceived
or abstract ontology:

> We suggest the following conclusions about the experiential grounding,
> the coherence, and the systematicity of metaphorical concepts:
>
> — Most of our fundamental concepts are organized in terms of one or
> more spatialization metaphors.
>
> — There is an internal systematicity to each spatialization metaphor. For
> example, *HAPPY IS UP* ("elated", "uplifted", "high spirits") defines a
> coherent system rather than a number of isolated and random cases.
>
> — There is an overall external systematicity among the various spatializa-
> tion metaphors, which defines coherence among them.
>
> — Spatialization metaphors are rooted in physical and cultural experience;
> they are not randomly assigned. A metaphor can serve as a vehicle for un-
> derstanding a concept only by virtue of its experiential basis.
>
> — There are many possible physical and social bases for metaphor. Co-
> herence within the overall system seems to be part of the reason why one is
> chosen and not another.
>
> — In some cases spatialization is so essential a part of a concept that it is
> difficult for us to imagine any alternative metaphor that might structure the
> concept.

— So-called purely intellectual concepts ... are often—perhaps always—based on metaphors that have a physical and/or cultural basis. The *high* in "high-energy particles" is based on *MORE IS UP*.

— Our physical and cultural experience provides many possible bases for spatialization metaphors.

— It is hard to distinguish the physical from the cultural basis of a metaphor, since the choice of one physical basis from among many possible ones has to do with cultural coherence.[32]

Lakoff places metaphor as the basis of the human conceptual system (embodying both language and ontology), and tries to refute the simple concepts of intersection and independence in the theories of *abstraction* and *homonymy*. The first view is that there is "a single, very general, and abstract concept" which is neutral to the different contexts in which a word may be used. The second claims that "there are two different and independent concepts".[33] The *metaphor* theory holds that one concept in one context is primary and that the other meanings of a word are derived from it. Lakoff supports this theory systematically and convincingly on the following basis:

Any adequate theory of the human conceptual system will have to give an account of how concepts are (1) grounded, (2) structured, (3) related to each other, and (4) defined.[34]

In the ontological and epistemological arena, we can also see the surprising importance of this supposedly literary device:

Metaphors, as we have seen, are conceptual in nature. They are among our principal vehicles for understanding. And they play a central role in the construction of social and political reality. Yet they are typically viewed within philosophy as matters of "mere language" ... Instead, philosophical discussions of metaphor have not centered on their conceptual nature, their contribution to understanding, or their function in cultural reality. Instead, philosophers have tended to look at metaphors as out-of-the-ordinary imaginative or poetic linguistic expressions, and their discussions have centered on whether these linguistic expressions can be *true*. Their concern with truth comes out of a concern with objectivity: *truth* for them means *objective, absolute* truth. The typical philosophical conclusion is that metaphors cannot directly state truths, and, if they can state truths at all, it is only indirectly, via some non-metaphorical "literal" paraphrase ...

We do not believe that there is such a thing as *objective* (absolute and unconditional) *truth*, though it has been a long-standing theme in Western culture that there is ... In a culture where the myth of objectivism is very much alive and truth is always absolute truth, the people who get to impose their metaphors on the culture get to define what we consider to be true—absolutely and objectively true ... It is for this reason that we see it as important to give an account of truth that is free of the myth of objectivism.[35]

There may be absolute truth, such as "2 + 2 = 4". But our knowledge is always contingent and such statements are understood in frameworks characterized by metaphor. Thus set theory is a metaphor *par excellence* whose obscurity belies the usual clarificatory intent of metaphor, since here it is intended to formalize the intuitive rather than to elucidate the obscure.

Notes to Chapter Eight

1. McNeill, David, "The Capacity for the Ontogenesis of Grammar", in Dan I. Slobin, *The Ontogenesis of Language* (Academic Press, 1971), pp.17-40.
2. Moore, Timothy A., *Cognitive Development and the Acquisition of Language* (Academic Press, New York, 1973), p.4.
3. Staats, Arthur W., "Linguistic-Mentalistic Theory versus an Explanatory S-R Learning Theory of Language Development", in Dan I. Slobin, *The Ontogenesis of Language* (Academic Press, 1971), p.108ff.
4. Narasimhan, R., *Modelling Language Behaviour* (Springer-Verlag, Berlin, 1981), p.71.
5. Brown, Roger, *A First Language: the early stages* (London, UK, Allen and Unwin, 1973), p.35.
6. *Ibid.*
7. Wexler, Kenneth, and Peter W. Culicover, *Formal Principles of Language Acquisition* (MIT Press, Cambridge, MA, 1980), p.2.
8. Winograd, Terry, "A Procedural Model of Natural Language Understanding", in Roger C. Schank and K. M. Colby, eds, *Computer Models of Thought and Language* (Freeman, 1973), p.183.
9. Piaget, Jean, *The Child's Conception of the World* (London, UK, Kegan Paul, Trench, Truber and Co., 1929), p.81.
10. Tanz, Christine, *Studies in the Acquisition of Deictic Terms* (Cambridge, UK, Cambridge University Press, 1980), p.4.
11. Hayes, P.J., "The Naive Physics Manifesto", in D. Michie, ed., *Expert Systems in the Micro-electronics Age* (Edinburgh U.P., Edinburgh, Scotland, 1979), p.242.
12. Hume, David, "Creating Interactive Worlds with Multiple Actors", *B.Sc. Honours Thesis, Electrical Engineering and Computer Science* (University of New South Wales, Sydney, November 1984).
13. Lettvin, J.Y., H. R. Maturana, W. S. McCulloch, and W. H. Pitts, "What the Frog's Eye Tells the Frog's Brain", *Proceedings of the Institute of Radio Engineers,* Vol.47 (November, 1959), pp.1940-1951.
14. Clark, Eva V., "What's in a Word? On the Child's Acquisition of Semantics in his First Language", in Timothy E. Moore, *Cognitive Development and the Acquisition of Language* (Academic Press, New York, 1973), p.70f.

15. Block, H.D., J. Moulton, and G. M. Robinson, "Natural Language Acquisition by a Robot", *Int. J. Man-Mach, Stud.*, Vol. 7 (1975), p.577.

16. Tanz, Christine, *Studies in the Acquisition of Deictic Terms* (Cambridge, UK, Cambridge University Press, 1980), p.70ff, 164.

17. McNeill, David, "The Capacity for the Ontogenesis of Grammar", in Dan I. Slobin, *The Ontogenesis of Language* (Academic Press, 1971), p.21.

18. Vanderslice, R., *The Prosodic Component: Lacuna in Transformational Theory* (Rand Corporation, Santa Monica, CA, November 1968), p.53.

19. *Op. cit.,* p.52f.

20. Wilks, Y., "An Artificial Intelligence Approach to Machine Translation", in Roger C. Schank and K. M. Colby, eds, *Computer Models of Thought and Language* (Freeman, 1973), p.118ff.

21. Partee, B.H., "John is Easy to Please", in A. Zampolli, ed., *Linguistics Structures Processing* (North Holland, 1977), p.287.

22. Anderson, John R., *Language, Memory, and Thought* (Lawrence Erlbaum Associates, Hillsdale, NJ, 1976), p.221.

23. *Op. cit.,* p.74.

24. *Op. cit.,* p.221.

25. Suppes, Patrick, "The Semantics of Children's Language", *American Psychologist* (1974), p.103f.

26. *Op. cit.,* p.105-6.

27. Anderson, John R., "Computer Simulation of a Language Acquisition System: A First Report", in R. L. Solso, ed., *Information Processing and Cognition: The Loyola Symposium* (Lawrence Erlbaum Associates, Hillsdale, 1975), p.298f.

28. Fillmore, C. J., "Scenes-and-frames semantics", in A. Zampolli, ed., *Linguistics Structures Processing* (North Holland, 1977), p.62.

29. Lakoff, George, and Mark Johnson, *Metaphors we Live By* (University of Chicago Press, 1980).

30. Braine, Martin D. S., "On Two Types of Models of the Internalization of Grammars", in Dan I. Slobin, *The Ontogenesis of Language* (Academic Press, 1971), p.173.

31. Fillmore, C. J., "Scenes-and-frames semantics", in A. Zampolli, ed., *Linguistics Structures Processing* (North Holland, 1977), p.70.

32. Lakoff, George, and Mark Johnson, *Metaphors we Live By* (University of Chicago Press, 1980), p.17ff.

33. *Op. cit.,* p.106f.

34. *Ibid.*

35. *Op. cit.,* p.159f.

Chapter Nine

The Mechanics of Language

This chapter moves from a descriptive characterization of language to examine attempts to provide a predictive explanation. We note the important distinction between phoneme and phone, according to whether a distinction was recognizable in the entire potential human speech repertoire and significant or not in a particular actual language. Phonology provided a basis for analyzing the sound systems of language, building from this distinction. Tagmemics extends this analysis to encompass the entirety of linguistically significant human behaviour, expanded and refocussed to include each level, hierarchy and perspective. Context, contrast and equivalence not only have roles in analysis of language but have potential functionality in language learning and development. The same features which help us distinguish between languages as analysts and learners of second languages would seem obvious candidates for a similar role as learners of a first language. The analysis traditionally applied to adult language can also be applied to child language, and proves consonant with the idea of consistent adherence to child grammars rather than just incorrect usage of adult grammar. The most simple of these supposed grammars can add insights to our view of language. We conclude the chapter with a discussion of the generalized and relatively dynamic tagmemic features introduced by Pike, and an illustrative consideration of the basic units of the phonological, grammatical and orthographical hierarchies.

The critical histories of modern linguistics in Lyons and Hockett[1] add detail to what we said in the last chapter. Hockett's assessment of the situation of linguistics before Pike and Chomsky is particularly interesting:

> We ignored the whole problem of the implications for language design of the fact of linguistic change and vice-versa ... Our model for grammar ... was item-and-arrangement ... though some of us were developing some doubts about too mechanical and complete a parallel between grammar and phonology ... Grammar and semantics were separable and should be separated. The traditional ... direct correlation of meanings on the one hand, formal features on the other, was incorrect; between semantics and phonology stood grammar-and-lexicon, as a separate and autonomous subsystem of the whole language ... It is now my opinion that on all three points the consensus was wrong and that any theory of language design that accepts any one of the three is faulty.[2]

Pike's insights and tagmemic terminology largely provide the linguistic framework for this research. But while the principles are important, the definitional relationships need to be sharpened:

> Pike has given us some remarkably important insights: phonological hierarchical structure is one; his brief exposition of linguistic-like approaches to the discussion of other phrases of culture ... is another. These contributions are all the more striking because they are couched in a terminology and style as confused, inconsistent, and redundant as I have ever encountered in any field of scholarly endeavour ... Tagmemics chokes on its own terminological complexity.[3]

Chomsky's insights and transformational generative grammar have provided the primary influence in contemporary linguistic and psycholinguistic research. In this case, whilst the general insights are important, the theory has tended to be too rigid and empirically unsupported. This work provides a foil against which contrasting proposals are pitted:

> Syntactic transformations, in either the Harris or the Chomsky version ... yield a special sort of item-and-process model of grammatical design that is not only more powerful but also, in my opinion, much more realistic than any item-and-arrangement model can be ... To be sure, transformational treatments of specific data are still usually too cumbersome and hard to follow, but we may hope that will pass. It is not uncommon for an innovation to be much more complicated than really necessary when it first appears! ... We must also remember that transformations are not a theory, but only a possible ingredient of a theory.[4]

In this chapter we review some of the influences of traditional and modern Linguistics. First, a pot pourri of elements of linguistic theory which are essential, but not normally accommodated within grammatical theory.

Contrast and Similarity: Emic *vs* Etic

> Heraclitus knew long ago that "into the same river we both step and do not step" ... A man cannot understand well what a thing is unless to some extent he simultaneously knows what it *is not*.[5]

No single action, utterance, event or object is exactly the same as any other. Atoms may be exactly similar, but they will always be distinguished by identity of composition and locus in time and space. In the macroscopic natural and artificial universe which constitutes our universe of discourse, this similarity is never complete. Within the domain of discourse itself, the same word is never said the same way even by the same speaker. The similarity or dissimilarity that we wish to perceive here is said to be *emic*, whilst the dissimilarity which we wish to ignore is said to be *etic*. The etic differences in speech may involve tone, loudness, rate of speech, as well as many more subtle variations. Similarly an object may have many variant forms, which may involve size, shape and usage, quite apart from accidental variation:

> The etic viewpoint studies behaviour as from outside of a particular system, and as an essential initial approach to an alien system. The emic viewpoint results from studying behaviour as from inside the system. (I coined the words etic and emic from the words phonetic and phonemic, following the conventional linguistic usage of these latter terms.)[6]

Etic variation from one perspective may be emic from another. Thus harsh, loud, rapid speech may be a reflection of anger or urgency. The form of a table will be influenced by its usage: whether dining-, coffee-, dressing- or bedside-table. Variation in speech may go unremarked or be noted as an accent, may be a result of phonological context or may be free and totally insignificant:

> With linguistic forms: -s, -z, and -es can each be variants of the same English plural suffix. And as for sentences, it is hopelessly less than adequate … to list changes in them by deletions, or additions, or transformation without instituting a search for some criteria to find which of them in some psychological or behavioral sense are emically the same; otherwise we are in grammar back to the stage analogous to that reached by phonetics before there was a technique and theory to pull together variants into units, symbolized in some way as explicit phonemes.[7]

Phonology was revolutionized, if not truly begun, with this distinction of etic and emic, and the development of an analytical methodology to examine the *phones* (the etic units) in context, and so identify the *phonemes* (the emic units). Phonetics identifies the characteristic features of sounds; phonemics identifies the significant classes of sounds *for a given language*.

Speech is not our focus here, but rather learning and analysis. The main work of phonemics must be the discovery of order in language at every level, including the development of ontology. This principle depends on the distinction between emic contrast and etic variation.

The best way to identify emic units is Contrast in Identical Environment (CIE).[8] This is to say, if two etic units occur in the same slot in a particular context so as to produce contrasting units at the higher level, they therefore must themselves contrast and hence represent two distinct emic units. Thus the phones *[p]* in /pull/ (an unvoiced aspirated bilabial stop) and *[b]* in /born/ (a voiced unaspirated bilabial stop) represent phonemes /p/ and /b/ since they contrast in the words /pit/ and /bit/, /pack/ and /back/, /pot/ and /bot/, /pout/ and /bout/, /pet/ and /bet/, /path/ and /bath/, *etc*. This is the ideal situation. Incidentally, the square and slope bracketing is the convention for distinguishing phonetic and phonemic transcriptions of units.

Unfortunately, we don't always have such a clear contrast in identical environments, and we must resort to Contrast in Analogous Environment.[9] Thus /past/ and /bask/ only show a contrast in an analogous environment. The point of articulation of the final consonant (contoid phone) is different. Other phonetic differences represent, in general, variation. In particular a phoneme may be made up of a number of phones in free variation (*e.g.* in the Australian dialect "tuna" is normally pronounced [t^{y}una], but owing to American influence may be pronounced [tuna].

There is also Complementary Distribution (CD) in which the same phoneme uses different phones in mutually exclusive environments. "Tuna" (in the Australian dialect) is an example of such a distribution for /t/, [t^y] before /u/, [t] elsewhere. However, there are counterexamples: "toot" CIE with "tute", "coot" CIE with "cute". In fact, this is a function of orthography rather than phonology. The correct segmentation would show the palatalization of "u" to a distinct phoneme /yu/ − *cf* Russian's vowel pairs and mutes b .

Now we have introduced the concepts of contrast and variation, etic and emic, in the context of phonology, we can go on to think about their role in other hierarchies. The general nominal unit corresponding to an emic unit is an *eme*, and the etic units which comprise it are its *allos*:

> The relationship of an eme to its allos is really one of *representation*. That is, the eme is *represented* by its allos on a different level. Thus the recognition of this type of relationship involves the recognition of separate levels … The eme has its existence on one stratum, its allos on the adjacent lower stratum.[10]

The distinction being made is one of level. However the distinction is not limited to one pair of levels in a hierarchy; it is a matter of standpoint. A given level, viewed as a system, has certain significant units, the emic units. These units are formed of the components which may themselves be emic in the level below. But they are etic in that they do not directly belong to the organization of the system of the given level. This corresponds to the initiated recognizing and correctly grouping units which are distinguished or even grouped incorrectly by the foreigner.

Examples which are only indirectly linguistic include "knowing the category cup (as opposed to glass or bowl)".[11] Probably the most famous example is the distinguishing of seven different types of snow (using seven different words) by the Eskimos. Fillmore argues that, in the language of an individual, there are no exact synonyms, and hence presumably that there is no free variation, at least at the word level. In the case where there is a variation, such as [suppozed] and [supposed] or [greazy] and [greasy]:

My understanding of what happens in these areas is that the two pronunciations sort themselves into separate frames, one having to do with
the literal original use of the word, one with its metaphoric derived use
... The no-synonymy insight, then, is one about the tendency for distinguishable frames to be paired with distinguishable scenes. The insight
about their not being synonyms is seen as an insight about the nature of
the frame-to-scene mapping.[12]

Clark considers the development of children's comprehension of
words, and finds that at first a child does not distinguish between the
meanings of *more* and *less*. They are treated as synonyms with the
meaning "more". Apparently the fact that quantity is in focus is understood clearly while the appropriate direction is not. Evidently the positive direction, appropriate to the unmarked word, is assumed in both
cases.

Other quite different examples are *tell* and *ask*, and *boy* and *brother*.
In this latter case, *brother*, according to Clark, develops from a synonym
of "boy", with features [+ Male, − Adult], adding [+ Adult], then [+
Sibling], then [+ Reciprocal] (*viz.* he recognizes that he is also a
brother).

Many would actually prefer not to add in a negative feature when the
positive feature is already part of the prior hypothesis. This is the usual
approach in Concept Learning, but there is support for a purely additive
deletionless paradigm − as if painting a canvas. Thus all concepts may be
learned contrastively, by distinguishing features which are significant,
and adding them conjunctively to refine the concept, or alternately by
allowing variation, extending the concept disjunctively. This last mechanism seems to be rather rarely required and just as rarely used. It is
very difficult to think of naturally-occurring concepts (as distinct from
classes) which require disjunction. This is one reason why we may be
wary of having the "plus or minus adult" feature above − this addition is
disjunctive.

To overcome the deletionless objection, we have to suppose that the
concept is relearned from scratch without the offending incorrect over-
specialization. This in fact turns out to be fairly natural, and is the way
our learning experiments work. What actually happens is that the development of the overspecialized concept hypothesis is blocked, and extant
but hitherto relatively low-likelihood concept hypotheses come to the
forefront and are available for further modification.

It would seem that contrast has several roles. It appears to be something of a driving force behind learning. And it certainly is a shaping
force: the concept without the distinction can be refined by the addition
of a new feature. If there is a clear contrast in evidence there can be a
twofold addition, with one concept being developed and associated with
the negative feature, and one with the positive.

Contrast can be a differential shaping force: the positive, variant examples prompt generalization; the negative, contrastive examples block further development of unhelpful or unpromising avenues of generalization. This part of the process would moreover interact with that outlined above, giving rise to a considerably more complex picture of the role of contrast. This complexity would be particularly necessary if the positive feature does naturally gain precedence as Clark suggests. This more complex proposal seems to deal adequately with the apparent inconsequence of correction and other forms of negative information for the child's language development.

Another example of the influence of contrast is its attentional, focussing aspect. The unresolved contrasts are identified and tackled, then Clark hypothesizes an increase in the weighting, speed and/or quantity of generalizations. Increasing the learning parameter in equations of plasticity would have all of these effects.

So far we have been talking about contrasts in the abstract, as if we were always presented with a pair of contrasting units. In general, this situation is rare. In fact, it is more usual that at least one part of the contrasting pair is present only in our memory. Kuczaj focuses on the child's imitation in terms of practice and knowledge acquisition, seeing imitation as:

> the means for children to practice contrasts that are not yet within their productive system in that the model utterance produced by another may exceed children's linguistic competence.[13]

Here the contrasting forms are respectively just within and just outside the child's current knowledge and capability. What is clear from psycholinguistic evidence is that contrast must be conservative in order for it to be useful. This suggests that contrast must be able to take a concept which is already within the child's competence, and allow the creation of the distinction by the contrasting refinement of redundant, parallel concept recognizers. A contrast which is too subtle or depends on concepts outside the child's competence will be ignored. Thus the child must understand the concept of *more* as "different in quantity" before it can possibly make the *more-less* distinction.[14]

Equivalence and Nuance: Antonyms and Synonyms

We remarked earlier on Fillmore's question mark over the existence of true synonyms at the word level, or even true variation within an idiolect or dialect at the phoneme level. At these levels, such observations are little more than interesting. But at higher levels, this becomes an important issue.

The transformationalist assumes that transformational variants of a sentence (such as the active and passive forms) are in some sense equivalent to each other, and in a sense this is no doubt true. But unfortunately it is frequently evident that the transformationalist thinks that in many cases (*e.g.* active – passive, but not interrogative – indicative) the variation is completely free and arbitrary. He fails to recognize that the form is actually dictated by context and purpose. In particular, to pursue the example of voice, the active is the norm and the passive brings a different entity, the undergoer of the action (the *patient*), into focus as the subject of the sentence and of the discourse at this point. Moreover there is frequently a cohesion between successive sentences whereby an adjunct (*e.g. direct* or *indirect object*) of the previous sentence is made the *subject* of the passive sentence.

English has a word for the synonymy that is achieved by such transformation. The word is *paraphrase*, and it implies a significant divergence from the original, although meaning is supposedly preserved. Unfortunately, all students of translation are only too aware of the differences in nuance suggested by different paraphrases with the same basic meaning. And all students of Machine Translation will be aware of the corruption of such sentences as "the spirit is willing and the flesh is weak" into "the wine is agreeable but the meat has spoiled" by an early two-way translation system for Russian.

Synonymy can never be absolute and complete. This is especially true when we depart from the morpheme and word levels and consider the sentence level and above. A fundamental error has been made by those linguists and psychologists who assume that multiple sentences can comprise an equivalence class which has the same deep structure. Thus rather than judge a theory on how well this equivalence classification can be made, models should be designed which are capable of capturing the subtle distinctions and nuances in the usage of apparently synonymous words and sentences. This is, of course, a tall order, particularly at the word level where individual differences in lexicon are especially evident.

Anderson offers motivation for invariance of representation under paraphrase, in terms both of "efficiency and psychological plausibility":

> It is more efficient when trying to retrieve information at the time of test if that information is only stored in one form and it is not necessary to consider the possibility of many paraphrases of the same information. (However, they can usually be shown to be able to discriminate better than chance.)

Anderson continues with two pragmatic reasons why the paraphrase invariance ideal is not viable – in essence that it is not realizable. We can go further and argue that it is neither essential nor desirable. The evidence for paraphrase invariance in humans is that paraphrases are discriminated "better than chance". The choice of voice conveys information about the focus of the conversation and generally has some cohesive relationship with any preceding and succeeding clauses. Further, the adjunct is more likely to have been newly introduced than the subject, and the adjunct is more likely to be the subject (or at least a topic) of a subsequent clause than is the subject of the verb form in question. A specific example may be helpful here:

> On my way home I was nearly hit by a car. It must have run a red light because for once I did have a walk signal.

versus

> On my way home a car nearly hit me. I almost jumped out of my skin because for once I did have a walk sign.

The first sentence of the second example is stilted because a degree of cohesion has been lost in introducing non-specifically "a car" as subject since "I" was the primary topic. Interchanging the second sentences of the examples stretches the anaphora slightly, resulting in stylistic degradation and subjective disjointedness. We can't press the examples too much, but they illustrate a point: that synonymy is the result of insufficiently global a viewpoint. Why do we ever use redundant variants of expression? The variability, with its distinctive nuances, has probably been learned as appropriate responses to different contexts. This is far more likely than that it has been arbitrarily and innately determined. The variant forms in which a question may be asked may be learned by a hypothesis-and-correction learning paradigm.

One final point concerns the opposite potential, antonymy. Here there are two things to balance. The first is that antonyms are differentiated from a common concept. And the second is that there is apparently no more complete antonymy than there is complete synonymy. This is illustrated by a number of phenomena. The most obvious is that there are so many forms of negation. Thus an adjective may be negated by the use of the word "not" or the prefixes "un-", "in-" and "a-" (as well as case-specific use of other prefixes). The negatives formed by these mechanisms are not equivalent—in particular "a-" has acquired a unique character. There can be negatives of opposite extreme, of absence of extreme, of denial of relevance, of interchanging of components, to name a few.

One of an antonym pair (usually the positive member) often describes the contrast dimension with a generality unmatched by its opponent, whilst using the other has a considerably greater degree of specific nuance. Thus asking how long, tall or old something or someone is fairly neutral, but asking how short, young or new someone or something has quite different and often negative overtones.

Homonyms: Homophones and Homomorphs

Related to the synonym — almost an antonym, in fact — is the homonym. Rather than being different names with the same meaning, we have different meanings with the same name. This name may be written the same (a homograph) or may sound the same (a homophone). Synonymy is not really a problem, since the word gives rise to but the one meaning, we assume. It can be a slight problem in generation, but only if the synonymy is not total. We should be able to assume that we could choose any member of an equivalence class of true synonyms. Unfortunately, there are always differences which appear primarily in the extensions of the meaning. These are the basis for puns and the cause of errors such as those involving the "spirit" and "flesh" example we gave previously.

But this is more a problem of lack of synonymy, or more precisely still, an example of the reverse phenomenon, homonymy. The fact that the same word has several meanings or extensions of meaning, only some aspects of which are synonymous with any other word, is an obvious problem. The "word" (as the unit of communication) does not convey all the information necessary to identify the intended sense. Note that we are primarily referring to the word here, although some puns, slips of the ear, and garden-path sentences extend beyond the word level (*e.g.* "Why did the fly? Because the spider spied her!")

So context and function are essential disambiguating factors. There has been a lot of deliberation on this question, since it is the obvious problem in constructing a plausible model. It is much discussed in the AI literature, but let us refer to only one linguistic study: Fillmore's treatment of "the various meanings of the English noun bachelor".[15]

A correctable learning system would clearly seem to be best equipped to deal with this problem. Just because confusion will be corrected, it must be assumed that the system will "learn" more than one sense for a word, and that a token will index a set of meanings, each of which may index a *different* sequence pattern. This means that the different meanings of a word may belong to different classes, since they are then very easily differentiated by usage. In most cases verb/noun pairs (and the like) have an element of commonality (*cf* "fly" in the above example). In many cases homonyms have a common ancestry.

What about the derivation of alternate meanings, and the extension of existing words? Etymology is a most interesting and surprisingly complex field of endeavour, but the derivation of most words in the English language is quite well understood. Families of words can be traced back to single parents in the English of several ages, and the linguistic influences of several nationalities. The process of extension of the meaning of words is continuous. It is also an integral part of our learning process. Just consider the impact of the several industrial revolutions, and recently of the computer: masses of new meanings for old words have been coined. Most are blatant borrowings, such as "word" in the computer sense. A very few are cleverly contrived, such as "byte". Some started as acronyms or other compositions, such as "modem". Some are a pun-like mixture, such as "bit".

The essence of all derivation by extension is analogy. An arbitrary and formerly meaningless word will have a hard time gaining acceptance. A brilliant or blatant analogy will run away with itself, even though the first accidental usage, or deliberate coinage, was quite consciously metaphorical.

It may be useful, in closing this section, to give one example of the breadth of words that can spring, apparently naturally, from a single root — and this metaphorical usage is particularly appropriate for the word "plant". Its modern meanings vary through many contexts, with meanings as diverse as a spy, a factory, and the vegetable matter that springs up from a root, which is its basic meaning. A little thought can show the connections throughout all of the diversity.

Paradigmatic Learning and Context

Our discussions so far have led us to see the importance of learning in varied contexts. We now think about the situation where we hold the context constant and vary the unit or units of interest. This is the paradigm, which we have already seen is integral to our analytic processes. It is also a traditional tool for language learning or, more accurately, teaching. It should then be a tool which is recognized and accommodated for the teaching and design of language-learning models or computers.

The old grammar text did this in a rather uninspired way, drilling short patterns, often single words or phrases, conjugating or declining the forms of a verb or noun. A more sympathetic approach simply provides a number of fixed contexts into which members of the appropriate subclass of word (*e.g.* 1st declension or 2nd conjugation) may be substituted, not necessarily drawing out the pattern formally. In both cases, the association of person or case with ending (or whatever) can be learned. And the broader the base for association the better.

The child's situation frequently provides a correlate of this paradigmatic context. As we saw earlier, the child's private crib speech and language play often takes a paradigmatic form. Paradigms provide "templates for analysis [and] stereotypes for generation",[16] and a "context [which] delimits the range of possible action".[17] This latter concept is very important in AI and Piagetian psycholinguistics, where it goes under names such as *frame, scene, scheme* or *schema*. Context, or Fillmore's frames, are very important in disambiguating homonyms.

Ervin-Tripp makes a contrasting point that we "must hear units in the diverse positions possible" to allow sufficient scope for generalization.[18] This is really the opposite of paradigm, but is still reminiscent of the template viewpoint, however the unit in focus is kept and the context is exchanged. This type of drill is also fairly common in language teaching, and very common in child experience.

Some workers think that paradigmatic analysis is enough to learn grammar without worrying about semantics. Indeed, our experiments have something of this flavour. Paradigmatic analysis is certainly a powerful tool, but it gives rise to a number of questions: "How powerful is it?", and "What assistance is required?"

> Attempts have been made to construct an algorithm for automatically generating a phrase structure grammar for a language solely by analyzing a text of the language. One approach uses the "distributional analysis" of Harris (1951, 1964) and Hockett (1958). Namely, one associates phrases which are found to occur in the same context, thereby defining phrase categories and simultaneously enlarging the set of contexts which can be considered equivalent; then one records how phrase categories are constructed by concatenation of phrase categories. Another approach ... uses "identification by enumeration" ... These attempts suggest the question, "Is there enough information in a text, even one of unlimited length, to allow the identification of a context-free language?" The results presented in Section 3 show that it is impossible to construct a learning algorithm for the entire class of context-free languages if the only information is an arbitrary text ... However, it would be useful to determine if there are interesting subclasses of the class of context-free languages which can be identified by either of these approaches.[19]

Let us now consider the more formal grammatical structure of language. Note that this does not mean that we are confining ourselves to the grammatical hierarchy. However, as vision was our model for neurological considerations, syntax and parsing provide the model for the linguistics. The biggest divergence between languages is in the grammatical hierarchy, both in terms of rules and morphs. The other main area of divergence is in cultural perspective, and we will turn first to this.

Multiple Language Applicability: e.g. Fixed vs Free Word Order

Our research should be applicable to any natural language. The difference between languages can be marked — not just in vocabulary, but in semantic categories and the concepts which are distinguished by the language. To give an example:

> The Japanese verb *kaku* and the English verb *write* are frequently acceptable translations of each other, but the scene-and-frame analysis of

the two words show them to be partly different ... In the case of the Japanese word, the nature of the resulting trace is left more or less unspecified ... The answer can identify a word or a sentence or character, or, just as well, a sketch or a circle or a doodle.[20]

This should not pose any real problem for a learning system, since if a model can learn the concepts important in a language like English, it should be able to do so in any other language. A range of specific and general concepts is present in every language, the difference lies in which are recognized, and which are most significant in the culture.

It is in syntax that the greatest difference lies. The most important contrast is between the specification of word order, and the specification of inflection. Both of these are cohesive in nature. Various restrictions are imposed on an assemblage of words and morphs according to the relationship between their roles. But most grammatical theories seem to be mainly concerned with word order; parsing usually just determines the order of subunits. This needn't be the case, but we don"t know of any grammatical theory that has adopted any other model.

Variations of word order occur in systematic ways, either according to the cohesion of a construct in the grammatical hierarchy, or to its role in relation to another hierarchy, usually the referential hierarchy.

Despite the differences, there is a large degree of commonality between languages — as there must be, given the common innate human mechanisms. McNeill proposes three specific universals:

Every language has a sound system ... of some 15 distinctive features ...

Every language contains the same basic syntactic categories ...

Every language adheres to the same basic grammatical relations among these categories ... [21]

These seem to have a descending order of likelihood. The first has a degree of freedom, plus or minus some small number. The second seems true at the gross level of noun and verb, subject and object, but less true at the level of small particles, subcategories *etc.* The third is either false or vacuous. It is either really referring to semantic or referential relationships, ontology rather than language, or some other bad definition of grammatical relationship. Or it ignores the two or three completely different systems of syntax.

This viewpoint is very heavily influenced by the TGG concepts of interlingua and deep structure. These presuppose that every human being has the same innate deep structure. It also presupposes that the same innate sets of possible transformations are available to choose from — specific and explicit innately specified sets, rather than a general and potentially learnable set. There are a few sources of evidence for an innate word order: *e.g.* that from creoles, and that reported by Slobin in studies of infants learning Russian:

> Even in a language with relatively free word order (Russian), the early constructions of children are ordered.[22]

However, we can make the converse argument that it seems to be empirical that *no* regularities are true of every known NL. So it seems sensible to model the NL mechanism by a mechanism which has *no* prior tendency to prefer some syntagms over others.

This subsection emphasized the importance of taking an approach which explains language in the context of all that is known about language, and is applicable to the acquisition of any Natural Language:

> Although such considerations seem elementary, the investigation of language acquisition has not proceeded in this way ... No theories of language acquisition of which we are aware are concerned with this demonstration.[23]

An example of a proposed restriction, which is universally applicable, is the TGG X-theory which claims that all phrase structure rules for a given language have a similar form. That is for all X-phrases the X has the same ordering relation with its arguments and specifiers (where X may be noun, verb, preposition, *etc.*).

Classes: Open *vs* Closed

As soon as children start to put two words together, their speech seems to obey rules which govern the ways in which particular words are used. Around 1963, Braine analyzed the distribution of vocabulary in a corpus of children's speech and concluded that there were two classes of words: a small "closed" class of "pivot" words and a much larger "open" class of words. The "open" class words were more likely to have been used in one-word utterances. The "closed" class words almost invariably occupied a fixed position in a two-word utterance:

> One first-position pivot, for example, is *allgone* ... in utterances such as *allgone shoe, allgone bandage, allgone outside* ... A common second-position pivot is *on*, as in utterances such as *shoe on, bandage on, fix on* ... Words such as *shoe* and *bandage* fall into the residual "open class" of words, freely occurring with both first and second position pivots ... All of the words in the open class can occur as single-word utterances, but some of the pivot words never do.[24]

This analysis provides us with at least three grammatical classes (two pivot, one open) and half a dozen rules. More recent evidence shows that things are not quite so simple as this:

The simple rules *Ps P* + *O* and *O* + *Ps P*, which summarize ... obtained and interpretable utterances ... also predict a large number of others ... Bowerman (1973) was one of the first and most detailed of what has become a flood of disconfirmation of pivot grammars in languages other than English. In all cases there seems to be the kind of frequency imbalance among words which is the starting point for the pivot-open distinction ... Then it turns out that ... the presumptive pivot class and ... the presumptive open class fail to manifest one, some, or all of the distributional relations they are supposed to manifest.[25]

This still leaves the question of why children start to build multi-word utterances in ways that have this "pivot look":

> There are always a few words which have, for semantic reasons, an extremely wide compositional potential ... The look derives from an impression that there is a sharp discontinuity of combinatorial features in the child's words: some, the pivots occurring in numerous different combinations and others, the open words occurring in very few combinations ... If, in addition, the pivot words in two-word combinations are at least usually found in just one position, first or second, then the pivot look is especially strong ... I want to offer here some data indicating that the pivot look ... is mainly due to the very wide utility of certain words and the accessibility to the child of their meanings.[26]

Brown's point concerns a view of the data which, in a more general sense, is a natural outgrowth of the generative approach. TGG tends to explain all distributional data in terms of syntax, without allowing for the semantic and referential in words.

So how might the classes be learned, assuming there is some basis for the distinction? The early nativist view of McNeill, since largely disavowed, was fairly deterministic:

> McNeill (1966d) has argued that there is a very strong initial constraint on the development of grammatical categories. A child is presumed to possess an initial categorical hierarchy which would "direct the child's discovery of the classes of English" ... At the top of the hierarchy two classes might be distinguished, pivot and open classes, and so a child would be led to discover those two classes in the speech sample he is exposed to.[27]

Leaving aside the innate determinism of this approach, such binary differentiation is quite plausible. The behaviourist explanation can also be simulated:

> Now when the child acquires his first words he probably does so as a function of simple conditioning or paired-associate learning. The parent places objects, including himself, before the child and labels them; he frequently indicates observable characteristics of those objects in adjective and verb forms; and he may even do such things as wave the

child's hand and say "byebye" ... Some of the single word utterances of the child may, however, occur under the same or similar stimulus conditions. For example, consider the environmental conditions in which the child's ball is on a shelf, in sight, but out of reach. The child may obtain the ball on the shelf by saying "want", and perhaps pointing, or he may obtain the ball by saying "ball". Sometimes he says "want" and sometimes he says "ball" and both utterances may bring about the desired result ... We have then the simplest case of response equivalence and the occasion for the occurrence of "want" to elicit "ball" and, thus, the two-word utterance is possible. But "want" may have been used interchangeably with "truck", and "dolly", and "horsie" in which case we have a class of words which go with "want". We have a pivot word "want" and an open class of items which a child may want at one time or another ... The open-open construction generally involves the omission of the pivot word necessary for communication. Thus, in the construction "man car" the pivot word "in" may be missing ... The utterance is possible through chaining from open to pivot to open word classes ... with the mediating pivotal word position omitted, but implied, in the utterance.[28]

This proposal for forming grammatical associations depends on similarities of referential frame. This is basic to our experiments, but none of those experiments tries to mimic the pivot-open class paradigm. More generally, the one- two- three-word sequence of stages requires a partial analysis approach, since children are not given actual models for the grammars at those stages.

Privileges of Occurrence: Class and Hyperclass

The division of words into classes which are syntactically equivalent is a fundamental property of grammar. All the words of a given class may substitute for any of the others in all possible contexts. Taking this strictly produces smaller *subclasses* (*e.g.* mass noun, intransitive verb, *etc.*) rather than the generally recognized *classes* (noun, verb, *etc*). Therefore, in the usual terminology, the term *classes* sacrifices this specificity:

> The fundamental notion in linguistic syntax is that the words of any natural language can be grouped into classes which are defined by the fact that the members of a class have similar "privileges of occurrence" in sentences. Certain very large and rough syntactic classes are traditionally called the parts of speech ... If a child has learned to organize words into such classes, to enter them on mental lists of syntactic equivalents, he will have a very powerful means of getting beyond his corpus.[29]

If we consider the class as filling a slot in a rule, or formula, we can use still wider types of classes. Thus, subject and object slots may be filled by noun phrases and pronouns. The sets of classes which may fill particular slots are called *hyperclasses*. The hyperclass of fillers for a given slot can also be called its *filler class*.

The concepts of hyperclass and "privileges of occurrence" suggest a paradigmatic definition of class, and this in turn suggests a behaviourist associative paradigm for learning classes. But it is precisely this sort of distributional mechanism which has been shown to be unfruitful, except in well constructed presentation of the data, or by well defined limitation of the model. However, the admission of semantic cues and referential structure produces a far more powerful system.

In general, the problems of development of ontology and of semantics are similar to those of the development of syntax. Thus, models which show learning of a phrase structure grammar corresponding to a simple constructed "referential" grammar are missing the prime source of difficulty. The real question is whether the processed sensory-motor fields are sufficiently ordered. This order is both physical and temporal, and reflects the order implicit in the universe, and explicit in the cortical mapping which allows such a process. There is little point in defining an arbitrary "Representation Language" just so that an isomorphic "Natural Language" can be learned. In fact, the prior question is the learning of such a "Representation Language", or ontology.

The learning of linguistic and ontological classes has been neglected in Computational Linguistics. It is much easier to learn "grammar" if the classes of words are given, or to extend "vocabulary" by classifying words into known classes. It is not possible to learn non-trivial languages, learning both classes and rules in parallel and *ab initio*, without recourse to interhierarchical association. There are theoretical objections suggesting that this is an impossible goal without such extragrammatical assistance. Our experiments, described later, represent the small distance we have been able to go in this direction, showing an example of partial learning of a "Natural Language" and a "Representation Language" without interdependence.

Formulae: Slot – Intrahierarchical Nature

We now turn to look at the rules, which correspond to the grouping of elements of one set of hyperclasses to become a unit which is a member of a higher level hyperclass. We will call these *formulae* after Pike. Despite our earlier remarks about order independence, word order seems to be important at many levels in all natural languages. It is easiest to define hyperclasses of formulae reflecting the different possible word orders rather than to define a single set of units with no implicit order. In any case, the function and determination of appropriate orderings are made explicit by *cohesion* in any implementation based on the tagmemic model. The omission or inclusion of optional and obligatory units is also assumed to be specified by *cohesion*.

The identification of the position of a unit within a formula is called its *slot*. In Pike's examples, this takes two forms, distinguished names, *e.g.* subject, predicate, adjunct; or binary centrality, *viz.* nucleus, margin. Since there may be more than one adjunct (*e.g.* direct and indirect objects) or margin (*e.g.* of time or location) according to Pike's formulation, the slot is not fully deterministic, and its specification is therefore completed by its conjunction with *role*.

From the point of view of a computational model, determining the slot independent of its role is essential. In our models no labels are used, but formulae are assumed to be binary, and slot is purely a matter of distinguishing first and second units within a formula. The binary approach is not completely natural, and has the effect of placing a further load on cohesion — since margins and adjuncts may have order constraints previously handled within a single formula. However, a recursive approach with accumulation of cohesive tags for occurrence in nominally lower level units is sufficient not to lose generality.

The Subjects of active sentences and passive sentences have completely different roles. There is a difference in meaning between "the dog bit the man" and "the dog was bitten by the man". In both cases "dog" is the nucleus of the subject, "bite" is the nucleus of the predicate, and "man" is the nucleus of the adjunct. However, the "dog" is respectively actor and undergoer, and the "man" is respectively undergoer and actor. The actor — undergoer labelling is a function of the referential scene, rather than the parse structure of the grammatical hierarchy. Thus the cohesive flagging of predicate, with respectively active and passive voice, determines the *role* of the subject and restricts the *role* of any adjuncts.

The actor of tagmemic terminology corresponds to the subject in Deep Structure in TGG. It has been suggested that the Agent-Action-Object order is the most natural for children, part of a language independent Deep Structure, and is an innate linguistic characteristic:

> In effect, the Government-Binding theory claims that simple N-V-N strategies never have to be abandoned, because syntactic form never deviates from semantic form, contrary to surface impressions. This confluence of representational levels has a prima facie appeal from the standpoint of acquisition, of course.[30]

Why is this order preferred? To explain this we use the concept of focus — in a sentence the subject holds the focus, and is usually the actor. Given a situation where a child wants his mother to get him a ball, the one-word sentences "ball", "want" or "get", "mummy" have different effects. The first gets attention from whoever is present and focuses that attention on the ball. Only prosody and repetition can make it do more than that. Either of the verbs expresses that the child actually wants something, but requires a deictic gesture to complete the semantic effect. The last sentence focuses attention on the person who can achieve the desired physical effect. If the sentence can have but one word and must identify the object, the choice is clear: object is most important. If the child can use two words and must identify in the context either actor or action as well as object, again the choice is made on that basis. In an imperative context, the actor must certainly come first if he or she must be specified. Since the actor is more closely associated with action than object we have that as a competing force to the greater relevance of the object, and a possible explanation for a natural word order. We also have an explanation of why other word orders can be used.

It is clear that *role* is identified by certain features of the sentence's form, whether it is transformed into another sentential form or related directly to a framework. *Role* is thus a useful characteristic to be identified in our grammatical formulae, but it is apparent that it cannot be understood purely in grammatical terms. It is *interhierarchical* in that it reflects *filler-slot* structure in another hierarchy.

Formulae: Cohesion — Transhierarchical Nature

The key to the usefulness of Pike's Tagmemic theory is *cohesion*. It extends to many of the problems for which transformations are used in TGG, but rather than extending the space of possible languages and running into problems because of excessive "power", *cohesion* limits the space of possible sentences for a particular language.

Cohesion, with *slot*, *role* and *filler class*, completes Pike's four-featured Tagmemic unit, the *tagmeme*. The most straightforward definition of *cohesion* is as:

> The feature of a tagmeme which controls the manner in which it affects (governs) or is affected (governed) by other tagmemes.[31]

Some straightforward examples are agreement of number within a noun phrase, and within a clause root. A more subtle form of cohesion is the subdivision of the verb into transitive, intransitive, *etc.* In this case there is a cohesive relationship between the formulae appropriate to a particular verb, and conversely the verbs appropriate to a particular formula. The transitivity cohesion is particularly important in a binary representation of Phrase Structure, since it may be propagated to where it must correlate with the direct or indirect objects.

Pike has queried whether cohesion is a restrictive feature. He sees his treatment of cohesion over the last few years as in a sense "representing the repository of all human knowledge as contained in that particular speaking individual". This claim for cohesion seems to leave little room for the other hierarchies, formulae, classes, *etc.* But cohesion, as "relationship" *par excellence*, is the organization which reflects relationships between the structural units of a hierarchy. Thus it captures the knowledge within that hierarchy. Role shares this importance, but mainly reflects relationships across different hierarchies, including semantic relationships.

The natural tendency of entropy is to uniformity. This, paradoxically, we describe as "disorder". "Order" involves an active process of structuring and differentiation. Reorganization and self-organization are ultimately anti-entropic. Between them cohesion and role represent our active self-organized and contextually impressed relationships. Hence they are the active repository of our knowledge. In the referential hierarchy, for example, or in our ontology, every physical law we "understand" is a cohesive relationship in the referential hierarchy.

Thus the essential nature of cohesion is that it imposes order, and it is learned according to the necessity for order or the potential for discrimination. This is illustrated by psycholinguistic data on the order of learning inflections in English:

> Interestingly, the possessive "-'s" and the third person singular present "-s" are among the inflections learned relatively late (Bellugi, 1964). In a sense, these inflections are redundant. Thus, the possessive may be indicated in the child's language by a simple rule ... The plural "-s" and the past ending "-ed", by contrast, carry semantic information that cannot be expressed by position rules, and these inflections appear earlier.[32]

Note that all of these inflections are redundant to a degree. Thus the most essential of them, the past tense, can also be implied by referential context (*e.g.* "yesterday"). This particular inflection has a cohesive relationship with such margins: its selection is restricted by the margin of time. The same inflection has a role relationship with the referential context: it has a semantic content "past" and selects or is restricted by a relationship which places the referenced event before the current conversational event. The essence of cohesion is that commitment to a particular paradigm is more widespread than the unit most directly affected, although there may be a direct semantic or role selection as well.

In closing, we consider an example which shows that complexity of the interaction of cohesion and role is not limited to the grammatical and referential hierarchies. The use of "a" and "an" before mutually exclusive classes of nouns is an example of cohesion, when viewed purely at a transhierarchical level. From an interhierarchical viewpoint, the phenomenon is morphophonemic since it ultimately depends on the phonetic character of vowels and consonants. However, the ambiguous position of the phoneme /h/, which was originally not always an alphabetic letter at all, but a "rough breathing" on the initial vowel in

Classical Greek, may indicate that the choice is made by a rule of cohesion. In the case of /h/, this is enforced or not according to social norms rather than morphophonemic laws: consider /an hour/ *versus* /a hospital/ or /an hospital/.

As a final point, cohesion acts along the lines of the *formula-filler* relationships. It does not reach arbitrarily between disparate points in a hierarchy. It operates within a single formula, but then attaches to the parent class, the head, or the right hand side of the formula, and to the implicated sibling classes. So it acts across a single level of the hierarchy, and through a single formula. This is not to say that it cannot be manifested between an arbitrary pair of tagmemes. On the contrary, it can be transmitted to a lower level through the children (subtended formulae) of an implicated sibling class. It can also be transmitted to a higher level through the parents of an implicated parent class. However cohesion can only extend between two units if it is carried by all formulae in the substructure of the parse tree connecting the two tagmemes.

Although Pike shows cohesion originating at a particular tagmeme such as the plural, this is not the only case. The plurality actually originates in the referential structure and affects the entire clausal structure, whether or not the subject appears first or at all. *Cohesion* and *role* relationships may well operate as parallel correlations inconsistent with such a serial viewpoint.

The Reality of the Word

Why are "a" and "in", in the sense of article and preposition, "words", whilst "a-" and "in-", in the sense of negation are "prefixes"? The answer has to do first with the limited class of words which can accept the prefixes. But there is a second and more important reason: whereas the prefixes are modifying a single word, the words relate to a larger grammatical unit. Many words can intervene between an article or preposition and the "noun" ultimately governed by it.

Phonetically, these small words may nonetheless merge with the word or words alongside to produce a single morphophonemic "word". This accounts for a sizeable portion of the connected speech problem in computer speech recognition. Small words which tend to attach themselves to neighbouring words are called "clitics". In many cases it is very difficult to distinguish between "clitics" and "affixes" (the class of prefixes plus suffixes plus, in some languages, infixes).

There is some arbitrariness about the choice of the word as the atomic unit in the sentence. It is not that we can't talk about affixes, or name them separately—we have just done just that. It is not that they are the smallest units of meaning—the morphemes are that. The distinction is fairly complex, and possibly historically fairly recent (the last few centuries perhaps).

As an example of the arbitrariness of the word, or at least of the difficulty of deciding what is a unit, consider a "word" class for the grammar determined for a child's speech:

all gone, broken, fall down, tired.[33]

All of these "words" have similar two syllable forms, and in the child's grammar, each may substitute for any of the others and produce a grammatical sentence — although semantics, and in particular animacy of the "subject", will constrain occurrence. For the child these are words. It is only as the distributional freedom or variation passes a certain level that the components are identified as separate morphs, and perhaps eventually as separate words.

We started out with the paradox that "in" is a word, and "in-" a prefix. The distributional criteria we gave were about the impossibility of intervention. There is however Australian dialectic which gives the lie to the "im-bloody-possibility of inter-bloody-vention". I have even heard multiple incursions into a single word!

There is a related question about minimal units and subunits of the phonological hierarchy. We have already observed that phonological words and grammatical words do not necessarily correspond, which is recognized in the label "clitic". What is the atomic unit of the phonological hierarchy? It cannot be the feature, since features cannot in general be articulated in isolation. For the same reason it cannot be the phoneme. The next level is the syllable, which seems to provide the best basis for an analytic approach to speech data. A child can select at an early stage from an "alphabet" of syllables, but not from an "alphabet" of features, phones, phonemes, morphs, morphemes, or words. The Chinese characters constitute such a syllabic alphabet.

Pike comments on the fundamental character of syllables:

> I would personally expect to hear syllables. To be sure, some scholars might disagree—since they think they can (or that they do) describe English elegantly without them ... But in my wildest nightmares I have not imagined any way to describe usefully all the data easily accessible to use about English conversation without using *some* kind of grouping of sounds into chunks which may include sequences of two or more sounds, such that the groups are distinguishable from one another by pauses, hesitations, contrastive peaks of intensity or "prominence", or other device; and these group units are often more or less comparable in length of pronunciation time, so that a *rhythmicity* is formed ... Such a rhythm unit, we add now, seems to be a part of human necessity ... No one is capable of making a long rational discourse having a string of identically-long sounds ungrouped, nonrhythmic. Rather this physical activity of speaking is hierarchical, as evidenced by this rhythm.[34]

Finally, we can also distinguish an orthographical hierarchy. The orthographical and grammatical hierarchies are not in precise isomorphism (or there would be no point in distinguishing them). An example is the word "no one" (as in the last quotation from Pike). This is a word, in the same way as "nobody". It just presents particular orthographical difficulties. We have also seen the transformation, over the last few decades, of "to day" into "to-day" into "today". The whole issue of hyphenation as an intermediate step in the formation of words is specifically pertinent.

Notes to Chapter Nine

1. Lyons, John, *Introduction to Theoretical Linguistics* (Cambridge University Press, Cambridge, UK, 1968); Hockett, Charles F., "Grammar for the Hearer", *Proc. Symposia in App. Math.*, Vol. XII (Amer. Mathl Soc., 1961), pp.220-236.
2. Hockett, Charles F., "Grammar for the Hearer", *Proc. Symposia in App. Math.*, Vol. XII (Amer. Mathl Soc., 1961), p.31.
3. *Op. cit.*, p.33.
4. *Ibid.*
5. Pike, Kenneth L., *Language in Relation to a Unified Theory of the Structure of Human Behavior* (Mouton, The Hague, Holland, 1954/1967), p.656n, 16.
6. *Op. cit.*, p.37.
7. *Op. cit.*, p.17.
8. Pike, Kenneth L., *Phonemics* (Summer Institute of Linguistics, Santa Ana, CA, 1947), p.80ff.
9. *Op. cit.*, p.73.
10. Lamb, Sydney M., "On the Mechanization of Syntactic Analysis", *1961 Conference on Machine Translation and Applied Language Analysis*, Vol. II (1961), p.675.
11. Fillmore, C. J., "Scenes-and-frames semantics", in A. Zampolli, ed., *Linguistics Structures Processing* (North Holland, 1977), p.56.
12. *Op. cit.*, p.78.
13. Kuczaj, Stan A., *Crib Speech and Language Play* (Springer-Verlag, New York, NY, 1983), p.16.
14. Clark, Eva V., "What's in a Word? On the Child's Acquisition of Semantics in his First Language", in Timothy E. Moore, *Cognitive Development and the Acquisition of Language* (Academic Press, New York, 1973), pp.65-110.
15. Fillmore, C. J., "Scenes-and-frames semantics", in A. Zampolli, ed., *Linguistics Structures Processing* (North Holland, 1977), p.67.
16. Wilks, Y., "An Artificial Intelligence Approach to Machine Translation", in Roger C. Schank and K. M. Colby, eds, *Computer Models of Thought and Language* (Freeman, 1973), p.116ff.

17. Schank, Roger C., "Identification of Conceptualization Underlying Natural Language", in Roger C. Schank and K. M. Colby, eds, *Computer Models of Thought and Language* (Freeman, 1973), p.189.

18. Ervin-Tripp, Susan, "Some Strategies for the First Years", in Timothy E. Moore, ed., *Cognitive Development and the Acquisition of Language* (Academic Press, New York, 1973), p.263.

19. Gold, E. M., "Language Identification in the Limit", *Information and Control*, Vol. 10 (1967), p.454f.

20. Fillmore, C. J., "Scenes-and-frames semantics", in A. Zampolli, ed., *Linguistics Structures Processing* (North Holland, 1977), p.64.

21. McNeill, David, "The Capacity for the Ontogenesis of Grammar", in Dan I. Slobin, *The Ontogenesis of Language* (Academic Press, 1971), p.21.

22. Kelley, K.L., *Early Syntactic Acquisition* (Rand Corporation, Santa Monica, CA, November 1967), p.49.

23. Wexler, Kenneth, and Peter W. Culicover, *Formal Principles of Language Acquisition* (MIT Press, Cambridge, MA, 1980), p.4.

24. Slobin, Dan I., *The Ontogenesis of Language* (Academic Press, New York, 1971), p.4f.

25. Brown, Roger, *A First Language: the early stages* (London, UK, Allen and Unwin, 1973), p.99.

26. *Op. cit.,* p.169.

27. Kelley, K.L., *Early Syntactic Acquisition* (Rand Corporation, Santa Monica, CA, November 1967), p.65.

28. Palermo, David S., "On Learning to Talk: Are Principles Derived from the Learning Laboratory Applicable?" in Dan I. Slobin, ed., *The Ontogenesis of Language* (Academic Press, 1971), p.48ff.

29. Brown, Roger, and Colin Fraser, "The Acquisition of Syntax", in C. N. Cofer and Barbara S. Musgrave, eds, *Verbal Behavior and Learning: Problems and Processes* (McGraw-Hill, 1963).

30. Berwick, Robert C., *The Acquisition of Syntactic Knowledge* (MIT Press, Cambridge, MA, 1985), p.89f.

31. Pike, Kenneth L., and E. G. Pike, *Grammatical Analysis* (Summer Institute of Linguistics and University of Texas at Arlington, Dallas, Texas, 1977), p.482.

32. Schlesinger, I.M., "Production of Utterances and Language Acquisition" in Dan I. Slobin, *The Ontogenesis of Language* (Academic Press, 1971), p.81f.

33. Brown, Roger, and Colin Fraser, "The Acquisition of Syntax", in C. N. Cofer and Barbara S. Musgrave, eds, *Verbal Behavior and Learning: Problems and Processes* (McGraw-Hill, 1963), p.186.

34. Pike, Kenneth L., and E. G. Pike, *Grammatical Analysis* (Summer Institute of Linguistics and University of Texas at Arlington, Dallas, Texas, 1977), p.21f.

Chapter Ten

The Ubiquity of the Sentence

This chapter considers the larger broader functions of language and grammar. The sentence is both the highest point of grammatical explanation to which traditional grammars aspire, and in its complexity and variety the stumbling block for elaborations based on any theory. The relationships between the major components of one or more sentences, and the possible variations and subtleties admitted by a language at this level, provide the basis for the enrichment of our linguistic theories. We look here at some of the hidden agenda which lies beneath the sentential surface, the expectation and anticipation which lie beneath our pronoun system, including the other understood omissions of anaphora and elision, and the class of humour represented by riddles involving puns and scenarios involving misinformation. We examine whether our grammatical assumptions in areas such as recursion and transformation are adequate, warranted or just simplisitic. Our conclusions are that these approaches gloss over certain semantic overtones and cohesive constraints. We end up questioning the validity of even trying to find a complete syntax and semantics which is invariant across both individual and time, and assert the importance of a dynamic model of grammar.

Moving up from the "word" toward the largest syntactically specified "chunk", we come to the "sentence". The sentence like the word is an arbitrarily defined unit; it is rarely as self-sufficient as is claimed. An alternate name for the linguistic unit we discuss in this chapter is *utterance*, which is used frequently in psycholinguistic studies — particularly of the corresponding unit in the phonological hierarchy.

The utterance is the first prototype for a sentence, and both utterance and sentence fit into larger hierarchies and do not represent the root of the phrase structure. The word "sentence" tends to be used in traditional grammars, and in TGG — which specifically defines a grammar as a mechanism capable of generating all and only all legal "sentences". We can extend this superstructure further:

> We can see ... that Mark and his mother, like any successful conversationalists, are engaging in a collaborative activity. Collaborative, firstly, in the orderly sequencing of speaking and listening taking *turns* to fill *slots*. Collaborative, secondly, in relating the meanings expressed in each turn to those in the turns that precede and follow. Collaborative, finally, in agreeing on the objects and actions in the shared situation to

which these meanings are intended to apply *role* ... As we have seen, one of the most noticeable characteristics of conversation is the orderliness with which participants take turns in speaking, rarely overlapping or leaving long periods of silence ... Ensuring a smooth transition from one speaking turn to the next is thus fundamental to the sequential structuring of conversation, and it depends upon several forms of behaviour.[1]

Pike suggests an extended hierarchy with paragraphs, monologues and exchanges. But even this structure is primitive. We have already discussed the features of the phonological hierarchy such as point of articulation and voicing, and of the referential hierarchy such as aspect and voice. We now turn to look at the grammatical hierarchy and to relate these to this proposed, Tagmemics inspired, model. This in some cases includes explanation of how the phenomena would arise from the hypotheses of Chapter Fourteen.

Pronouns and Anaphora

The closed pronoun class is one of the best illustrations of the interrelation of the tagmemic features. The pronoun class is a component of the hyperclass which is the filler class in, *inter alia*, the subject slots of the formulae defining the clause-root hyperclass. It is not clear how Pike sees the selection of case, but he seems to regard the filler class for the subject slot as including only pronouns in the nominative and, of course, noun phrases. Here we can simply treat the slot in the formulae as having a cohesive feature which specifies nominative case – in the same way that gender and number agreement with the referent of the pronoun might specify masculine gender and singular number. These three cohesive features determine the choice of a pronoun, and in other languages they would also determine the inflection of articles, adjectives and nouns.

Pike distinguished in his notation three classes of cohesive relationships: governs (originates), governed (affected only) and transitive. As we have said earlier, there is a case for not associating any direction with cohesion, but treating it only as a declaration of consistency. The case for specifying government is strongest when the cohesion is an arbitrary function (such as neuter gender for female referent) and it seems clear that a choice of word has actually determined the gender of the agreeing pronouns. But Pike associates government with the specific tagmemes which compose a formula.

The primary objection to assigning direction in this way is that in principle the direction is not a function of the tagmeme. The formulae and phrase structure are almost identical in "before I read it, I knew it would be a good book", "before I read it, I knew the book would be a good one", and "before I read the book, I knew it would be a good one". The only difference is where the noun phrase is slotted, and whether a pronoun is substituting for a noun or a noun phrase. Thus the direction of the cohesion cannot be a function of formula and slot.

The first and second person pronouns introduce further complexities in languages like English, French, German, *etc.* where second person pronouns are used in plural form with singular meaning. A still more complex phenomenon is the usage of self-reference and addressee-reference.

Cohesion in anaphora serves to disambiguate the possible referents of a pronoun. There is thus an opportunity for contrast, which is essential to the learning of the class, its semantics, and its cohesion. Note that the cohesion of anaphora in the grammatical hierarchy reflects cohesion of identity in the referential hierarchy. Anaphora is a specific case of a more general cohesion of topic which applies at clause-root level and above.

Interpretations: Puns, Trick Questions and Garden Paths

Some sentences, though syntactically correct, cannot at first be understood unambiguously or logically—such sentences as nonsense sentences, garden path sentences, puns and trick questions. Trick questions have stated preconditions or logical implications which are simply not true. A good natural language system "checks for this type of "loaded question" which presupposes things that aren't true" and thus SHRDLU responds: "I CAN'T EXPLAIN A NON-EXISTENT EVENT".[2]

In general a human may accept a faulty assumption for some time before realizing the fallacy, which illustrates the difference between logic and meaning. The system should try to understand the precondition in relation to the intended referents, and it should be able to detect an anomaly and take appropriate action. Humans recognize and act on such inconsistency consciously, although it is triggered by processing at a subconscious level.

Winograd also points out that nonsense sentences such as Chomsky's "colorless green ideas sleep furiously" would be eliminated easily by an attempt to make sense of the sentence, or any one of the anomalous collocations.

Puns and trick sentences are sometimes cited as evidence of parallel processing. There is some form of homonymy in this phenomenon, either at the word level, in the case of the pun, or at the sentence level in the case of the garden-path sentence. However, the relationships between selection of interpretation, parallelism and backtracking are much more complex than the inventors of garden-path sentences suggest. Parallel processing and thresholding imply that the subconscious understanding processes for the alternate parses or associations are not particularly noteworthy. But in fact the way a pun works is that the dual association is brought to consciousness, and the paradox of a garden path sentence (such as "The horse raced past the barn fell") is that there is a conscious failure to understand at first, and then backtracking and reparsing happen. Thus Schank asserts:

> A system ... should, in principle, never find more than one meaning for a given sentence at one time. Whereas this idea is contrary to the traditional one taken by researchers in this area in the past, we again call on the notion of human modelling as defense. That is, humans simply do not see all the ambiguities present in a given sentence at one time. Rather they see one meaning, and then they see another if the circumstances are right.[3]

We can now consider a possible explanation of these phenomena. The argument is that there is a lot of subconscious parallelism in the processes of parsing and assigning meaning. The different types of parsing for each modality, and between hierarchies, all proceed simultaneously. Activation and expectation play a part in which parses and interpretations are enhanced or masked. If a thresholding happens only one meaning will emerge. But if a second interpretation is also highly enough activated we will perceive a pun.

Once it has been used, an interpretation's degree of activation reduces, it enters a refractory state, and is temporarily removed from the focus of attention. Simultaneously, in the case of the pun, the interpretation will have increased the activation of the context, thus maintaining or increasing the activation of the competing interpretation. But in the more usual case, the successful interpretation will not support alternate interpretations. The expectations will be confirmed for the primary interpretation, and disconfirmed for the secondary interpretations.

The case of the garden path sentence is simpler, but uses these same mechanisms. In this case it is the unexpected unit (word) which disturbs the current parse structure and interpretation. In the case of less vicious examples, the alternate parse may be readily available as a parallel hypothesis, but in the vicious example cited above, a reparse is started with a different set of expectations for the syntactic role of what is being parsed.

In all these cases, the special contingency and emergency procedures are brought to conscious attention. In general, there are often many alternate parses and interpretations for sentences, but normally the selectivity imposed by the context is sufficient to avoid error — presumably by selective activation of associated concepts, and deactivation of inappropriate concepts. Thus although the process is basically parallel, it is usually quite deterministic. Furthermore, the thresholding of alternatives does not happen just at the top level or any other particular level. It happens at many levels throughout the hierarchy. If any of the same neural elements are involved in different interpretations, they cannot proceed in parallel. The relative activations must change to allow a different thresholding of concept at whichever levels are involved. Only one coherent network of cohesive relationships can be active at any given time. But once it proves incoherent (*i.e.* incohesive), new cohesive alternatives come into play.

There is no evidence for backtracking, which is usually an alternative to parallelism, at the subconscious level. Despite the arguments of linguists that garden path sentences require backtracking, the very fact that the sentences are only understood after conscious intervention implies that backtracking is *not* a subconscious parsing and interpretational process. On the contrary, the sentence is rehearsed again, and armed with the foreknowledge of the unexpected word category, the expectations are tuned so as to allow successful reparsing.

Some people never see the sense of "the horse ... fell". Many students read in an extra word "the horse raced ... *and* fell". Some interpreted "barn" as an adjective qualifying the noun "fell" as a particular field or hill. The correct interpretation requires a correct answer to "who fell?" before successful reparsing happens. Even then, subjects who are ready to assume and correct an error will not try to reparse the whole sentence. Those who saw "fell" as a possible noun asked "which fell?" and came up with a reasonable explanation—the fell near the barn as opposed to the fell near the pond, say. These failures would be hard to explain in a context of automatic subconscious backtracking or latent parallelism. The correct parse doesn't follow automatically when you recognize that you have made an incorrect parse.

We can now turn to the more usual case where there are potential ambiguities which are usually understood subconsciously by context or common sense. Again cohesion is essential to this disambiguation. A well known example is "time flies!", and artificial derivative sentences for which four meanings are distinguished (*e.g.* "time flies like an arrow!"). A better example is "he shot the man with the gun". But normally the intent of such a sentence would be better integrated into the context, and the sentence would take a less ambiguous form. But the use of the definite article implies prior knowledge of the gun and the man, and hence of who was holding the particular gun of interest. Of course as a literary device sometimes such ambiguities are used to create suspense.

There is also a class of problem construction where there is apparently no ambiguity, but the syntax does not of itself specify the meaning completely. Thus Schank considers two syntactically similar sentences:

2.John's love of Mary was harmful.

3.John's can of beans was edible.

Or to achieve our contrast in more identical environments, consider

4.John's can of beans was dented.[3]

It is clear that the cohesive patterns associated with "harmful", "edible" and "dented" are responsible for determining to which noun the adjective applies. Note again that this cohesion is referential rather than grammatical, and hence any purely syntactic approach is doomed. It is possible, in theory, to classify the adjectives and nouns in terms of which can govern which – but in practice there will always be exceptions. If not, language is sufficiently dynamic that we can invent some (*e.g.* "dollie" transcends the animate–inanimate classification). The inventions themselves are not primarily linguistic. Thus a toy-manufacturer created the doll. Similarly, a confectioner may have created a candy can for jelly beans, reversing the selection of governed noun in sentence 3. We can even make sense of Chomsky's little masterpiece of incoherence about "colorless green ideas" – there were some quite good entries in a competition to write a poem which included the line.

Note too that in sentences 3 and 4 the choice of anaphora for either includes both of

5.Mary's can was not.
6.Mary's beans were not.

Recursion of Syntax and Parsing

Clearly the child does not learn some finite number of patterns, say for adjectival position of the form:

Det + N "The man"
Det + Adj + N "The old man"
Det + Adj + Adj + N "The strong old man"

Rather he has learned a recursive rule that allows for an unbounded number of adjectives in that position.[4]

This obvious, simple and common proposition seems self-evident, but is probably wrong! There are some considerable limitations on the ordering of adjectives within a noun phrase. Again, there are pragmatic reasons why we should not unreservedly subscribe to Chomsky's assumption that the sentences of English are countably infinite. Syntax is not necessarily recursive, and there are certainly limitations on the extent of apparent recursion.

Can we deny that syntax could be learned after the form decried by Kelley above? But it also seems quite feasible linguistically that the rules are recursive, with grammatical cohesion, and ultimately referential cohesion, determining word order.

From a neural perspective, it is more difficult to see how a recursive formula would be implemented. Reverberating circuits do not seem adequate to the task. In fact, recursive grammars have theoretical difficulties in learning by any means. Many of the problems which we met during our experiments were mainly with direct or indirect recursion. This makes it more likely that what looks like recursion is merely a result of a tendency to use the same pattern at many levels of the hierarchy. In other languages than English matters can be more complex. For example in French some adjectives belong before the noun and others after. Our models avoided learning generalization of recursive rules by providing that only new concepts could be learned directly. Disjunctive concepts or rules could not. This corresponds to the first, "reflecting", "intensive", "comprehensive" stage of abstraction proposed by Piaget. However, a subsequent consolidation process can be introduced to merge similar classes with a high degree of overlap and thus introduce direct or indirect recursion. This corresponds to Piaget's second, "reflected", "extensive" form of abstraction.

There is no direct evidence that a recursive rule can be learned by consolidation process in humans. But given that a recursive rule can be learned by such a consolidation process, one hypothesis is that parallel activated concepts on the surface give rise to exactly one "adjectival concept" which exceeds threshold. This is helped by the influence of referential cohesion, which in this case corresponds to common sense about which concepts associate most directly. Once an adjective has been generated for this concept, its activation level drops. Because of the recursive rule, the circuit can be looking for either an adjective or a noun. If more descriptive features remain to be expressed which have not yet been deactivated, the most active of these will have surpassed threshold, with common sense order cohesion still suppressing the noun and those adjectives most directly associated with it. The process will therefore repeat. In this case recursive rules are possible because once they have triggered generation of a word, they become available again for reuse in the changed activational environment.

Note that this proposal again emphasizes the restricting, restraining nature of cohesion. Recursive rules are the most powerful and potentially unruly of all formulae, and emphasise the unconstrained explosive nature of the *formula–slot* phrase structure part of syntax.

Comparison and Comparatives; Adjectives and Word Order

> Lashley (1951) believed that one function of structure in the production of speech is that it controls the serial order of events in the action of speaking. By means of a structural schema, the speaker is able to organize elementary linguistic units ... into a strict sequential order, and do this as part of a single integrated action ... The notion ... will prove to be most useful ... We are guided by a variety of grammatical rules for establishing certain orders, but even when no rule applies (as in non-grammatical sequences), there must be an order, hence an organizational schema ... Intuition confirms that speech can be produced as it is organized. An experiment by Marslen-Wilson (1973) demonstrates this directly and convincingly ... The production of speech must itself be organized by schemas for action ... What is necessary is that the child should be able to use the action schema for cognition to organize the action schema for the content to be expressed; the latter then will guide and organize the former, and this process makes syntagms. The structure for the action that is schematized in the child's model of representing the world at this stage can be used to give structure to the production of utterances that describe this world.[5]

In this subsection we are going to discuss word order directly, concentrating on adjectives as a key example. The general point of view we will take here is similar to Piaget's: there are some natural constraints on word order which come from the referential framework itself. We are also proposing that cohesion in the referential hierarchy is largely responsible for the order of adjectives.

There are many fundamental differences in order between different languages, and indeed the significance of order, like stress, pitch, or indeed any phoneme, varies from language to language. The order of creoles, and of children's grammar is of particular interest here. The differences between this and the adult order of pedigree languages is an interesting study in historical and comparative linguistics in itself. There are two levels at which we can seek to understand the differences: at the level of a child learning with a parental model, and at the level of the evolution of a particular language.

The latter conformation is assumed to be primarily a result of consolidatory, compacting and communication efficiency considerations. The emergence and disappearance of inflection is particularly intriguing. The function of inflective cohesion is to assist the matching up of tagmemes whose semantics should reflect a relationship, and to restrict the choice of alternatives. So it presumably developed mainly for comprehension rather than production purposes. Grammatical cohesion itself suggests a semantic correlation involving referential cohesion. This is helpful because word ordering can be influenced by emphasis, focus and higher level cohesion. Thus cohesive markers possibly develop to distinguish the roles appropriate to different word orders, or more accurately and simply, to distinguish different role orders. However, common role orders reflecting common orders of emphasis could lead to word order based language with a minimum of inflective or other cohesive markings.

At the level of learning from a model, the process is much simpler since there is no need to invent grammatical cohesion rules for inflection or to distinguish word orders. The child will simply discover the appropriate ways of binding together concepts in the order he requires. Here the desired order comes first, but is eventually accompanied by cohesion and role cues to the corresponding referential structure. So what is a problem for which TGG proposes transformations between sentential forms?

So let us look at, now, the case of ordered adjectives in the apparently recursive noun phrase:

> The question of the ordering of adjectives in English has been studied extensively by Vendler (1968). He concludes that there is relatively strict and complex ordering involving 19 classes of adjectives. Adjectives in a higher class must precede adjectives in a lower class if they both occur in a noun phrase ... These adjective classes are not at all arbitrary but are correlated with semantic features. It seems that the more noun-like the adjective class is, the closer it can occur to the noun. Thus, for instance, adjectives that refer to substance like *foam* follow adjectives that refer to absolute properties like *white*, which follow adjectives like *big*, which refer to relative properties, which follow adjectives like *comfortable*, which refer to features of the noun's use.[6]

The most active adjective is usually the focus of a noun phrase and hence comes first, modifying the entire residual specified noun phrase. Sometimes apparent synonyms can be restricted. For example, try interchanging "small" and "little" in the following: "the little red fire-engine", "the reddest little fire-engine", "the small little boy", "the little green block", "the green little block". Note that "little" does not appear to be able to carry much focus. It may be that it is less qualitative: it can act as noun ("a little"), it is more an opposite of "much" than of "big", and it is etymologically associated with the comparatives "less" and "least" (as "much" is with "more" and "most"). The word "little" appears to want to attach to the noun or noun group, as a diminutive in a way that "small" does not.

It will be very interesting to see what rules are discovered by the first model to succeed in learning adjective usage.

Text Analysis, Corpus and Literary Criticism

The results of using computers for literary criticism vary from tempered validity to untempered numerology. The computer is used to calculate various probabilistic and distributional metrics to quantify the notion of style, and for author identification. It has also been used for some time on ancient manuscripts to help determine the grammar and lexicon of unknown languages. The computer is very helpful in such research; scholars can piece together a language from fragments of text and rare examples of glosses (*e.g.* the "Rosetta Stone"). But are these techniques deterministic enough to apply to learning arbitrary Natural Languages from text?

The short answer seems to be "no". Workers such as Wisbey report only unrelated and *ad hoc* techniques applicable to specific problems.[7] The researchers who decipher ancient languages must use useful techniques, but it seems that this expertise is in the form of heuristic methods. They are absorbed rather than learned from papers, or they are linguistic insights from our natural language propensities. In most cases there seem to be few short cuts through the maze of trial and error.

The resounding "no" of Fillmore and Gold reflects the theoretical impossibility of analyzing grammar without extra-grammatical information.[8] A weaker "no" stems from the unintuitive idea of a child assembling all the data and making a statistical distributional analysis at one point. Perhaps the flow needs to be in the other direction. Once human language learning processes are better understood this may provide an armoury of techniques to text analysts.

The starting point for language modelling is the traditional Phrase Structure Grammar (PSG) which refers to the straightforward decomposition of a "phrase" into its components at each level of a hierarchy. It is the basis for the traditional "subject–predicate" type of formulae, and the classification of words as "noun", "verb", "adjective" *etc.*

PSG is completely adequate for assigning a structure to any given "sentence". The problem is that sometimes there are two or more different structures which may be assigned to identical or similar sentences: *e.g.*

1. Visiting professors can be dull.
2. John is easy to please.
3. John is eager to please.
4. The shooting of the hunters was atrocious.

The problem in these examples is that in each case there is a difference of actor or active subject of the implied subsidiary clause — who is doing the visiting and the pleasing.

In the example 1, a PSG probably gives identical parses for the two distinct interpretations. All that differs between the two interpretations is the semantic role of "visiting", the relative nuclearity of the slots of "visiting" and "professor", and the labelling of the subject as a formula class within the hyperclass acting as filler class for the subject. The ambiguity only arises because number cohesion doesn't explicitly constrain the produced form of this verb form. Some workers try to distinguish the decompositions of the "sentence(s)" according to the nature of the decomposition of the subject.[9] Transformational Generative Grammar (TGG) simply transforms the "sentence(s)" into quite different Deep Structures.

Notice that Block does not assign distinct parse structures in the case of example 4, but claims that it is:

> better reserved for lexical and pragmatic information ... The difference hinges on the *nature* of the relationship to the shooting.[10]

In the case of examples 2 and 3 above, some people try to assign a different parse structure to the two sentences, and TGG once again assigns disparate Deep Structures. Note that coordination is possible:

5.John is both eager and easy to please.

This is easily accommodated by TGG, as coordination of the adjectives can be derived by a transformation of the coordination of the original sentences. It is not so easily accommodated by a theory which proposes alternate parse structures. This is one of the strongest examples Chomsky has put up to demonstrate the need for transformations.

In tagmemic terms, the distinction might originate in referential cohesion, marking a word as more or less passive. The range of fillers for the nucleus of the complement slot of example 3 includes "keen", "quick", "slow" and "a fanatic" (which have active cohesion, giving John the actor role). Alternatives to the corresponding slot of example 2 include "awkward", "impossible", "a joy", and "a cinch" (with the passive cohesion, giving John the undergoer role). Conceivably there could exist a filler for the slot in which either cohesion could be assigned according to context.

This is illustrated in a different paradigm by the word "shooting" in the example 4. It could be substituted by "murder" or "aim" which would resolve the ambiguity one way or the other according to the cohesion attaching to the filler in context. A less neutral preposition, *e.g.* "by" with "murder", would be required to reverse the sense of the cohesion.

Notwithstanding these weaknesses, PSG is still the main component of any grammatical theory. In the case of Tagmemics, PSG describes a more general language, which is then restricted by cohesion. In the case of TGG it is seen as describing a more specific language, which is then exploded by transformation.

Transformational Grammar; Generative Grammar

Around 1957, Chomsky brought to linguistics a formal mathematical basis. Generative Grammar also revolutionized linguistics by providing a clear statement of the problem: a grammar should be able to generate all the acceptable sentences of a language and none of the unacceptable sentences. In fact the traditional goal of generating all the syntactically acceptable sentences and none of the syntactically unacceptable was always implicit. One danger implicit in this formulation is that the syntactic and semantic aspects of acceptability can be confused, and the term "grammatical" extended to encompass both classes of acceptability. This is both unnecessary and unhelpful, and uses an inadequate account of semantics. This is helped by the fact that Transformational Generative Grammar does not propose semantics, but provides only a postulate of equivalence.

A reasonable alternative to a generative grammar is any acceptive grammar which can test sentences and decide if they are grammatical. It is trivial to define a mechanism which can generate all acceptable sentences but also generates unacceptable ones — given a dictionary, it only needs to successively generate all collocations of 1, 2, 3 ... words! An acceptor mechanism can be combined with such an exhaustive generator to produce a generative mechanism. It is not, in general, possible to convert a generative grammar into an acceptive grammar. It is easy enough to verify an acceptable sentence by generating all sentences in sequences until it is found. But this technique cannot be used to establish that a sentence is not acceptable if there are an infinite number of acceptable sentences, as Chomsky claims. Perhaps it would be more correct to describe Chomsky's goal as an acceptive grammar.

Chomsky has made an important step in introducing a degree of mathematical formalism to linguistics. But has he retained the philosophical bases of empirical science? Many critics answer no:

> I explore in these chapters the legitimacy of the view, at present widely accepted in linguistics, that "generative grammar is very much in keeping with contemporary views on the philosophy of science" (Langacker, 1967, p.10), and conclude as the result of that study that, in almost every detail, precisely the opposite is true.[11]

The problem is that Chomsky makes many assertions. At times he seems to treat these as facts rather than as hypotheses. However, to be fair, he has at times referred to simplifying assumptions — perhaps in accommodation to mounting contrary psycholinguistic evidence, and to criticisms such as these:

> Is linguistics then, after all, an empirical science like Chemistry? Or is it a formal discipline, like Logic and Mathematics? ... With no hesitation whatsoever, I answer that linguistics is an empirical science; that "conclusions" reached about language on any other basis are worthy of scientific consideration only as hypotheses ... The alternative answer, however, is attractive to some temperaments ... It was particularly appealing in the atmosphere ... at the turn of the half-century, and perhaps most of all to those within Harris's sphere of influence. Apparently it was this second alternative that Chomsky chose ... Having done so, Chomsky was in due time led to refine the Bloomfieldian–Saussurean vague "rigidity" of language ... into the mathematically precise "well-definition". Point C10 asserts that the grammar of a language is a well-defined system. Chomsky nowhere says so explicitly, but I believe that this point is absolutely crucial for his whole theory. If it is true, or if one accepts it on faith, then all that Chomsky says is rendered at least plausible. If it is false, then everything falls to pieces ... I cannot accept the proposal on faith, for that is not what a scientist does. But I can enter it as a hypothesis, and try to see whether its consequences are in accord with experiential and experimental fact.[12]

This argument is a little unfair since Chomsky would claim to be empiricist in his approach, as well as being theoretically disciplined. Unfortunately, it true that Chomsky did make some claims for which he gave no empirical support, nor tried to assure testability. Even the considerable influence his theory has had on psycholinguistics seems to have been largely at cross purposes to the order that naturally emerges from the discipline.

For a sympathetic viewpoint underlining the influence of Chomsky, the spread of TGG, and the degree of acceptance among linguists, see Lyons.[13]

It is a difficult step to reject the preeminent views of the day, but this is the stand we have taken. To the extent that we deal with the same language data, there are obviously useful results from the TGG school, but the interpretation and use of this data can be varied to fit other theories:

> My dilemma is very much the one described by Koestler (1967, p4): "If one attacks the dominant school in [some field] one is up against two opposite types of criticism. The first is the natural reaction of the defenders of orthodoxy, who believe that they are in the right and you are in the wrong—which is only fair and to be expected. The second category of critics belongs to the opposite camp. They argue that, since the pillars of the citadel are already cracked and revealing themselves as hollow, one ought to ignore them and dispense with polemics. Or, to put it more bluntly, why flog a dead horse?" We suspect that the number of

scholars in the second of these two categories with respect to Chomsky's views is larger than the average transformational-generative grammarian might like to think. There are some people (and not all of them ill-informed or irrational), who find little or nothing which is compelling in Chomsky's work to be worth the trouble of criticizing.[14]

This latter category of reader is welcome to skim or omit this section. But the reader who is by choice or tradition Chomskian, will hopefully read on. We hope he or she will consider the lack of concrete evidence for many of Chomsky's proposals, and indeed the difficulty of making any scientific evaluation of them.

The spread of TGG would make an interesting research topic for a student of mass communication. There are many factors behind the phenomenon. First there is generalization of reputation, and influence beyond their original area. In the case of Chomsky, his introduction of mathematical formalism to linguistics and his criticism of behaviourist theories is the origin of his reputation. Unfortunately, the mathematical formalism, excellent and applicable in itself, seems to have proved a shroud and a barrier to the linguist who is unable to probe past a veneer of mathematical respectability. The linguist should be able to accept that the previous traditions of linguistic methodology have validity, and that mathematics is but one very artificial form of description which has its own intrinsic limitations, not the least of which may be its obscurity.

At the beginning of the 1970s, virtually no psycholinguist wrote without some reference to TGG, either as the guide for their research, or to discuss their departure from it. This represents the peak of TGG's influence in psycholinguistics. In the 1980s there is an increasing reluctance for those outside the direct influence of linguistics to subscribe to TGG. Many of those who went along with TGG in the early 1970s were rejecting it by the mid 1970s:

> During most of the last two decades, computational linguists and AI researchers working on natural language have assumed that phrase structure grammars, despite their computational tractability, were unsatisfactory devices for expressing the syntax of natural languages. However, during the same period, they have come to realize that transformational grammars, whatever their linguistic merits, are computationally intractable as they stand. The assumption, unchallenged for many years, that PSGs were inadequate for natural languages is based on arguments originally advanced by transformational linguists in the late 1950s and early 1960s. But recent work has shown that *none* of those arguments were valid. The present paper draws on that work to argue that (i) there is no reason, at the present time, to think that natural languages are not context-free languages, (ii) there are good reasons to think that the notations needed to capture significant syntactic generalizations will characterize phrase structure grammars or some minor generalization of them, and (iii) there are good reasons for believing that such gram-

mars, and the monostratal representations they induce, provide the necessary basis for the semantic interpretation of natural languages.[15]

It is particularly interesting to note the comments of some of those who originally espoused TGG, around the time when they came to be dissatisfied with it:

> The transformational structure corresponds to the speaker's intuition that pronouns have definite referents, but it suggests an implausible mechanism if it is assumed to describe the processes that supposedly take place during speech production ... While it is undoubtedly the case that a speaker knows the definite referent of the pronoun he utters ... it is implausible to claim that because he knows this, he generated a nonpronomial underlying form first. It is more plausible to be guided again by intuition, and to say that the pronoun appears in pronominal form from the first in the production of the sentence.[16]

The list of examples is quite considerable, covering many different stumbling blocks for TGG, in the linguistic and logical domain as well as the psycholinguistic:

> Chomsky (1965) proposed the theory according to which sentences had underlying structures generated by a context-free base component. The sentences themselves were obtained from these by the application of transformational rules which did not, however, have any effect on meaning. Optional transformations made it possible to derive sets of two or more sentences from the same underlying structure, but, in these cases, it was claimed that all the sentences in the set would have the same semantic interpretation. It was an appealingly simple view and constituted a strong claim about the nature of human language. But it proved impossible to uphold this claim. It soon appeared that certain aspects of semantic interpretation, notably those concerning quantifiers, depended in crucial ways on the surface forms of sentences. So, for example, "Every command is represented by a single code" is to be interpreted quite differently from "A single code represents every command" ... However, it rapidly became clear that there was a great deal more than quantifiers and related logical problems to embarrass the theoreticians.[17]

Wells examines the question of innateness after examining the impact and ramifications of Chomsky's approach, and setting this against the considerable assistance that is available from the child's environment.[18]

It seems to us that Transformational Generative Grammar is founded upon a wrong emphasis and an incorrect perspective. Whilst there is a great deal of truth in the transformational view of linguistics, and there is a good case for a transformational view of neurolinguistics, we think that there is an immense discrepancy between such a view and the Chomskian view.

In essence, Chomsky's TGG derives from the "rewrite rules" of formal language theory, a commendable mathematical borrowing, but one which has been a mixed blessing in its application to linguistics. As a hypothesis, it has stimulated much useful linguistic and psycholinguistic research, but its overapplication is dangerous to linguistics. The Chomskian fallacy derives from adoption of a parochial linguistic application of this theory, rather than employment of an interdisciplinary application drawing on a psycholinguistic and neurolinguistic viewpoint.

Our view is diametrically opposed to Chomskian Transformational Grammar at a number of points. Let us pick on two. First, the "innate fixed nucleus" — Deep Structure and the Language Acquisition Device are unjustifiable. From the point of view of transformations, the problems come from the choice of a particular level as the innate one, which is hence incapable of decomposition. This is accompanied by a failure to consider neurolinguistic transformational processes, which ignores the sensory-motor level as the ultimate source of reference and semiotic significance. It also ignores the fact that language is continuous with other brain processes. Chomsky supposes that the language acquisition process is completely distinct from the other processes of the brain, and the rest of the animal kingdom. To do this, he needs the extreme and completely untenable dogma of TGG that Deep Structure, as the interlingua — the common core of all human languages — is innate. On this view, languages are not so much learned, as that specific features which are used by a particular language (the baby's mother tongue) are selected out from the core, whilst those not used are submerged.

This is an extraordinary view to take. On this definition the interlingua, supposedly a common core of human language becomes no longer an intersection but an entangled union of all human languages. Transformational grammar ironically presupposes a shortsighted selection hypothesis, whilst a more neurolinguistically and psycholinguistically consistent view would be far more transformational in nature.

Second, the intralanguage "rewrite rule" approach has limitations. The interhierarchical, and transhierarchical aspects of language are emphasized. The crux of language is the representation and expression of relationships amongst every aspect of human experience. These range from extrinsic sensory-motor experiences, to intrinsic emotional, motivational, cognitive experiences. The primary transformations are from the different "languages of the brain" to the particular natural human language. The fundamental transformations are not between different forms of, say, English, such as the active and passive forms, or the indicative, interrogative and imperative forms.

There is, in fact, no evidence that such transformations occur, and introspection leads to the contrary conclusion. The TGG view is, it seems to us, based on a simplistic idea of synonymy. In fact, choice of form is not arbitrary. It is determined by the content to be expressed, and it is far more plausible to believe that the factors that produce, say, a passive form influence the building of that form right from the start. This means that the mechanism is selection rather than transformation.

Hence we have two very interesting contrasts—in one case TGG adopts an explanation involving selection, whereas we take a transformational approach. In the other case, TGG goes for a transformational view whilst we hypothesise a selection process.

Chomsky himself disclaimed any intention of psychological, neurological or physiological validity for his theory. But by the very nature of the theory, any attempt to make use of it implies a claim to such validity. Indeed, Chomsky's criticisms have been directly instrumental in bringing TGG into those areas.

Even the earliest attempts to use Chomsky's proposals as a basis for psycholinguistics charted a rather muddy course. This is illustrated in the work of Brown and his colleagues at the stage when they were seeking to conform to transformational ideals. Their transformational approach really had very little to do with TGG:

> The interaction between mother and child is, much of the time, a cycle of reductions and expansions. There are two transformations involved. The reduction transformation has an almost completely specifiable and so mechanical character ... What kind of instructions will generate the mother's expansions? The following are approximately correct: "retain the words given in the order given and add those functors that will result in a well-formed simple sentence that is appropriate to the circumstances"... The expansion encodes aspects of reality that are not coded by the child's telegraphic utterance.[19]

The types of transformation we suggest do seem to be occurring, do bear some relation to those proposed for transformational grammar, and in the case of the adult are operating generatively. The fundamental difference is that unlike in TGG *per se*, there is no need for all the information in the surface form to be represented to the deeper form, or that these forms should have the same linguistic character. It is also clear that the transformations have a semantics associated with them, and they have a direct function in expressing sensory/motor relationships.

Our transformational model, therefore, has related generative and acceptive modes. It is conceived as passing through a number of levels from the sensory/motor level where contentives arise, through higher levels where functional and focal morphemic and syntactic recombinant transformations take effect without any of the apparent arbitrariness of transformational grammar. The big problem with TGG is the absence of real semantics, whereas even a simple phrase structure grammar is capable of capturing better the idea that different components are combined, and can thereafter proceed through subsequent recombinant transformations as a unit.

We also propose that units are inviolable and apparent interspersion actually occurs at a low enough level so that it is achieved by adjacent recombination or simple alternation. This runs into the most problems at the word level. In English, the root changes (*e.g. ride/rode/ridden, ring/rang/rung, run/ran/run*), but this is not regular enough for conclusions to be drawn, and anyway cannot be described in terms of infixes. Evidence from other languages suggests that alternation of word stems is governed by morphophonemic or morphoprosodic transformation. An example is the durative morph, and the process allomorph of the past time augment, the temporal augment, in some Greek verbs.

Another limitation of TGG is that it is mainly concerned with word order, when a big advantage of transformation is that it needn't be. The problem is that TGG is overly concerned with transforming between supposedly semantically equivalent surface forms, whilst failing to consider reduction and expansion properties including addition/subtraction of functional particles and inflections. To distinguish this sort of transformation from the TGG type, we call it Combinatorial Grammar (CG).

Individual Differences: Learning Process and Idiolect

We have already noted Chomsky's assumption "that adult speakers have internalized the same grammar", although he recognises individual variation.[20] This is in the face of evidence that no two people learn exactly the same semantic or even syntactic categories or rules. But these individual differences have enormous implications for the nature of language and its role in communication, specifically for understanding the role of context.

Such a deliberate false assumption completely ignores the implication that language is dynamic and that no fixed set of grammatical rules, whether of phrase structure or transformation, can be adequate. It can be argued that a snapshot of the grammar at any given time can be described by a grammar. But it does not take account of variation in perspective, or the question of acquisition, which is where most problems lie.

The differences between idiolects are themselves useful data for the study of the processes involved in the development of language – in the fact of the acquisition of those idiolects. The history of language, including the ongoing development of an individual dialect, is thus always a source of useful data, and an important aspect of the testability of a theory of language. The underlying processes are analogy or metaphor, and the phenomena of homonymy or equivalence. The selections are allied to the process of successive generalization and abstraction, which move language away from the directly affective. These choices are likely to follow Lakoff's proposals for the originals of metaphorical language constructs: "The prime candidates for concepts that are understood directly are the simple spatial concepts such as *up*. Our spatial concept of *up* arises out of our spatial experience".[21] Undoubtedly, the most important work in this area is Lakoff's and Clarke's which we frequently refer to.

Speech Understanding *vis-a-vis* Speech Recognition

A very considerable amount of money has been spent by ... the US Department of Defense on research directed towards speech understanding. Speech understanding is to be clearly distinguished from speech recognition in that it aims to go beyond the recognition of isolated spoken words and to respond in some potentially useful way to connected speech ... Very early in this work, it became clear that the established view that a linguistic processor could consist of a series of components, each taking as input the output of the one before, was no longer viable. Recognition of phonetic units in the acoustic signal required not only the data in that signal, but also predictions about what later parts of the signal might contain based on a syntactic and semantic analysis of what had already been heard. It was necessary to devise schemes whereby the components could work essentially in parallel, each being prepared to accept and deliver partial results, hypotheses, and predictions, even at a very early stage of the analysis.[22]

Newell's ideas were a great influence on our research. The model has not yet been applied in the area of the phonological hierarchy, but this conclusion provided the first of many examples of the impossibility of forcing clear distinctions between the various levels and hierarchies associated with language — and also of the importance of taking account of the interdependence of different aspects of language.

Notes to Chapter Ten

1.   Wells, Gordon, *Learning through interaction: The study of language development* (Cambridge University Press, Cambridge, UK, 1981), p.26.
2.   Winograd, Terry, "A Procedural Model of Natural Language Understanding", in Roger C. Schank and K. M. Colby, eds, *Computer Models of Thought and Language* (Freeman, 1973), p.166.
3.   Schank, Roger C., "Identification of Conceptualization Underlying Natural Language", in Roger C. Schank and K. M. Colby, eds, *Computer Models of Thought and Language* (Freeman, 1973), p.190f.
4.   Kelley, K.L., *Early Syntactic Acquisition* (Rand Corporation, Santa Monica, CA, November 1967), p.63.

5. McNeill, David, "Semiotic Extension" in R. L. Solso, ed., *Information Processing and Cognition: The Loyola Symposium* (Lawrence Erlbaum Associates, Hillsdale, 1975), p.354ff.

6. Anderson, John R., "Computer Simulation of a Language Acquisition System: A First Report", in R. L. Solso, ed., *Information Processing and Cognition: The Loyola Symposium* (Lawrence Erlbaum Associates, Hillsdale, 1975), p.336.

7. Wisbey, Roy A., *The Computer in Literary and Linguistic Research* (Cambridge University Press, Cambridge, UK, 1971).

8. Fillmore, C. J., "Scenes-and-frames semantics", in A. Zampolli, ed., *Linguistics Structures Processing* (North Holland, 1977), p.61; Gold, E. M., "Language Identification in the Limit", *Information and Control*, Vol. 10 (1967), p.454f.

9. Block, H.D., J. Moulton, and G. M. Robinson, "Natural Language Acquisition by a Robot", *Int. J. Man-Mach. Stud.*, Vol. 7 (1975), p.586.

10. *Ibid.*

11. Derwing, Bruce L., *Transformational Grammar as a Theory of Language Acquisition* (Cambridge, UK, Cambridge University Press, 1973), p.21f.

12. Hockett, Charles F., "Grammar for the Hearer", *Proc. Symposia in App. Math.*, Vol. XII (Amer. Mathl Soc., 1961), p.56f.

13. Lyons, John, *Introduction to Theoretical Linguistics* (Cambridge University Press, Cambridge, UK, 1968).

14. Derwing, Bruce L., *Transformational Grammar as a Theory of Language Acquisition* (Cambridge, UK, Cambridge University Press, 1973), p.7ff.

15. Gazdar, Gerald, "Phrase Structure Grammars and Natural Language", *Proceedings 8th IJCAI* (1983), p.556.

16. McNeill, David, "Semiotic Extension" in R. L. Solso, ed., *Information Processing and Cognition: The Loyola Symposium* (Lawrence Erlbaum Associates, Hillsdale, 1975), p.353f.

17. Sparck-Jones, Karen, and Martin Kay, "Linguistics and Information Science: A Postscript", in Donald E. Walker, Hans Karlgren and Martin Kay, *Natural Language in Information Science: Perspectives and Directions for Research* (Scriptor, Stockholm, 1977).

18. Wells, Gordon, *Learning through interaction: The study of language development* (Cambridge University Press, Cambridge, UK, 1981).

19. Brown, Roger, and Ursula Bellugu, "Three Processes in the Child's Acquisition of Syntax" in E. Endler, L. Boulter, and H. Osser, eds, *Contemporary Issues in Developmental Psychology* (Holt, Rhinehart and Winston, New York, 1968), p.418.

20. Hockett, Charles F., "Grammar for the Hearer", *Proc. Symposia in App. Math.*, Vol. XII (Amer. Mathl Soc., 1961), pp.220-236, p.39.

21. Lakoff, George, and Mark Johnson, *Metaphors we Live By* (University of Chicago Press, 1980).

22. Sparck-Jones, Karen, and Martin Kay, "Linguistics and Information Science: A Postscript", in Donald E. Walker, Hans Karlgren and Martin Kay, *Natural Language in Information Science: Perspectives and Directions for Research* (Scriptor, Stockholm, 1977); Lakoff, George, and Mark Johnson, *Metaphors we Live By* (University of Chicago Press, 1980), p.186.

Chapter Eleven

Computer Science and Artificial Intelligence

This chapter takes a step back to place our problem of Natural Language Learning in the historical and theoretical perspectives of Artificial Intelligence. For this purpose we distinguish this engineering tradition of AI from the empirical approaches of Cognitive Science. This then provides a bridge to those techniques and theoretical stances which are not grounded in Linguistics, Psychology or Neurology. The Turing Test provides a foundational metric for AI which focuses our understanding of the term intelligence on this language and learning facility. However, the methodological focus of engineered intelligence is the application of heuristics in a search paradigm. Since virtually any problem can be set up as a problem of choosing an appropriate path through a decision tree, this is an appropriate base for AI. Expert Systems and Natural Language systems traditionally have programmed deterministic rules which largely eliminate the search component and reduce the generality of the systems. But the addition of a general Problem Solving or Machine Learning component returns such systems to the fold of heuristic search. Such systems differ in the way they are read, taught and criticized, how they obtain and make use of positive and negative examples, and in the extent to which they are expected to be error-free and intuitive.

Natural Language of Machine Learning are venerable members of that loose association of difficult problems popularly known as "Artificial Intelligence". This chapter focuses on the relationships of this book to the wider context of AI, the main questions and problems of AI, and the history of AI research on learning.

> The ultimate goal that motivates work discussed in this book is a model for a well-balanced, thinking, intelligent, flexible cognitive system. Such a model must be able to communicate in a natural language like English, perceive and recognize objects in its external environment and respond appropriately to them, draw inferences from what it sees, knows and remembers, solve problems, and, in general, learn to conduct itself in such a way as to maximize those things it values. This is the case whether we want to model human beings or build (or grow) intelligent computers.[1]

Although it is a complicated and diverse subject, we think we can distinguish two main types of approaches to AI. One is the "nuts-and-bolts", "systems development" approach, which we can think of as the engineering perspective.[2] This is the approach which says, in effect, "Here is a hard problem. It looks like it requires intelligence to solve it. How can I design a computer program/system to solve it?"

Because this perspective is so common within computer science, as soon as there are some useful techniques to solve a problem, it tends to be taken away from AI and become common lore. From the engineering perspective, the most distinctive feature of AI is the inapplicability of deterministic algorithms, and the consequent necessity of heuristics: the "rules of thumb", even "rules of guesswork", which guide the algorithmic process. Moreover, AI has spawned calculi for quantifying heuristics and manipulating them deterministically.

The other main perspective sees AI more as a branch of Cognitive Psychology than of Computer Science. This cognitive science perspective uses computers as a modelling tool to give us greater understanding of human (or more generally, animal) intelligence and behaviour.[3] This version of AI sees it as a subject of suppositions, questions and aims such as:

> The abstract logical character of a program which matches feats of human intelligence must be very similar to that of the human mind ...
> To build models of human information processing which predict features of human behaviour.[4]

Our approach in this book includes both engineering achievement and psycholinguistic insight. Our most basic claim is that algorithms, heuristics, mechanisms and processes which solve problems when used by human intelligence should have analogues which will solve the same problems when used by computers. The converse claim, of course, is not necessarily true. There is no reason why engineering solutions should contribute to psychological insight unless they are guided by psychological considerations.

The Turing Test

The pioneer in AI, whose contribution spanned mathematics, computer science, neurology and psychology, was Alan Turing. We have already discussed the famous test he proposed for the question: "Can computers think?"[5] This test, we should remember, effectively equated language capability with proof of intelligence.

The Turing test supposed that a certain mechanism, candidate for attribution of thought, might be connected to one of two terminals manned by an adjudicator. The other terminal was to be connected to a human person. The adjudicator's role was to judge, purely on the basis of typed interaction through the terminals, which terminal was connected to the computer and which to the human.

This test avoids the problem of defining thought or intelligence. It essentially leaves them implicitly defined as something which humans have which characterizes their behaviour. There are however many objections to the paradigm—it is actually a test of two other attributes of humans. We do want to teach our computers to talk (or in this case type) in a Natural Language, but do we really want to teach them to dissemble? This, in turn, begs another question: "Can computers lie?"

From the point of view of Natural Language research, the Turing test provides a rather elaborate demonstration of the linguistic capabilities of a system. It also has another range of application: to test intelligence, thought, or language in animals. In this case, the terminal may need to be modified to something more suited to the organism, but chimpanzees have been taught to use a form of keyboard.

Incidentally, the terminal was introduced so that the physical characteristics of the computer could be hidden. But in fact long before a serious demonstration of computer intelligence could be arranged, cosmetic and robotic advances will make this secrecy unnecessary. By the way, the test was not necessarily meant to be carried out, but was posed as a "thought experiment" begging the answer: "Yes! It is possible to conceive of a machine, with sufficient breadth of programming and data, that could pass the test!" A cynic has quipped: "Why test the human?". The answer is simple: "It is the human that is paranoid about losing this last vestige of his pre-eminence".

Problem Solving and Heuristic Search

The most general characteristic of the AI problem domain is clearly the heuristic method, and the metaphor for AI problems which has proved most useful for the study of heuristics is the search tree. Perhaps the most easily examined AI problems are the artificial ones—games like Chess, Draughts (known also as Chequers or Checkers), Go and a myriad of specifically designed or revived games and sub-games (such as Chess end-games). In general, an AI problem can be seen as a decision tree, whether it is a matter of which of N legal moves may be made from a given position according to the rules of Chess, or which of N phrasal collocations may be employed in a given context according to the rules of language.

A decision tree branches out from a given initial configuration (the root) towards many possible final configurations (the leaves). The final positions in games can be win, lose or draw, or in other contexts, consistent or inconsistent, right or wrong, true or false. There are also indeterminate results, stalemates or other draw states, and cycles where the same states recur. It is interesting that Chess avoids cycles with a rule that it is a draw if a position recurs twice, and this distinguishes identical states by a recurrence count. The 50-move rule has a similar effect by adding the number of moves since the last pawn move.

For some game trees (*e.g.* NIM) there is a deterministic winning strategy, but in general there is no way of knowing for certain which choice will win. But there are many heuristics, such as the assignment of weights to the different chess pieces and the maintenance of relative piece counts. Our intuitions are a particular form of heuristic, and in linguistics this amounts to asking "what humans *think* their methods of procedure are".[6]

In games, heuristics are usually applied to global features of the current state of the board, where the set of possible moves does not change during the game and is specified by the rules. In the case of "Expert Systems" the rules can often only be guessed at, many intermediate variables may be introduced, and the majority of the heuristics refer only to local features dependent on a subset of the variables.

Knowledge Representation and Expert Systems

Two of the AI "buzz words" of the 1980s are "Knowledge Engineering" and "Expert Systems". Indeed, even the primitive results of today have so successfully captured the popular imagination that this subdomain of AI is rapidly developing into a field in its own right. And the current approaches are very primitive since one important ingredient, whose importance has been realized for at least the best part of a decade, is still largely missing.

In this context, Knowledge Representation means mainly the storage of heuristics and procedures, the techniques and "rules of thumb" used by the model. More generally, it refers to the storage and organization of all the information relevant to the domain. The Expert System mechanisms, or "shells", consist essentially of an inference engine usually supplemented by some species of relational, probabilistic or possibilistic calculus. Basically, they use the same heuristic search repertoire as the rest of AI. Most shells employ the production-rule paradigm: a rule is fired and a consequent validated if an antecedent condition is satisfied. What characterizes them as "Expert Systems" is the "Knowledge Engineering" process whereby the heuristics used by an existing human expert are captured and represented as rules.

Since most people are expert language users, Natural Language would seem to be a suitable domain for application of Expert Systems technology. Unfortunately the "Knowledge Engineering (KE)" approach has met with only limited success, particularly in linguistics, but also in AI in general. In these cases where the expertise is so deep-seated, subconscious, ubiquitous and fundamental an outcome of human development, rather than formal education or apprenticeship, as much as with any domain where there are no experts, the Knowledge Based Systems cannot be developed with interview style knowledge engineering: "Why is that wrong?" "How do you work that out?" *etc.* In a sense, KE is what linguists have been doing for centuries — it is just that they have only recently begun to use computers to exercise their rule systems. What is most urgently needed is an expert system *for* Knowledge Engineering. Some work on concept learning can be looked at like this — such systems are expert systems for capturing concepts. Most, like any expert system, require interaction with users who are to some degree sympathetic. A further jump is to an expert system which operates without supervision or interaction. In the case of the concept capture expert applied to natural language, this becomes a child-like language learner, automatically relating and recognizing concepts, relationships and rules as it is exposed to them.

There has been some movement towards this viewpoint. Michie, for instance, has been advocating and developing a "learning" approach to expert systems in recent years[7] and Quillian's ID3 system has proved quite effective for certain classes of problem.[8] ID3 depends on ready access to the significant features which are the basis for classification, coupled with direct feedback. These are not readily available in a hierarchical application, such as language.

Natural Language and Parsing

The other traditional domain of AI is Natural Language (NL). This includes not only Natural Language understanding and programming, but Machine Translation (MT), and speech recognition. There are also the areas of computer science and mathematics concerned with artificial languages, formal languages, and parsing.

Computational and representational ideas provide the metaphors describing different parsing strategies: notably, top-down, bottom-up and middle-out. These terms are more generally applied to reasoning processes, and come from the general search-tree paradigm. The most appropriate parsing strategies seem to be composites of top-down and bottom-up, giving rise to an "end-in" search strategy. This is illustrated, for example, in Schank's proposals.[9] He sees the hearer as a bottom-up parser aggregating "words", rather than a top-down parser, decomposing expectations about "sentences". He proposes a model which will extract meaning bottom-up until it can "shift gears" and match up with the top-down analysis of expectations. The NL work which is most relevant is that of the Yale group, especially since they have considered the role of learning and have developed a theory of meaning.

Many of the more interesting models did not originate in a computer science framework. Interestingly, the parsing paradigm suggests a bottom-up analogy for concept learning. There are a number of other areas at the fringes of AI which also relate to language learning research. Automatic programming involves the provision of specifications and/or examples, leaving the machine to work out a way to achieve the results. Such a system may compile its input specifications and examples into a conventional algorithmic program, or it may build up rules and execute interpretively.

Another area of AI work is mathematico-logic, and the attempt to get computational help in theorem proving. This is a classical search paradigm. Rules of logic, deduction, inference, *etc.* provide the possible choices for combining the original and previously derived "facts" to produce further "facts". The theorems are notionally the leaves of the tree and the lemmas are interior nodes *en route*. On this basis the search criterion is for a statement of the particular theorem required. In fact, theorems are themselves interior nodes to the extent that corollaries are derived from them and further theorems are built from them. The terminology is really quite arbitrary. The "proof by contradiction" paradigm has proved most useful for automatic theorem proving, particularly as enshrined in the *resolution* principle, and corresponds to goal-orientated search.

These two independent avenues of automatic programming and automatic theorem proving have come together over the last decade to bring about a new force in computer science, the logic programming paradigm, the basis of the so-called "Fifth Generation Computer System". This synthesis originated in application to Natural Language research.[10] The Logic Programming language, PROLOG, is the medium for the design and implementation of much Natural Language learning research.

Learning

> By "machine learning" we mean the modification or construction by program of stored information structures, so that the machine-deliverable information becomes one of the following:
>
> - More accurate
> - Larger in amount
> - Cheaper to obtain …
>
> To put this in other terms, a learning algorithm seeks to improve either the *quality* or the *quantity* or the *economy* of the solutions which the machine is capable of getting.[11]

The most important theme of this research is the emphasis on learning as the basis for human acquisition of Natural Language, and hence as an appropriate basis for computer acquisition of Natural Language. In this section, we look at the different facets of learning within AI, and in particular learning of language in AI systems. In Michie's definition above, the emphasis is on the program's improvement of its own performance by making adjustments to its own behaviour — whether by adjustment of variables (which are regarded as data) or rules (which are regarded as program). It is even possible for the program to improve the learning algorithm itself. Notice that this definition of learning excludes mere data acquisition, which is like rote learning.

The main type of learning studied in AI is Concept Learning (CL), although this was not the earliest. Concept Learning involves a program learning whether or not a given example is or is not an instance of a specified concept, *e.g.* an arch. CL programs learn by taking into account information about positive and/or negative examples. The examples may be supplied either by a teacher,[12] or by the CL system itself.[13] The approval, or disapproval, of the examples can be given by a teacher as with all current CL systems, or by the CL system itself.

The positive information is used for the expansion or generalization of the concept, if it is not already part of the definition. The negative information contracts the concept — by showing that it not completely appropriate.

An example of a language learning program which gets reinforcement internally is Zbie.[14] It has a grammar which represents the external environment or a previously learned ontology. This structure is what is therefore impressed upon the learned structure. Such learning compares both linguistic and ontological structures associated with a pair of paradigmatically related scenes: discovering and systematizing the minimal differences between the paradigmatic structures of both modalities. The process of differential minimization has been examined in our research and we will discuss a minimal difference procedure in the last chapter.

Learning with and without a Teacher

Two functions are needed in a learning system which come from the parent or teacher, if not the child. These are the functions of model and critical learning.[15] The model is needed to compare with the theory or currently hypothesized description of a concept (or grammar of a sentence). The criticism is needed to give direction to the learning process — the positive or negative information so necessary to learning. Cohen is an example of learning with a teacher (who provides both functions) whilst Sammut is an example of learning with a critic (who provides the latter function, with the system itself generating most of the examples).

There are many examples of all the important concepts in the language and environment. What is critical are the questions of attention, focus and criticism. These are all provided by the environment, despite the fact that criticism from human intermediaries seems to have little direct effect.

The child's or the program's attempts to generate utterances which fit its hypothesized description of a concept are examples of the generation of the concept. Our proposal of "anticipated correction" would be an example of the generation of the criticism by the child or system. In this case two basic classes of potential mechanism may be distinguished. The child may generate criticism on the basis of stored or synthesized information from within the same modality, or on the basis of stored or synthesized information from other modalities.

Thus a sentence may be rejected for one of three reasons: because the utterance produced does not "sound" like the memory trace of sentences heard, because of a semantic inconsistency resulting from the interaction of the syntactic recognition grammar and the semantic referential target, or because of an explicit form of negative reinforcement, whether linguistic or social.

Whilst the notion of the "sound" of a memory trace is vague, the possibility of a recognition grammar which is distinct from and more advanced than the production grammar seems to us to suggest an appealing mechanism. The second class of criticism might appear to be more relevant to semantic learning, but if the semantics associated with syntactic features suggests a contra-indicated referential correlate, the production grammar which produced the utterance will be negatively reinforced. If an externally generated sentence met with such an inconsistency, it would be the recognition grammar that was negatively reinforced. The third possible reason for rejecting an utterance corresponds to the controversial correction paradigm, but again a degree of independence and separation between the recognition and production grammars would explain the empirical lack of direct effectiveness of explicit correction.

We have seen that all three of these forms of criticism are feasible given separate recognition and production grammars and hierarchies. However, this suggests the further problems of just how the production grammar comes to be inconsistent with the recognition grammar, and how, conversely, the recognition rules migrate to the production grammar at all. We propose that, logically, the recognition grammar feeds the production grammar those rules which have exceeded some threshold. Physically, the entire transfer may take place by a feedback-based inter-hierarchical learning mechanism.

The only completely criticless models are the self-organizing networks, but these networks themselves function only through the interaction of excitatory and inhibitory effects, the latter being negative information of a kind. We also need to recognize that neural self-organizing systems need not actually be learning systems. They can be genetically determined systems whose precise internal configuration is determined by the interaction of boundary conditions with random noise input. Where self-organizing systems do learn, this is mainly a change in the relative proportion of the network devoted to recognizing the given pattern.

Learning Strategies: Conservative *vs* Radical

Boundary conditions are not only important in connectivist models, but in general psycholinguistic models. Thus Fillmore is concerned with boundary research into apparent homonyms.[16] The more instances of a common concept to which we are exposed, the more we are likely to distinguish between them. There are various natural external boundaries in language, both referential (including motor), and linguistic (including phonological). The internal contrasts are learned as contrasts corresponding to perceived contrast in external input.

Traditional CL in AI does not consider the learning of contrasting concepts. These are the cases in which the positive and negative examples for the one have duals in the other. They get inverse reinforcement when the contrasting (as distinct from common) features are significant. In the absence of such contrasts, CL systems have difficulty knowing how far to generalize. Given that a dozen features may be significant, do we generalize as if almost all may be significant or as if almost none are significant?

If we make the latter assumption, we would generalize radically, and would probably have overgeneralized (as the class of everything has its uses, but more specific classes are more common). If we make the former assumption, we would generalize conservatively, and would probably undergeneralize, by choosing to generalize on an insignificant feature (*e.g.* that colour was not significant to the concept "box"). The generalization is correct, but being conservative we did not generalize size, as we should. This dilemma really only applies if the model must select its own examples. Under this arrangement, the model should test the generalization by choosing examples in the newly extended part of the concept. This conservative strategy makes the process fairly deterministic for reasonable concepts.

If the examples are provided externally, it is possible to generalize features which differ between two instances, and develop a generalization to the set or range which contains all the features. In real life, there may be probability factors, as well as more complex cohesive relationships (*e.g.* "tall" is 5' 9" or more for women, 6' 2" or more for men; "black" represents almost complete absence of light and colour for cloth, and a quite widely varying function of perceiver and perceived for skin[17]).

In human learning, both radical and conservative strategies can be inappropriate. But associations between features, and associations between associated sets of features in varying hierarchies, seem to be the best basis for generalization. Children, in fact, seem to use a fairly radical form of generalization strategy.

When children do overgeneralize, it seems quite logical. Children do not choose arbitrarily to overgeneralize features: they either overgeneralize radically to supersets, or they supplant the exceptions which cause problems for the rule. This second way is illustrated by overgeneralization of the application of the past tense suffix "-ed" to irregular verbs. The first case is illustrated by the use of the word "horsie" for cows, or "woof" for cats. In this case, not only has the child correctly generalized features such as size and colour (which he or she knows may be specified separately with other words), but he or she seems to have generalized aspects of shape. One explanation for such radical generalization, if it indeed is at all helpful to think of it this way, is that the child is failing to specify those features which he does not yet recognize.

To learn a concept a child needs to have an indicator (whether word or function or occurrence) that the concept is significant, and a recurrence of the significant association. Thus the words "want" and "dollie" will together be associated with the one sort of scene,[18] but individually with different sets of scenes. They will therefore come to be associated with the common features of the respective sets of scenes. This is generalization involving purely positive information. Negative information cannot be employed until the focus is clear, and the focus is made clear by contrast in an identical or analogous environment (*e.g.* between horse and cow).

Once a feature is shown to be emically significant by the discovery of contrasts involving it, negative information can then be usefully used (although it need not be immediately reflected in self-correction). Once there is a name for the negative examples, the principle of synonym avoidance leads to implicit negative reinforcement.

A variant of the radical–conservative criterion is also used in human language and concept learning. This is "the complexity hypothesis" of Clark, which is that the "less complex" is learned before the "more complex".[19] This asserts that correct recognition of contrasts involving a single feature or dimension should be learned before those involving more than one feature or dimension (*e.g.* length contrasts should be learned before volume contrasts, as illustrated in Piaget's experiments on understanding of conservation of liquid volume in children). This does not deny the obvious fact that it is easier to distinguish concepts which contrast in more than one feature (e.g. "dada's" beard, eyes and voice). Contrasts of single features should be learned before contrast between clusters of associated features. This is especially true where the contrast cannot be correctly made by considering a single feature (*e.g.* the height of the water level in glasses of different diameters).

Generation of Examples and Counter Examples

If a CL is to provide useful examples for testing its hypotheses, they should be chosen so as to be falsifiable, by choosing them within the hypothesized concept but outside the pre-generalized concept.

This does not transfer directly to the case of the child as CL, since it is not at all clear that a child has any intention of providing utterances for criticism or correction. On the contrary, the child generates sentences in order to communicate. This motivation may itself be enough to encourage the child to produce the most detailed sentence of which it is capable, but naïve observation suggests the opposite view, that the child uses the least effort necessary to communicate the message.

But there is also the phenomenon of play, and in particular crib speech, a unique form of language play. In this the child generates utterances purely for his own entertainment. Possibly this also exercises hypothetical rules of production, perhaps for comparison with the recognition rules, perhaps for comparison with some rote memories of sentences. Since it seems that not all children play in this way, it may not be significant.

Learning by Probabilities: Signature Tables and Network Models

The earliest attempts at machine learning used optimization of weightings. Samuels' checker-playing program worked by optimising the weightings of a linear polynomial involving 16 of 38 conceivably pertinent factors.[20] A more general and older tradition originates in brain modelling rather than computer science. This gave the Perceptron class of devices which used a cell which learns local connectivity weightings in a plastic way.[21] This model became the basis for theoretical studies of learning, and conclusions about what could and could not be achieved by probabilistic learning.

Samuels' revised checker-playing program used a three level "signature table" scheme which corresponded to a three layer Perceptron network.[22] In this method "parameters which are thought to be somehow related"[23] are grouped together into small subsets of, in different versions 3, 4 or 5 parameters, whose level-1 linear polynomial outputs become the parameters for level-2. They are then grouped as 3 level-1 parameters for each level-2 linear polynomial, whose level-2 outputs in turn become the level-3 parameters in the single level-3. The parameters at all levels are then reinforced according to a normalized correlation coefficient with the "book move" which is supposedly one of the best in that context.

One of the best introductions to the theory of learning machines for the classification of patterns is Nilsson.[24] The particular approach uses weighting, summation and threshold elements falling within the Perceptron family. One basic unit capable of binary linear classification is the building block for the discussion. Our models have a statistical *vs* neural classification, whilst Nilsson has made a parametric *vs* non-parametric classification.

Nilsson also looked at the convergence of three weight adjustment schemas for the TLU in learning a linear classification: the *fixed-increment rule* in which the weights are modified by a constant amount in the appropriate direction, the *absolute correction rule* in which the weights are adjusted in the appropriate direction until the threshold is passed and the pattern would now be correctly recognized, and the *fractional correction rule* in which the weights are adjusted a specified proportion of the way to the threshold. All techniques are convergent, the first two after a guaranteed finite number of adjustments.

Our approach, and that of Samuels corresponds to the third technique, although our approach is more complex and has some features of the first. The original version of our program was closer to the first technique.

Learning Word/Morpheme Classes

Let us look a little more specifically at the application of Concept Learning and Probabilistic Learning techniques to Natural Language Learning. We will discuss the development of grammatical categories, which are themselves a specific form of concept.

The concept learning process reflects McNeill's conclusion as to the two possible hypotheses by which grammatical categories are "elaborated": "differentiation and feature-assignment".[25] We argued earlier that differentiation is primary, as differentiation of features must precede feature assignment. When we are considering classification into grammatical categories (*i.e.* into word and morpheme classes) we suggest that semantics are essential to the process. By contrast, McNeill sees the syntactic hierarchy independently of meaning, and hence considers only the determination of features (corresponding to *slot* and *filler class*) which are implied by the syntactic context.

The alternative which McNeill puts forward is that of "a universal hierarchy of categories"[26] into which words are classified by successive differentiation, level by level, first into pivot and open, later more finely.

Ignoring McNeill's nativist leanings at this stage, and noting that semantic occurrence is significant, we can see a natural mechanism for Concept Learning to apply to differentiation of categories at a largely semantic level.

Thus at the one-word stage, a child comes to recognize Palermo's "response equivalence" between "the pivot word "want" and an open class of items which a child may want".[27] This distinction occurs before any overt expression of syntax. The differentiation is on the basis that a specific member of the open class applies to the scene where a specific object is desired, whilst the pivot word "want" is more general and applies to any member of the set of scenes in which an arbitrary object is desired. Thus "want" is reinforced in relation to a large number of scenes, but any open class word is reinforced only in relation to a small number of scenes.

The hypothesis is that at the two word stage the child starts to produce both words appropriate to the situation, with or without any cohesion determining the relative order. Given that two concepts are known to the child, cohesion may be learned by association between individual concepts. This is a fairly standard behaviorist explanation. Thus "Jenkins and Palermo ... describe some paradigms which ... explain how words elicited in the same contexts will tend to elicit each other".[28]

The questions this leaves is whether words are actually put into classes, and if so how. The evidence for the specific pivot and open classes is in dispute, but the evidence for classes seems convincing nonetheless. It is certainly evident at a higher level as new words met in one context are generalized to all slots using the same filler class. There is still the question as to how the child ""puts" the word into the cognitive class and thereafter uses the word in novel ways that obey the "rules" of the class".[29]

There are probably times when grouping by slot and cohesion features takes place. We outlined the mechanisms of this proposed consolidation phase in an earlier chapter, and use it in our experiments, although without the initial semantic based difference categorization. One proposal, apparently never actually implemented, which utilized such initial semantic differentiation is that of Block.[30]

The Syntax Crystal is a departure from traditional phrase structure in that it is, in tagmemic terms, cohesion based. There is no direct learning of *slot*, but this is construed only for purposes of comparison of the resulting parse structures with the corresponding traditional phrase structures.

The use of the consolidation process involves the grouping not only of words into classes, but of single word oriented rules into class connecting formulae. This is arguably the more important part of the process. So much so that one system which does employ a consolidation-like technique does not automatically import all instances into the newly consolidated classes.

This interesting feature of the complete Zbie algorithm is that, using the "Match Back" process, a new translation rule is developed.[31] This comes from a rule which gives a "close" partial parse, and the component classes are not inherited, but are only discovered, by the "Try Learn More" process, as they recur. Such inheritance clearly can easily be achieved. The question is therefore how computationally advantageous or psycholinguistically plausible it is to impose such a restriction. Two areas to consider are the phenomena of forgetting and "overlay" which may be consistent with the restriction. However, the "overlay" phenomenon (whereby learning a new rule seems to wipe out various correct, normally irregular forms) seems more like an instance of overgeneralization rather than undergeneralization as provided by this restriction.

Once classes have been determined, it is trivial to allocate new words or usages to be allocated to the correct class.

Learning and Representing Syntax

The learning of word classes is the first stage of the learning of syntax, and the Consolidation Hypothesis can clearly serve both to group word/concept associations into word classes, and to group word/word or class/class associations into formulae. However the class-formula model of syntax is not adequate on its own, and this common element of both TGG and Tagmemics and other linguistic theories meets widespread agreement. Cohesion is the key to meeting this inadequacy, to use the Tagmemic formulation. However, it is claimed here that the key function is one of restriction. The problem is not that Phrase Structure Grammar (PSG) is not capable of generating all grammatical sentences, but that it is not capable of restricting to grammatical sentences only. Some formulations of TGG also recognize the fundamental role of restriction, particularly in some of the more recent and computationally oriented discussions.[32]

It is surprising that the importance of restriction has so often been lost sight of, since under-restriction of PSG is the foundational point of Generative Grammar. However, the answer provided by so-called Transformational Generative Grammar is to add an even more general and more powerful mechanism to grammar. This serves to increase the number of classes of languages which may be generated, without demonstrably increasing the power to restrict the class of languages. We pointed out earlier that this has been recognized as a fault in TGG.

We proposed earlier that the restriction of language is mediated through cohesion, and that this cohesion is derived from negative information. In an earlier paper,[33] we gave very strong support for the role of negative information in the face of the theoretically intolerable contrary psycholinguistic tradition. We claimed that the only reason a child learns English (as opposed to French, or Chinese) is that his or her learning is corrected by a native speaker of English. The child may be considered to be anxious to please, avoiding error for this reason, based on inferences about what is likely to be acceptable. Simply hearing the sounds of the language may not be enough. Grammar, on this theory, is *nothing but* correctness.

Some older work has proposed a restrictive formulation of grammar, but has not tied this in with the correction paradigm.[34] Block's proposed system incorporates both cohesion-like and correction paradigms.[35] Our current learning models do not take into account correction, since they currently have no concept of semantics. We propose to introduce general semantics and syntactic correction independently at first, to allow us to examine the contribution of each to the efficacy of the system.

Learning and Representing Semantics and Relationships

We can now look at the learning of Semantics; we have already considered how semantic information may contribute to the learning of syntax. Semantics arises from relationships within the sensory-motor hierarchy and interrelationships with the linguistic hierarchy are fundamental to Hayes' ontological proposals. They are also fundamental to Narasimhan's and Kuczaj's language learning proposals,[36] although this and related work by Sembugamoorthy and Siklossy use a simplistic formal representation rather than a serious and meaningful attempt to equip the model with a basis for the development of ontology.[37] These latter projects demonstrate no recognition of the role of functionality and the motor modalities.

By contrast, Hayes is anxious to clear away the toy structures and provide a world in which the model can interact meaningfully; but the design of NL systems, and in particular, NLL systems is beyond the scope of his manifesto. His proposal does however capture the locus of meaning and meaningfulness for a general class of AI systems, in contrast with the arbitrary representation approach:

> The meaning of the tokens is defined by the structure of the formalisation, by the pattern of inferential connections between the assertions ... It is worth emphasizing that the view of meaning espoused here differs profoundly from the view which holds that tokens in a formalisation are essentially words in a natural language (Wilks, 1977). According to this latter view, the tokens *do* represent the concept intended, by *fiat*: they

are "semantic primitives", out of which all other meanings are composed.[38]

The first reasonably adequate presentation of the various interrelationships between the different facets and hierarchies of the NLL task is Block's:

Natural language acquisition requires the learning of complex information. For our purpose, we can consider this information to be of three types. (1) Lexical—the formation of an association between each concept and the lexeme ... which names it ... (2) Syntactic—the development of a system which can signify a relationship among concepts by a relationship among lexemes. (3) Pragmatic—learning whether particular concepts and/or their instantiations can be related to each other in a given situation.[39]

A final point, which we must recognize, is that the linguistic hierarchy is itself part of the ontology. All linguistic relationships which are recognized are themselves concepts which may be associated with a word. Furthermore, new words need not be learned directly by association with their respective sensory-motor experiences, but may be learned through conversation, illustrating that "meanings" are usually composites of both linguistic and sensory-motor experience. There are many words in our vocabulary which we understand, but where we don't have first-hand experience (*e.g.* "murder" and "rape"). There are similarly concepts which we do not have words for, but do understand since we recognize the concept once someone supplies a word (*e.g.* the "tip-of-the-tongue" phenomenon, where the meaning is recognized before the apt phrase is encountered, let alone a fully declinable noun and verb). This is Russell's technical distinction between "knowledge by acquaintance" and "knowledge by description".[40] We can distinguish "dictionary definitions" from "empirical" and "artificial" referential concepts, using a simplistic "primitive definition" *vs* "dictionary definition" dichotomy. Alternatively, we could argue that the redundancy of concept definitions is such that associations of every sort are potentially involved in every concept. But in a learning program, an object in the program's experience is a relationship between words. Relational word-senses are the normal principle of dictionary definition. The advantage of this for a computational mechanism is that it closely mirrors what must, of necessity, happen in a program. Dictionaries (mostly) do not have pictures: programs (mostly) do not have eyes. The use of relational meanings also enables a program to look up meanings in an on-line dictionary, created for human use, and receive definitions of a familiar kind. This simplification minimizes the sensory-motor requirements of the system. It is difficult to see how such a simplification could be viable in the initial stages of a learning system, but once an initial training stage has been passed it is feasible that the system could be blinded and learn solely through "dictionary definition". This would allow the system to be exported for use in simpler configurations.

Frame Problem: Frames and Schemas

We can now consider some of the specific problems which have arisen in AI (Artificial Intelligence) for which there is no clear cut solution. This final subsection of this chapter includes a review of some of the formal results relating to algorithms and languages.

We think it is convenient to consider questions of context, semantics and relationships in terms of frames, scenes and schemas, and we have used these terms quite freely — the last in Piaget's sense, and the first mainly following Fillmore's usage. The main idea is that words belong to particular linguistic frames, and correspond to various sensory-motor scenes. This allows, for example, explanation of the disambiguation of homonyms or, more generally of the appropriate nuance or denotation of a word in a particular context.

Anderson points out the unlikelihood "that any fixed set of frames will be appropriate to all possible situations",[41] showing the need for a dynamic perspective on language. We are also left with the problem of which facts to store with which frame. This problem is reminiscent of "the frame problem" in AI.

The term "frame" is used in AI in the domain of problem solvers and planners. In this context the main problem with frame-based systems, termed the "frame problem", is the difficulty of knowing, or keeping track of, which parts of the environment will be affected by an action.

But the real problem is how to represent the scene before and after an action, and how to represent the class of possible side effects (consider a chair which can be placed on or beside a box and would move when the box was moved if and only if it was on or in the way of the box). Two opposing options on representing the before and after frames are to specify anew all the features of the new frame, or to respecify only those features which changed. This latter option requires removing facts from the database and adding new ones, the former implies respecifying the entire database, which is in general extremely inefficient as only a small portion would actually change.

This is best illustrated from the visual system. We perceive a portion of our environment as the whole scene, yet the information we receive is in that still smaller part of it which changes, or in the systematic nature of the change (*e.g.* the view through a train window). Our visual system has evolved to be exceptionally sensitive to even small changes.

Thus the ideal of transmitting information as quickly as possible requires in the sensory modalities transmission of changes. The millions of bits in television frames (still orders of magnitude below retinal capacity) can be captured in a few bits with rotational and translational information about an object, or at intermediate cost by encoding pixel change. In the planning domain we need to understand the empirical consequences of motor activity. This however leaves a choice of transmitting all consequent changes indiscriminately, or a "lazy" approach where rules may be employed to determine the whereabouts of an object at the point where that knowledge is needed. This appears to be the way humans work—with sensory data primary (where we saw something last) and consequence consideration secondary (when we think through consciously what might have happened to something). But we can however note when we do something that it has a particular effect the importance of which we anticipate—this is the essence of a plan.

This leads us to another aspect which should be made explicit: the time factor. The scene and frame are not adequate, since without temporal information a state is not specified completely. We can thus consider state as a function of time and frame. There is a case for requiring that state information should never be deleted, since historical facts are perpetual. One important capability we must retain is the ability to determine the last known state of a feature, and to consider the hypothesis that it is still current. It may however be expedient to impose restrictions on access to past states.

All of these facets of frames, scenes, states and schemas are subsumed by the relationships which we propose here as the sole mechanism of representation. The sensory-motor scene is far too complex to be handled in full detail at every instant, and cohesive relational associations are presumed to embody the ontology necessary to allow elaboration of those features of a scene which are in focus.

The top-down linear search strategy employed in the PROLOG database is quite suited to a deletionless time-stamp strategy in which an implicit assumption is that the most recent fact recorded is still current, and the relational notion of "projection" and its corresponding non-unit clause definition in PROLOG, has the potential for capturing the delayed "lazy" determination of consequences which corrects this assumption. The best illustration of the need for such deferral will be a consideration of the part-whole problem.

Environment: Reality, Games and Toy Worlds

We have stressed both the importance of the sensory-motor hierarchy, and the need for the development of an ontology. Such a recognition underlay our earlier discussions, although AI research has typically been concerned with inadequate ontologies which do not always exercise systems appropriately. The best example of the common deficiencies in this area is in the semantics for NL systems. The ontology has tended to be a pale reflection of language rather than even a simplistic reflection of the environment.

Games and toy worlds are legitimate domains for AI research, but we believe that it is necessary for an ontology to approach the human ontology in order to realize a meaningful NL system. This needs to be more than an afterthought, an expedient to "resolve the dilemma by picking a tiny bit of the world".[42] The understanding of UNL (Unrestricted Natural Language) requires extensive world knowledge, indexed in intelligent ways. It proves necessary, for instance, to apply both world and syntactic knowledge to drive the selection between numerous word-senses. Whatever system of representation is used, however, word-sense disambiguation presents a major challenge to an UNL system.

The most coherent, and outspoken, exponent of an adequate ontology has been Hayes, who has outlined "The Naive Physics Manifesto":

> Artificial Intelligence is full of "toy problems": small artificial axiomatizations or puzzles designed to exercise the talents of various problem-solving programs or representational languages or systems. The subject badly needs some non-toy worlds to experiment with ... The formalism we propose should have the following characteristics ...
>
> (i) *Thoroughness*. It should cover the whole range of everyday physical phenomena: not just the block world, for example ...
>
> (ii) *Fidelity*. It should be reasonably detailed. For example, such aspects of a block in a block-world as shape, material, weight, rigidity and surface texture should be available as concepts ...
>
> (iii) *Density*. The ratio of facts to concepts needs to be fairly high. Put another way: the units need to have *lots* of slots ...
>
> (iv) *Uniformity*. There should be a common formal framework (language system, *etc.*) for the whole formalisation, so that the inferential connections between the different parts (axioms, frames ...) can be clearly seen, and divisions into subformalisms are not prejudged by deciding to use one formalism for one area and a different one for a different area.[43]

Hayes's manifesto is essential reading because the development of a reasonable basis for ontology is so fundamental. Hayes recognizes many of the important factors which we have emphasized, including the immensity of the problem of which the so-called "frame problem" is just a fragment. He also recognises the fundamental role of relationships in ontology, and the importance of reflecting not only the power but also the restrictions of the human sensory-motor and linguistic systems.

The visual "see" hierarchy is just another representation unless it can be linked to a good referential model of some sort. An initial implementation has been completed recently by Hume, and further development of this system as an environment for Sammut's 1981 concept learner has been described recently in Sammut's 1985 paper.[44]

Hayes's manifesto does not stop at the sensory level, but includes a physics which interacts also at a motor level. It is essential for NLL that the learning system has an adequate sensory and motor environment, as the relationships to be learned are partially functional.

There is an established tradition in Psycholinguistics (quite apart from Piaget's approach) which emphasizes the essential referential role.[45] However, although some implementors have paid lip-service to the principle of a sensory-motor referential basis (*e.g.* Siklossy[46]) there is actually little departure from the representation language approach:

> The systems we have been discussing had the common property that they could process successfully only carefully constructed sentences about the very narrow subject matter for which they were designed. They were designed around what has come to be known as a *micro-world*. The extent of their contribution to linguistics, computational or general, is therefore very much an open question.[47]

The projects which have had the most effective referential interaction in an NLL context have been those of Anderson and Block, as well as the earlier and related work of Harris: "L. Harris (1972) successfully simulated some aspects of language acquisition ... according to the maxim: "The parts of speech are the parts of the robot" (p.87)."[48]

Block demonstrates this approach to ontology with a toy language learning situation with an intriguing twist: parent-robot/baby-robot teams compete to teach/learn a language fastest in a chessboard environment.

Part-whole Problems: Intersecting Taxonomic Hierarchies

A special instance of the frame problem concerns those entities which normally have a fixed relationship, and which as a group have a separate identity and label. This instance is so general that it accounts for almost every object in our sensory-motor environment. Classical examples are people, lampstands and arches, having heads and bodies; stand, bulb and shade; supports and crosspiece. Even an amorphous blob has a perimeter and a centre. For the purposes of this discussion we generally stop short of the microscopic (*e.g.* cells, atoms, electrons) and concern ourselves solely with what can be perceived and/or affected directly as a unit. The differentiated subunits themselves admit of further subdivision (*e.g.* person – body – arm – hand – finger – nail) and in general units admit of multiple subdivisions. Each human sensory-motor modality and each field of science defines a different taxonomic hierarchy. Thus a person not only has a head and a body, but a characteristic voice, a characteristic footstep, a characteristic heartbeat, *etc.* He or she not only has a gross physical anatomy, but a cardio-vascular system, a nervous system, a musculo-skeletal system, *etc.* Schubert uses the example of a lamp, with its structural system and its electrical system, distinguished on the grounds of functionality, and its general apparent visual configuration, which hierarchy transcends the other two.[49] Thus if we focus on the light bulb, we see it is present in all three systems, it is supported by the structural system, it is powered through the electrical system, it is perceived in the visual configuration.

In tagmemic terms, the bulb plays different roles in different slots in different formulae in different hierarchies, bound by different cohesive relationships (*e.g.* cohesion of support of bulb with socket; cohesion of lighting of bulb with state of switch — this latter in both electrical and visual hierarchies).

Thus, the first problem with parts is that there are many taxonomies of any given object and, in general, of any given part. The second problem is the generic hierarchy. For example, animals have a head and a body, kangaroos are animals and therefore have a head and a body. This is equivalent to the "Socrates is mortal" syllogism, and exemplifies the need for a logical calculus. Although it has a major role in Schubert's analysis, it is mainly a matter of properties. This is generally true of the problems of parts. Why should we distinguish the properties that John has a head and a head has two eyes from the properties that teeth are white (or yellow or decayed) and eyes are blue (or brown or small)? The primary answer seems to have little to do with the special nature of the physical connectedness property, after all we could say that irises have pigment (or a particular molecular structure with specified absorption properties).

The main difference appears to be one of cohesion, norms and disjunction or gradation. We can say a unit has features or properties, but the aggregate of these features associates with the label ("name") for the unit. All men have two arms, but only some men have green eyes. Green eyes help us to distinguish John — and on analysis this distinction arises on the basis of norms. One-armed men exist, for various reasons — but we do not distinguish them with a single word for they are rare and a specific case of a named class (*e.g.* amputee or mutant). Nor do we distinguish green-eyed men with a single word, but we do distinguish pink-eyed blonds as "albinos". We also distinguish the classes of animals with no, two, four, six, eight and myriad legs. We thus come across the problem of disjunction in defining the physical taxonomy for a generic animal. But there is no significant difference between our identification of a number of legs and eyes for a specific individual, and identifying the pigment of his eyes.

Thus one can assume parts includes all inalienable properties (but this is still normative, one can lose an arm or dye one's hair, for example). In terms of the frame problem there is, for the most part, little point in distinguishing the relationship of the hat on the head from that of the head on the shoulders. Both can be attached quite firmly: one by a strap, the other by a neck. Both can be detached: one can be blown off by the wind, the other by a shell.

So in relation to the frame problem, the part-whole analysis merely identifies that there may be thousands of units affected by a single emic operation. Thus when John moves across the room, so do his teeth and his toes (or for that matter his dentures and his shoelaces, and even the yellowness of the tartar on his teeth). The point is that there is an invariance property which should allow us to avoid itemizing the effects in terms of the smallest distinguished units, but allow us to discover the whereabouts of John's toes or his dentures.

The final observation is that there are things which we don't localize at all, but which we may gain or lose (*e.g.* John's charm). These we always identify as properties of John. We will thus assume that parts are handled by relative cohesive relationships, and that people learn whether or not hats and heads should be dealt with in relative or absolute coordinates, and if relative, whether relative to John or to the hatstand.[50]

Notes to Chapter Eleven

1. Uhr, Leonard, *Pattern Recognition, Learning, and Thought: Computer-Programmed Models of Higher Mental Processes* (Prentice-Hall, Englewood Cliffs, NJ, 1973), p.16f.

2. Raphael, B., *The Thinking Computer: Mind Inside Matter* (Freeman, San Francisco, 1976).

3. Boden, M., *Artificial Intelligence and Natural Man* (Harvester Press, Hassocks, Sussex, UK, 1977).

4. Anderson, John R., *Language, Memory, and Thought* (Lawrence Erlbaum Associates, Hillsdale, NJ, 1976), p.1-2.

5. Turing, A.M., "Computing Machinery and Intelligence", *Mind*, Vol. 59 (1950), pp.433-460.

6. Wilks, Y., "An Artificial Intelligence Approach to Machine Translation", in Roger C. Schank and K. M. Colby, eds, *Computer Models of Thought and Language* (Freeman, 1973), p.115.

7. Michie, D., "The state of the art in machine learning", in *Introductory Readings in Expert Systems* (Gordon and Breach, 1982), p.218.

8. Quillian, J.R., "Word Concepts: A Theory and Simulation of some Basic Semantic Capabilities", *Behavioral Science*, Vol. 12, pp.410-430.

9. Schank, Roger C., "Identification of Conceptualization Underlying Natural Language", in Roger C. Schank and K. M. Colby, eds, *Computer Models of Thought and Language* (Freeman, 1973), p.190f.

10. Colmerauer, Alain, "An Interesting Subset of Natural Language", *Logic Programming* (Academic Press, 1982), pp.45-66.

11. Michie, D., "The state of the art in machine learning", in *Introductory Readings in Expert Systems* (Gordon and Breach, 1982), p.208f.

12. Cohen, Brian L., *A Theory of Structural Concept Formation and Pattern Recognition*, Ph.D. Thesis (University of NSW, Sydney, Australia, 1978).

13. Sammut, Claude, *Learning Concepts by Performing Experiments*, Ph.D. Thesis (University of NSW, Sydney, Australia, 1981).

14. Siklossy, Laurent, "A Language-Learning Heuristic Program", *Cognitive Psychology*, Vol.2, Pt.1 (1971), pp.479-495.

15. Widrow, B., K. G. Narendra, and S. Maitra, "Punish/Reward: Learning with a Critic in Adaptive Threshold Systems", *IEEE Trans. Sys. Man and Cyb.*, Vol. SMC-3 (September, 1973), pp.455-465.

16. Fillmore, C. J., "Scenes-and-frames semantics", in A. Zampolli, ed., *Linguistics Structures Processing* (North Holland, 1977), pp.55-81.

17. *Op. cit.*, p.69.

18. *Op. cit.*, p.62.

19. Clark, Eva V., "What's in a Word? On the Child's Acquisition of Semantics in his First Language", in Timothy E. Moore, *Cognitive Development and the Acquisition of Language* (Academic Press, New York, 1973), p.55.

20. Samuels, A.L., "Some studies in machine learning using the game of checkers", *IBM Jour. R & D*, Vol. 3 (1959), pp.211-229. Reprinted in Feigenbaum and Feldman, eds, *Computers and Thought* (McGraw-Hill, 1963).

21. Rosenblatt, F., "The Perceptron: A Probabilistic Model for Information Storage and Organization in the Brain", *Psych. Rev.*, Vol. 6 (November, 1958), pp.65ff; Block, H.D., B. W. Knight, and F. Rosenblatt, "The Perceptron: A Model for Brain Function", *Reviews of Modern Physics*, Vol. 34, No. 1 (1962), pp.135-142; Minsky, M., and S. Papert, *Perceptrons* (MIT Press, 1969).

22. Samuels, A.L., "Some studies in machine learning using the game of checkers II - recent progress", *IBM Jour. R & D*, Vol. 11, No. 6 (1967), pp.601-617.

23. *Op. cit.*, p.610.

24. Nilsson, Nils J., *Learning Machines: Foundations of trainable pattern-classifying systems* (McGraw-Hill, New York, NY, 1965).

25. McNeill, David, "The Capacity for the Ontogenesis of Grammar", in Dan I. Slobin, *The Ontogenesis of Language* (Academic Press, 1971), p.23.

26. *Op. cit.*, p.25.

27. Palermo, David S., "On Learning to Talk: Are Principles Derived from the Learning Laboratory Applicable?" in Dan I. Slobin, ed., *The Ontogenesis of Language* (Academic Press, 1971), p.48f.

28. Kelley, K.L., *Early Syntactic Acquisition* (Rand Corporation, Santa Monica, CA, November 1967), p.61.

29. Staats, Arthur W., "Linguistic-Mentalistic Theory versus an Explanatory S-R Learning Theory of Language Development", in Dan I. Slobin, *The Ontogenesis of Language* (Academic Press, 1971), p.125f.

30. Block, H.D., B. W. Knight, and F. Rosenblatt, "The Perceptron: A Model for Brain Function", *Reviews of Modern Physics*, Vol. 34, No. 1 (1962), p.573f.

31. Siklossy, Laurent, "A Language-Learning Heuristic Program", *Cognitive Psychology*, Vol.2, Pt.1 (1971), pp.479-495.

32. Berwick, Robert C., *The Acquisition of Syntactic Knowledge* (MIT Press, Cambridge, MA, 1985).

33. Turk, Christopher C. R., "A Correction NL Mechanism", *ECAI-84: Advances in Artificial Intelligence* (Elsevier Science Publishers, 1984), p.8.

34. *e.g.* Lamb, Sydney M., "On the Mechanization of Syntactic Analysis", *1961 Conference on Machine Translation and Applied Language Analysis*, Vol. II (1961), p.679f.

35. Block, H.D., J. Moulton, and G. M. Robinson, "Natural Language Acquisition by a Robot", *Int. J. Man-Mach. Stud.*, Vol. 7 (1975), p.574, p.582.

36. Narasimhan, R., *Modelling Language Behaviour* (Springer-Verlag, Berlin, 1981); Kuczaj, Stan A., *Crib Speech and Language Play* (Springer-Verlag, New York, NY, 1983).

37. Sembugamoorthy, V., "Analogy-based Acquisition of Utterances relating to Temporal Aspects", draft submitted to IJCAI-7 (1981); Siklossy, Laurent, "A Language-Learning Heuristic Program", *Cognitive Psychology*, Vol.2, Pt.1 (1971), pp.479-495.

38. Hayes, P.J., "The Naive Physics Manifesto", in D. Michie, ed., *Expert Systems in the Micro-electronics Age* (Edinburgh U.P., Edinburgh, Scotland, 1979), p.245f.

39. Block, H.D., J. Moulton, and G. M. Robinson, "Natural Language Acquisition by a Robot", *Int. J. Man-Mach. Stud.*, Vol. 7 (1975), p.572.

40. Boden, M., *Artificial Intelligence and Natural Man* (Harvester Press, Hassocks, Sussex, UK, 1977), p.248.

41. Anderson, John R., *Language, Memory, and Thought* (Lawrence Erlbaum Associates, Hillsdale, NJ, 1976), p.446.

42. Winograd, Terry, "A Procedural Model of Natural Language Understanding", in Roger C. Schank and K. M. Colby, eds, *Computer Models of Thought and Language* (Freeman, 1973), p.154.

43. Hayes, P.J., "The Naive Physics Manifesto", in D. Michie, ed., *Expert Systems in the Micro-electronics Age* (Edinburgh U.P., Edinburgh, Scotland, 1979), p.242ff.

44. Hume, David, "Creating Interactive Worlds with Multiple Actors", B.Sc. Honours Thesis, Electrical Engineering and Computer Science (University of New South Wales, Sydney, November 1984); Sammut, Claude, *Learning Concepts by Performing Experiments*, Ph.D. Thesis (University of NSW, Sydney, Australia, 1981); Sammut, C.A., "Concept Development for Expert System Knowledge Bases", *The Australian Computer Journal*, Vol. 17, No. 1 (February, 1985), pp.49-55.

45. Fraser, D., U. Bellugi, and R. Brown, "Control of Grammar in Imitation, Comprehension, and Production", *Journal of Verbal Learning and Verbal Behaviour*, Vol.2, No.1 (1963). p.134.

46. Siklossy, Laurent, "A Language-Learning Heuristic Program", *Cognitive Psychology*, Vol.2, Pt.1 (1971), pp.479-495.

47. Sparck-Jones, Karen, and Martin Kay, "Linguistics and Information Science: A Postscript", in Donald E. Walker, Hans Karlgren and Martin Kay, *Natural Language in Information Science: Perspectives and Directions for Research* (Scriptor, Stockholm, 1977), p.187.

48. Block, H.D., J. Moulton, and G. M. Robinson, "Natural Language Acquisition by a Robot", *Int. J. Man-Mach. Stud.*, Vol. 7 (1975), p.577.

49. Schubert, L.K., "Problems with Parts", *6th International Joint Conference on AI* (1979), pp.778-784.

50. Hume, David, "Creating Interactive Worlds with Multiple Actors", *B.Sc. Honours Thesis, Electrical Engineering and Computer Science* (University of New South Wales, Sydney, November 1984).

Chapter Twelve

Heuristics and Analytic Intransigence

This chapter looks at some of the particular problems associated with the computational demands of AI. The frame problem is a serious pragmatic problem characteristic of AI and NL, in which we must consider tradeoffs in time and space efficiency relating to storage and recall of information. More generally, we consider the question of efficiency and just what can and cannot be achieved in a given time frame. This is contrasted with the intransigent problems for which no efficacious algorithm can guarantee a solution in any time frame. Heuristics may be used to trade a fast probable solution against the possibility of failure in both these cases.

We also consider the limitations for specific mechanisms and applications. In particular various classes of language and presentation sequences face limitations of learnability independent of mechanism, whilst various mechanisms face specific limitations of applications, functions or languages learnable. Bearing in mind these theoretical limitations we review existing attempts at language learning and present syntheses of new approaches from well known computational formalisms and theoretical standpoints, which form the basis of our own experimental work.

We now turn to consider limitations on what computers can do, or on what algorithms can do. It is convenient to partition these difficult problems into two classes, which we may call the improbable and the impossible; respectively these are the focus of the next sections.

First we look at "needle-in-the-haystack" type problems, theoretically possible problems for which we are not likely to be able to find a solution in a reasonable amount of time. But we could definitely find a solution after an arbitrarily large finite time by following a well-defined search procedure.

For example, consider a trivial search problem in which one must make a score of binary decisions (*e.g.* a maze in which there are 20 T-junctions on the desired route). If one made a correct decision every second, it would take 20 seconds to achieve success, but if one made random choices or followed an exhaustive strategy it could take a month. Make it 30 decisions and the difference is 30 seconds versus a century. 20 more and it is 50 seconds versus a million years.

Many problems in AI map into some sort of search strategy like this. In a 20 move chess game there are two players and hence 40 decisions, few of which are even binary: the first involves a choice out of 20 possibilities (8 pawns and 2 knights each with 2 potential moves).

Problems for which there is no more efficient algorithm than exhaustive search are said to be non-deterministic-polynomial (NP). Sorting by trying exhaustively all possible permutations (decisions about order) and then checking if it is sorted is an exponential (non-polynomial) algorithm. But there are better algorithms. Selection sort, scanning to find the smallest, putting that first, and then sorting the rest the same way is one. The amount of work is polynomial, being proportional to the square of the number of elements, or the minimum number of decisions. With an oracle to allow you to go straight to the smallest item, you make only this minimum number of decisions and achieve the sort in $o(N)$ time. The theoretical and practical best order (sequential) sort is somewhere between these two at $o(N \log N)$.

In general we don't have oracles, but we can use rules-of-thumb or heuristics to guide the search in ways which may be profitable (*e.g.* "Hug the left wall!"). In a game like chess we use heuristics about the relative number, potential and mobility of the pieces retained by each side, and chess masters seem to recognize features of positions which are currently beyond such characterization.

Even parallelism is no panacea for overcoming the NP order of algorithm. The most it could achieve is to replace the term $exp(N)$ by the term $exp(N/k)$, where k is the number of parallel elements working on the problem. In practice even this is seldom achievable.

Automata and Formal Languages

There are also problems which are impossible. The best known and definitive member of this class is "the Turing machine halting problem". Can we write a program which when given an arbitrary program and its data can determine conclusively whether or not that program will stop when run? Suppose such a program exists, and we incorporate it in another such that if it decides "no" it stops, and if it decides "yes" it does not. If we then arrange to apply the program to itself, it must stop if it decides it will not, and it must continue if it decides it will stop. This contradiction implies that our assumption of the existence of such a program was invalid.

A more relevant example concerns language. Suppose we are to write a program which will learn an arbitrary language from examples. Assuming there are an infinite number of sentences in the language (as Chomsky claims) but a finite number of rules. Given any number of examples there will always be more than one grammar which will generate all those sentences, and others beside. With random positive examples and no negative information, it is impossible to restrict to a single grammar defining all and only the sentences of the language (we ignore the fact that there may be more than one grammar defining a given language).

This shakes up some of the common assumptions of linguistics and psycholinguistics (see Wexler[1] for a comprehensive and readable account of formal linguistic results). Gold derives some fundamental results about the learnability of different classes of languages under various conditions (following on from earlier landmark presentations of Miller and Chomsky) which contrast markedly with such attempts at language learning as had been made earlier (*e.g.* the quite reasonable approach of Lamb).[2]

So now let us consider Gold's study:

> Recently, psycholinguists have begun to study the acquisition of grammar by children (*e.g.* McNeil, 1966). Those working in the field generally agree that most children are rarely informed when they make grammatical errors, and those that are informed take little heed. In other words, it is believed that it is possible to learn the syntax of a natural language solely from positive instances, *i.e.* a "text". However, the results presented in the [final] Section show that only the most trivial class of languages considered is learnable (in the sense of identification in the limit) from text.[3]

This assumes that the lack of observed explicit negative information may be equated with a lack of restriction from the environment, that lack of immediate conformation to the rare examples of explicit negative information equates with a failure to utilize negative information, and that as a result the stream of information the child receives is no different in essence from an arbitrary text. In view of our earlier discussion, it is not surprising that the results indicate that languages can only be learned if either the language or the text is highly constrained. The weaknesses in these assumptions are implicit in his careful summation leading to one or more of the following conclusions:

> 1. The class of possible natural languages is much smaller than one would expect from our present models of syntax. That is, even if English is context-sensitive, it is not true that any context-sensitive language can occur naturally. Equivalently, we may say that the child starts out with more information than that the language it will be presented with is context-sensitive ...

> 2. The child receives negative instances by being corrected in a way we do not recognize. If we can assume that the child receives both positive and negative instances, then it is being presented information by an "informant". The class of primitive recursive languages, which includes the class of context-sensitive languages, is identifiable in the limit from an

informant. The child may receive the equivalent of negative instances for the purpose of grammar acquisition when it does not get the desired response to an utterance ...

3. There is an *a priori* restriction on the class of texts which can occur, such as a restriction on the order of text presentation. The child may learn that a certain string is not acceptable by the fact that it never occurs in a certain context. This would constitute a negative instance.[4]

We must be cautious with such results, which claim that it is impossible to learn language, in at least two respects. First, the constructions used take no cognizance of semantics and do not take into account that sentence generation is not arbitrary, but expresses some particular sense. Second, they assume that a human should have a complete mastery of the language by some specific age. The results relating to texts are negative precisely because, on the one hand, it is possible to proceed indefinitely far through a text without encountering a particular characteristic of the language, and on the other hand, it is possible to overgeneralize. The first symptom is not unexpected: it is quite usual to continue to meet new words and constructions throughout one's life, and indeed even the language itself is undergoing continuous change. The second problem, overgeneralization, is well known: in this case it is suggested that some sort of negative information must be used by the learner—whether by way of explicit correction, or by reassertion of the previously expressed forms which had been overlaid.

Anderson has extensively reviewed the implications of these results in relation to contemporary NLL proposals and systems, and also produces a set of three possible conclusions:

1. The class of possible languages can be much more restricted than the class of context-sensitive languages.

2. The learner can make certain assumptions about the information sequence. For instance, he may expect to see certain kinds of grammatical structures early or see certain structures used with some constant probability.

3. There may exist information other than the sentences in the information sequence. This information may serve to provide valuable clues as to the structure of the language.

He notes further that

These three sorts of ideas have been used in those past induction algorithms that have had some success in language learning situations ... They have shown that relatively efficient, constructive algorithms are possible for interesting language classes if the algorithms have access to information about the sentences' surface structure. The problem with their work is that this information is provided in an *ad hoc* manner. It has the flavour of "cheating", and certainly it is not the way things happen with respect to natural language induction. There is also a sense in which the work of Pad, Crespi-Reghizzi, and others is irrelevant to the task of inducing a natural language. They have, as their goal, the induction of the correct syntactic characterization of a target language. However, this is not what natural language learning is about. In learning a natural language the goal is to learn a *map* that allows us to go from sentences to their corresponding conceptual structures and vice-versa.

Anderson drives home this last point by reference to some impressive research into the contribution of referential information to the learning of syntax:

> The importance of semantics has been very forcefully brought home to psychologists by a pair of experiments by Moeser and Bregman (1972, 1973) on the induction of artificial languages. They compared language learning in the situation where their subjects only saw well-formed strings of the language versus the situation where they saw well-formed strings plus pictures of the semantic referent to these strings. In either case, the criterion test was for the subject to be able to detect which strings of the language were well formed—without the aid of any referent pictures. After 3000 training trials, subjects in the no-referent condition were at chance in the criterion test, whereas subjects in the referent condition were essentially perfect.[5]

The other main area where there are relevant results as to the possibility or impossibility of learning is in relation to the Perceptron. Minsky and Papert were quite critical of some earlier work with perceptron-like devices, but were very careful to indicate that there was still much potential for the network type of model, and indeed they both have continued with research with network models. Unfortunately those who have heard of their critique (and such lore spreads quickly) often have a quite unwarranted negative attitude to network models, and indeed to learning models in general, supposing that "all of that was laid to rest years ago by Minsky".

In setting the record straight, we will not refer to subsequent work by Minsky and Papert here, nor to ignorant references to Minsky in the subsequent literature, but directly to the original monograph.

First, some of their criticism is quite severe:

> Our discussion will include some rather sharp criticisms of earlier work in this area. Perceptrons have been widely publicized as "pattern recognition" or "learning" machines and as such have been discussed in a large number of books, journal articles, and voluminous "reports". Most of this writing (some exceptions are mentioned in our bibliography) is without scientific value and we will not usually refer by name to the works we criticize. The sciences of computation and cybernetics began, and it seems quite rightly so, with a certain flourish of romanticism. They were laden with attractive and exciting new ideas which have already borne rich fruit. Heavy demands of rigour and caution could

have held this development to a much slower pace; only the future could tell which directions were to be the best. We feel, in fact, that the solemn experts who most complained about the "exaggerated claims" of the cybernetic enthusiasts were, in the balance, much more in the wrong. But now the time has come for maturity, and this requires us to match our speculative enterprise with equally imaginative standards of criticism.[6]

However, following presentation of some theorems highlighting one characteristic (and now notorious) limitation of the perceptron (which we will get to shortly) they note:

> These critical remarks must not be read as suggestions that we are op-posed to making machines that can "learn". Exactly the contrary! But we do believe that significant learning at a significant rate presupposes some significant structure. Simple learning schemes based on adjusting coefficients can indeed be practical and valuable when the partial func-tions are reasonably matched to the task, as they are in Samuel's checker player. A perceptron ... properly designed ... will have a good chance to improve its performance adaptively. Our purpose is to ex-plain why there is little chance of much good coming from giving a high-order problem to a quasi-universal perceptron whose partial functions have not been chosen with any particular task in mind ... It may be ar-gued that *people* are universal machines and so a counter-example to this thesis. But our brains are sufficiently structured to be programm-able in a much more general sense than the perceptron and our *culture* is sufficiently structured to provide, if not an actual program, at least a rather complex set of interactions that govern the course of whatever the process of self-programming may be.[7]

This is an extraordinary example of any authors' concern to present their criticisms in a way which could not be misunderstood. They devote an entire chapter (13) to the whys and wherefores of how to interpret the results. This chapter is in the form of questions and answers. From one comment it seems that they were already starting to receive extreme reactions to their work.

The particular notorious and, at first, surprising result which showed the perceptron limitations was the task of recognizing whether a pattern was convex or connected. (Convex, in the mathematical sense, means that if two points are part of the pattern, then all points on a straight line connecting those points are also part of the pattern. Connectedness is more general, requiring only the existence of a possibly quite circuitous line within the pattern and connecting the two points.)

It turns out that Perceptrons can distinguish a convex pattern, but cannot distinguish a connected pattern. This is quite a paradox, since whilst people seem to have a natural understanding of connectedness, they tend to find convexity quite an artificial concept. It looks on the surface to be disastrous for the Perceptron as a model of human pattern recognition.

The proof is very simple. The point about Perceptrons is that they are local. Each one processes information from only a small number of (surrounding) points, k say (*viz.* it has order k which is considerably less than the total number of points resolved in the retina). The proof compares a pattern consisting of parallel stripes with another in which the intervening gap is filled in. On the first figure at least one Perceptron must return false (not connected), but all must return true (connected) on the second figure, and that includes this same Perceptron. But that Perceptron depends on only k points, so there must be at least one point in the gap which it does not take into account. This point can provide a bridge, making the pattern connected, but this Perceptron would still indicate that the pattern is not connected.

The answer to the paradox is that humans don't have a natural conception of convexity because that is handled subconsciously. Connectivity, on the other hand, requires a conscious search procedure. If we could determine connectivity so easily there would be no market for "can the bunny get to the carrot?" type mazes in our newspapers — this is precisely the example of an intransigent problem. The figures in Minsky (p.6) illustrating connected and unconnected patterns are quite small and simple, but nonetheless, in the case of one contrasting pair at least, require careful tracing to determine connectivity. Thus the result is totally unsurprising.

Methodology: Implementation *vs* Experimentation

We devote the rest of this chapter to a number of notes about implementations and systems: sundry factors and perspectives in the realization of an AI model, the testing of theory, and the development of techniques.

First we should think about the purpose and value of an implementation in AI and cognitive science. Unfortunately, many AI programs are written in an *ad hoc* fashion without either rigorously testing any realistic hypothesis, or advancing the state of knowledge significantly. Hayes complains:

> It is tempting to make such demonstrations from time to time. (They impress people; and it is satisfying to have actually *made* something which works, like building model railways; and one's students get Ph.D's that way.) But they divert attention from the main goal. In fact, I believe they have several more dangerous effects. It is perilously easy to conclude that, because one has a program which *works* (in some sense), its representation of its knowledge must be more or less *correct* (in some sense). Regrettably, the little compromises and simplifications

needed in order to get the program to work in a reasonable space or in a reasonable time, can often make the representation even less satisfactory than it might have been ... I emphasize this point because there is a prevailing attitude in AI that research which does not result fairly quickly in a working program of some kind is somehow useless, or at least, highly suspicious. This may be partly to blame for the dearth of really serious efforts in the representational direction, and the proliferation of programs and techniques which work well (or sometimes badly) in trivially small domains, but which are wholly limited by scale factors, and which therefore tell us nothing about thinking about realistically complicated worlds.[8]

Hayes argues this case in great detail. What is needed is to explore many methods in simple experiments, involving arbitrarily complex domains. They can then be evaluated and developed efficiently without developing a "castle in the clouds" for each one. Predicate calculus is a useful starting point for this. Combined with a reasonably complex world model such that language, learning and control methods may be examined quickly and non-trivially, this is the approach taken here: exploring several, rather than a single one, of the proposals arising from the hypotheses we have outlined here.

It is unfortunate, but evident, that AI has been a number of "extended forays into the unknown", and relatively little was being done to "advance the foundations". We would argue that relatively little has been learned from the previous AI work on NL — mostly the approaches have already been pushed to the extreme without opening up avenues for the development of more powerful systems. There was no way of building on them. Their structure was arbitrary, being built up solely for the purposes of a single demonstration. So there was very little gain for those that followed.

For these reasons, our research which is described in the last chapter sought to move on a broad front, examining many relevant factors, with the drawing of them together as a long term goal, and the development of small experiments to examine specific aspects as appropriate as intermediate stages. Hayes's methodological exposition, and Block's multimodal approach, are milestones of encouragement towards a more broadly scientific approach.

Multi-processing

Parallelism plays an important, although only partially understood, role in cognitive and linguistic processing. But we have already shown multiprocessing is no "panacea" to solve our problems of intractability. There have been a number of explorations of parallelism in different contexts: some integral and some more tangential to the general tenor of this research. Generally the approach espoused is the development of multi-processing systems which are capable of capturing and utilizing "natural parallelism".

The first level of "natural parallelism" available is the existence of independent processing in the low levels of each modality—*e.g.* we could have separate vision and acoustic modules in parallel with other processing. The second level is the intramodal parallelism implicit in the existence of many relationships between different units and levels and hierarchies. There is apparently some interference when the same cell would be involved in responding to more than one association, so a thresholding preferential service effect is hypothesized. This scheme corresponds to the standard interrupt priority arbitration arrangement of most computer architectures. Once the highest priority is dealt with, whether accepted or rejected, the next highest interrupt still waiting for service is considered.

The neural and statistical language learning models use such a technique, with PROLOG clauses representing cells and connections. However, Powers' model is designed to be able to exploit this parallelism. It retains logical clauses as cells and adds the concept of links as associations being recognized and captured by a cell in the connection graph paradigm.[9] The current model (CONG) is designed to simulate around 1000 processors which handle non-interfering links. These 1000 processors are far too few, but ideally should correspond to the number of cells required in the underlying neural model. The 1000 is a compromise to allow simulation on a uniprocessor, and in current research characterization of performance on up to 6 concurrent processors. In the connection graph paradigm, clauses which no longer form a complete association are disabled and links form new clauses. Ideally, a given processor should be available for one specific association based on the changing aspect of the Herbrand universe according to the environmental interaction with the sensory-motor modalities. Such a parallel predicate calculus representation does appear to be capable of capturing ontological and linguistic interassociations.

While there seems to be a potential relationship between parallelism, and links in connection graphs, and also between parallelism and associations in neural networks, such consideration has been deferred until a fully operational parallel connection graph (CONG) is available. The logic programming paradigm appears very promising as there are 6 distinct types of inherent parallelism of which at least 5 can be exploited using connection graphs.

Cybernetics and Robotics

The field of robotics has separated from the mainstream of AI to a considerable extent. Commercially, it is more closely related to assembly lines than to Cybernetics. However, we see that the most obvious and logical extension, application and implementation of AI principles is the robot. To learn language, the computer must be embodied as an intelligent robot, or at least be a simulated robot or embedded in a simulated environment or some form of sensory-motor application.

We have emphasised that associations between the sensory and motor hierarchies characterize human cognitive processes, and must characterize computer/robot intelligence. The associative aspect has typically been demonstrated with a sensory emphasis — with the associative network organization most clearly apparent in relation to vision. However, associations apply to the motor modalities, and conditioning and habituation exemplify the motor association. Indeed, meaning is embodied primarily in functional association rather than abstract or even sensory associations.

Since association provides a mechanism for learning functional motor control, it is potentially applicable to robotics irrespective of any linguistic aspirations.

Language Learning Systems

We now turn to highlight briefly the most significant proposals and models for Natural Language Learning systems. An important consideration is their referential basis, and the best approach seems to be to provide, like Block, a robotic referential basis.

Block's proposal is to spend the effort setting up a robot in an environment, and set it learning using an associative technique, the "Syntax Crystal Learning Algorithm". This is much like the rules of dominoes, except that duplicates of existing tiles may be made as required. Also, adjacency is topologically stretched so that new words or larger constructs, treated as a unit, can substitute for a constituent (labelling external edges to match the adjacent edges). In general, unlabelled edges are labelled when an adjacency becomes apparent. In the case of this substitution paradigm, the new construct is assumed to generalize to all places where the displaced constituent fitted. There are instructions concerning discarding or devaluing cards, and inventing new labels which apply when attempted (over)generalization results in an ungrammatical string. This provides the opportunity for feedback from the teacher to influence the correctness of the grammar. Normally, all labels must be matched to produce a grammatical crystal. There is however provision for optional codes for which this requirement is relaxed.

The instructions relating to ungrammatical strings and feedback are a bit vague, but could be tightened up. There are a number of other respects in which the algorithm is not immediately ready for computer implementation, including a few gaps concerning initial and new labelling which become more apparent only through examination of his examples. In addition, some of his grammatical labellings are unconventional, but, of course, these are not generated by the algorithm, but are glosses for the benefit of the reader. Similarly his rule notation for transcribing strings includes certain redundancies and unnecessary complexities, and also exposes some redundancy in the algorithm—in terms of producing different but equivalent Syntax Crystals and card sets. And likewise this is irrelevant to the implementation of the algorithm.

A step away from experiential learning is book learning—Zbie is an example. However the translation of the pictures in the book to a highly structured and very simple representational language reduces the impact of important results which might have been achieved:

> We have not tried to simulate the acquisition of a first language by a child. We have investigated the capabilities of an information-processing system to express situations under the assumption that the system possesses a way to perceive and internally represent situations. In the remaining parts of this article, we describe, through some examples, the representational device FL, and illustrate the operation of Zbie by exhibiting its learning of English and Russian.[10]

The Zbie system is presented as two situations represented as tree structures in the FL language and by sentences in the target natural language. If the trees are similar, Zbie builds a generalized super-tree. Later, in the test phase, situations are presented in FL and compared with the stored patterns, and an attempt to produce a corresponding NL sentence is made by Zbie. A significant feature of the system is that a "correct" sentence is then provided, and the system attempts to compare its own attempt with the experimenter's "correction" to build on its knowledge of NL.

Despite, or possibly because of, the well defined, highly restricted representation language (FL), the general NLL capability of Zbie is little more than that of our early experiments, which used only syntactic information. The approach bypasses the more general problem of how to understand the environment and develop an ontology. A clear implication of the evidence presented in the debate on innateness is that if the structure is not innate, but learned, then it must be impressed from the environment. It is impossible for a more complex system to be learned or developed from a simpler one.[11]

An older approach by Kelley attempts syntactic learning without semantics or ontological assistance.[12] What made it interesting was the attempt to build up through the psycholinguistic one-, two- and three-word stages, with a deletion scheme to allow turning of model adult sentences into telegraphic child speech. Another interesting feature was that if the sentence was not consistent with what the child already knew, no attempt at learning from it was made.

This system manages to learn to produce up to three-word telegraphic sentences. The type of three-word sentence produced is S-V-O, along with other expected forms such as Adj-S-V and V-Adj-O. The partial analysis ensures that the more directly functional words receive a priority, and a deeper structure is reflected. The innate stages provide very strong constraints which provide enormous guidance: stage two in relation to verbs, and stage three in relation to subjects. One wonders what is the impact on performance of removing the intervention and changing the learning algorithm at each stage.

A far more recent project, with some quite sound theoretical assumptions but a completely inadequate attempt at implementation, is described by Kucera.[13] The use of a teaching program is of minor interest, since it merely saves the experimenter doing the job himself. But as such it is an appropriate mechanism to use, although only in either an *ad hoc* manner, or to determine systematically the learning capabilities of a system for various classes of languages and classes of presentation.

The output of the child machine is reinforced either positively or negatively by the parent machine (which acts both as teacher and critic). The learning process operates by making modifications to the sentences the child machine has "heard": by either substitution or interchange of vocabulary.

Although there is some controversy over the role of imitation and correction, the idea of the machine attempting to speak, and the parent providing correction is consistent with the position we argued for, although more overt than is empirically justifiable. The generated imitation is further removed from the original sentences than it is in Kuczaj's "modification",[14] but it is varying the utterance in a way which should be guided by semantics.

This model is interesting, but it is not clear that class and state discoveries were performed simultaneously — it appears that they were achieved in two stages. The state discovery algorithm has not been fully described, although we are told that it was "directly modeled after the word-class discovery algorithm". The discovery of word classes seems to occur by substitution and permutation of the given sentences, allowing paradigmatic discovery of word classes using the direct positive/negative reinforcement of the teacher. This type of teacher is probably more powerful than is justified, and the word-class discovery algorithm is largely pattern matching and seems not to make use of grammatical rules. The research is completely independent of semantics, and this aspect of language acquisition is not discussed.

The learning process uses a concept which Kuczaj calls "abduction" to introduce hypotheses in a process similar to the conjecture and refutation approach. It is not clear whether this is strictly the classical abduction process of hypothesizing the condition given the consequence (*i.e.* using legitimate inference "backwards"). Nor is it clear how abduction is used, except in the relatively unintelligent sense of the paradigmatic pattern-matching approach to word-class discovery.

Sembugamoorthy's approach, and in particular Narasimhan's, also have much to commend them in theory, yet are disappointing in practice. The "learning" technique of Sembugamoorthy's PLAS is quite gross, and goes outside the bounds of what can be regarded as reasonable simplification. It is far more objectionable than Siklossy's representational oversimplifications criticized earlier. The experimenter as teacher is involved at every level in identifying the associations between the language and the simulated teaching environment.

Suffice it to say that the learning, and in particular, the teaching, varies significantly from our approach, and the system is thus not really making an attempt at the problems we address. What elements there are in common with our approach have not been developed in this model sufficiently to contribute to an understanding of them. This is not to decry the research framework in which this work was carried out. But we must be clear that PLAS does not learn language from a conversational and interactional environment, but by direct association of language constructs with sensory/motor tokens through the use of a specific set of predefined *"tags"*. PLAS has no ability to handle verbs, other than the copula. There are claimed, and to an extent valid, real-life analogues of this aspect of the model:

- pointing to an individual object/agent while simultaneously uttering a name or name-expression;
- pointing to a collection of objects/agents while simultaneously uttering a name or name-expression;
- the use of intonation to mark the topic part of an utterance in contrast to the comment part.

We agree with these analogues, and we also agree that such direct or indirect ostensive behaviour is essential to any model of child language learning. But we think they are overdone in PLAS to the extent of "cheating": it gives the machine equivalences for words and phrases. Pragmatically, too, it is problematic, in that it becomes little different from the traditional approach of feeding the machine dictionaries and grammars. But it has provided a base from which other problems have been tackled, and it is in this that the value of PLAS lies.

Database Theory and Entity-Relationship Models

One particular area of computer science where the graphical models are particularly close to the associative network model is in Database Theory. The current trend in databases is towards relational models in which redundant storage is avoided and separate relationships involving a common domain can be "joined". This has been extended into a formalized entity-relationship model, which is essentially an analogue of the associative network. Quite a detailed theory has been built up for such models, including issues such as integrity and consistency, and recently even relationship to NL concepts.[15]

This work by Sowa is a comprehensive attempt to integrate cognitive science and AI, merging philosophy, linguistics and psychology with Logic Programming, Expert Systems and Database Theory, and emphasizing in particular representational aspects.

The relational model is in a sense the database answer to the database equivalent of the frame problem. The basic idea is to obviate redundant storage in a data base, and to allow access to information in an efficient and consistent manner. Thus if another 747 is added to a fleet of aircraft, it is not necessary for either the plane or the flights to which it is allocated to be annotated with the number of passengers it can carry. Similarly, if a flight leaves its origin and arrives at its destination, it is not necessary to copy over the aircraft type or the flight manifest, and in the latter case the actual and booked manifests are available indexed by port of call.

Another analogue of the frame problem with an associated solution is in a PROLOG interpreter. Here literal frames are kept on a stack, and the problem of excessive redundancy is solved in some systems by structure sharing in which what is stored in each frame is not actually the complete set of new data, but the framework of the structure containing new material where necessary, and pointers to the inherited structures otherwise.

Deletionless Strategies

One other database strategy is also of interest. This is what in accountancy is known as an audit trail. In particular, no information is ever permitted to be thrown away. If an error is identified in the records, it is not erased and corrected, but a new pair of entries are put through to cancel the incorrect transaction and perform the new.

In Computer Science this is not usually done directly, but file editing and deletion combined with automatic archiving of backups means that a similar effect, albeit on a coarser-grained time-scale, is often achieved.

Even banks do not normally keep all information directly accessible indefinitely, but discard the information once a statement is issued.

A more direct approach to an audit trail would be a non-deletion strategy using timestamps.[16] This simply adds a new entry so that it is found in preference to the original entry. It is also possible to use a structure sharing approach, and store the framework of an entry, and the new information, with pointers back to the information which has not changed. Keeping things forever has the disadvantage that memory is tied up with out of date information, but consolidation and archiving can be done periodically.

Such a structure-shared and/or time-stamped non-deletion strategy is easily implemented. In a language like PROLOG where there is no intrinsic distinction between program and data, this is easy. It also has properties which are useful in relation to the frame problem. The technique is particularly suited to write-once devices such as the current generation of optical disk technology.

There is evidence that human memory operates with some sort of non-deletion strategy. Under hypnosis or electrical stimulation of areas of the brain, it appears that memories can be brought back vividly in perfect detail. The pattern of child language development and overgeneralization errors also has the character of a painting, in which strokes are laid one on top of the other and there is no deletion as such.

This remains a strategy which could be looked at again. A non-deletion strategy, with timestamp and periodic consolidation, is used in our experiments reported in the next chapter. Some recent developments have also been made in Logic Programming following this principle.

Formalisms

> It is *not* proposed to develop a new formalism or language to write down all this knowledge in. In fact, I propose ... that first-order logic is a suitable basic vehicle for representation ... which also has the advantage of a clear, explicit model theory, and a well-understood proof theory.[17]

This subsection and the next are not an essential part of the theoretical background to research into Natural Language Learning, but they do focus on the particular disciplines used to implement most of our experiments. As Hayes points out, the particular formalism is not a matter of great importance in itself. What is important is to standardize on a formalism. There has been a *de facto* standard for AI research for more than two decades, but LISP has spawned a great number of non-portable non-comparable systems of representation, and it is currently being ousted from its place by PROLOG (although in the listing of recent parsing systems in *Computational Linguistics* [Vol 8, No 3-4, 1984] LIS-Pish implementations still outnumbered PROLOG implementations almost two to one.

While there is still much scope for differences between representational systems in PROLOG, there is the advantage that in PROLOG all data and procedural entities have a common logical relational structure. They form a relational database which can be simply converted into other formalisms. LISP, by contrast, has a common structure and notation which is functional and constitutes a functional program.

PROLOG has the part-advantage, part-disadvantage, that it is relatively young and pure, and there are many classes of problems, the solution to which in PROLOG is not readily apparent (and which have not yet been studied). LISP lost its purity long before it gained any widespread acceptance, and most AI programs don't have many of the nice theoretical properties which pure LISP programs should have. Interestingly, the inventor of LISP, John McCarthy, predicted (in about 1960) that the basis for Computer Science in the next century would be formal logic, in the same way as formal analysis was the basis for Physics in the last.

These following notes are not a broad introduction to Logic, Logic Programming or even PROLOG. They are introductory, but make brief specific points about the Logic Programming paradigm.

Truth Values and Predicates – the Calculus

Given the position that the essence of the NLL phenomenon is the acquisition of cohesive relationships, the NLL problem becomes a matter, first, of how to represent and, second, of how to acquire such relationships.

A relationship is expressed in logic by noting that a particular set of entities have a particular relationship with each other. A set of such entity-relationships may be associated with a particular concept, and have an analogous structure. Such a relationship structure identifies or names a relationship, and may for convenience be associated with a constant symbol, a "functor" or "predicate name", and a characteristic (finite) number and ordering of components. Strictly speaking, the predicate name and arity (the characteristic number of components) are themselves entities in the relationship. These distinguished constants define the notation for a "predicate".

In the predicate calculus, predicate names are usually selected from the set of upper case Roman letters, and functors from the set of lower case letters, in both cases possibly followed by other alphanumeric characters. In the PROLOG notation used here (the Edinburgh syntax), functors and predicate names are not distinguished, but the first letter of either must be lower case. The name is in either case followed by the appropriate number (its arity) of parenthesis-grouped arguments, representing the related entities, which may themselves be constants or predicates. A constant may be regarded as a function of zero arity. The constants, functions and predicates are collectively called literals. Thus in PROLOG notation, the following are two legal literals.

> cat   bit(cat, dog) saw(boy, bit(cat, dog))
>   equals(she, mother(cat))

The last involves nested functions. The general concept of a function involves a mapping from the arity-dimensional space of constants to the single-dimensional space of constants. Thus in the fourth example the two arguments may be regarded as equivalent. The first order logic on which PROLOG is based demands textual (rather than functional) equality for equivalence. Thus the term "function" is not helpful. Predicates have intrinsic truth values. A function merely represents a substructure.

The predicate calculus also includes variables which may be universally or existentially quantified in a "sentence" according to whether the sentence is claimed to be true for all substitutable literals (not one counter-example), or some substitutable literals (at least one example). Sentences are simply quantified predicates, or else quantified predicates composed of such things using the distinguished axiomatic logical predicate names "and", "or" (both diadic — of binary but recursively extensible arity) and "not" (monadic — of arity one).

In general, a sentence can be restated in a form in which all variables are universally quantified. This form also consists of a conjunction of independently quantified clauses ("and"ed to form the sentence), where each clause is a disjunction of interdependently quantified terms ("or"ed to form the clause). Each term can also be a negated predicate ("not"ed to form the term). Any sentence of the predicate calculus may be expressed in this Conjunctive Normal Form (CNF) in First Order Logic (FOL). We call this clausal form, and the disjunctions, clauses.

In PROLOG (the Edinburgh syntax), variables are written as alphanumeric strings commencing with a capital letter, and are assumed to be universally quantified. Using this convention, and without showing quantifiers, the following is an example of a sentence in conventional notation using "−" for "not", "*" for "and" and " + " for "or":

$$(a(X, Y, Z) + b(X, Z)) * (b(X, Y) + -a(X, Z, Y))$$

Omitting the operators "−", " + " and "*", writing the separate disjunctive clauses of the conjunctive sentence on distinct lines, and separating the positive and negative literals by a colon ":" with the right-hand side containing the negative literals marked by a single "–", we obtain the most usual form of clausal notation as used in PROLOG.

a(X, Y, Z), b(X, Z).
b(X, Y) :\- a(X, Z, Y).

There are well-defined truth-preserving principles and operations for manipulating and transforming sentences of the Predicate Calculus. We will discuss some essentials of this logical calculus now, although the standard operations and transformation of Boolean logic will be assumed.

Inference and Unification; Syllogism and Resolution

Let us consider the question of an inference rule now, and for simplicity, let us first consider it in the propositional logic (without the complication of variables):

(1) h
(2) m :– h
(3) m

(1) and (2) are given. They are clauses which must both be true. The first states that h is true, the second states that m is true or h is false. Since the first clause contradicts the second part of the second clause, the conclusion (3) is obtained. This leads to a general inference rule, since the addition of any number of true alternatives to either (1) or (2) will result in a conclusion obtained by the addition to (3) of these same alternatives.

Consider the famed syllogism:

(4) Socrates is Human
(5) all Humans are Mortal
(6) Socrates is Mortal

This may be expressed as above if Socrates is the implied referent. In predicate form, it may be expressed

(7) human(socrates).
(8) mortal(X) :– human(X).
(9) mortal(socrates).

In order to apply the inference rule an additional step is needed. It needs to be recognized that a specific instance of (8) may be found by substitution of the universally quantified variable X by the specific instance socrates, *viz.*

(10) mortal(socrates) :– human(socrates).

Once we have achieved a "ground instance" of a clause, our predicates become simple textually distinguished propositions, and the example of (7) – (9) reduces to that of (1) – (3).

The substitution which is required is that which leads to otherwise identical terms of opposite sign in the two terms being "resolved upon". The processes of making two literals identical is called "unification". The combination of unification with this syllogistic logical inference step is the basis of the "resolution" theorem-proving technique.

Example and Counter-Example: Proof and Refutation

Note that in (1) – (3) the inference step depended on the avoidance of a logical inconsistency by the cancelling of contradictory terms. If it were not for the existence of one or more additional terms in the two axioms (1) – (2), in that case "m", the axioms would have indeed been irredeemably inconsistent. The inference rule may still be deemed valid if we define that the empty clause (the result of resolving inconsistent axioms) is false. Then if we can prove "false", we have demonstrated an inconsistency in the set of axioms. When we use the Predicate Calculus, the particular set of substitutions which result in such a contradiction denotes a counter-example to the series of axioms proposed.

It is possible to add to our believed axioms certain hypothesized proposition(s) which are to be examined. If it is now possible to find a contradiction whereas the axioms were themselves formerly consistent, we have succeeded in disproving the (set of) hypotheses, and we have found a counter-example. This is negative information, and failure to find a contradiction may or may not in general constitute a proof that one does not exist. It is possible to hypothesize the antithesis of the theorem to be proved, in which case discovery of a contradiction *does* constitute a proof, and the unifying substitution found denotes that proof.

This still leaves the possibility that the proposition is true, but that no proof has been found. However, a *complete* proof procedure will not terminate if no finite proof exists within the formalism.

Clauses: Horn and Non-Horn, Unit and Non-Unit

We have already noted that the CNF FOL formulation has all the expressive power of the Predicate Calculus. The clausal form has an additional advantage in that it is quite natural and easy to understand, and conveniently itself reflects the notion of logical implication. Thus (8) may be read:

mortal(X) if human(X).

The colon ":" separator and negation "–" marker conveniently coalesce to form a single symbol reminiscent of the implication sign, which may itself be used as an alternate notation, *viz.*:

mortal(X) :– human(X).

A special case of clausal form, which again has the full expressive power of Predicate Logic, is the Horn Clause, in which the additional restriction is imposed that exactly one term in each clause must be a positive literal. There may be zero or more negative literals. The clauses above are almost all Horn Clauses. A clause with exactly one (positive) literal is called a unit clause. In PROLOG a clause with no positive literal is used as the goal, the negated theorem.

Lemmas, Recursion and Tautologies

Another class of theorem provers makes use of lemmas. The unification and inference rules may be used to generate further propositions, called "lemmas", which may themselves be used to generate further possibilities. The Model Elimination proof procedure of Loveland is particularly noteworthy.[18] The connection graph proof procedure also makes use of arbitrary resolvents, although the term "lemma" is not usually applied in this case.

It is possible that recursive rules, relationships and structures will map into clauses with unifiable positive and negative literals within the one clause. Such recursive clauses can result in fruitless infinite searches in a different disjunctive branch of the search space when depth-first proof strategies are used.

It is possible that, whether by unification with such a legitimate recursive clause or otherwise, a clause has otherwise identical positive and negative terms. Such a clause has no utility whatsoever, since it is a tautology and trivially true. This is because any term is either true or false, and the disjunction of positive and negative instances must in one case be true.

It is also possible that unifiable terms of the same sign occur in a clause. This does not cause a problem in the Horn Clause paradigm, but can result in cycles in general *e.g.*:

a(X), a(Y).
:– a(X), a(Y).
a(X) :– a(Y).

In this case any two of these clauses resolve to one of the set. Although the clauses are inconsistent, this will not be found by the use of resolution alone. A counter-example is found by considering the instance obtained by instantiating X = Y = b, in either or both of the first two clauses (in the last a tautology would result). A process which may be systematically applied to such clauses to allow resolution to complete a proof is factoring, which amounts to noting that the first two of the above clauses respectively imply:

a(X).
:– a(X).

These resolve directly to an empty clause. Unfortunately indiscriminate application of the factoring rule can lead to an explosion in the number of clauses to be considered.

Systems: LUSH and PROLOG

The Horn Clause, the Unification and Inference operations, and the method of proof by contradiction, lead to a well defined and deterministic (but not complete; see Kowalski[19]) algorithm for obtaining a proof. This procedure (obscurely called "LUSH") involves the presentation of the negation of the theorem as a disjunction of negated literals (or goals, comprising the query). Note that this clausal notation also suggests the negation of a positive conjunctive formulation of the theorem itself.

Each goal is tried successively in turn, left to right, against the single positive heads of the Horn Clauses in the database of axioms, top to bottom. Note that axiom clauses containing no negative literals are especially useful, since successful unification leads to direct elimination of the goal (by the resolution inference rule). These single-term clauses are called unit clauses. Non-unit clauses whose positive terms (heads) are unified with a goal entail the inheritance of the negative literals as additional subgoals.

In LUSH, which is used by PROLOG, these new subgoals are given priority over existing goals. If any goal fails to unify or resolve, backtracking seeks another clause whose head will unify with it, and its negative literals become the current set of subgoals to eliminate. At this point the goal which matched the head has been resolved (proved, or more strictly, contradicted), and the succeeding goal or subgoal from the same clause is considered.

This results in a top-down, depth-first search procedure of the proof space. If the goals were queued and resolved in the order they were set, rather than resolved stack-wise in reverse order, the search would be breadth-first. The LUSH procedure is, however, very simple to implement and quite natural in terms of the propensity which humans have for completely solving one subproblem before going on to the next.

Connection Graphs

The resolution operation is not intrinsically limited to serial use or deterministic evaluation order. In general, in a database of clauses, Horn or non-Horn, there are at any given time many different pairs of terms which are unifiable. The Connection Graph theorem-proving paradigm maintains a record of "links" between all unifiable pairs of literals. These may be selected in any order, resolved, the link removed, and the inferred clause added to the database, along with copies of links inherited by the new clause from its "parents".

Links between terms of the same clause are special — they indicate recursive rules and possible tautologies. One rule is that they are never resolved upon directly, but they will be inherited as normal links between the clause and its "children".

It has been shown that, in the absence of factorization or some other augmentation, the non-Horn Connection Graph procedure is neither complete, nor sound.[20] The CONG extension of the Connection Graph procedure[21] extends the link concept to terms of the same sign, and thus allows the investigation of subsumption links and factor links which bear the same relationship to each other as do the normal and pseudo links between terms of opposite sign.

One clause subsumes another if it logically entails it, such as the subsumed clause being identical except for the addition of some terms, the substitution of some variables. In either case the subsumed clause may be omitted without affecting the possibility of a proof, or precluding the possibility of independent solutions not themselves subsumed by other more general solutions.

A potential efficiency factor in the Connection Graph procedure is the elimination of clauses which cannot contribute to a solution. This includes elimination of clauses containing terms without links, since these can obviously never be eliminated. CONG extends this with subsumption and tautology tests. The elimination of tautologies has been associated with the unsoundness of the procedure, but can be retained by imposing various constraints. CONG, and other proof procedures without the HORN and LUSH restrictions, allow the potential of exploiting parallelism, macroexpansion of rules and simultaneous exploration of alternative parses.

This chapter completes our discussion of the theoretical and implementational issues in the engineered acquisition of NL. In the last chapter we present some practical experiments arising from these arguments.

Notes to Chapter Twelve

1. Wexler, Kenneth, and Peter W. Culicover, *Formal Principles of Language Acquisition* (MIT Press, Cambridge, MA, 1980).
2. Gold, E. M., "Language Identification in the Limit", *Information and Control*, Vol. 10 (1967), pp.447-474; Miller, George A., and Noam Chomsky, "Finitary Models of Language Users", in R. A. Luce, R. R. Bush and E. Galanter, eds, *Handbook of Mathematical Psychology*, Vol. II (Wiley, New York, 1963), pp.419-491; Chomsky, Noam, "Formal Properties of Grammars", in R. A. Luce, R. R. Bush and E. Galanter, *Handbook of Mathematical Psychology*, Vol. II (Wiley, New York, 1963), pp.269-321; Lamb, Sydney M., "On the Mechanization of Syntactic Analysis", *1961 Conference on Machine Translation and Applied Language Analysis*, Vol. II (1961), pp.674-685.
3. Gold, E. M., "Language Identification in the Limit", *Information and Control*, Vol. 10 (1967), p.453.
4. *Op. cit.,* p.453.
5. Anderson, John R., "Computer Simulation of a Language Acquisition System: A First Report", in R. L. Solso, ed., *Information Processing and Cognition: The Loyola Symposium* (Lawrence Erlbaum Associates, Hillsdale, NJ, 1975), p.297-8.
6. Minsky, M., and S. Papert, *Perceptrons* (MIT Press, 1969), p.4.
7. *Op. cit.,* p.16f.
8. Hayes, P.J., "The Naive Physics Manifesto", in D. Michie, ed., *Expert Systems in the Micro-electronics Age* (Edinburgh U.P., Edinburgh, Scotland, 1979), p.243f.
9. Powers, David M. W., L. Davila, and G.Wrightson, "Implementing Connection Graphs for Logic Programming", *Cybernetics and Systems '88* (Kluwer, 1988), pp.959-964.
10. Siklossy, Laurent, "A Language-Learning Heuristic Program", *Cognitive Psychology*, Vol.2, Pt.1 (1971), p.480.
11. Fodor, Jerry, *The Language of Thought* (1975).
12. Kelley, K.L., *Early Syntactic Acquisition* (Rand Corporation, Santa Monica, CA, November 1967).
13. Kucera, Henry, "The Learning of Grammar", *Perspectives in Computing*, Vol 1, No. 2 (1981), pp.28-35.
14. Kuczaj, Stan A., *Crib Speech and Language Play* (Springer-Verlag, New York, NY, 1983).

15. Sowa, J.F., *Conceptual Structures: Information Processing in Mind and Machine* (Addison Wesley, 1984).

16. Copeland, George, "What if Mass Storage Were Free", *IEEE Computer* (July, 1982), pp.27-30.

17. Hayes, P.J., "The Naive Physics Manifesto", in D. Michie, ed., *Expert Systems in the Micro-electronics Age* (Edinburgh U.P., Edinburgh, Scotland, 1979), p.244f.

18. Loveland, Donald W., "Theorem-Provers Combining Model Elimination and Resolution", *Machine Intelligence*, Vol. 4 (1969), pp.73-80; Loveland, Donald W., "A Unifying View of Some Linear Herbrand Procedures", *JACM*, Vol. 19, No. 2 (April, 1972), pp.366-384.

19. Kowalski, Robert, "A Proof Procedure using Connection Graphs", *JACM*, Vol. 22, No. 4 (October, 1975), pp.572-595.

20. Kowalski, Robert, *Logic for Problem Solving* (North Holland, New York and Oxford, 1979), p. 176.

21. Powers, David M. W., L. Davila, and G.Wrightson, "Implementing Connection Graphs for Logic Programming", *Cybernetics and Systems '88* (Kluwer, 1988), pp.959-964.

Chapter Thirteen

Postulates, Claims and Hypotheses

This chapter pulls together all the threads we have been considering in this volume and presents a consolidated set of practical conclusions from our study of Natural Language Learning. The proposals collected here are intended to provide the basis for a programme of experimental work. We emphasize the fundamental importance of ontology and relationships from the sensory-motor level up. We consider that the essential prerequisites for relationships to be learned are constancy, consistency and usefulness. These correspond to roles in learning for reinforcement, prediction and bootstrapping—in a mixed metaphor based on behaviourist, scientific and engineering methodologies.

We separate out the production and recognition processes, grammars and acquisition paradigms, and propose that interaction between those two centres can allow comparison of heard utterances with recognition expectations and potential production forms, and also permits comparison of spoken utterances with actual and anticipated recognized forms. We propose that these different feedback loops will eventually explain the empirical data about errors in, and localization of, grammatical and semantic function. We next emphasize the positive face of restriction, and hypothesize that the shaping together of natural languages and human cognitive processes allows and ensures the learning of natural languages through natural learning methods based on contrast and similarity detecting mechanisms, self-organization, reinforcement and consolidation.

We have tried to bring together ideas in many different fields and the work of other researchers from many disciplines. We have levelled criticism at certain specific proposals, and more fundamentally at any dogmatic viewpoint which seeks to exclude a class of possible approaches without complete justification. Similarly, we have dealt ruthlessly with proposals which assert a specific rationale without attempting to reconcile it with the available multi-disciplinary empirical evidence, and without demonstrating that it admits experimental testing.

This chapter collects together a number of the more significant proposals and counter-proposals that have been discussed in the last chapters, and makes some additions. Mostly these are original hypotheses, but there is hardly one which is without precedent in the work of others.

This is as it should be. They comprise quite an unique and significant crystallization of the important principles of language acquisition.

Although we have only argued loosely about many of these proposals so far, the arguments will not necessarily be tightened here. This chapter presents primarily hypotheses, the "proof" of which will lie in their experimental and predictive usefulness. The starting point for such "proof" is the series of experimental programs we developed, and the broader programme of experiments carried out at Macquarie. Of course, there is a place for theoretical analysis, both to steer research away from fruitless avenues and to suggest feasible implementation techniques. But we must understand such work in the context that computer science is not the only source of information about possible processes and mechanisms. The empirical work of many of the other disciplines is directly applicable, and inherently experimental.

Let us look first at some fundamental propositions about language, and the language acquisition mechanism which underlie our further proposals. The main one of these is the sensory-motor basis of meaning. Meaning is embodied in the relationships present between sensory-motor perceptions and activities – language is ultimately derived from relationships of this nature. Thus all words are defined by processes of metaphor, extension and inter-relationship from a spatio-temporal basis derived from sensory-motor experience.

Thus a prerequisite for the acquisition of language is the acquisition of ontology, commencing with direct sensory-motor ontology and extending eventually to all aspects of the complete adult ontology. Something has to be understood, or at least recognized, in order to be discussed. Our thesis is that in the final analysis our entire ontology is founded on the affective and effective natures of our sensory-motor modalities.

Our second proposition is the relational basis of language. In general, child development and acquisition of language concerns relationships – relationships, whether syntactic, semantic or pragmatic, are learned and give rise to learned concepts. The earliest relationships learnt are those with direct sensory-motor significance. The relationships learned define our view of the world, and our interaction with our environment. Thus our ontology is built up from, and consists of, such relationships.

Language is subsumed by our ontology. It is reasonable to think that we understand words combining together to form a sentence in much the way we understand features combining together to form a face. In other words, the understanding process performed by the brain is heavily weighted towards the recognition of relationships.

In the visual system, we have relationships between receptors in a limited locus; relationships expressing a preferred orientation of a line; relationships expressing a preferred direction of motion; relationships expressing a preferred size; *etc.* In the conditioning paradigm, relationships are learned on the basis of spatio-temporal association: whether it is that a bell precedes the arrival of food; or that a left turn leads to water. Similarly for language, semantics expresses the relationship between the language modality and the ontological relationships being discussed; prosody reflects a semiotic relationship between the sentence and the ontological reference (*e.g.* tone indicating an affective state or stress indicating a focal point); syntax expresses relationships between parts of the sentence; role expresses relationships between syntactic and semantic structure; and cohesion expresses relationships between syntactic structures.

In general, we can understand a parse-tree as reflecting both the relationships perceived between the units at one level, and the use of these relationships as the units of a higher level.

All learning happens by the correlation of hypotheses about, and refinement of, currently recognized concepts — including those which may themselves be held as tentative hypotheses. Since relationships are fundamental to all language and ontology, it is relationships which must be learned.

Apparent relationships between entities (which are in general themselves relationships) are proposed as hypotheses and reinforced under appropriate circumstances.

The Scientific Metaphor of Learning

Recognition of concepts or constructs carries on even while they are only held as tentative hypotheses. The usefulness of such hypotheses is the main ground for their reinforcement. Since relationships may be systematic or fortuitous, recurrent or unique, significant or irrelevant, there must be a mechanism for ensuring that only useful relationships are learned, and the infinity of possible, but useless, relationships are not.

Our central proposal, in summary, is that the mechanism for learning relationships is akin to scientific method. First, note that a learned concept, in association with its *name* (or recognizer), is a relationship. The relationships which are to be learned should have three properties: constancy, consistency, and usefulness. The first of these properties, constancy, declares that a relationship must hold at all times in all contexts. The second, consistency, asserts that the relationship must hold for all possible applications or instantiations in all contexts. The third, usefulness, asserts that the relationship holds some significance to the learner.

On a static view, relationships would have all of these properties, and would be remembered long term. On a dynamic view, it must be recognized that change occurs. Thus a chair can break; a face can be marked or scarred; a word can acquire a new meaning.

The constancy property corresponds to learning by repetition. A relationship between specific entities which may be construed at one specific time should not be retained, but a relationship which is evident whenever all the components are present should be learned. The *name*, or recognizer, of the relationship and the "word" which accompanies it are all part of this relationship. If the *name* is present, it must be in proper relationship with the other entities present (which may themselves be *names* of other relationships). This allows for the learning of relationships by what Piaget calls "assimilation" of "coordinations".[1] This first level of abstraction requires the presence of exactly (or almost exactly) the same set of entities (or *names* in the sense of recognizers).

The consistency property concerns relationships which have been generalized to refer to classes of objects. During an intermediate stage a relationship may be learned as a disjunction of specific instances. This is what Piaget calls "reflective" or "constructive" abstraction. Eventually, through generalization of common components of this and similar disjunctive concepts, a consolidation may take place. Piaget calls this generalization process "empirical abstraction", and the result will be that the interchangeable components are grouped together as a common class, with a class "name" (or recognizer). The final stage of the process is what Piaget terms "reflected" or "completive" abstraction, and involves the generalization from the disjunction of specific instances to a (non-disjunctive) formulation involving the generalized class. In general, it is possible for over-generalization during either induction of the class, or completive abstraction of a relationship involving the class. The consistency property specifies that all instances of a generalized relationship are appropriate. It is essential not to retain inconsistent relationships.

The usefulness of a relationship is the participation of a relationship (or its "name" or recognizer) in other relationships. If a relationship takes part in a "successful" sensory-motor interaction, it should be reinforced. If the relationship is of no practical consequence and participates in no successful processes, it need not be learned.

The proposal here is that the learning process involves hypothesizing of relationships (the assignment of "names" or recognizers) which may not turn out to be useful through violation of one of these properties. For it to be reinforced, a relationship must recur, must specify correct instantiations, and must participate in sensory-motor interactions. It must further be capable of being negatively reinforced, or superseded if over-generalization has occurred and it is not consistent (*viz* it specializes to some incorrect instantiations).

Note that because of this proposed usefulness reinforcement criterion, a tentative relationship must be capable of use as a hypothesis, including being used as a component in the hypothesizing of further tentative relationships. This learning process is clearly similar to the scientific method, since it involves the making of hypotheses which must prove useful in achieving some end, and must be purportedly consistent and capable of invalidation on the basis of failure of their predictions (instantiation by a counter-example).

Partitioned Nature of Language

Humans have common, but in practical effect partitioned, production and recognition "grammars". The recognition and production processes both employ relationships and tentative hypotheses, but the relationships produced for the one need not be reflected in the other. Rather, it is likely that recognition and production are focussed in entirely disparate regions of the brain, and so they must be regarded as independent hierarchies which do not so much overlap as interconnect. They probably do this through the *arcuate fasciculus*, with the innate expression and/or learned construction of interhierarchical relationships. Furthermore, certain functions of language do appear to reside more in one hierarchy than the other. Thus Broca's *aphasia* appears when there is damage to Broca's area, near facial (speech producing) areas of the motor cortex. It shows as the inability to understand or express relationships denoted by closed class "words" (*e.g.* prepositions and inflections). Speech thus takes on a telegraphic quality, and is also marred by poor production of speech sounds. These relationships are obviously essential to understanding speech, but appear to be understood somewhat after the understanding of, and multi-word production of, "sentences" involving open class "words". Presumably they are learned only when it becomes necessary to communicate such relationships (perhaps by a conditioning-like process).

By contrast, we have seen that damage to Wernicke's area, near the primary auditory cortex, results in a different syndrome, in which the speech production is quite undistorted and fluent. The problem is that the patient has difficulty finding the right open class words, and his speech is thus verbose and circumlocutory. Presumably association of open class words with sensory-motor concepts initially proceeds independently of attempts at production.

There is thus some bridging needed between recognition relationships and production relationships. Thus articulation must be learned by comparison of the results of one's own articulatory motions with the language of others. Once the basic pronunciation rules (*i.e.* inter-hierarchical articulation relationships) are learned, imitation of words heard is possible. Thus once a new open class word is associated with a context it is immediately available for use.

However, in order to learn closed class words with a mainly relational function, and especially those involving grammatical or cohesive restrictions, one must assume a gradual process of hypothesizing of production rules, and testing of the output by the recognition rules, which reflect the usage of others. This is an interesting reversal of the "Recognition by Synthesis" approach advocated by Newell et al.[2] Moreover, we propose that synthetic feedback of the deep structure-like form within present competence allows contrastive association with the present (surface structure) form embodying the new cohesive and role relationships being learnt, in a positive form of 'Analysis by Synthesis'.

Note, too, that there is a difference in the precision required of recognition and production processes. The recognition process is tolerant of errors of various sorts, but in production they are readily apparent. Thus consider the child who knows a host of verbs with their respective regular or irregular past tense forms. When he generalizes the "-ed" rule, this will augment his recognition processes with a rule that allows separate recognition of individual regular and irregular past tense forms to be bypassed. During this period, there is no interference between any of these rules. Incorrect inflections will be quite happily accepted. Suppose this rule is made part of the production grammar. It will then, as a very common rule, tend to take priority over the various irregular forms and produce the over-generalization phenomenon.

It is proposed here that the production grammar borrows from the recognition grammar, not necessarily by duplication of the grammar, but perhaps by relating appropriate portions of the two hierarchies. This raises questions in two areas where further elaboration is required. The first of these areas concerns the nature of the inter-relationships between the production and recognition grammars, given that they are separate but interrelated hierarchies. The second relates to the correction of over-generalizations and other incorrect usages which emerge in production.

Threshold of Concepts

Using concepts or constructs in production only happens for definitive hypotheses which have exceeded some threshold of usefulness for recognition, and have been successfully related to the existing structure of the production hierarchy. This proposal assumes a degree of separation between the recognition and production grammars, and defines a practical mechanism by which the two may be related. This process is reminiscent of the interning of symbols in computer languages like LISP and PROLOG.

The model that we are working with uses a shared grammar where hypotheses automatically become available for production once a certain threshold of credibility is passed. This is no doubt overly simplistic. A more accurate reflection of the interaction may be that there is importation as soon as an appropriate inter-hierarchical relationship can be formulated. This naturally requires the components of the relationship, on each side of the relational bridge, to have some degree of stability.

The thesis we are elaborating in these experiments concerns the importing into the production grammar of rules learned within the recognition hierarchy. This is itself possibly only one side of the relationship, and it is quite conceivable that there is communication in the reverse direction in terms of the export of rules, or positive or negative feedback of some sort. For example there is the evidence of aphasiacs already cited, which suggests that closed class words and syntax may actually be developed in the areas of the brain concerned with production rather than in those concerned with recognition. This may mean that syntactic understanding does revert to the "Recognition by Synthesis" paradigm.[3]

Sensory-Motor Restriction of Learning

Natural languages can be learned because their structure reflects the richness and restrictiveness of the total man-environment system.

There are theoretical results which seem to prove that certain classes of language cannot be learned under specific conditions from negative information. But the theorems fail to take into account peculiar restrictions in three domains: natural language; the systems which interact with language; and the language learning mechanisms.

Fodor argues strongly for the view that no system can learn to become more powerful than it originally was, and that therefore language must be an innate capability which then becomes restricted (as claimed by Chomsky) to suit the mother tongue.[4] The contrasting claim made here is that natural language bears a very direct and natural relationship to the structure of the environment. The acquisitive child thus learns his ontology by an abstractive learning process: he or she assimilates the structure of his or her environment. The sensory-motor environment includes the language of others, and therefore as part of the ontology they develop, the learners learn their own idiolect. The experiments and representations of the final chapter demonstrate that similar forms of analysis may be applied to both language and non-language modalities.

The most straightforward argument in support of this thesis, other than appeal to its plausibility, is the apparent absence of constructions or words for which one cannot propose a fairly obvious relationship with the referential hierarchy. Assuming that there is no such counter-example, and surely that is the basis of semantics, it is certainly appropriate to propose a constructive methodology for learning such relationships.

Human Restriction of Learning

The natural limitations of the human mind, and in particular of memory, attention, comprehension, *etc.,* are essential to the human process of learning natural languages. Thus it may, counter-intuitively, be helpful to limit the power of the mechanisms and theories proposed to emulate or model human language acquisition. The assumption that restrictions are always bad is a fallacy. Whilst it is fairly obvious that restrictions on the class of possible natural languages may make it feasible to learn them, it may not be so obvious that restrictions on the learning mechanism may be required to reflect this information.

In this case, it is proposed that most of the restrictions common to all language are reflections of restrictions on the human language acquisition mechanisms. This relationship is again plausible, but more self-evident than formally arguable. However, it should be clear that restrictions on the nature of the human language acquisition mechanism would limit the class of learnable languages in an appropriate way. And it is theoretically straightforward to show that there are classes of restriction which can direct a language learning algorithm in more profitable directions than it might otherwise take. Indeed, this characterizes the formal approach whereby, if it is known or suspected that a language belongs to a particular formal class, a parser may be restricted appropriately.

Whilst such a viewpoint may not be natural to linguists, psychologists, philosophers and neurologists, it is very natural to workers in AI (Artificial Intelligence), since a common technique of the field has been the employment of heuristics to limit search space. It is interesting that the only areas where these AI techniques are used are those in which problems are theoretically insoluble or intractable.

Mechanisms: Minimal Differences of Concepts

We can now examine anew the processes of language acquisition, and the essential components of the language acquisition mechanism. In this section, we summarise the mechanisms responsible for certain functions in language acquisition, before we turn to a specific model of the processes.

We argue that language and non-language modalities can be parsed in similar ways, and that there must always be a direct correspondence between an utterance and its referent. We therefore propose that, given a text with referents (as in a picture book), it is possible to determine the concepts which are the referents of individual words (and then phrases, clauses *etc.*).

The particular mechanism we propose is based on the concept of etic and emic distinctions. We suppose that it is reasonable to assume a helpful order of presentation — an assumption explicitly rejected by Gold and labelled "anomalous text" because it turned out to be more powerful even than learning with a tester/teacher.[5]

For example, consider a scene: a spatio-temporal sequence of frames. The ideal situation is the before/after paradigm beloved of advertisements for exercise machines, cosmetics, and hair/baldness treatments. Successive pages in a picture book would have the same effect. Consider a presentation of the following pairs of sentences, accompanied by the appropriate pictures: "John can run. See John run." "John can skip. See John skip." "John can jump. See John jump."

Each of the different actions will be associated with the differences between the pictures, *viz.* the different things John is depicted as doing. Consider any sequence of events in the child's life, and the accompanying commentary. Whether it is talking about the smelliness of nappies, or the activity of meals, or the colour of toys, there is usually an accompanying sensory-motor contrast between these scenes which corresponds with the contrast between the parental utterances. In addition, there may be other cues and roles for contrast, including pointing fingers and hunger pangs, but these all fit into the fuller sensory-motor framework of the referential ontology.

The experiments described in the last chapter determine parse structures for both language and non-language modalities, and include the study of differential minimization as a mechanism for determining association of meaning. Since all structures may be assumed to be finite, and indeed since the significant parts of the structures are in general quite small and the constant subtrees quite easily separated off, differential minimization is a deterministic, effective process. Further restrictive information by way of semantic or referential focus can provide useful heuristics for the guidance of the procedure, and the structure sharing used within PROLOG not only provides a natural solution to the frame problem but allows the immediate discarding by the differential minimizer of inherited equal subtrees.[6]

Conservative Nature of Reinforcement

Semantic, syntactic, cohesive and pragmatic relationships are all reinforced according to the degree of confidence in the composing substructures. Thus, situations or models with multiple features beyond the child's competence will allow little learning, whilst those close to the model will allow for significant reinforcement of feasible generalizations. This proposition accords with the evidence concerning imitation phenomena. A child will only imitate sentences, or parts of them, which are close to the level of his or her spontaneous production.

The proposal is that, for any set of existing recognizers which give rise to concept *names*, the only new relationships which can be recognized will be at an existing or adjacent level, using existing *names* as direct input. Thus, if a new formula involving new classifications is required, it cannot be learned until all the required subclasses are recognized. However, those classifications can be effectively learned independently of the new formula, since they are readily apparent as the parts of the utterance which do not have recognizers (or concept *names*). They contrast with the parts of the input which are already within the recognition competence, and independently capable of being parsed effectively. Thus, recognizers can be hypothesized for such new "words", and once the "words" have a class "name", formula recognizers can start developing.

This thesis is that hypothesized class recognizers develop only once the component *names* are reasonably well established. The initial weighting given to a hypothesis is a function of that of the component *names*. This ensures that the concept formation and reinforcement process is rather conservative. Long chains of reasoning cannot be undertaken until new hypotheses have gained some credibility.

Note that the proposed hypothesis and reinforcement paradigm is effectively a bottom-up conjunctive process — it recognizes spatio-temporal agglomerates of *names*. We propose that generalization of different *names*, whether for "word" classes or "formulae", to a common hyperclass takes place *via* a consolidatory mechanism. Such consolidation is primarily a top-down disjunctive process performing aggregation of alternative parse structures (*names*) into hyperclasses.

It is also possible to produce conservative hypotheses by a composite top-down and bottom-up (*viz.* "end-in") process. This is done on the basis of the hypothesis of a link between the results of well-attested bottom-up parses as previously described, and the parse structure of well-attested top-down parses. It has the effect of using expectations from top-down analysis to guide the utilization and formulation of parse structures by bottom-up analysis. This process is employed in the second experiments of the following chapter.

Innate Organization of Learning

The neural networks of the brain are largely self-organized within levels and local areas. The inter-relationships between areas and between organs are basically genetically determined. This is the neural correlate of the psycholinguistic innateness hypothesis. The debates of both psycholinguistics and neurology concerning the issues of innateness and self-organization are discussed in detail in earlier chapters. At this point we clarify specific assumptions relating to these issues.

First, it is common ground that the general localization of brain functions and the neural connections to particular sensory-motor receptors and effectors is innately and genetically determined. It is not clear whether the topologically conservative mapping is directly determined genetically, or is maintained by the function of known self-organizational processes (which need not be dependent on external sensory-motor interaction). In either case it is still innate to the extent that it is not dependent on interaction with the environment.

It is difficult to justify excluding all self-organization at this level, and whilst it may be regarded as innate organization (in the sense that it is not learned), it is not especially helpful to regard this as genetic determination since there is still scope for variation between individuals, even within the specifications of a given set of genes.

Second, there is no need for specific innate determination of the preferred "concepts" recognized by individual neurons within a level of an area of the brain. It can still be true that the general neural connectivity and anatomy of major regions of the brain is genetically controlled. However, the precise connectivity within a region must vary. The recognition function and precise field of a neuron must be learned, even if its general location and size are probably innate.

Third, the general neural structure throughout the cerebral cortex is basically fairly uniform, although differences obviously exist between areas of the cortex. These differences are in the sensory-motor or other functions, in their connections to other organs and other areas of the brain, in their density, thickness and topology. Therefore it is reasonable to assume that the mechanisms proposed for sensory-motor or cognitive hierarchies are universally applicable.

Fourth, in view of this, the neurally motivated models constructed as part of this project have been based on a self-organizing neural network involving modification of plastic synapses, and all the models have depended on the ability to process all modalities and hierarchies in a similar manner.

Cohesive Consolidation of Concepts

Independent, intensive conjunctive abstractions are effectively coalesced to form coherent, possibly disjunctive concepts with the potential for extensional usage. This is a basically cohesive procedure, and an area where this theoretical basis is at variance with the pragmatic programming techniques used in some of the experiments of Chapter Fourteen. In this model, consolidation is used as a periodic expedient to speed the disposal of useless hypotheses, and to coalesce redundant rules. It is quite successful in doing this.

However, others of our experiments develop disjunctive word classes and formula classes by the use of *expectation*. Thus, if a particular parse tree or relationship *name* is required to complete a parse, whatever is parsed will be hypothesized to be of that class. Thus, hypotheses are made to join the results of partial top-down and bottom-up analyses. A roundabout, but more neurologically plausible, route for such links is postulating (*viz.* developing recognizers or *names* for) all possible parses. There should be only two or three of these under conservative conditions. These hypotheses would later either be reinforced or decay according to whether or not they were successfully employed.

In the case of the *expectation* mechanism, a separate consolidatory process is needed to relate independent parse structures which share components which have been consolidated, or which differ in a highly paradigmatic way. In the case of the supposed neurological mechanism, we propose that generalization from the fillers of the paradigm to a class would occur, so that this case now reduces to the former case of formulae with shared consolidated components. In this former case, exactly the same type of generalization will occur if these structures fill similar slots in higher level formulae.

This generalization produces a new *name* for a (hyper)class of fillers for analogous slots. Formulae utilizing this new *name* will be reinforced much more consistently than those which directly utilize the several individual fillers, which will therefore decay. This produces a natural consolidatory effect. However, it may be that fillers which are members of the same class for some purposes include irregularities which need to be handled separately at some level. Here we must assume that some type of negative feedback eventually comes to cause the rejection of the (over)generalized rule for this form. We can also assume that such negative feedback has an additional activating effect for the alternate form, whether or not it is overtly produced. Note that it is unlikely that much of this negative feedback will be available before attempts are made to use the rule for production.

If a known filler occurs in a new context, separate rules involving the *name* of the filler and the *name* of the filler class will be hypothesized — perhaps with comparable weight, perhaps not. In any case, the hypothesized rule involving the filler class is a latent generalization, and empirical evidence indicates that words of the appropriate class will be tried in the new slot. Similarly, if a new filler occurs in an old slot, a hypothesis of its membership in the appropriate filler class will be made, and its usage will extend to all slots where such a filler class is appropriate. Empirical evidence exists for such learning behaviour.

Note that the starting point for such cohesive behaviour is the cohesive effect of similarities between paradigmatic environments, and is complementary to the differentiation process and the contrastive activational effect. Thus contrast in identical environments leads to distinctions amongst what are emically fillers, whilst classification and consolidation lead to their (re)union into filler classes. Consolidation most needs more theoretical consideration and empirical investigation.

Cohesive Effect of Refraction

A possible linguistic correlate of neural refraction is that the use of a *name* causes temporary deactivation of the recognizer. This will reduce the immediate inhibitory effect of that cell, and hence enhance some which were being suppressed. This may be responsible for the successive nature of production, the generation of the next unit being triggered by the completion of the last. It may also explain the later availability of alternative parses or senses.

Such interaction of inhibition and refraction is another cohesive mechanism, involving control by application and removal of restriction. This is a rather speculative proposal, and there is a lack of direct neurolinguistic evidence, although Gigley's effective computational neurolinguistics model uses refraction in a similar way.[7]

Contrast has a role in attention ("focus") and activation ("motivation"). We have already seen that contrast in corresponding modalities is a powerful basis for the learning of concepts. It also seems that areas of change are very important, and that specific mechanisms exist for focussing on the area of change. The area in focus is then primary in subsequent processing and other areas are largely ignored whilst they are "out of focus".

Contrast is activational; not only does contrast cause "focus" on the contrasting features, but it prompts an increased "effort" to resolve the contrast. This fact is captured by Klopf's use of the metaphor of a pleasure-seeking pain-avoiding Hedonist.[8]

Neither of these facets of contrast have yet been incorporated into any experimental models, or into this research programme, although we recognize that attentional and activational parametization of the model's learning is desirable.

Robot Model of Learning

We now move to focus more closely on how learning happens, extending our view to the processes and the broader philosophy of language understanding and production, together with further consideration of language learning *per se*.

The successful language learning system will be, or will appear to be, a robot. We have already seen how important the sensory-motor modalities are in providing a referential basis for language. We have also seen how essential such referential information is in guiding and motivating the learning of language.

The logical conclusion of this is that language is intimately bound up with the entire ontology of sensory-motor and cognitive processing. Thus, the best language learner is obviously a human, or a system with similar sensory, motor, motivational and reasoning capabilities, as well as the expected specifically linguistic capability. Provide a computer with these additional capabilities, and you have designed (built or simulated) what is essentially an intelligent robot.

In fact, build such a system without explicit linguistic capabilities, and the robot should itself devise and/or recognize some form of symbolic communication. There is a sense in which language is a consequence of pure cognitive power, directed by activational and attentional manifestations, acting on sensory and motor modalities. The interesting questions thus concern the relationship between the particular class of learnable (recognizable and generable) human languages, and the particular set of cognitive manipulations and modal interconnections which defines this class of languages and determines also the class of possible natural (evolvable) languages and the class of possible artificial (devisable) languages. The main additional component required, over and above sensory-motor and cognitive capabilities, is motivation to communicate. Interestingly, there is no solid evidence of animals seeking to communicate spontaneously at a meta-level, let alone any report of experiments to see whether animals who have been taught a language will attempt to teach it to others, whether human or of their own kind.

Whilst this observation is interesting and quite possibly valid, the main attribute of the cognitive and sensory-motor structures of the ostensive robot is their systematic recombination. Furthermore, the main process involved in learning is the capability of recognizing similarities between different and recurring frames. And finally the main process involved in cognition is the ability to construct relationships between hierarchies, and to logically manipulate such modal relations.

Thus, the ideal non-human language learner would be a robot with the propensity for language-like parse-structuring of its sensory-motor environment, a logic for the generation and manipulation of relationships, and a partial-associative memory capable of recognition of similarity and contrast, and hence of abstractive generalization.

Creative Invention of Language

The child or language learning model must be able to invent analogies and usages. As we observed about the intelligent robot, motivation to communicate and a high level of cognitive ability combine to allow the devising of forms of communication. The contrastive and generalization paradigms automatically lead to manifestations as metaphor and extension.Goldschlager offers an explanation of creativity as a direct consequence of the associating and generalizing properties of the memory surface in his cognitive model.[9]

The essential point here is that the mechanisms for the transmission, invention and development of language in the individual (*viz.* acquisition) and in the society (*viz.* evolution) are similar. The mechanism of metaphor is fundamental to the nature of language, and is not simply a literary device. The act of creation is fundamental to the learning of language.

Language learning is substantially different from rote learning of phrases, as from a phrase-book. The nature of language is completely different from the quoting of texts. Most of what is communicated is originally conceived, if not actually novel. Most of what is learned is created afresh by generalization from similarities between frames. The recognition ("naming") of the concept is frequently accelerated by the relationship-augmenting association of the common feature instanced in the application of a particular "word" to the frame in the usage of others .

Parse Structure of Modalities

The parsing paradigm for structural analysis is applicable to all sensory-motor modalities, not just to speech. All cortical processing, and much other brain processing, suggests a parse-like decomposition. The basis of semantics is relationships between the structures parsed in the different modalities. We adopt this approach, despite the recognized inadequacies of traditional parsing. We are fully aware of the brain's transformational nature, although this is not to be confused with the TGG imputation of transformations between forms of language, the associative paradigm, and possibly even the syntax crystal approach.

This proposal is worth comparing with Fodor's notion of the "Language Of Thought" (LOT), by which he does not refer to language in the sense of a communication medium, but as a formal structured representation, nor thought in the sense of a stream of consciousness, but as a subconscious process. Fodor's language metaphor is primarily motivated by the evident logical semantic relationships which are clearly formally expressible in the language of logic. Fodor considers LOT to be essentially equivalent to "First Order Logic" (FOL).[10] Our proposal is mainly motivated by the relevance of the syntactic mechanisms of formal linguistics to all such relationships, and the evident constituent structure of any logical system. This thesis that all modalities should be regarded as similarly and comparably structured is the cornerstone of the experimental program presented in the last chapter.

Spontaneous Production of Language

The child is motivated in spontaneous production according to a primary focus. Thus, his or her first single-word utterances will be directly concerned with the nuclear focus of his or her attention. It may be, for example, the object that he wants or sees (*e.g.* "truck"), the action which he wants or perceives (*e.g.* "bye-bye"), the fact that he wants something, or the agent whom he wants to influence. A secondary marginal focus at this stage may be indicated by other expedients (*e.g.* by pointing), and it is also possible for the primary focus to be indicated redundantly. Note that the referents of these foci need not have the same nuclearity ranking.

In the two-word stage, both the primary and a secondary focus will be expressed. Thus although closed class words may help in learning by indicating the open class words, they are (not surprisingly) omitted by children who can as yet string only a very few words together. There is thus a strong connection linking the child's motivation and focus with the first "words" and utterances he or she produces. This should be reflected in any language learning system, and failure to do so is probably responsible for much of the poor performance of such systems.

Conservative Focussing of Learning

A child can generally only learn one rule (of a given type) at a time. Note, however, that when a new formula, word class and situation are highly correlated, they may not be separable. Thus hypotheses in different hierarchies or levels must be made together, and reinforced by the co-occurrence correlation. However, these hypotheses will emerge simultaneously to the extent that they cannot occur separately. They may or may not actually reach production threshold at the same time.

We have argued that the conservative nature of reinforcement would tend to propose classes before formulae. This is because only in an end-in, expectation-driven, strategy involving a class which occurs only in an unique slot need formulae and classes be developed simultaneously. The conservative focussing strategy depends on the condition that only a few hypotheses are being tentatively considered at any one time, strictly speaking only one. If there is only one hypothesis which is open to refutation, then there can be no ambiguity about the rule to blame for incorrect predictions, and it also becomes possible to construct examples designed to test the specific hypothesis.

If multiple hypotheses are being tested, they may nonetheless be tested by examples which exercise subsets of them. In these, inconsistency in an example will negatively reinforce all the members of the corresponding subset of exercised hypotheses. The closer we can come to the ideal of examples exercising a single hypothesis, the more useful the negative information obtained. We can compare the more analytic, "perfect-memory", "bull-cow" guessing technique.[11]

In the complex ontologico-linguistic context, the focussing effect of contrast, prosody, and other features of the form in which the negative information is provided may further (heuristically) direct disapprobation to the implicated hypothesis. But in the case where a class is used only in a given formula (and other instances of multiple hypothesis testing) it may well be that the most appropriate action is negative reinforcement of all the hypotheses concerned. This corresponds more to the signature table approach than to conservative focussing.

Complementary Processes of Language

The generalization of template clusters, and the contrasting of features are essential and complementary analytic learning processes. The use of contrast and similarity between recognition templates allows for consolidation (development of subsuming generalizations and decaying of subsumed recognizers). The use of contrast between recognizers and new input allows the abduction of new categories. The use of contrast between generators and new input allows the synthesis of (intended or unintended) negative information from expansion, correction, *etc.*

Generalization by its nature is an expansive process, and although passive thresholding and normalizing mechanisms may be employed, it is important to make use of active techniques for respecializing, eliminating and consolidating generalizations. Contrast between inputs of different modalities, or between inputs and outputs, or of inputs or outputs with generalizations, provides a constant active source of cohesive information.

The significance, and hence the role, of contrast or similarity within a single modal hierarchy is in general ambiguous, and must be disambiguated by reference to other hierarchies. In the absence of inter-hierarchical correlations, some of our experiments implicitly assume that all formular contrasts are significant, but those of others assume that some arbitrary level of class overlap is sufficient to warrant consolidation.

Complexity Hypothesis of Language

Another potentially useful proposal is Clark's Complexity Hypothesis.[12] This hypothesis proposes that the simpler concepts are learned before the more complex. Whilst we don't adopt it as axiomatic, it is a logical consequence of the assumptions we make. The conservative hypotheses, the role of contrast and focus, the effects of cohesion, and the mainly bottom-up but occasionally expectation-driven abstraction and generalization process are all used. Each contributes to a tendency to prefer those hypotheses which are most directly related to the sensory-motor hierarchies, and which are primarily dependent on the most well-attested existing hypotheses.

There is also a sense in which the Complexity Hypothesis is a direct consequence of the proposal that all modalities, and hence all concepts, have a parsable constituent structure.

The inherent character of language gives the empirical phenomenon of constituent parse structure which may be characterized as an interaction of a combination of processes. The sense to be communicated must relate to real or irreal sensory-motor events which have some internal representation involving an effect on neural states which correspond to the basic linguistic units, the open-class morphs. These states are evidently organized through a number of neural levels, producing a corresponding hierarchical organization of related open class morphs by combination into successively larger formular units.

These formular units are supplemented by additional recognizers which correspond to closed class morphemes and cohesive and syntactic features. There is apparently no intrinsic semantic difference between these recognizers and the formular recognizers, but syntactically they differ in the characteristic type of relationship recognized. The formular unit recognizes a relation of sequence, and acts as a constituent in relation to other formular recognizers. The cohesive and role recognizers are concerned with inherited properties of units rather than with sequence. Like daemons, the non-formular recognizers transcend the constituent structure. In different languages the different types of recognizers can be associated with different language functions.

The combinatorial structure of grammar thus involves both sequence-dependent and sequence-independent recognizers operating in a limited parallelism with focus-directed serialism, utilizing both daemon-like and state-oriented processing.

Parallel Blocking of Generalizations

We hypothesize that recognizers of different parse combinations operate in parallel, in conjunction with a selection process which normally allows only one parse to be accepted and blocks any other possibilities. Blocking of parallel but unhelpful parse trees and generalization sequences accords with neural evidence of self-organization, psycholinguistic evidence of the apparent ineffectiveness of correction, and formal linguistic proofs of the necessity of negative information.

The phenomena of puns and garden-path sentences illustrate the vying of parallel (multi-modal) parse structures where two or more interpretations come to our attention. This parallelism must therefore be a characteristic of the language process, and as such allows for multiple hypotheses to be evaluated, both in the course of language use (primarily understanding, but also production) and during the process of language learning.

In adult language usage, such alternatives would be selectively weighted according to the context, resulting in one coming to the forefront of consciousness before the other. During language acquisition, some may well be incorrect. In the case where a rule is under-generalized, the more general one will be utilized more, and hence reinforced more. The less general one will be superseded and eventually decay. The fact that it was a second best may actually lead to negative reinforcement. Where a rule has been over-generalized and is deactivated by negative feedback from some source, the less general one will be allowed to come to the fore. It may even be positively reinforced.

The proposal made here is that these learning phenomena are mediated by inhibitory blocking. Specifically, active recognizers tend to block other potentially active recognizers in their vicinity. The use of a *name* is intrinsically reinforcing to a recognizer. Inability to use a name is hypothesized to be highly disapprobatory, and to immediately quench the firing recognizer and hence remove the blocking on the second most active, which now becomes the most active. This now allows the new *name* to be reinforced.

On the other hand, recognizers which were never preeminent would always be negatively reinforced, or not at all, according to the strength with which they asserted recognition (*i.e.* fired). Most should, indeed, be suppressed below the threshold for reinforcement so that the blocking leads only to decay but not to overt negative reinforcement.

Note that the power of mutual inhibitory blocking is quite remarkably demonstrated in Rummelhart, where automatic learning of visual recognition of the alphabet and aural recognition of phonemes has been achieved using such a network.[13] We can now conclude this section on hypotheses with a brief look at some useful consequences of these assumptions and proposed mechanisms.

Partition Explanation of Correction

The apparent conflict between theoretical results (which supposedly demonstrate the necessity of negative information) and empirical observations (which seem to show that children fail to use correction) is a legacy of the partitioning of production and recognition "grammars". This separation tends to buffer the effects of any input and delay the appearance of modified forms. Correction is a more complex paradigm than has been recognized in many psycholinguistic studies, and includes also the expansion and reduction phenomena which are clear evidence of the child's attempt to make use of correction.

Given that there is a degree of separation between the recognition and production mechanisms, and hence differences in their grammars, we can only expect correction to be used profitably when the original utterance is reasonably close to the correcting model. It also needs the recognizers and potential generators for this model to exist, and be fairly close to threshold (but not necessarily the most "credible" alternative). If the contrast between original and model is too great, or the form is too novel, correct imitation cannot be expected.

Even if imitation happens, the effect will only be that certain hypotheses (probably but not necessarily including the best one) are reinforced. If the separation between recognition and production grammars is purely a matter of threshold (as modelled in Battery Five of Chapter Fourteen), it is faintly possible that this reinforcement could have some short-term or long-term retention. But if the separation between the two hierarchies is mediated by independently consolidated relationships, it is most unlikely that any retention at all will be observed.

In either case, it is more likely that further positive input would be responsible for the appearance of any "new" rule. It is also possible that a "new" rule would surface during a period of consolidation or language play.

In other cases it is likely that some existing hypothesis would need to be abandoned first. This will only occur once the devaluation of the faulty rule takes its "credibility" below either a production threshold, or the "credibility" of an alternative ("new") rule. Thus, it is evident that the partitioning hypothesis suggests that correction would *not* usually be immediately reflected in production rules, although there would be cases where straightforward imitation results in reproduction of the corrected form.

Idiolect Explanation of Language

The meaning of a word is not identical for different individuals, but is part of the network of sensory-motor relationships from which the perception and production of the word comes. There is however for each language/dialect/locale a common core meaning for the word. Such a core concept, however, will not correspond identically with that of any word in another language/dialect/locale. This is entirely analogous to the variation between individuals.

This principle operates not just at the four levels pinpointed, but generally. There is a continuum wherein each logical grouping produces another shade of refinement or generalization of the core meaning. Furthermore, this phenomenon is clearly *not* limited to the domain of concepts and semantics. Similar phenomena apply throughout the syntactic and semantic level, but in their more gross forms give rise to the discrimination of different languages and dialects.

Syntax cannot be learned independently of semantics. It may well be possible to come up with a grammar for a given idiolect at a particular point in time such that this may be expressed independently, but analysis or learning cannot take place independently. This is illustrated by the "Rosetta Stone" and thus could be called the "Rosetta Principle".

This principle is one of the main motivations for our research, since traditional approaches have not tried to give an adequate account of the role of semantics in the learning and use of syntax. This is the area where most further work needs to be done. Whilst some of our experiments have been explicitly concerned with semantic interrelationships, and alternate hierarchies, this area has still not been adequately explored.

Word order and inflection are functions of the interrelationship of role and cohesion, and *vice-versa*. The close relationship between the referential framework and the linguistic hierarchies is through parse relationships and inter-hierarchical relationships between constituents of different modalities. This implies that constraints on word order, and requirements for inflection, may derive fairly directly from the referential framework.

If word order and inflection have any purpose, they must have a semantics and hence a referential correlate. This implies that particular word orders and inflections have significant *role* relationships (assuming that they are unlikely to have concrete semantic referents). Similarly, the role of *cohesion* is to ensure consistency of referential correlates of cohesively restricted components. This is a significant advance on the implicit TGG attitude that choice of one particular grammatical word order over another is essentially insignificant and arbitrary, and is mediated by transformations for which no semantics have ever been proposed.

The question of the specificity and rationality of word order is quite interesting—we discussed it earlier with examples from the ordering of adjectives and comparatives, demonstrating the function of *cohesion* and *role* in determining word order.

Sensory-Motor View of Innateness

We can now conclude with some final comments on the implications of these proposals for the nativist. In general, the innate hardware/firmware of the human cognitive system is directly related to the sensory-motor system, and this gives rise to innate concepts. Innate limitations of physiology or environment also lead to restrictions present in natural language.

Thus our earlier proposals give a clear statement on the question of what aspects of language and language acquisition are innate. All the sensory-motor and neural apparata are innate, and at a gross level genetically specified. That the neural connections are innate, in the sense that they are not learned, is also granted, although not their complete genetic determination. Indeed, there is considerable evidence of differences of detail in the neural connections of identical twins (or identical litter mates) in several species.

To look briefly at the implications for an innate organ of language as proposed by Chomsky, were there an actual physical organ, the issue would already have been covered by the previous discussion. As it is, the argument needs to be closed with a consideration at the level of mechanisms and processes. The question, so framed, has been answered in the discussion up to this point. Language is a direct consequence of our sensory-motor and motivational processes, in combination with our powerful cognitive capabilities. Thus, there need be no innate language acquisition system or innate language other than the cognitive logic model constructed in our neural processes. This process includes the logical consistency of the associative, generalizing and contrastive processes.

These cognitive mechanisms are themselves innate consequences of the fundamental neurological mechanisms and connections within and between local levels, areas and regions of the brain which correspond with levels, branches and modal hierarchies.

The Artificial Subsumes the Natural

The original motivation for our research in the area of Natural Language Learning is twofold, although a majority of researchers have approached it from only one of the two perspectives. These perspectives masquerade under the names "pure" and "applied": the Natural Sciences of psychology, linguistics and biology; and the heritage of AI (Artificial Intelligence) from engineering and high technology. In this work, we are trying to give our computers the "natural flavour" of Natural Language. We have the choice of trying to induce this in an *ad hoc* manner using whichever engineering techniques and technologies are feasible; or of trying to make use of the results of pure psychological, neurological and linguistic research.

There is no particular scientific or moral ground for insisting on the use of "natural flavourings" rather than "artificial flavourings", but the general question of economics means that we choose whichever is likely to achieve the result we want most cheaply and effectively. The processes plagiarized from nature are merely a subset of the full range of mechanisms at our disposal in seeking to artificially endow computers with the facility of Natural Language.

Our research, which is motivated mainly by the dictates of engineering but secondarily by the fascinations of theoretical science, assumes that we are unwise to proceed in any engineering task without taking into account the full range of knowledge at our disposal. In this case, there is the added motivation toward a learning approach which arises from the complexity of the task, and our understandable desire to allow the computer to carry out as much of the accumulation and analysis of data as possible. Unfortunately that subtask has seemed to many to be practically, if not theoretically, too difficult. But every baby appears to achieve it in a painless and effortless natural way! Hence the need to at least consider the natural processes in Natural Language and Language Acquisition as possible pointers to engineering solutions to this task.

Notes to Chapter Thirteen

1. Piaget, Jean, "The Psychogenesis of Knowledge and Its Epistemological Significance", in M. Piatelli-Palmarini, ed., *Language and Learning: The Debate between Jean Piaget and Noam Chomsky* (Routledge and Kegan Paul, 1979), p.27.
2. Newell, A., J. Barnett, J. W. Forgie, C. Green, D. Klatt, J. C. R. Licklider, J. Munson, D. R. Reddy, and W. A. Woods, *Speech Understanding Systems – Final Report of a Study Group* (North-Holland Pub. Co., Amsterdam, Holland, 1973).
3. *Ibid.*
4. Fodor, Jerry, *The Language of Thought* (1975).
5. Gold, E. M., "Language Identification in the Limit", *Information and Control*, Vol. 10 (1967), pp.447-474.
6. Boyer, R.S., and J. S. Moore, "The sharing of structure in theorem-proving programs", *Machine Intelligence 7*, ed. D. Michie (Edinburgh University Press, Edinburgh, UK, 1972), pp.111-116.
7. Gigley, H.M., "Neurolinguistically Based Modeling of Natural Language Processing", Presented at the *Linguistic Society of America*, Association for Computational Linguistics Meeting (New York, 1981); Gigley, H.M., "A Computational Neurolinguistic Approach to Processing Models of Sentence Comprehension",

COINS Technical Report 82-9 (Computer and Information Science, University of Massachusetts at Amherst, September, 1981); Gigley, H.M., "Artificial Intelligence meets Brain Theory: An Integrated Approach to Simulation Modelling of Natural Language Processing", in R. Trappl, ed., *Proceedings of the Sixth European Meeting on Cybernetics and Systems Research* (North-Holland, 1982).

8. Klopf, Harry, *The Hedonistic Neuron: A Theory of Memory, Learning and Intelligence* (Hemisphere, Washington DC, 1982).

9. Goldschlager, Leslie M., *A Computational Theory of Higher Brain Function* (Computer Science Department, Standford University, Standford, CA, April 1984).

10. Fodor, Jerry, *The Language of Thought* (1975).

11. Powers, D.M.W., "Playing Mastermind more Logically or Writing PROLOG more Efficiently" , *SIGART, #89,* pp28-32 (July, 1984).

12 Clark, Eva V., "What's in a Word? On the Child's Acquisition of Semantics in his First Language", in Timothy E. Moore, *Cognitive Development and the Acquisition of Language* (Academic Press, New York, 1973), p.29.

13. Rummelhart, and McClelland, "Syllable learning", *SPIE'88*; Hirai, Y., "A New Hypothesis for Synaptic Modification: An Interactive Process between Postsynaptic Competition and Presynaptic Regulation", *Biol. Cyb.*, Vol. 36 (1980), pp.41-50; Hirai, Y., "A Template Matching Model for Pattern Recognition: Self-Organization of Templates and Template Matching by a Disinhibitory Neural Network", *Biol. Cyb.*, Vol. 38 (1980), pp.91-101.

Chapter Fourteen

Computer Modelling Experiments

This chapter presents the experimental framework and research which the authors have pursued to explore the theory and methodology outlined in the preceding chapters. It is deemed essential that language be presented in a full context so that the interhierarchical relationships can be learnt, and can provide cues for intrahierarchical learning. The ideal compromise for this work is a toy world in which the learner can act and be acted upon. It can then learn language in a rich context which avoids the need for the experimenter to laboriously construct semantic sequences to accompany text, and obviates the need for full pattern recognition and robotic dexterity in the prototype.

However, most of our experiments to date have been learned in a single or dual modality simulation. Some of the initial experiments studied neural learning in a visual context or associative memory in the abstract, whilst subsequent experiments established a framework for parsing both language and other modalities, explored learning in neural, statistical and linguistically motivated models, and extended some of these to simple experiments in learning semantic relationships between modalities. In addition to the obvious extension and elaboration of these experiments, we present proposals to copy the child's staged and telegraphic grammars and to interface with actual vision and speech subsystems.

The next two sections present the programme of experimental work done at New South Wales and Macquarie Universities. The emphasis is on the model, and on the areas worthy of further investigations, rather than the experiments which were actually performed. Thus we regard the main product of the research as a framework for long term investigation, rather than the completion of certain specific experimental programs.

These notes sketch some of this research programme. The first battery of experiments represents the explorations in many different directions and languages before adoption of the general PROLOG or FOL approach of Batteries Two to Seven. The experiments of Battery Two are mainly concerned with semantics and representation. The learning experiments of Batteries Three, Five and Six are simulations of learning within a single modality (*viz.* syntax learning only, or its equivalent when applied to other modalities). The final battery of experiments is tied together by a use of an explicit critic in conjunction with retention of dis-confirmed hypotheses, providing a primitive combination of actual and anticipated correction.

Preliminary Results

None of the experiments presented here represents an attempt to build a working Natural Language system. Rather, they were intended to en-hance our understanding of the field, and complement our theoretical discussion. The experiments divide quite clearly into seven batteries, which represent distinctly separated stages in the work. Each usually started by the writing of completely new programs from completely dif-ferent perspectives, and consisted of the development of a series of ver-sions of a program focussing on one particular feature.

These generalizations are not, of course, completely accurate. In particular, the initial battery of experiments consisted of many different programs, explored different proposals, were written in different lan-guages, and in general were not specifically oriented towards language learning, and so will not be described in any detail. Furthermore, Bat-tery Two was rewritten preparatory to adding the learning capabilities of Battery Three, and the results presented for Battery Two derive from this rewrite. Batteries Five and Six are also very closely related. They differ in that Six is a rewrite of Five, produced some time later to reflect a more systematic and neurally-motivated mechanism than its *ad hoc* probabilistically-driven precursor.

With the exception of the first battery of experiments, all of these ex-periments are implemented within the Logic Programming paradigm. Working within this paradigm, the programs which are produced tend to be short and pithy, directly reflecting our understanding of the problem. In each major sequence the initial program and each subsequent version was written, run, analyzed and modified until it became quite cumber-some, but the understanding of the problems encountered enabled the quick writing of a completely new and quite elegant program which allowed further development. Thus these sequences each comprise sev-eral independent programs resulting from these "fresh starts", as well as various modifications of each such progenitor.

Battery One — Preparatory Experiments

Having discovered the literature on holograms, parallelism, and the modelling of self-organizing neural networks, we spent time tracking down applications of these metaphors to human memory and language. We did some mathematical analyses and experimental implementations

to explore these areas. Since these early studies bear little direct relationship to the later batteries of experiments and the present experimental framework, they are mentioned here only briefly, merely to
give a complete picture of the course of our work.

Our experimental work was commenced at UNSW and continued in
the Artificial Intelligence and Cognitive Science group at Macquarie
University. Initially we focused our attention on the association problem
in streams based on superimposed coding[1] and non-holographic memory.[2] The approach involving holographic/associative memory and multi-
processors/parallelism was also explored by a number of programs tabu-
lating and plotting the results of various mathematical analyses, and approximations to the expected absolute and relative performances of particular configurations. Extensions of the associate net to D-dimensions
with k-keys were specified, and optimal values for other parameters
determined, for each N (keeping the expected number errors in the system bounded by 1). The analysis is not shown, but represents simple extension to D-dimensions of that of Longuet-Higgins and Willshaw.
Whilst we do think that this approach does have some significance and
promise as an associating technique, the analysis showed that its storage
efficiency held up only if ridiculous extremes of redundant storage were
used as a reference (*viz* it is assumed that other storage techniques can
only index on a specified set of keys, and other access paradigms require
redundant storage). More importantly, it was difficult to see how such a
model could be related to the problem of language and language learning; and more specifically, neurally motivated network models were then
investigated. This work was therefore no longer in the direct path of research.

Another set of preliminary programs provided a view of the simulated retina and cortex presented to a self-organizing neural model
based on the interaction paradigm. This will not be discussed in any detail here. Input consisted of a sample of retinal images of lines in nine
different orientations. The self-organizing network was provided with
repeated presentations of these nine images in various random and systematic orderings. The results showed each cell developing one or more
preferred orientations after as few as three presentations of each orientation. The slowness of such simulations precluded larger experiments
with examination of interactions between many layers.

Battery Two – Simple Two Sense Hierarchy Parsing

Turning more directly to language and parsing, our first concern was for
a common form of representation and parse structure to allow for a
common mechanism for all aspects of semantics, consistent with the relational basis of language, and the sensory-motor basis for ontology. This

resulted in a series of simple and fairly conventional parsers which were, by contrast, quite unconventionally applied not only to the language stream but also to an arbitrary number of the other modalities. Furthermore, consistent techniques and representations were explored for expressing both intra-hierarchical and inter-hierarchical relationships, the former being expressed as cohesive relationships between subtrees of a given hierarchy, and the latter being expressed as role relationships between subtrees of arbitrary hierarchies.

The implementation and representation language for this battery of experiments is PROLOG. As will be seen by the representation of the grammar for the simple example from the language modality (called the "hear" hierarchy), PROLOG allows a fairly standard representation of traditional phrase structure rules.

```
class(hear,the,article).
class(hear,fox,noun).
class(hear,dog,noun).
class(hear,quick,adjective).
class(hear,brown,adjective).
class(hear,lazy,adjective).
class(hear,jumps,biverb).
class(hear,over,preposition).
formula(hear,[article,spnounphrase],nounphrase).
formula(hear,[noun],spnounphrase).
formula(hear,[adjective,spnounphrase],
              spnounphrase).
formula(hear,[nounphrase,biverbphrase,
              prepphrase],biclauseroot).
formula(hear,[biverb],biverbphrase).
formula(hear,[preposition,nounphrase],prepphrase
```

*Figure 14–1: Examples of hear classes and formulae for
              Battery 1*

% Parse:This is a parse algorithm which is designed to be operable both top-down and bottom-up or both. Operation is to determine the class of the first word (bottom-up) and determine an inclusive sequence of classes dependent on the specified class list (top-down). The expected class is recursively transmitted in a list which must be satisfied by a successful parse. Any variables are capable of instantiation by the algorithm.

% HyperFormula: This subfunction is used to provide an effective formula connecting an expected class to a list head actual class.

```
parse(Sense,RTail,[],RTail).
parse(Sense,[Word,..WTail],[EClass,..ECTail],
        STail) :-
    class(Sense,Word,Class),
    hformula(Sense,[Class,..CTail],EClass),
    parse(Sense,WTail,CTail,RTail),
    parse(Sense,RTail,ECTail,STail).
hformula(Sense,[Class],Class).
hformula(Sense,[Class,..CTail],EClass) :-
    formula(Sense,[IClass,..ITail],EClass),
    hformula(Sense,[Class,..JTail],IClass),
    append(JTail,ITail,CTail).
```

Figure 14–2: Simple early parser for Battery 2

Similarly, we can see from this that implementation of a standard phrase-structure parser in PROLOG is quite straightforward and very brief. Moreover, this parser will, thanks to the backtracking capabilities of PROLOG, operate both top-down and bottom-up. Indeed it can quite usefully interchange between the two modes of operation as appropriate.

Note that the interpretation of the grammar rules is not grossly inefficient compared with the compilation of Definite Clause Grammars, and leads to additional flexibility, particularly in relation to the learning variants developed in subsequent Batteries.

The definition and restriction functions of both cohesive and role relationship trees are straightforwardly handled by PROLOG's unification algorithm, without requiring differentiation of the restricting and restricted tagmemes as would be normal in most programming paradigms. However, such relationship trees make use of assumed ontological concepts of ordering and magnitude which have been provided here as innate, but which would more properly be recognized increasingly during the learning process—if not actually learned as concepts because of their significance. These concepts thus may not themselves be innate. However, we see a direct relationship between them and various consequences of the physical and physiological nature of the brain and, in particular, of the visual system. The trees and the minimal differentiation procedure are not illustrated here as the trees become complex and huge very quickly, only a naïve, exhaustive and fairly standard search for closest match was implemented, and no significant use has yet been made of the metric or of relationships between semantically dependent trees.

Battery Three – Simple Parsing with Learning of Classes and Formulae

The next logical stage (overlapping with the developments of the previous battery) was the parsing programs with learning capabilities. Such programs are not as rare as we believed when we first undertook these experiments, and we refer to three or four programs in the review chapters. There is quite an overlap between these and some of the experiments performed in this battery. But, in general, our experiments are simpler, isolating the problem of learning syntax in a way reminiscent of some of the earliest attempts.

The experiments in this battery extend Battery Two by learning the class of new "words", independent of semantics or other hierarchies. We use "words" here in the generic sense of a lower level Tagmeme. The experiments have not been limited to the "hear" hierarchy, but the "hear" modality was host for the most complex "grammars" studied.

```
Sentence   clause root nounphrase article: the
                        spnounphrase noun: mouse
                        null
                        predicate biverphrase biverb: ran
                        null
                        prepphrase preposition: around
                        nounphrase article: the
                        spnounphrase noun: cat
                        null
null
```

```
P = pt(sentence, pt(clauseroot, pt(nounphrase,
              pt(article, the, slass),
              pt(spnounphrase, pt(noun, mouse, class),
              null)),
              pt(biverbphrase, pt(biverb, ran, class),
              null),
```

```
                    pt(preppphrase, pt(prepostion, around, class),
                    pt(nounphrase, pt(article, the, class),
                    pt(spnounphrase, pt(noun, cat, class),
                    null))))),
        null)
```

*Figure 14–3: Example of word class learning and parse tree for
           Battery 3*

Modifying the PROLOG parser to learn a new word was straighfor-
ward; the result was that a new class predicate was asserted, as illustrated in the run of Fig. 14–3. The main new complication in this version
was the separation from the main parser of a predicate which first did
bottom-up pre-processing. The final bottom-up post-processing assigned
classes to words on the basis of initial and augmented class definitions.
Several other variations have now been produced.

Modifying the parser to learn a new word of a completely new class
is much more complex. Consider the sentence

(1) "The fox jumps over the dog".

Suppose that this sentence lies within the bounds of the grammar
understood — it is encompassed by the grammar of Fig.14–3. We can also
suppose further that the grammar does not cover adverbs — neither of
the grammars illustrated does. How then should the system respond to
sentences like:

(2) "The dog quickly jumps over the fox".
(3) "The dog jumps quickly over the fox".
(4) "The dog jumps over the fox quickly".
(5) "Quickly the dog jumps over the fox".

The new class could be associated with several components in each
of these sentences. Semantics would presumably tend to suggest association with the "verb" in sentence (3), and with either "verb" or "predicate" in sentence (2), although the "subject" and "prepphrase" would
both be candidates from a syntactic viewpoint. In cases (4) and (5), the
semantic association would be the clause, or arguably in (4) the "predicate", but other syntactic possibilities include respectively "subject" and
"prepphrase". In general, in all these cases there are other possibilities
in trying to bind the word to a single "noun" or "article".

To handle any of these uses of an adverb, there are thus many possibilities which need to be hypothesized and evaluated in the light of fur-

ther experience. This thus requires some sort of heuristic evaluation technique, and suggests numerical strategies which are implemented at quite a low level in Batteries Five and Six. It is, however, possible for such techniques to be used in the context of the basic model and framework inherited from Battery Two.

But there is also another problem. Consider the nature of the modification to the formulae to handle the "adverb" in the context of sentence (2) above. The result of attaching the "adverb" to either the "verb" or the "predicate" (to leave out less semantically desirable associations) is that an extra level is introduced into the parse tree. Consider the attachment to the "predicate". We must somehow allow the "clauseroot" to subtend either a "predicate" or an "adverbialized predicate". The "adverbialized predicate", however, itself subtends a "predicate". So it is more appealing to allow for the omission of an "adverb" by removing the possibility of a "clauseroot" subtending a "predicate" directly, and hence allowing an "adverbialized predicate" to reduce to a "predicate". This involves the insertion of an extra level between the existing levels of the parse structure.

The resulting grammar could therefore become entirely analogous to that shown above where the "specified noun phrase" is introduced to allow the option of an "adjective". Note that an alternative to having two rules for "spnounphrase" or "adpredicate" is to use the concept of a zero morph.

So let us now consider the problem which occurs with PROLOG's control mechanism as a result of the introduction of the ability to intersperse new formula classes between existing levels. This capability introduces the problem of ensuring that the interspersion does not happen unnecessarily—as ultimately this can lead to infinite recursion without the introduction of tighter controls than used in the simple parser inherited from Battery Two and the word class learner.

The appropriate restriction seems to be to preclude unary (single class) rules and augment the marginal class with a zero morph to compensate. This creates problems for probabilistic learning where a hypothesized rule may be discarded, and is also quite counter-intuitive in many cases. It leads to complex parse-trees cluttered by many additional terms which need not always occur.

For example, we do *not* seem to assign significance to the absence of an "adjective" or an "adverb" (as indicating that, respectively, the "fox" or the "jumping" was not quick). But we do see significance in the absence of an "-s" on a "noun" or a "verb" (indicating it is not plural or not third-person singular, respectively). Thus it would appear that the zero morph is really only appropriate as a member of closed classes.

Another problem with such a simple formulation is that there is the need to invent names for the new classes, and that even after a successful parse (with or without an attempt to associate a new word with an existing class) there will always be more possibilities to try. And the more such gratuitous and spurious hypotheses are made the more parse structures there will be for a given sentence which will also be the basis for further nefarious hypotheses. This again points up the need for a calculus of possibility or probability.

This battery of experiments is really starting at a half-way point. The object was to gain an understanding of what needs to be addressed to allow learning of grammar, without actually having to consider the difficult questions concerned with getting started. How do we learn our first classes and formulae?

So the problems and goals pointed up by this battery of experiments, and the necessity for use of some sort of calculus, were not immediately pursued at this level, but were allowed to influence the course of the experiments performed at a lower level in Batteries Five and Six.

Battery Four – Parrallel Logic Programming and Parsing

One of the main weaknesses of PROLOG is the arbitrariness of its control mechanisms. The studies of Battery Two indicated the flexibility of PROLOG and the simplicity and naturalness of logic as both representation and implementation language. In a fully defined system (which by definition, learning systems are not), it is possible to have beautifully simple parsers, and to program without use of any of the devices which lead PROLOG away from the purity of First Order Logic. The implementation of PROLOG is concerned with defining orders of evaluation. Parsing is not. We are wanting the most likely parses, where these are functions of particular interrelationships, not just of the grammar in the abstract. In fact, we are quite happy to have multiple parses with evaluation of their corresponding likelihoods. Learning will then occur when a parse cannot be completed but involves high likelihood components, notwithstanding that other less likely parses may conceivably be completed.

The parallelism of various network models is thus quite appealing. The experiments of Batteries One, Five and Six use neural-like associative networks. Other network formulations include Petri Nets and Data Flow, which have some useful properties. We find the Data Flow concept relates quite well to the sort of parallelism which occurs in parsing.[3] But we also find the representational solutions of Logic Programming too essential to leave behind. The Connection Graph Model is an essentially parallel network implementation of Resolution Theorem Proving. It is like the Data Flow model in that the links between any pair of potential resolvents may be acted upon at any time. It appears to be naturally suited to heuristic programming since there is no need to worry about control. The only variable is the order of processing, and unlike PROLOG, it is possible to guarantee that a solution (in this case a parse, more generally a path) will be found if one exists. It is thus amenable to the application of appropriate heuristics to the ordering of processing of links, or, equivalently, the allocation of processors to links. In the case of the language and ontology learning paradigm, there is plenty of such information available. There is not only the potential for the application of a calculus of likelihoods, but there is the implicit and restrictive interaction of semantic, cohesive and role relationships. Thus it was decided to investigate the solution of vestigial problems with the Connection Graph paradigm, and a Connection Graph system with effective augmentation was designed and partially implemented, prior to and interspersed with the work on Battery Three. It became apparent that this was quite a major and independent undertaking in itself, and completion of the system[4] was postponed until Batteries Five and Six had been completed. Programming in a connection graph system is itself a whole new art and leaves much to explore.

Battery Five – Probabilistic Semantic Free Syntax Learning

Following the partial success of the representational and grammar learning experiments of Batteries Two and Three, the UNSW/Macquarie group felt it appropriate to defer study of learning of and restriction by interhierarchical relationships until it had a better understanding of the areas in which syntactic learning was inadequate. There were three main areas of syntactic learning yet to explore. The first was the appropriate level and basic units of language which were appropriate to study and to utilize as the "atoms" for a production grammar. The syllable was considered the most appropriate starting point from a theoretical and empirical perspective, and this indeed defined one of the hierarchies studied as part of Battery Two. However, it seemed expedient at this stage of the experiment to maintain the fiction of the "word" as the atomic unit of language. This we continued in Batteries Five and Six, however work below the word level has been commenced at Macquarie, concentrating on inflections in English and German.[5]

The area which we were most keen to explore was the area of interaction between hierarchies, but the satisfactory exploration of that area, commenced in Battery Two, required the assistance of the computer at the level of simulation of the modalities in an interactive environment. Although such a system has been developed,[6] we have not yet fully linked it in to the programs and representations of Batteries Two and Three.

The third area to investigate was the implementation of some type of calculus of likelihoods, possibilities or probabilities, or indeed some species of neurally motivated calculus. This is the area investigated in the experiments of Battery Five and Battery Six respectively. One of the points which emerged from Battery Three was the necessity of in some way restricting the number of hypotheses which could be made. And the idea of the calculus is somehow to ensure that only the most promising are made at all, and that extant hypotheses are evaluated, positively reinforced, and/or negatively reinforced. The primary restriction built into the system is based on the "magic" number seven. The system has a Short Term Memory for each modality which consists of seven tags, each of which is able to hold a possible parse tree, along with information about its sequence (each tree occupies a position between two time-stamps or other spatio-temporal equivalents). As it stands, the system requires strict sequence (a parse requires the second time-stamp of the first unit to unify with the first time-stamp of the second unit). It is apparent from the phenomenon of telegraphic speech that this is not necessarily appropriate in the early stages of a language learning model, and it is proposed to relax this criterion to mere sequence (spatio-temporal "after") in further experiments. It would then appear that once learning reached the stage where all information was being parsed, the telegraphic quality would disappear and the connectedness would be complete. However, if ever the Short Term Memory was swamped, there could be lapses in various forms of cohesion (and this happens frequently in the more convoluted attempts at producing sentences). Whenever a new unit becomes available, whether it is a "word" or the result of successful parsing, the tag with the lowest expectation of utility is dropped in favour of the new parse-tree. Only parse-trees extant on tags are available for incorporation by formulae or classification. The procedures which achieve this are responsible for determining the utility factor for the new parse-tree (or tag) according to the expected validity and utility of the component subtrees found on the tags.

the dog.
this dog.
the cat.
the rat.
a cat.
the cat.
this rat.
a dog.

*Figure 14–4: Sample three-word sentences for
              Batteries 5 and 6*

Formulae and classifications are reinforced when ever they are current (in the sense that constructed parse-trees still occupy tags) and tag utility decays with time (slower or faster according to whether or not, respectively, there is a connection to a tag with a current time stamp).

% Sense, Class, Cred, Components

        formula(lang, 39, 18, [26, 12]).
        formula(lang, 38, 18, [16, 26]).
        formula(lang, 37, 15, [16, 36]).
        formula(lang, 36, 15, [20, 10]).
        formula(lang, 35, 16, [16, 20]).
        formula(lang, 34, 15, [16, 18]).
        formula(lang, 33, 15, [10, 31]).
        formula(lang, 32, 15, [10, 30]).
        formula(lang, 31, 15, [12, 29]).
        formula(lang, 30, 15, [12, 28]).
        formula(lang, 29, 16, [16, 13]).
        formula(lang, 28, 15, [23, 12]).
        formula(lang, 27, 15, [10, 25]).
        formula(lang, 26, 17, [10, 24]).
        formula(lang, 25, 21, [12, 23]).
        formula(lang, 24, 73, [17, 10]).
        formula(lang, 23, 31, [16, 10]).
        formula(lang, 22, 16, [1, 20]).
        formula(lang, 21, 15, [1, 18]).
        formula(lang, 20, 37, [10, 17]).
        formula(lang, 19, 15, [14, 16]).
        formula(lang, 18, 17, [13, 16]).
        formula(lang, 17, 76, [12, 16]).
        formula(lang, 15, 17, [1, 13]).
        formula(lang, 14, 17, [11, 12]).
        formula(lang, 13, 36, [10, 12]).
        formula(lang, 11, 19, [1, 10]).

% Sense, Class, Thresh, Set

        formula(lang, 24, [[17, 10]])

formula(lang, 17, [[12, 16]])

*Figure 14–5a: Raw and thresholded formulae
produced in Battery 5*

class(lang, 16, 53, a).
class(lang, 10, 72, rat).
class(lang, 10, 76, cat).
class(lang, 16, 72, the).
class(lang, 16, 76, this).
class(lang, 12, 76, ".").
class(lang, 10, 76, dog).
class(lang, 1, 28, the).

% Sense, Class, Thresh, Set

class(lang, 16, [a, the, this])
class(lang, 10, [rat, cat, dog])
class(lang, 12, ["."])

*Figure 14–5b: Raw and thresholded classes
produced in Battery 5*

Variants on this model have been tested with several reinforcement schemes and on a variety of input data and orders of presentation. Generally, the system learns the first few classes and formulae fairly quickly, but does not retain them well once confused by further input. This implies that some sort of fixing is needed whereby demonstrably useful hypotheses have their decay functions weakened. It is quite difficult to see how to do this without introducing arbitrary intervention at various stages. The order of learning is also quite interesting. After three presentations of 24 three-"word" sentences, the first eight of which are shown in Fig. 14–4, the formula and classification summarized in Fig. 14–3 are produced. Interestingly, the first word learned (*viz.* passing threshold) is ".", and the second is "the". Furthermore the rules (formulae 17 and 24) may be summarized respectively as:

- "An article follows a punctuation mark" or perhaps
- "A sentence begins with an article" and
- "A noun follows the article at the beginning of a sentence".

This is not our impression of the order in which children learn words. It is however an obvious and expected result of the data provided. Factors which are omitted in this experiment which should be significant include the more obvious semantics of nouns, the one-word stage which precedes attempts at multi-word sentences, the telegraphic nature of the first multi-word sentences, and the general influence of semantics. Note that (1) reader's speed at boundaries is higher then, (2) there is psycholinguistic evidence of the importance of prosody, and (3) there is neurolinguistic evidence of the importance of poles and boundary conditions. Quite different results may be expected once partial analyses are attempted and semantics, motivation and reference are introduced. Children do seem to make extensive use of the marking of the beginning and end of sentences, as shown in reading, for example, in the speeding up of their scan when nearing the end of a sentence, and their slowing down when moving into the middle. This suggests that these closed class "words" may assist the child in focussing his attention on the important parts of a sentence, but that he will not find it expedient to use these in production until he has solved the problem of producing the important open class words which convey the core of his intended meaning.

Battery Six—Neural Model Semantic Free Syntax Learning

The probabilistic calculus model of Battery Five suggests the neural network model of Battery One. There is a sense in which each of the PROLOG clauses representing formulae, classifications and tags is operating similarly to a neuron.

To examine this insight, a rewrite of the model totally on neural principles was instigated, and the initial version of the resulting much simpler program is shown in Fig. 14–6. (Note that it makes extensive use of a very dangerous built-in PROLOG predicate "adjusti" which was added to PROLOG precisely to simplify and increase the efficiency of such programs. The predicate "adjusti" actually changes an integer value within a stored clause to another, saving retracting and reasserting the clause as was done in the systems of Battery Five. Furthermore, the program uses half-cut "$" which prevents backtracking on the head without restricting backtracking in the body of a clause). This language learning program is based directly on the neural model of Barto and Klopf.[7] The model depends on synaptic efficiency being modified according to correlations between the change in activity of a neuron and the immediate history of the cell which synapses on it.

```
defop(700,xfx,lim)!
V lim E :- T is E.
bound(-30000,T,30000,V).
bound(A,B,C,A):- A, B, !.
bound(A,B,C,C):- B, C, !.
bound(A,B,C,B).
clim(3).
do(S):-
     repeat,
     ratom(W),
     inword(S,W), !.
     inword(S,W):-
          yclass(S,C,Y,YT),
          fixwclass(S,C,W,WC),
          fixxclass(S,W,X,XT),
          XX is 9500,
          adjusti(X,XX),
          YY lim (Y + 2*WC*X/10000),
          adjusti(Y,YY),
          fail.
     inword(S,_):-
          yclass(S,C,Y,YT),
          yclass(S,F,XN,X),
          F/=C,
          fixwclass(S,C,F,WC),
          YY lim (Y + WC*X/10000),
          adjusti(Y,YY),
          fail.
     inword(S,W):-
          genint(S,C),
          clim(L),
          C < = L,
          fixwclass(S,C,W, ),
          fixxclass(S,W,X,XT),
          fixyclass(S,C,Y,YT),
          wclass(S,C,W,WC),
          WWC is 1500,
          adjusti(WC,WWC),
          fail.
     inword(S,_):-
          yclass(S,C,Y,YT),
```

```
        wclass(S,C,W,WC),
        xclass(S,W,X,XT),
        WWC lim (WC + (Y-YT)*(XT/2 + X)/10000),
        adjusti(WC,WWC),
        fail.
inword(S,_):-
        yclass(S,C,Y,YT),
        yclass(S,F,XN,X),
        F/= C,
        wclass(S,C,F,WC),
        WWC lim (WC + (Y-YT)*(XN/3 + X/2)/10000),
        adjusti(WC,WWC),
        fail.
inword(S,_):-
        xclass(S,W,X,XT),
        XXT lim (6000*XT)/10000 + X,
        adjusti(XT,XXT),
        XX is 0,
        adjusti(X,XX),
        fail.
inword(S,_):-
        yclass(S,C,Y,YT),
        YYT lim (200*YT + 9800*Y)/10000,
        adjusti(YT,YYT),
        YY is 0,
        adjusti(Y,YY),
        fail.
fixwclass(S,C,W,WC):-
        wclass(S,C,W,WC),
        $.
fixwclass(S,C,W,WC):-
        WC is 500,
        assertz(wclass(S,C,W,WC)).
fixxclass(S,W,X,XT):-
        xclass(S,W,X,XT),
        $.
fixxclass(S,W,X,XT):-
        X is 9500,
        XT is 0,
        assertz(xclass(S,W,X,XT)).
```

```
fixyclass(S,C,Y,YT):-
    yclass(S,C,Y,YT),
    $.
fixyclass(S,C,Y,YT):-
    Y is 450, YT is 0,
    assertz(yclass(S,C,Y,YT)).
```

*Figure 14–6: Example of language learner based on a
            neural model*

Each neuron in the PROLOG model of Fig. 14–6 has a current level
of activity for inputs and output, denoted respectively, X and Y, and
traces representing its history of recent activity, XT or YT. Each synapse
has a weight WC. The words take the place of a retina, and are the inputs to the network, and the classes are the outputs. There is assumed to
be a "receptor" cell which recognizes each distinct word ("xclass") and
fires on recognition. The program is seeking to learn to distinguish the
words into classes (and in the program of Fig. 14–6 the number of different classes which may be distinguished is limited to three by the predicate "clim"). The set of neurons in focus ("yclass") are those responsible
for this classification. In reality there would be many neurons responding to under-distinguished classes in the early stages of learning, but for
simplicity, the number of neurons is kept to a minimum in the hope that
each will learn a distinct class. The program is an example of a failure
driven program, with the predicate "inword" doing most of the work,
and apart from the case handled by its first clause each clause will be attempted for each word. This predicate is set up so that any word will not
only match clauses which process that word (those with W in the head),
but will also trigger a cycle of interactions and decay, matching clauses
(with – in the head) which calculate (in order):

- mutual excitation by traces of other neurons;
- modification of synapses from receptors on the basis of the
  correlation of change in the neuron with the traces of the receptors;
- modification of synapses with other neurons on a similar basis;
- decay of receptors and update of input traces;
- decay of neurons and update of output traces.

Interestingly, the ability to recognize classes from presentation of the
same sets of input as given to the programs of Battery Five is remarkably
comparable. Note that the decay functions provide some of the function-

ality of the tags without, however, any direct correlate of either tags or formulae. There is considerable room for further study of such models and comparison with those of Battery Five.

Battery Seven — Learning with a Critic and Anticipated Correction

The experiments in this battery have in common the use of a critic and represent extensions of the experiments of Batteries Two and Three in diverse directions.

The interference of the critic is not intuitive in this type of problem and we find it adds a taste of "artificiality" to the experiments. Attempts have been made to obviate the use of a critic in other machine learning research through statistical measures or neural models. As applied to language learning the probabilistic approach involves correlating syntactic patterns, and hypothesising and reinforcing word classifications and formulae that give a correct parse. Such work, *eg* Lamb (1961), had severe theoretical limitations (Minsky and Papert, 1969), (Chomsky and Miller, 1963) and (Chomsky, 1963). Hence further research using autocorrelative models must steer clear of such pitfalls. Use of a critic avoids any necessity to face these issues while allowing investigations of different aspects of language learning.

One important finding that emerged very early on in the experiments is the limitation presented by PROLOG to the learning systems due to its *negation as failure* approach. This is very limiting since it means that PROLOG does not provide differentiation between negative information and no information at all. One system takes this into account, and overcomes the problem by storing extra knowledge. The knowledge base still uses the *class* and *formula*, but it also makes use of *notclass* and *notformula* to note previous encounters or attempts that had been deemed wrong on examination by the critic. In this manner mistakes were limited to one occurrence only. This negative information also helped in allowing a single word to fit multiple classifications: that is, a word could fit any class as long as this relation was not prohibited in a *notclass* clause.

This pragmatic approach provides an *ad hoc* form of anticipated correction. It is quite possible that matches develop in children which recognize forms which have repeatedly been negatively reinforced. This will occur if a hypothesis forms associations positively and negatively, rather than just of varying positive strength.

Three main critic-driven systems have been completed to date. The first, HAL, focuses its attention on certain sentence sections. The focusing allows greater accuracy in the learning of a new formula, and is analogous to the natural language learning in humans, who as babies focus their attention on small subsets of sentences, and once proficient with these look at how the small sections are related. The teacher/critic provides the focusing necessary, by giving HAL the name of the section to be learnt. At any stage where the system derives a new rule, the teacher/critic is asked for approval. More complex sections are learnt by analysing and collating the existing grammar rules and word classes.

Once sufficient has been learnt about a concept, the program is allowed to develop and refine its grammar rules, using an *evolutionary* learning strategy. This strategy aims to consolidate what has been learnt by either generalising or specialising grammar rules, or sections thereof. Using this algorithm, any wrongly portrayed rules will not remain so forever, only until they can be superseded by better ones.

Testing of this section involved learning both grammar rules and words simultaneously, with an empty initial knowledge base. From this stage HAL was taught to recognise complex sentences, incrementally adding new knowledge to the knowledge base.

Sense: bear
Give me a description: the bad dog
What should I call the concept to be
                        learnt: nounphrase
Are any relationships to be learnt: n
HAL > Is this a suitable grammar rule:
HAL > article + spnounphrase is a nounphrase
HAL > y
HAL > parse tree for hear hierarchy
nounphrase
         |–> article:the
         |–> spnounphrase
              |–> adjective:bad
              |–> spnounphrase
                   |–> noun:dog

Figure 14–7: Teaching HAL about nounphrases

HAL teaches us various lessons. The most obvious is the important part focusing attention plays in speeding up the learning process. And secondly it reinforces that learning systems, as a general rule, should be incremental, and should provide the facility to adapt any rules already in the system, as more information comes to hand.

In the second system this approach differs from the previous in that whole sentences are processed. The whole sentence is analysed and restructured in as many ways as is required for it to be acceptable to the critic. From the critic's point of view, having to patiently turn down all the possible incorrect structures that may be produced from a given sentence is quite unacceptable. This situation is prevented from occurring by keeping, and learning from all information about previous attempts, whether it was productive or otherwise.

Fred is made up of two separate stages. In the first stage it attempts to parse a sentence with the formulae it has. Only when there is no way for this to succeed will the second stage fire off. This second stage is simply the capability to ignore an input word, in which case its knowledge base will be extended by fitting this new word's class into a formula that finally allows it to parse; or ignore an expected word class, and so create a formula similar to the one that was proposed for parsing this word, only with this particular word's class omitted. When the sentence finally parses, the parse tree created is analysed, to check whether any new formulae are needed. If this is the case, the sections this new formula will be made up of are parsed from the bottom up, trying to find the highest level constructs that will fit the actual combination of classes. For example in adding knowledge about adjectives in noun phrases, we find we need a higher, recursive formula, as it is correct to place as many adjectives as one wants before a noun. In learning about adverbs and verbs however, see Fig.14–8, we find that we need a lower level, non-recursive formula as normally only one adverb is allowed before a verb.

Two nodes *pred* and *verbp* can be used by Fred in the formula generation. Similarly we need the skeletal structure in parsing simpler sentences, since we need to be able to remove nodes that are not essential in our given example. The reason why this is a disadvantage is that there are a multitude of ways of structuring a given sentence and a correspondingly large set of possible initial grammars.

Fred was extended in this manner to attempt to find relations between parse trees. To simplify this problem and at the same time provide an excellent example of an application to this approach, Fred was given the task of learning relations between two senses, called *English* and *Spanish*. These senses are both grammatical parsing of language, obviously the English and the Spanish languages respectively. This application simplified the problem due to the fact that sentence structures do not differ that much between these two languages.

Sense: hear

Input: the dog quickly jumps
Is dog an adjective? n
Is quickly a verb? n
I do not know about the word "quickly".

What is the class of this word? adverb

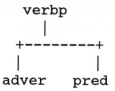

```
        verbp
          |
     +--------+
     |        |
   adver    pred
```

Is the above a correct construct?n

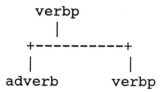

```
        verbp
          |
     +----------+
     |          |
   adverb     verbp
```

Is the above a correct construct?   n

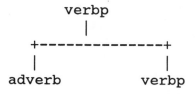

```
         verbp
           |
    +--------------+
    |              |
  adverb         verbp
```

Is the above a correct construct?   y

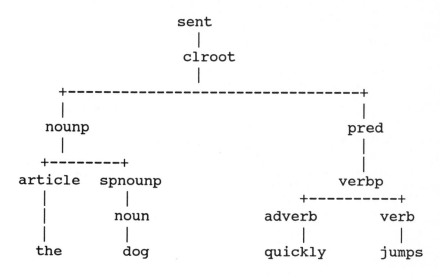

```
                      sent
                       |
                     clroot
                       |
     +----------------------------------+
     |                                  |
   nounp                               pred
     |                                  |
  +--------+                            |
  |        |                            |
article  spnounp                      verbp
  |        |                      +----------+
  |      noun                     |          |
  |        |                    adverb      verb
 the      dog                     |          |
                               quickly     jumps
```

```
Is this the required structure?    y
```

Figure 14–8: Teaching Fred a non-recursive relation—adverbs

```
Sense: hear
Input: the quick brown fox jumps over the
       lazy dog.
I do not know about the word `over^.
What is the class of this word? prep
```

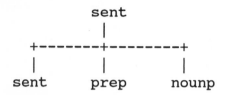

```
                sent
                 |
        +--------+--------+
        |        |        |
      sent      prep    nounp
```

```
Is the above a correct construct?   n
```

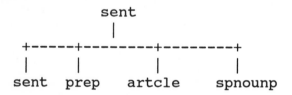

```
                sent
                 |
     +------+---------+--------+
     |      |         |        |
   sent    prep    artcle   spnounp
```

```
Is the above a correct construct?   n
```

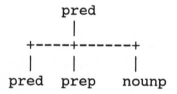

```
              pred
               |
       +----+------+
       |    |      |
     pred  prep   nounp
```

```
Is the above a correct construct?   n
```

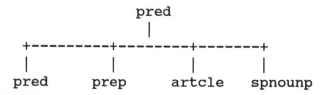

```
                pred
                 |
    +---------+--------+-------+
    |         |        |       |
  pred      prep    artcle   spnounp
```

Is the above a correct construct?   y

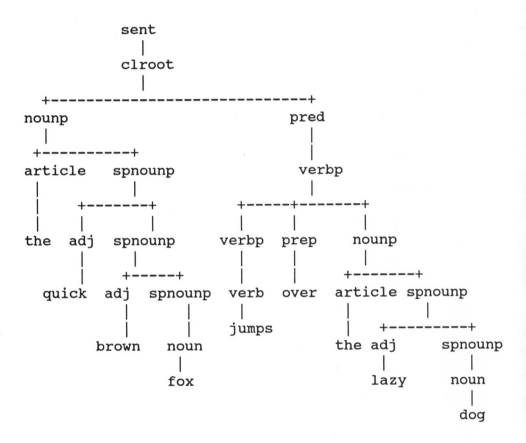

Is this the required structure?   y

Figure 14–9: learning a complex structure—the recursive verb phrase

```
Sense:   English
Input:   the black dog jumps.
Sense:   Spanish
Input:   el perro negro salta.
```

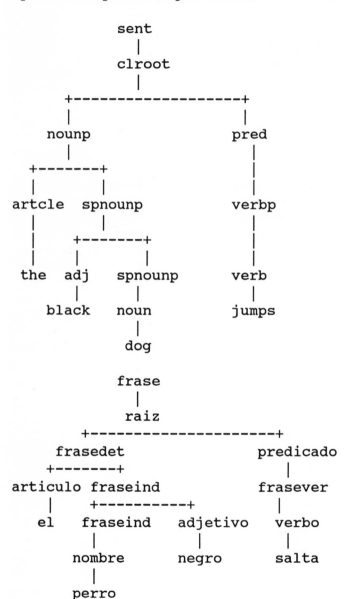

```
                      sent
                       |
                    clroot
                       |
          +--------------------+
          |                    |
        nounp                 pred
          |                    |
     +-------+                 |
     |       |                 |
  artcle   spnounp           verbp
     |       |                 |
     |       |                 |
     |    +-------+            |
     |    |       |            |
   the   adj   spnounp        verb
          |       |            |
        black   noun         jumps
                  |
                 dog


                    frase
                      |
                    raiz
          +----------------------+
       frasedet                predicado
       +-------+                  |
   articulo fraseind           frasever
       |      +----------+        |
      el   fraseind  adjetivo   verbo
              |          |        |
           nombre      negro    salta
              |
            perro
```

Is this the required structure? y

Is "black" in the "English" sense, related to
"fraseind" in the "Spanish" sense? n

Is "adj" in the "English" sense, related to
"adjetivo" in the "Spanish" sense? y

Is "black" in the "English" sense, related to
"negro" in the "Spanish" sense? y

Figure 14–10: Learning connection between
Spanish and English adjective use

The third system attempts to mimic human learning of language, and
in doing so limits itself to two word, *telegraphic*, sentences. It then
devotes its attention to propagating cohesive constraints amongst words.
As far as general natural language processing systems go *cohesive constraints* play a very important part in the parsing stage, and even more so
in the generation stage. Language learning programs for the most part
steer away from this topic as it is a non-trivial exercise to implement.

In the first stage *Learn* accepts individual words as if they were single
word sentences. These words are then processed by extracting common
roots amongst similar words, and creating dictionary entries of the form
word = root + suffix. These dictionary entries are represented as PRO-
LOG clauses, see Fig. 14–11, each indexed by a unique number. This
knowledge is kept so that it may be applied in later developments to semantically constrain words in sentences.

```
transform(1, object,[s] ).
transform(2, action,[e,s] ).
transform(3, action,[s] ).
transform(4, adjective,[s,r] ).
transform(5, adjective,[e,s,t] ).
```

Figure 14–11: Some transforms generated by Learn.

The more complex sentences are parsed with each word analysed
using the known transforms and then processed as a root and a suffix. In
this way legal combinatorial knowledge is stored, see Fig. 14–12, where
each combination, or *formula* is indexed by a unique number and con-

tains the word classes that may occur together with lists referencing the allowed transforms on words that fit these classes. This gives the system the ability to intercept invalid sentences at some later stage, and to generate better ones.

formula(1, [pronoun,object]).
formula(6, [action,where]).
formula(2, [adjective,object,[0,1]]).
formula(3, [action,how,[2,1]]).
formula(4, [action,when,[2,0]]).
formula(5, [object,action,[1,0],[0,3],[0,2]]).

Figure 14–12: Formulae and Transform constraint pairs generated by Learn

We have now completed our description of our preliminary experiments and results.

Learning with a Generalized Toy World Package

We wanted to test the learning programs in a fairly rich simulated environment modelled as a robot world. The specifications of this world are used as part of Battery Two, but it was hand simulated. The model was designed to handle multiple objects of various kinds, any number of which could be:

- *mobile* — capable of moving themselves: self-propelling, capable of acting on other objects: pushing or attaching;
- *motile* — capable of being moved: not self-propelled, capable of being acted on by other objects: pushed or attached;
- *fixed* — incapable of movement, capable of being collided with and stopping a moving object.

Objects may have "eyes" which give them (or their controlling PRO-LOG program) information about the environment. They may also have "parts" which may be relatively fixed, or rotatable about a single fixed pivot point. Importantly, the "eyes" may be constrained to a particular field (angle) of view, and may be parametrized to return information in absolute or relative coordinates and in a raw geometric form or in a named and structured form. This allows, for example, a learning program to receive information which doesn't give away the structure and is relative to the appropriate viewpoint, so that it is able to learn its onto-

logy for itself. The view of other "eyes" may be displayed in the main
window, or one of three smaller windows. Similar choices apply to the
way in which motor-control may be specified by the program governing
a motile object. In the unstructured relative mode used for sensory-
motor control by the language and ontology learning programs, information is conveyed in terms of sequences of keywords (*e.g.* xcoord) and
numbers according to grammars such as that used for the "see" hierarchy in Battery Two. At this point the system has been used with a variant of Winston's algorithm to learn verbs such as run, jump and fly from
positive or negative examples. There is further ongoing work with this
system as an environment for simulation of a complex world in which to
further investigate Concept Learning using Sammut's MARVIN model.[8]
Some simple examples of non-learnt semantics have been demonstrated.

The next logical extension is to combine the models of the first two
Batteries with each of Batteries Three, Five and Six. In this way, we can
explore the intermodal learning capabilities and the effectiveness of
contrast techniques in guiding the learning of an individual modality as
well as the entire ontology. The best initial paradigm may well be the
more difficult "bringing up baby" simulation. The basic mechanism used
will be the differential minimization of parse-trees of pairs of modalities.

The learning of structure within the visual hierarchy has however at-
tracted more of the present effort, both with and without an explicit visual simulation, and also in the context of a simulator based on current
dedicated image processing hardware.[9] The child's picture book is an excellent tool for and paradigm of learning. It is possible to build straightforward situations, and simple but progressively more complex contrasts
to investigate the responsiveness of various learning techniques. This experiment is thus a specific paradigm for investigations of the class just
discussed.

Development of Partial Analysis and Deletionless Approaches to NLA

Another essential ingredient of a learning system, which may be studied
separately as an extension of Batteries Three, Five and Six, takes into account the phenomenon of "telegraphic speech". It does this by examining techniques by which the child/model will focus on and learn the important open class words (with or without recognition of the closed class
words as pointers to the focus), and discard the words which seem irrelevant. Currently no selectivity is employed, and it is difficult to see how
useful partial analysis can be performed in the context of learning within
a single modality, since there the only available guide would be expecta-

tion. This approach is necessary for any attempt to achieve the one word, two word, three word stages of production discussed earlier.

The *Learn* system described as part of Battery Seven has a focus at the telegraphic level, although no automatic focusing process has been employed to discard irrelevant details.

The child language acquisition evidence is suggestive of a deletion-less strategy being employed; there may be a level of decay, but there are indications that nothing is ever lost completely. Similarly, there are applications in which deletion is inappropriate. Masking, in the style of the overlaying of a painting or tapestry, is the appropriate mechanism. Moreover, PROLOG has many theoretical problems relating to its control — certainly the use of "retract" gives rise to many undesirable properties in PROLOG programs and represents a significant departure from the pure theory of First Order Logic. As a consequence it has seldom been adequately well-defined in existing PROLOG systems. This, interestingly, has resulted in "bugs" and "features" of the PROLOG implementation I have used which have necessitated the improvisation of a number of "kludges" which mar the source of some of the programs developed. We have various proposals for avoiding retraction completely, both in the framework of the LUSH Horn-Clause-based execution of PROLOG, and more particularly in the context of the Connection Graph paradigm, where the proposal also allows dispensing with "assert".

Future Development of an NLA System

The proposals we are about to discuss are all at least another level further removed from those experiments attempted to date. Some of the later ones should require reasonably good indications of success in their prerequisites before being attempted, and complete success would represent the graduating of STANLIE to a "HAL".

Although the simulated robot environment avoids much of the chore in providing hand simulated input to an NLL program, it is still necessary to devise an entire program of scenarios for teaching the system. This raises the question of whether a learning program can be devised which, given a grammar, can present the acquisition model with appropriate examples. A simple teaching program could be devised quite straightforwardly, but there are several open questions about teaching method and correction paradigm. A sophisticated learning/teaching system would require both the learning model and the teaching model to reflect appropriate choices. For example, a teacher could give no feedback, yes/no feedback, obedience response feedback, punishment and reward by sensory-motor interaction, expansion and/or correction feedback, *etc.*

Similarly, the learning system may or may not be adjusted in an attempt to optimize responsiveness to a particular teaching method. In addition, the teacher could adjust its syllabus to the rate of learning of the system, or it could seek to present at a fixed rate of increasing complexity or with no accommodation at all to the learning stage of the learner. Further, both learner and teacher could work on continuous parametrizations, or fixed or threshold determined times of transition between parametrizations of teaching or learning. Thus a good teaching/learning system could be a lot more sophisticated than a trivial (multimodal) sentence generator. It could also play an active part in developing understanding of the learning and teaching processes, and be much more than just a utility to save me some time.

It has become increasingly apparent that an NL user is essentially an expert in language use, and an NL system can be seen as an Expert System. This is more than just a casual analogy. Both an Expert System and an NL System have databases of rules with complex interactions. Both the Expert System and STANLIE involve some sort of probabilistic interaction between rules, and involve evaluating alternatives on their relative merits. So then, can an Expert System be produced to handle Natural Language? Also, once we have achieved some degree of NL capability, what do we do? We are not advocates of NL programming; and NL access to databases is a research area in its own right. The first problem is to think of a way of using NL for database access which is not incomparably more cumbersome than (say) a Fourth Generation Language. This requires use of sophisticated procedures for getting from a user's higher level form of request to the action required. This is again an appropriate job for an Expert System, with the database as the referential system for the NL system. Thus an Expert System model of NL could emphasize consideration of application as well as handling of the Natural Language interface.

One of the problems with the learning models is their lack of parametrization of learning. It is really necessary for the rate and ease of learning to be varied according to factors relating to importance, relevance, and need. It is also apparently necessary to provide for some means by which learned concepts may be stabilized. For example, there is evidence that nerve growth factor is present in early childhood but disappears completely eventually. This may affect the degree of plasticity of the brain. It may also be that banks (or layers) of neurons become activated progressively; that there are innate determiners of learning stages. Or, more simply, there may be a progression by which, somehow, utilized neurons cease to be available for learning new concepts and other unused neurons do become available — note that, apart from some very recent new evidence from a study of the canary, the general consensus has been that no new neurons are born after the first week or so; they can only die. Surely learning cannot be explained by every neuron retaining its original pliability, and the whole network somehow being kept stabilized in some balance. Or is there actually some sort of RNA linked stabilization process as may be suggested by some of the data?

Application of NLA Process to Actual Speech and Visual Data

Once useful simulated results are available, it will be useful to apply learning procedures to the actual phonological hierarchy, whilst retaining control of the semantics and/or learning of general ontology. Quite independent of questions of speech recognition, we are interested to see how the analytic techniques implemented by the various models deal with real phonetic data.

It will also be useful to apply the techniques to actual visual data, with standard (ASCII) language input. Much the same considerations apply as for actual speech data. Once success is achieved here, it will be appropriate to link to both actual speech data and actual visual data. Serious consideration should be given to linking motor control to an actual robot. Current experiments by the Macquarie group link a speech processor board to a "micromouse" mobile robot.

Conclusions

None of the experiments presented here represents an attempt to build a working Natural Language system. Rather, they were intended to enhance our understanding of the field, and complement our theoretical discussion. The experiments divide quite clearly into seven batteries, which represent distinctly separated stages in the work. Each usually started by the writing of completely new programs from completely different perspectives, and consisted of the development of a series of versions of a program focussing on one particular feature.

The last seven years have been explosive for the Computer Industry: years of unprecedented developments for Personal Computers, microprocessors, memory and disk technology; years of excitement and controversy about the Japanese Fifth Generation Computer Systems proposals; years in which PROLOG has developed from an AI language virtually unknown outside of Marseilles and Edinburgh to the heir apparent to LISP, and the basis of the kernel language of the FGCS; years in which old dreams and new expectations for computers have become formalized into a new field. Eight years ago saw the first publication of a truly interdisciplinary debate on "the cognitive sciences", and the beginning of its recognition as an interdisciplinary field of study.[10] The same period has seen the development of centres for Computational Linguistics around the globe. Now, for the first time, the disciplines which we have tried to draw together in this volume are being recognized as interdependent, and interdisciplinary Cognitive Science groups are starting to form. As yet there has been little fruit. The interaction is just beginning. Our education has just begun. We hope we have drawn together and demonstrated the importance and interrelationships of these various disciplines. We have demonstrated that we are now at the point where our centuries of pursuit of knowledge have finally reached the stage where we may be able to reproduce, artificially, just those first distinguishing steps of intelligence that each newborn baby takes.

Notes to Chapter Fourteen

1. Colomb, Robert M., "A Clause Indexing System for PROLOG Based on Superimposed Coding", *DCS Report 8506, Dept of Computer Science, EECS, University of NSW* (Sydney, NSW, Australia, May, 1985); Colomb, Robert M., "Design of a Prolog Machine", *DCS Report 8503, Department of Computer Science, EECS, University of NSW* (Sydney, NSW, Australia, 1985); Colomb, Robert M., "Storage of Prolog Clauses on Disk", *DCS Report 8507, Department of Computer Science, EECS, University of NSW* (Sydney, NSW, Australia, October, 1985); Colomb, Robert M., "Extended Syntax for Prolog Based on Superimposed Code Indexing", *DCS Report 8603, Department of Computer Science, EECS, University of NSW* (Sydney, NSW, Australia, April, 1986); Colomb, Robert M., "Application of Indexing Features in Prolog-SCX", *DCS Report 8604, Department of Computer Science, EECS, University of NSW* (Sydney, NSW, Australia, September, 1986); Colomb, Robert M., "Prolog Implementation Engineering", *DCS Report 8605, Department of Computer Science, EECS, University of NSW* (Sydney, NSW, Australia, October, 1986); Colomb, Robert M., "A Hardware-intended Implementation of PROLOG Featuring a General Solution to the Clause Indexing Problem", *Ph.D. Thesis* (Department of Computer Science, Sydney, NSW, Australia, October, 1986); Ramamohanarao, Kotagiri, and John Shepherd, "Answering Queries in Deductive Database Systems", *Logic Programming: Proceedings of the Fourth International Conference* (February, 1987), pp.1014-1033.
2. Longuet-Higgins, H.C., David J. Willshaw, and O. P. Buneman, "Theories of Associative Recall", *Qutly Revs Biophysics*, Vol. 3, No. 2 (1970), pp.223-244; Willshaw, David J., O. P. Buneman, and H. C. Longuet-Higgins, "Non-Holographic Associative Memory", *Nature*, Vol. 222 (7th June 1969), pp.960-962.
3. Ackerman, W.B., "Data Flow Languages", *IEEE Computer*, Vol. 15, No. 2 (June, 1982), pp.15-25; Agerwala, T., and Arvind, "Data Flow Systems: Guest Editors' Introduction", *IEEE Computer*, Vol. 15, No. 2 (June, 1982), pp.10-13.
4. Wise, Michael J., and David M. W. Powers, "Indexing PROLOG Clauses via Superimposed Code Words and Field Encoded Words", in D. De Groot, ed., *International Symposium on Logic Programming* (Atlantic City, New Jersey, February, 1984), pp.203-210; Powers, David M.W., Lazaro Davila, and G.

Wrightson, "Implementing connection graphs for logic programming", *Cybernetics and Systems '88*, Robert Trappl (ed.) (Kluwer, 1988), pp.957-964.

5. Davila, Lazaro, David M.W. Powers, Debbie M. Meagher, and David Menzies, "Further experiments in computer learning of natural language", *1st Australian Joint Artificial Intelligent Conference* (1987), pp.458-468.

6. Hume, David, "Creating Interactive Worlds with Multiple Actors", *B.Sc. Honours Thesis, Electrical Engineering and Computer Science* (University of New South Wales, Sydney, November 1984).

7. Barto, A. G., and R. S. Sutton, "Landmark Learning: An Illustration of Associative Learning", *Technical Report #81-12* (Dept of Comp. and Inf. Sci., U. of Massachusetts, 1981); Klopf, Harry, *The Hedonistic Neuron: A Theory of Memory, Learning and Intelligence* (Hemisphere, Washington DC, 1982).

8. Sammut, C.A., "Concept Development for Expert System Knowledge Bases", *The Australian Computer Journal*, Vol. 17, No. 1 (February, 1985), pp.49-55.

9. Powers, D.M.W., "A PROLOG simulator for studying visual learning", *Proc. 7th SPIE Conf. on Intelligent Robots and Computer Vision* (1988).

10. Piatelli-Palmarini, M., ed., *Language and Learning: The Debate between Jean Piaget and Noam Chomsky* (Routledge and Kegan Paul, London, England, 1979); Gardner, Howard, "Cognition Comes of Age", pp.xixff, in M. Piatelli-Palmarini, *Language and Learning: The Debate between Jean Piaget and Noam Chomsky* (Routledge and Kegan Paul, 1979), pxix.